COLLECTOR'S ENCYCLOPEDIA OF
DEPRESSION GLASS

SEVENTEENTH EDITION

America's #1 Bestselling Glass Book!

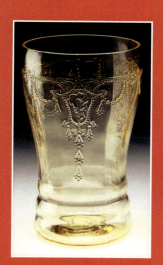

GENE & CATHY FLORENCE

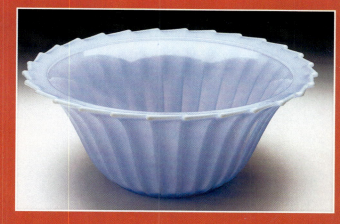

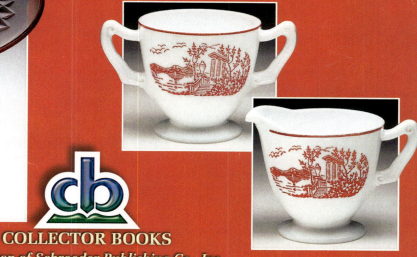

COLLECTOR BOOKS
A Division of Schroeder Publishing Co., Inc.

PRICING

All prices in this book are retail prices for mint condition glassware. This book is intended to be only a guide to prices as there are a few regional price differences that cannot reasonably be dealt with herein. You may expect dealers to pay from 30% to 50% less than the prices quoted. Glass that is in less than mint condition, i.e., chipped, cracked, scratched, repaired, or poorly moulded, will bring only a small percentage of the price of glass that is in mint condition — if wanted at all.

Prices have become reasonably well established due to national advertising by dealers, the Depression glass shows held from coast to coast, and the Internet. I have my own web page operated for books and glass (www.geneflorence.com). However, there are still some regional differences in prices due partly to glass being more available in some areas than in others. Companies distributed certain pieces in some areas that they did not in others. Generally speaking, prices are about the same among dealers from coast to coast.

Prices tend to increase swiftly on rare items and they have increased as a whole due to more collectors entering the field and people becoming aware of the worth of Depression glass.

One of the important aspects of this book is the attempt to illustrate as well as realistically price those items that are in demand. All items listed are priced. The desire is to give you the best factual guide to collectible patterns of Depression glass available.

MEASUREMENTS

To illustrate why there are discrepancies in measurements, I offer the following sample from just two years of Hocking's catalog references:

Year	Item	Ounces	Item	Ounces	Item	Ounces
1935	Pitcher	37, 58, 80	Flat Tumbler	5, 9, 13½	Footed Tumbler	10, 13
1935	Pitcher	37, 60, 80	Flat Tumbler	5, 9, 10, 15	Footed Tumbler	10, 13
1936	Pitcher	37, 65, 90	Flat Tumbler	5, 9, 13½	Footed Tumbler	10, 15
1936	Pitcher	37, 60, 90	Flat Tumbler	5, 9, 13½	Footed Tumbler	10, 15

All measurements in this book are exact as to some manufacturer's listing or to actual measurement. You may expect variance of up to ½" or 1 – 5 ounces. This may be due to mould variations or reworking worn moulds or changes by the manufacturer as well as rounding off measurements for catalog listings.

On the front cover:

Top left, New Century tumbler, 4¼", 9 ounce, green, $22.00. Middle, Cameo tumbler, 15 oz., yellow, $350.00. Top right, Sierra bowl, 8½", Delphite, $125.00. Bottom left, Diamond Quilted cake salver, tall, 10" diameter, pink, $95.00. Bottom right, Lake Como sugar, footed, $30.00. Bottom right, Lake Como creamer, footed, $30.00.

On the back cover:

Various pieces of green Old English. See pages 158 – 159.

Cover design by Beth Summers
Book design by Terri Hunter

Collector Books
P.O. Box 3009
Paducah, KY 42002-3009
www.collectorbooks.com

Gene and Cathy Florence

P.O. Box 22186   P.O. Box 64
Lexington, KY 40522   or   Astatula, FL 34705

Copyright © 2006 by Gene and Cathy Florence

Searching For A Publisher?

We are always looking for people knowledgeable within their fields. If you feel that there is a real need for a book on your collectible subject and have a large comprehensive collection, contact us.

CONTENTS

ACKNOWLEDGMENTS

We would like to thank everyone for the information that dealers, collectors, and readers have communicated to us through writing, e-mailing, calling, and talking to us at shows in different areas of the country. Thanks for sharing those newly unearthed pieces for documentation and sending pictures of your discoveries. E-mail has made pictures more convenient for us to keep records of what you are finding. Thanks for letting us know of Internet auctions with rare or unlisted items. Thank you for the promotional 1930s coupons that you've shown or sent us copies which advertise products from seeds to farm equipment with Depression glass as "incentives." Thank you also for your unique and outstanding knowledge regarding glassware you collect and what you are finding and can't find in the areas where you live. Longtime collectors of a particular pattern usually know more than we do about that one pattern. All this has certainly been invaluable to us and, we hope, to collectors as a whole. All our mutual labors have vastly added to the ever expanding information pertaining to Depression glass.

We have treasured the shows that Depression glass clubs and show promoters have invited us to participate in over the years. Shows have helped add an inestimable amount of knowledge about glass. However, we will be eliminating many of the shows we've been honored to be a part of in the past as some health problems for both of us are imposing restraints. Without Cathy, these 95 books on collectibles would not exist. She has worked years at my side as my chief editor, critic, and proofreader but, most recently, research assistant. She is the workforce end of unpacking, packing, sorting, and labeling the glass. As our job categories stretched over the years, so did our stress levels, which are not being aided by our unbelievably hectic agenda. Writing more books each year and traveling less, doesn't seem to be the answer; so we will even be cutting back from the four or five books written yearly as soon as our current schedule is completed. Changes are always difficult and the book industry is ever-changing with deadlines and concepts. It is becoming too arduous to keep the pace needed to do all jobs at the caliber we require of ourselves. Eyes are rather important and mine have suddenly made those 16 hour days staring at our computer monitor (which I need to do to make deadlines), nearly impossible.

Individual thanks regarding this book need to go to Dick and Pat Spencer, Dan and Geri Tucker, Janet and Wendell Martin, Bret Bonck, and Gary D. Smith. Additionally, there have also been bits and pieces forthcoming from readers outside the United States, including Australia, Canada, New Zealand, The Philippines, and England. We always enjoy hearing about "finds" from other countries.

Any way you slice it, there's an enormous amount of work that must be accomplished by many hands before these books come to you with a wealth of current information. Photographs herein were artistically accomplished by Richard Walker of New York, Charles R. Lynch of Kentucky, and Dan Tucker of Ohio. Richard and Charles toiled extremely long hours over hundreds of setups during one 10-day session and several unplanned smaller sessions throughout the two-year period since the last book.

Glass arranging, unpacking, sorting, carting, and repacking was completed by Jane White, Zibby Walker, Dick and Pat Spencer, Sarah Henry, and Cathy Florence. Members of the Collector Books' shipping team simplified loading and unloading vans. In addition, Jane White and many of the crew previously mentioned helped on several other photography sessions for our books when we were not even there. Thanks for the expertise of the editorial department at Collecto Books, especially Terri Hunter, who knew what was neede from our offerings to make these pages come to fruition a you see it.

If you write us, please enclose a SASE (self-addressed stamped envelope) that is large enough to return your photos you wish them back. Writing books from January through Ma attending shows and visiting markets, malls, and shops leave insufficient time for answering the stacks of letters that arriv each week. E-mails that can be answered quickly, are. answers have to be researched, they are usually filed to b answered when time permits — which may take months.

We wish to thank the thoughtful people who send postcard with the possible answers to their questions for us to check o the correct response. Those are a joy. We want to inform peopl who forget to include the SASE that they'll not be answered. C course if you send the SASE a couple of weeks later, it is some times difficult to remember the previous letter which was cor signed to file 13. We want to encourage you to send pictures c items you hope to have identified, preferably ones where th pattern can be seen or even pencil rubbings of the patterr rather than descriptions. There are millions of pieces of glas and pulling one out from a description is a long shot.

We want to make clear that our expertise, such as it is, lies knowledge of the patterns presented in our books. We know quit a bit about the collectible patterns we have researched and w gladly help you any way we can with those when time permits. W honestly do not know the names, manufacturers, line numbers and worth of every single piece of Depression glassware mad nor do we have the time to research them for you. We now hav four *Glassware Pattern Identification* books on the market tha contain almost 2,000 patterns identified for you by names, date colors, companies, and how many pieces were made if knowr They should save you searching in over 300 books on your ow No, we don't provide lists or prices for those patterns. The book are for identifying your patterns only. We're trying to documer those "wonder who made this" type pieces you see at market but never in major books. Please know these words are not s much sour grapes as self-preservation. We're receiving a wave c questions about bottles, violins, pottery, metallic objects, an clocks that we have no knowledge of.

Please don't send an envelope full of pictures asking us t identify each piece with a price and information as to where yo can sell it. We don't mind a question or two, but 30 or 40 is jus out of the realm of possibility. We would hate to come to th place where we would discourage your writing us at all; bu these questions on everything other than the glassware in ou books is giving us pause to consider that.

As we go to press with this seventeenth edition, thank yo once again, our readers, for making this America's #1 bestsellin book on glass. We encourage you to inform your friends abou Depression glass. Point them to, or give them, a book, prefer ably this one. It appears that only a few of us realize this glass intrinsic, as well as monetary, value. We receive letters regularl from people who have just learned about Depression glass — c who just discovered they basically gave away some family trea sures at a sale. Also, if you get a chance, educate and thorough ly delight yourself by attending a Depression glass show Collecting is satisfying, stimulating, exasperating fun! We wis you very good luck in your searching for this colored treasur that daily continues to attract new admirers.

Information for this book comes from over 34 years of research and selling experience, via communication with fellow dealers and collectors throughout the country, and over 1,650,000 miles of traveling the country, hunting and locating glassware. I must say that some of the most interesting (and surprising) information has come directly from readers, sharing catalogs, magazines, photographs of glass, and the glass, itself. Information for this book is accumulative and likely never-ending.

We still finding out about this beautiful, old Depression era glassware. We have to try to educate them with all the information we've gathered and to do it in a way that the readers who have heard it all before, are not totally disinterested. It is an intimidating task. For those who don't know, these books have been rewritten every two years to include all the latest facts, finds, prices, and changes noticed in the market — and there are always some.

Depression glass as defined by this book is the colored glassware made primarily during the Depression era in colors of amber, blue, black, crystal, green, pink, red, yellow, and white. There are other colors and some glass made before, as well as after, this time frame; but essentially, the glass within this book was manufactured from the late 1920s through 1940. Further, this publication is mostly concerned with the inexpensively made dinnerware turned out by machine in bulk and sold through smaller stores or given away as publicity or premium items for other products of that time. Depression glass was often packaged in cereal boxes and flour sacks or given as incentive gifts for buying tickets or products at the local movie theaters, gasoline stations, and grocery stores. Merchandise was offered with magazine subscriptions, for buying (or selling) certain amounts of seeds or in return for amounts of coupons garnered with butter or soap purchases.

We are running out of space in this book for adding more patterns after the additional ones herein. If we have to add more pages, the book is going to have to increase in price, something we have tried diligently not to do through these many years of color production. (Have you noticed that nearly all new books rolling off the presses have only a few pages of color clustered in the center of the book, and then miles of black and white photos and/or history filling page after page, and cost more than this one?)

Significant changes in collecting Depression glass have occurred since our first book was published on this subject in 1972. Prices overall have increased faster than stocks; seemingly, plentiful patterns have been gathered into countless collections throughout the world and removed from the marketplace. Collectors, rather than accumulating complete sets of dishes are collecting a rainbow set (many colors) of one, or more, patterns. Smaller Depression patterns and previously ignored crystal and satinized wares have attracted patrons. Glass is now sold daily on the Internet, which has had a great impact on the collectibles market. Well educated glass collectors are more the norm than the exception, and they are crossing fields and branching into other areas of glass appreciation.

There were elegant, etched tablewares being manufactured during this 20s through 60s time frame which, today, are highly collectible; those have been covered in our *Elegant Glassware of the Depression Era* book which is now in its 11th edition.

Collectors have also been seeking later made patterns encompassing the time from 1940 to the 1960s, which has led to a companion book, entitled *Collectible Glassware from the 40s, 50s, 60s...*, now in its seventh edition. However, to correctly date glassware from this latter period, it was necessary to move some patterns previously exclusive to this Depression glass book into the time frame encompassed by the 50s book. If your pattern is no longer found within this Depression book, you should seek it in the *40s, 50s, 60s....* We still get letters starting out why is Holiday or some other pattern not in your Depression glass book? They haven't been there for 14 years.

We have also written a book on kitchenware items of the Depression, on extremely rare glassware of those times, not to mention Hazel-Atlas, candlesticks, glass kitchen shakers, a book on novelty shakers, and four books on pattern identification. Regarding these last four, we have had dealers write or seek us out to express their appreciation for saving them endless hours of searching through their libraries of books to identify some new piece they've acquired. One dealer told us that those books are the only one she carries with her on buying trips.

These words of encouragement are certainly appreciated, but truthfully, not as ego swelling as it sounds because we realize that the books are not just our work anymore. They have evolved into something of a community project at this juncture with us acting as liaisons to compile the information.

Over 35 previously unknown pieces have been added to the listings since the last edition, as well as some undocumented colors in several patterns. Those of you who feel nothing new is ever found should look closely at your favorite pattern. On the other hand, there have been deletions of a more than a dozen pieces that have never been found.

In this book, we need to address some decreased pricing that is apparent in some pattern pieces. Remember, we don't just make up these prices; rather we record or acknowledge what is happening in the market. We seriously study prices and over the years of our writing, we have noticed some trends evolve regarding other book prices. If a collector writes a book about items they collect, the items shown are usually wonderful but prices tend to be overstated. If a dealer writes a book on items that they specialize in, there is a tendency to over price common items and under value rare ones. Also, those who price their books by Internet auction results cover only a small percentage of items and create large discrepancies in others, neither being a good indicator of what is really happening in the marketplace. The reason for that may be that in any auction, items that at least two people want may go for a higher price than even a rare or hard to find item does when only one bidder sees it. In other words, we don't feel auction pricing is a solid indicator of overall markets. We attend shows around the country and are always in and out of malls and shops wherever we find them. We're always studying prices and we have tried to price items for what they are actually selling for and not with "hoped-for" prices. We often "spot" items in malls we visit three or four times a year. If the item is gone at the second viewing, the price was at a sellable range. If its there at fourth or fifth viewing, its overpriced. That is one of the reasons we get dealers input in pricing, as they are more aware of what they can get for a piece they've sold repeatedly. This points to another flaw inherent in over pricing the true market values. It often has the scurrilous effect of *depressing* prices for the items being promoted. We've seen it happen in baseball cards, Jim Beam bottles, and Beanie Babies, and in some areas of Depression glass with high blown priced books being churned out helter-skelter. When people get seriously "burned" on pricing — word spreads like wildfire, and this turns potential collectors off that area all together. Everybody loses in that scenario — collectors, dealers, promoters, and the interested public. Some downturn in market prices lies with ill informed pricing be it by authors or dealers.

One last note, if there's a Depression glass show within 100 miles of you; you should make an effort to attend it at least once. It's an awe-inspiring ticket to seeing our artistic past.

ADAM, JEANNETTE GLASS COMPANY, 1932 – 1934

Colors: pink, green, crystal, some yellow, and Delphite blue (See Reproduction Section.)

Jeannette's Adam has Deco era styling including triangles, squares, and lines, combined with a kind of Art Nouveau scrolled center motif of fern-like leaves surrounded by a festoon of petite flowers. There were diverse pieces made in a three-year period. When we started writing in 1972, nearly every booth at markets or shows displayed pieces of Adam. Today, you are lucky to come across a few pieces. You must be conscious that it will likely take some time to gather a complete set piece by piece. However, one cool thing about collecting these days is that table settings don't have to match. Any woman's magazine you pick up shows myriad combinations of wares delightfully presented.

Adam remains one of the most sought patterns in Depression glass. Pink is easier to find, but there is presently not enough to supply every collector who wants harder-to-find candy dishes, candles, iced teas, or vases. All of those pieces are equally difficult to find in the green except the vase which does surface occasionally. The green butter dish remains elusive.

New collectors continue to write us worried about Adam reproductions. Only the pink butter was reproduced and a description of how to distinguish that reproduction, as well as those in other patterns, is shown in the back of this book. You can only use the butter dish information to distinguish that parti,cular piece of old from new. That does not apply to any other piece of Adam. Prices on pink butters dipped temporarily when the reproductions first appeared, but they are back to as normal as can be expected 20 plus years later. Green butters were never reproduced.

Adam pitchers come with both square and round bases. The square has the motif on the base while the round has only concentric rings. These round-footed pitchers are usually very light in color and are sometimes less desirable to collectors due to that. They are much rarer than their counterparts, but do not fetch prices comparable to their rarity. Lack of demand keeps these reasonably priced.

Candy and sugar lids are interchangeable. Every round Adam plate or saucer you stumble upon is rare. There are at least five different pieces found in crystal, i.e. pitcher, ashtray, coaster, divided relish, and grill plate, and almost nobody cares at present even though they are truly rare. If there are not enough pieces found to collect a set, collectors often forego gathering these few pieces available.

Inner rim damage is found regularly on bowls, having been used and stacked in cabinets for over 70 years. If you see a description that says "irr," it means "inner rim roughness." You do not want to pay mint prices for damaged merchandise.

There exists a rare pink butter dish top that displays both the Adam (outside) motif and the Sierra (inside) mold design. One top contains two designs. The first one found sold for an eyebrow-raising $250.00 back in 1974. You can see that it has escalated quite a bit since then by the price shown below. There is also a rare, seldom seen lamp made from a frosted sherbet with a bulb attached to a metal cap.

	Pink	Green			Pink	Green
8 ▸ Ashtray, 4½"	28.00	25.00	3 ▸**Cup	30.00	25.00
12 ▸ Bowl, 4¾", dessert	22.00	22.00	Lamp	495.00	495.00
11 ▸ Bowl, 5¾", cereal	65.00	60.00	Pitcher, 8", 32 ounce	45.00	45.00
13 ▸ Bowl, 7¾"	27.50	28.00	Pitcher, 32 ounce, round base	75.00	
Bowl, 9", no cover	50.00	50.00	10 ▸ Plate, 6", sherbet	8.50	11.00
Bowl cover, 9"	20.00	45.00	9 ▸ ‡Plate, 7¾", square salad	18.00	16.00
Bowl, 9", covered	70.00	95.00	16 ▸ Plate, 9", square dinner	32.00	32.00
14 ▸ Bowl, 10", oval	35.00	40.00	21 ▸ Plate, 9", grill	27.00	24.00
Butter dish bottom	28.00	60.00	2 ▸ Platter, 11¾"	30.00	33.00
Butter dish top	72.00	330.00	22 ▸ Relish dish, 8", divided	20.00	25.00
Butter dish & cover	100.00	390.00	24 ▸ Salt & pepper, 4", footed	90.00	115.00
23 ▸ Butter dish combination			4 ▸ ‡‡Saucer, 6", square	6.00	7.00
with Sierra pattern	1,700.00		19 ▸ Sherbet, 3"	30.00	38.00
17 ▸ Cake plate, 10", footed	28.00	30.00	5 ▸ Sugar	20.00	25.00
25 ▸ *Candlesticks, 4", pair	100.00	115.00	6 ▸ Sugar/candy cover	25.00	45.00
26 ▸ Candy jar & cover, 2½"	125.00	130.00	18 ▸ Tumbler, 4½"	30.00	30.00
1 ▸ Coaster, 3¼"	22.00	20.00	20 ▸ Tumbler, 5½", iced tea	75.00	72.00
7 ▸ Creamer	25.00	28.00	15 ▸ Vase, 7½"	495.00	125.00

* Delphite $225.00   ** Yellow $100.00   ‡ Round pink $60.00; yellow $100.00   ‡‡ Round pink $75.00; yellow $85.00

6

"ADAMS RIB," LINE #900, DIAMOND GLASSWARE CO., c. 1925

Colors: amber, blue, green, pink; some marigold; milk and crystal w/marigold iridescence, vaseline; and colors decorated w/gold, silver, white enamel, florals; and flashed colors of blue and orange w/black trim

"Adam's Rib" is a Diamond Glassware pattern that is beginning to be noticed by collectors and dealers alike. The #900 line was one of their most distributed wares. When we were searching for pieces of "Adams Rib" for our book, most of the items we purchased were in antique malls or shops. Few pieces were being seen at shows, but in the last three years that has changed. More is being displayed — and sold. Collectors seem to like the diversity of colors as well as those tall candlesticks. We keep adding pieces to our inventory, but I doubt that the listing below is complete. You may find other items and I would very much appreciate a notice of such.

Many of the pieces listed below were shown in a 1928 Sears catalog that advertised six orange and black "ribbed" pieces for $1.32. Indications are that orange was a really big color craze in the country during that time.

Fenton made a pedestal candy that closely resembles that of "Adam's Rib." The knob of the Diamond Company's candy has a tiny protrusion on the top of the knob, whereas the one made by Fenton is smooth.

Flat-bottomed bowls were often offered on a black, three-toed pedestal base. Black bases were a vogue of the time. The marigold pieces are treasured by carnival glass collectors; so, you will have rivalry for those. There are iridized blue and green pitchers that most collectors have not found mugs to accompany. Keep your eye out should either of those colored mugs surface. A non-iridized mug is pictured.

Though Diamond had been a fixture in the glassmaking business, it became one of those unfortunate factories that was leveled by fire in the early 30s.

	Non Iridescent	Iridescent			Non Iridescent	Iridescent
Base, black, pedestal, 3 toe			3 ▸	Cup	18.00	
(for flat bowls)	15.00		2 ▸	Creamer	25.00	45.00
6 ▸ Bowl, vegetable, flared (belled)				Mayonnaise, 6", w/ladle	45.00	
rim	60.00		12 ▸	Mug (or lemonade)	35.00	85.00
Bowl, flat, rolled edge	40.00		11 ▸	Pitcher, lemonade, applied handle	225.00	350.00
Bowl, 8", 3-footed, salad	45.00			Plate, dessert	10.00	
Bowl, 10½" console, pedestal foot	55.00	175.00	1 ▸	Plate, lunch, 8"	18.00	
Candy, 3-footed bonbon w/lid	45.00			Plate, cracker, w/center rim	30.00	
Candy, oval, flat	65.00		4 ▸	Saucer	6.00	
7 ▸ Candy, footed jar and cover	55.00			Sandwich, center flat top handle		50.00
Candle, blown	30.00	50.00	10 ▸	Sandwich, center ½ hex handle	30.00	55.00
5 ▸ Candle, tall, 9"	40.00	60.00		Shakers, pr.	75.00	
Cigarette holder, footed	25.00			Sherbet, flat rim	20.00	
Compote, cheese, non-ribbed	25.00			Sugar, open	25.00	45.00
9 ▸ Comport, flared	30.00			Tray, oval sugar/creamer (8½x6¼")	20.00	35.00
8 ▸ Comport, small, rimmed	35.00			Vase, fan	45.00	65.00
Comport, 6½" tall	40.00	80.00		Vase, 8½", footed, flair rim	75.00	110.00
Comport, large fruit	60.00	100.00		Vase, 9¾"	95.00	150.00

"ADDIE," "TWELVE POINT," LINE #34, NEW MARTINSVILLE GLASS MFG. CO., c. 1930

Colors: amethyst, black, crystal, cobalt, green, jade green satin, pink, red; and w/Lotus Glass Co. silver decoration

"Addie" may be found in amber. We have had a couple of e-mails suggesting that, but no pictures to confirm it. Since there were multiple e-mails, it seems likely. A confirming photograph to my website www.geneflorence.com would be appreciated. The name we've frequently heard this pattern called in the marketplace is "Twelve Point," simply because it has that many points. We found that 20 years ago author William Heacock had christened the pattern in tribute to Addie Miller, a pioneer author for New Martinsville Glass Company wares. The company gave it a line number (#34), but we will continue the name tribute.

The Lions/heraldry design as shown in our *Elegant Glassware of the Depression Era* is etched on this Line #34 as well as the New Martinsville Moondrops Line #37. This begs the question, is it a Lotus or a New Martinsville decoration?

"Addie" impresses more people in the cobalt blue or red color when we have it for sale at shows. Once collectors are shown the jade green satin, it may capture major attention. Unfortunately, there is a shortage of that color today. Everything close to jadite colored ware has been seized in the last few years. New Martinsville's jade green was marketed with black, an arresting color combination — and certainly in keeping the bi- or tri-colored glass productions of that era.

Once more, it is possible you are going to find other colors or pieces and we'd appreciate hearing about what you find. In addition, all measurements you could supply would be helpful.

	Black, Cobalt, Jade, Red	All other colors
Bowl, large flare rim, vegetable	50.00	35.00
Candlestick, 3½"	30.00	20.00
6 ▸ Creamer, footed	17.50	10.00
Cup, demi	18.00	
4 ▸ Cup, footed	15.00	8.00
Mayonnaise, 5"	30.00	15.00
7 ▸ Plate, lunch, 8"	12.50	8.00
3 ▸ Sandwich tray, 2-handle	35.00	25.00
5 ▸ Saucer	5.00	2.50
Saucer, demi	8.00	
1 ▸ Sherbet, footed	18.00	10.00
2 ▸ Sugar, open, footed	17.50	10.00
Tumbler, footed, 6 oz., juice	15.00	10.00
Tumbler, footed, 9 oz., water	22.50	15.00

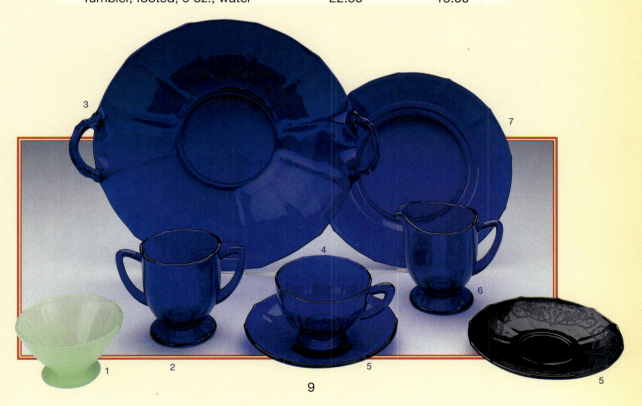

AMELIA, "STAR MEDALLION," "BOXED STAR," LINE #671, IMPERIAL GLASS COMPANY, c. 1920s

Colors: amber, blue, Clambroth, crystal, green, pink, Rubigold iridescent, Smoke; Azalea, Turquoise, and Verde, 1960s; pink carnival, 1980s

Line # 671, Amelia, began production in the 1920s, but not all pieces were made in all colors. Items we see most often at markets are the milk or hotel pitcher and sugar in either crystal or Rubigold, Imperial's name for their marigold carnival color. There are wide ranges of pricing on the pitcher, especially the Rubigold. People see a carnival colored ware and dollar signs go off in their heads. The Rubigold varies in shades from deep marigold to a very light color as depicted in our photo.

Another Amelia piece being found is a pink carnival, crimped rim compote that frequently turns up in malls and flea markets. These were made in the late 1970s and are not as old as many seem to believe.

Both the Rubigold custard cup and nut bowl are difficult to find. Actually, only the pitcher is regularly noticed in this carnival color.

We are not finding colored Amelia very easily — including the 1960s colors, which seems to indicate a scarcity in the market at present. That could mean owners are keeping it or Imperial did not produce mass quantities of it in the first place.

	Clambroth	Rubigold	Smoke	All other colors			Clambroth	Rubigold	Smoke	All other colors
Butter w/cover, round				45.00	10 ▸	Creamer				20.00
13 ▸ Bowl, 5", lily				15.00		Celery, 2-handle				30.00
Bowl, 5½", square	25.00	30.00	45.00	15.00		Celery vase, footed	80.00	90.00	150.00	40.00
Bowl, 5½", deep nut, ftd.		35.00		20.00	1 ▸	Goblet, cocktail				15.00
11 ▸ Bowl, 6", round nappy	20.00	25.00	40.00	15.00	2 ▸	Goblet, wine		50.00	75.00	20.00
8 ▸ Bowl, 6", 2-hdld. jelly				15.00		Pitcher, milk or hotel	33.00	40.00	80.00	25.00
Bowl, 6¼", oval preserve				25.00		Plate, 6½", dessert		35.00		12.00
Bowl, 7", oval				25.00	3 ▸	Plate, 9½", lunch	40.00	50.00	70.00	25.00
7 ▸ Bowl, 7½", berry, flare					9 ▸	Sherbet				10.00
(belled) rim			25.00			Spoon holder				
6 ▸ Bowl, 8", round berry				35.00		(open sugar)				20.00
Candlestick				25.00	12 ▸	Sugar w/cover				30.00
Cup, custard		22.00		11.00	4 ▸	Tumbler, 4"		30.00	40.00	20.00
Compote, straight rim				20.00	5 ▸	Tumbler, 4½", lemonade,				
Compote, crimped rim						flare rim	30.00	40.00	40.00	
(late)	35.00	35.00		15.00						

AMERICAN PIONEER, LIBERTY WORKS, 1931 – 1934

Colors: pink, green, amber, and crystal

American Pioneer is suffering from a lack of supply which means prices are remaining rather steady for common pieces, but increasing for the scarce items. Candy jar lids are identical even though the two candies are fashioned in different ways. One looks like a typical footed candy, the other is taller and has the profile of a footed vase. There are two styles of cups, one being a bit more flared than the other. One has a 4" diameter and is 2½" tall; the other has a 3⅜" diameter and is 2⅜" tall. These discrepancies are very minute and may well be mold differences; but collectors have noticed them enough to say the flared rim cup is the more frequently found.

Vegetable bowl covers are rarely seen; and we have observed two sizes (8¾" and 9¼") but there are reports of a third size. Stay tuned!

There are few pieces in amber, but both sizes of urns have surfaced in that color. Amber cocktails have been discovered in two sizes; none have surfaced thus far in other colors. Under liners for the hard-to-get urns (or pitchers in today's terminology) are the regular 6" and 8" plates. However, a 6" pink plate is rare. Candlesticks, which are handled, are in demand by collectors of candles, but do not appear as often as they once did. Dresser sets are desirable pieces in American Pioneer and a crystal one was finally discovered. Admirers of powder jars and colognes vie with American Pioneer collectors to add these to their sets.

It's exciting to know that 70 years later, and with hundreds of thousands of people collecting Depression glass, heretofore unknown items and colors are still showing up. This is what makes collecting exciting. There is the real possibility that any collector can find something rare in the next shop or market.

The American Pioneer design does need to have those plain banded, horizontal ribbed areas in order to be American Pioneer. Various companies made hobnailed designs that are analogous, but without the bands.

Liberty Works was originally designated a cut glass works. Indeed that was a part of its name. We've been assured by devotees of American Pioneer that this is "better glass" than your run of the mill Depression era wares and should be treated as such and placed in our *Elegant Glassware of the Depression Era* book. It probably should be, but I inherited its acceptance as Depression glass when we started writing in 1972. Unfortunately, the plant experienced fire damage in 1931 and could not recover financially from this blow. Fire seemed to be an ever-present problem of glassware manufacturing facilities back then.

AMERICAN PIONEER

	Crystal, Pink	Green
* Bowl, 5", handled	25.00	25.00
Bowl, 8¾", covered	110.00	150.00
11 ▸ Bowl, 9", handled	30.00	35.00
16 ▸ Bowl, 9¼", covered	125.00	165.00
Bowl, 10¾", console	60.00	70.00
Candlesticks, 6½", pair	110.00	135.00
Candy jar and cover, 1 pound	95.00	110.00
4 ▸ Candy jar and cover, 1½ pound	100.00	135.00
Cheese and cracker set (indented platter and comport)	55.00	65.00
Coaster, 3½"	35.00	35.00
2 ▸ Creamer, 2¾"	20.00	22.00
8 ▸ * Creamer, 3½"	20.00	22.00
14 ▸ * Cup	11.00	11.00
Dresser set (2 colognes, powder jar, indented 7½" tray)	495.00	495.00
Goblet, 3¹³⁄₁₆", 3 oz., cocktail (amber)	40.00	
Goblet, 3¹⁵⁄₁₆", 3½ oz., cocktail (amber)	40.00	
Goblet, 4", 3 oz., wine	40.00	55.00
Goblet, 6", 8 oz., water	50.00	60.00
Ice bucket, 6"	65.00	75.00
13 ▸ Lamp, 1¾", w/metal pole, 9½"		75.00

	Crystal, Pink	Green
Lamp, 5½", round, ball shape, amber $150.00	175.00	
Lamp, 8½", tall	140.00	180.00
5 ▸ Mayonnaise, 4¼"	55.00	80.00
6 ▸ Mayonnaise plate	14.00	14.00
Pilsner, 5¾", 11 ounce	150.00	150.00
1 ▸ ** Pitcher, 5", covered urn	175.00	225.00
3 ▸ ‡ Pitcher, 7", covered urn	195.00	250.00
Plate, 6"	12.50	15.00
* Plate, 6", handled	12.50	15.00
19 ▸ * Plate, 8"	14.00	14.00
9 ▸ * Plate, 11½", handled	30.00	40.00
15 ▸ * Saucer	5.00	5.00
Sherbet, 3½"	16.00	20.00
17 ▸ Sherbet, 4¾"	40.00	45.00
12 ▸ Sugar, 2¾"	20.00	22.00
7 ▸ * Sugar, 3½"	20.00	22.00
Tumbler, 5 ounce, juice	35.00	40.00
Tumbler, 4", 8 ounce	40.00	50.00
Tumbler, 5", 12 ounce	50.00	60.00
10 ▸ Vase, 7", 4 styles	125.00	150.00
Vase, 9", round		250.00
18 ▸ Whiskey, 2¼", 2 ounce	40.00	85.00

* Amber — Double the price of pink unless noted

** Amber $300.00   ‡ Amber $350.00

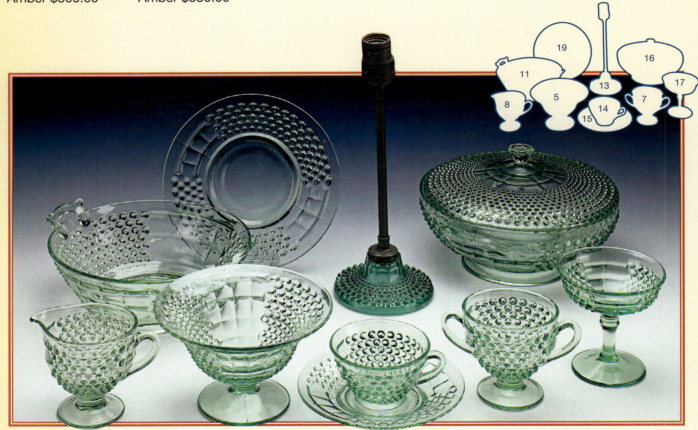

AMERICAN SWEETHEART, MacBETH-EVANS GLASS COMPANY, 1930 – 1936

Colors: pink, Monax, ruby, and cobalt; some Cremax and color-trimmed Monax

American Sweetheart was copiously produced during its seven-year run and was durable as is confirmed by the remaining pieces found. Prices on commonly seen luncheon pieces (cups, saucers, and plates) have diminished. The advent of the Internet has exposed a more abundant supply of some patterns than were previously known. American Sweetheart is one of those patterns. However, there are still pieces that are not turning up; so those items are increasing in price. These rarely found items include the sugar lid (with two different styles of knobs), and large (18", triple wide, flat rim) or small console bowls that appear in Monax; the larger console was also produced in red and blue.

Both pink and Monax (white with translucent edges) shakers are rarely found. You will find plates in Monax that come with and without a center motif. Plates vary in size due to the number of years this pattern was made. Moulds wore out and were reworked. There may be a $1/16$" or even an $1/8$" size discrepancy. I had a stack of dozens of American Sweetheart plates in my shop. Several collectors tried to find six or eight plates to match exactly, and did so with great difficulty.

We in the trade tend to feel that everybody knows about Depression glass by now, but they do not. The sadder ones are those who just gave it away, sold it for pennies at a garage sale, or trashed their aunt or grandmother's dishes because they had no clue they were valuable.

Monax luncheon pieces were trimmed in gold near the end of production, but are not as accepted by today's collector. If the gold is a distraction, you can remove it with an art gum eraser. Monax pieces are found with colored edgings of yellow, green, pink, and smoky/black, any of which is extremely collectible.

Even though this dinnerware is rather fragile looking, it was miraculously long lasting. A Louisville Tin & Stove Company catalog, dated 1937, offered a 32-piece set of Monax American Sweetheart for $2.75 as well as a 42-piece set (including a two-piece sugar) for $4.15. You must also remember that a day's wages in the 1930s were in the range of twenty cents to a dollar a day. These sets cost three to 20 days work for an average worker; so many people only owned the pieces that were give-a-ways or premiums for buying necessities.

Pitchers and water tumblers came only in pink and there are similar shaped pitchers having no design that were sold with plain, Dogwood shaped tumblers. These pitchers are not American Sweetheart, though some people do buy them to go with their sets. If it does not have the pattern, it is not considered to be American Sweetheart. These plain pitchers usually sell in the $50.00 range.

Ruby, cobalt, and Monax colors were used for tidbit servers (plates drilled in center connected with a metal rod), 15" sandwich plates, and the 18" console bowl.

Sherbets are found in two sizes, with the smaller 3¾" harder to find. Sherbets also appear in crystal with metal holders.

Cremax (beige color) items were made by the company in the mid-30s, ostensibly to compete with the china trade. Cremax does not seem to appeal to today's collectors and that is just as well since it is fairly rare.

AMERICAN SWEETHEART

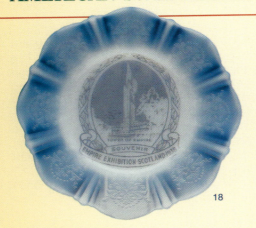

18   18   18

	Ruby	Cobalt	Cremax	Smoke & Other Trims
Bowl, 6", cereal			16.00	50.00
Bowl, 9", round berry			50.00	250.00
Bowl, 9½", soup				165.00
Bowl, 18", console	1,100.00	1,250.00		
Creamer, footed	185.00	210.00		110.00
Cup	120.00	150.00		110.00
Lamp shade			495.00	
Lamp (floor with brass base)			795.00	
Plate, 6", bread and butter				22.00
Plate, 8", salad	115.00	135.00		30.00
Plate, 9", luncheon				45.00
Plate, 9¾", dinner				100.00
Plate, 12", salver	165.00	265.00		125.00
Plate, 15½", server	325.00	425.00		
Platter, 13", oval				225.00
Saucer	25.00	30.00		17.50
Sherbet, 4¼", footed				
(design inside or outside)				110.00
Sugar, open footed	185.00	210.00		110.00
Tidbit, 2 tier, 8" & 12"	250.00	335.00		
Tidbit, 3 tier, 8", 12" & 15½"	625.00	750.00		

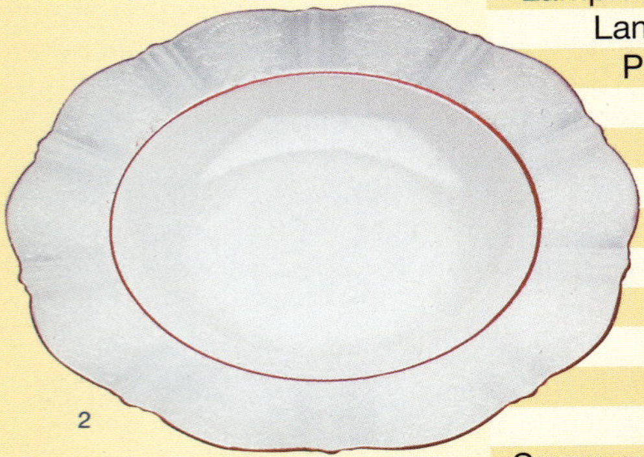

		Pink	Monax
23 ▶	Bowl, 3¾", flat berry	85.00	
21 ▶	Bowl, 4½", cream soup	87.50	120.00
1 ▶	Bowl, 6", cereal	18.00	20.00
20 ▶	Bowl, 9", round berry	60.00	75.00
2 ▶	Bowl, 9½", flat soup	74.00	87.50
13 ▶	Bowl, 11", oval vegetable	70.00	80.00
	Bowl, 18", console		495.00
10 ▶	Creamer, footed	14.00	12.00
11 ▶	Cup	17.00	8.00
	Lamp shade		495.00
8 ▶	Plate, 6" or 6½", bread & butter	6.00	6.50
18 ▶	Plate, 8", salad	12.50	10.00
	Plate, 9", luncheon		13.00
17 ▶	Plate, 9¾", dinner	35.00	25.00
25 ▶	Plate, 10¼", dinner		28.00
	Plate, 11", chop plate		21.00
24 ▶	Plate, 12", salver	23.00	22.00
	Plate, 15½", server		250.00

		Pink	Monax
5 ▶	Platter, 13", oval	55.00	70.00
6 ▶	Pitcher, 7½", 60 ounce	1,050.00	
19 ▶	Pitcher, 8", 80 ounce	795.00	
7 ▶	Salt and pepper, footed	595.00	495.00
12 ▶	Saucer	5.00	2.00
3 ▶	Sherbet, 3¾", footed	25.00	
22 ▶	Sherbet, 4¼", footed		
	(design inside or outside)	19.00	22.00
	Sherbet in metal holder		
	(crystal only)	3.50	
9 ▶	Sugar, open, footed	14.00	8.00
	*Sugar lid		500.00
4 ▶	Tidbit, 2 tier, 8" & 12"	60.00	60.00
	Tidbit, 3 tier, 8", 12" & 15½"		325.00
16 ▶	Tumbler, 3½", 5 ounce	97.50	
15 ▶	Tumbler, 4¼", 9 ounce	95.00	
14 ▶	Tumbler, 4¾", 10 ounce	135.00	

*Three styles of knobs.

2

ARDITH, PADEN CITY GLASS COMPANY, c. 1920s

Colors: amber, black, crystal, cobalt, green, pink, ruby, yellow

Ardith floral design can be found on several Paden City mould blanks. It appears frequently on the squared (#412) and round (#890) Crow's Foot blanks, the squared, cropped cornered #411 Mrs. B line, the #211 four Spired line, the #210 Stacked paneled line, the lined #215 Glades, and the #555 "Teardrop and Bead" line. You may find Ardith on other blanks.

Don't be deluded into believing this is regularly found even though the flowered motif seems to have been a popular etching considering the number of pieces on which it can be found. Finding it today is not an easy task. The few pieces I see are usually unidentified by the seller, but priced highly in case it might be something "good." Many sellers use that theory, and do not understand why their glass does not sell quickly. If you are not willing to research what you have, price it based upon what you paid for it and move on down the road to find another treasure which you do know. You may turn a dozen profits while you "wait" on that unidentified piece to lure a buyer.

I am using only one price for all colors and lines. Realize that red, black, and cobalt blue will fetch 20% – 25% more and crystal 50% less.

	*All colors			*All colors
Bowl, 5⅝", 2 hdld.	50.00	7 ▸ Cup	50.00
Bowl, 9", ped., ftd., sq.	125.00	Cheese & cracker, 10¼" plate; 5" sq. stand	130.00
Bowl, 9½", sq. ped., ftd.	125.00	Ice bucket w/lid	195.00
Bowl, 10", rolled edge console	75.00	Mayonnaise, w/ladle & liner plate	60.00
Bowl, 10", sq.	80.00	Pitcher, 7¼"	210.00
Bowl, 10", 2 hdld.	100.00	Plate, 5⅞"	15.00
1 ▸ Bowl, 10½", sq.	75.00	3 ▸ Plate, 8⅜", sq.	40.00
Bowl, 12", sq.	80.00	Saucer	20.00
Bowl, 12½", 4-toed console	85.00	Sugar, flat	45.00
2 ▸ Candle, 4", rolled edge	125.00	Sugar, ftd.	50.00
Candle, 4⅝", sq. flattened top	45.00	Tray, 7½", 2 hdld.	50.00
Candle, 5¼", keyhole	45.00	6 ▸ Tray, 9", cupped center hdld.	100.00
Candle, 6", "wings"	60.00	Tray, 10" sq., center handle	90.00
Candle, 6", center circle	60.00	Tray, 10¼", sq., center handle	90.00
Candy, w/lid, 2-part	100.00	Tumbler, 3 oz.	45.00
Candy, w/lid, 3-part	100.00	Vase, 3", high	185.00
Candy, w/lid, 8", ftd.	155.00	5 ▸ Vase, 4¼", ivy/rose, ftd.	75.00
Cake stand, 9¼", ped., ftd.	75.00	Vase, 5½", elliptical	150.00
Compote, 6½" high, sq.	65.00	Vase, 7½", bulbous bottom	135.00
4 ▸ Creamer, flat	45.00	Vase, 8½", horizontal ribbed	150.00
Creamer, ftd.	50.00	Vase, 10"	175.00

*Crystal 50% less

16

"ARTURA," PATTERN #608, INDIANA GLASS COMPANY, c. 1930s

Colors: crystal and w/color decoration, green, pink

"Artura" is another of Indiana's numbered lines. It is a comparatively small pattern which was promoted in 15-, 21-, and 27-piece sets to use for breakfast, luncheon, or bridge type get-togethers. Its distinguishing trait is a double rib which occurs at each of the nine points in its design. It may be the only nine-sided glassware from this period.

"Artura" has a wonderful Deco linear look, which is alleviated by "question mark" curving handles. It's truly a shame they didn't fashion more items in this delightful pattern. "Artura" often sits unrecognized, but we see more of it in Midwestern antique malls than any place we travel. Collectors seem to be attracted to the crystal decorated pieces. There is a small luncheon set of crystal decorated with black accents that is rather striking. If you find crystal undecorated ware, price it about 30% lower than the prices listed — for now!

		Green, Pink, Crystal Decorated			Green, Pink, Crystal Decorated
6 ▸	Cup	8.00	1 ▸	Sugar, open	12.00
3 ▸	Creamer	12.00	5 ▸	Tray, sandwich w/ornate center handle	35.00
4 ▸	Plate, 7½", salad	6.00		Tray, sugar and sugar	12.50
7 ▸	Saucer	2.00	2 ▸	Tumbler, ftd.	15.00

AUNT POLLY, U.S. GLASS COMPANY, Late 1920s

Colors: blue, green, and iridescent

Aunt Polly's collectibility is beset by some minor problems which put off some collectors. There are no cups or saucers. Many pieces have rough seams from the mould, and there are noticeably different shades of green and blue found. Observe the color variations shown in the photos. This would not be much of a problem if more Aunt Polly were available to pick and choose. However, avid collectors accept these idiosyncrasies as normal characteristics of the pattern. One long-time collector told us it "just added to the character of the pattern" as far as she was concerned.

That two-handled covered candy (lid interchangeable with sugar) pictured in green has never been found in blue although it has been spotted in iridescent. The footed, double handled, blue, open candy pictured in front is very desirable. It is missing in most Aunt Polly collections as are the oval vegetable, sugar lid, shakers, and butter dish. That Aunt Polly butter bottom is the same as other U.S. Glass patterns of the time, specifically Floral and Diamond, Strawberry, Cherryberry, and U.S. Swirl; but none of those patterns were made in blue. Consequently, blue Aunt Polly butter bottoms will always be scarce.

Some Aunt Polly creamers come with a more pronounced lip than others, due to the fact these were made by hand with a wooden paddle while the glass was still hot. Quality control was not high on the agenda for this cheaper glassware, so variations abound.

No reports of additional ruffled vases being found have been forthcoming. This vase was created from the regular vase mold. I'm sure it was experimental or an employee play thing.

		Green, Iridescent	Blue
1 ▸	Bowl, 4¾", berry	7.00	15.00
3 ▸	Bowl, 4¾", 2" high	16.00	
8 ▸	Bowl, 5½", one handle	15.00	25.00
7 ▸	Bowl, 7¼", oval, handled, pickle	15.00	35.00
2 ▸	Bowl, 7⅞", large berry	20.00	50.00
9 ▸	Bowl, 8⅜", oval	75.00	150.00
3 ▸	Butter dish and cover	240.00	225.00
	Butter dish bottom	90.00	100.00
	Butter dish top	150.00	125.00
9 ▸	Candy, cover, 2-handled	70.00	
5 ▸	Candy, footed, 2-handled	30.00	60.00

		Green, Iridescent	Blue
14 ▸	Creamer	35.00	60.00
1 ▸	Pitcher, 8", 48 ounce		235.00
8 ▸	Plate, 6", sherbet	6.00	12.00
4 ▸	Plate, 8", luncheon		20.00
10 ▸	Salt and pepper		250.00
7 ▸	Sherbet	10.00	10.00
15 ▸	Sugar	25.00	35.00
16 ▸	Sugar/candy cover	50.00	155.00
2 ▸	Tumbler, 3⅝", 8 ounce		30.00
6 ▸	Vase, 6½", footed	35.00	55.00

AURORA, HAZEL-ATLAS GLASS COMPANY, Late 1930s

Colors: cobalt blue, pink, green, and crystal

Deep Aurora blue bowls (4½") have doubled in price in the last ten years. How many of your stocks have done that? Of course, the lack of small, deep bowls being marketed in cobalt has forced that spiraling price. However this remain one cobalt blue set that can be obtained for less than a small fortune. Here, in Florida, many windows display coba glassware as a decoration. It does absorb heat, so be careful about putting it in direct sunlight. I've heard a couple of stories about pieces of glass "just exploding." Of course that also happens at shows when coats, purses, or bags dra by a booth of glass. "Did you see that? That glass just jumped on the floor! I didn't touch it!" Leaping glass disease is th scourge of glass dealers.

The few items found in pink bring a price comparable to the blue due to their scarcity. The deep bowl, creamer, an tumbler have so far never been found in pink. Canadian collectors testify that pink and green are more readily foun there than in the States. Both green and crystal cereal bowls, cups, and saucers have been found. So far, only collector of cups and saucers have been very excited over this turn of events.

A number of readers have recommended that any pattern with a creamer and no sugar, such as this one, shoul have the creamer listed as a milk pitcher. Milk pitchers normally hold at least a pint and this one definitely does no However, lending credence to that idea, a collector reported that creamers were given away as premiums for buying breakfast cereal in her hometown. I guess the small bowls did not hold enough cereal to warrant a give-away status of they would be more plentiful today. By the way, while we were doing research for *The Hazel-Atlas Glass Identification an Value Guide*, we noticed that a Hazel-Atlas catalog from the 50s shows that deep bowl in crystal listed as a "utility" bow So, if you can't find it in cobalt, you might try the latest glass fashion and mix in a crystal one.

		Cobalt, Pink				Cobalt Pink
1 ▸	Bowl, 4½", deep	68.00		Plate, 6½"		10.00
2 ▸	*Bowl, 5⅜", cereal	17.00	5 ▸	‡Saucer		4.00
3 ▸	Creamer, 4½"	25.00	4 ▸	Tumbler, 4¾", 10 ounce		26.00
6 ▸	**Cup	16.00				

*Green $8.00 or crystal $5.00   **Green $8.00   ‡Green $2.50

Colors: pink, green, crystal; white, 1950s; yellow mist, burnt honey, and water sets in myriad frosted and transparent colors for Tiara Home Products, 1974 – 1998 (See Reproduction Section.)

Indiana's #601 line was initially called "Sweet Pear" by authors of pattern glass books. Early Depression glass authors called it "Avocado."

As popular as "Avocado" is, there isn't enough of the older green and pink surfacing these days for new collectors to become captivated. Prices were stable for several years, but of late, these have been stumbling on all but rarer pieces. Newer collectors often seek less expensive patterns to start their collecting and "Avocado" is not an inexpensive pattern.

The infrequently found pitcher and tumblers are missing in many collections due to rarity and the fact that old ones are expensive. Be aware that Indiana reproductions of these two items abound in pink, but the pink repro is frequently an orange tinted pink. Be sure to read the Reproduction Section in the back depicting the various "Avocado" items and colors produced by Indiana for the Tiara Home Products line during their 1970 – 1998 life span. You don't want to be caught paying collectible prices for more recent wares. One such color was a striking yellow.

We are pricing crystal "Avocado" but only those items we can document as being made. If you see additional items, please let us know. A few pieces of white were made in the 1950s, but only pitchers and tumblers are seen regularly. We know a frosted pitcher and tumblers were made since 1980 for Tiara, as well as myriad other frosted colors not originally produced.

Every piece of green "Avocado" is pictured below except the pitcher; and with our new "legend" format, you will be able to identify each piece without difficulty. Hopefully, this will aid new collectors though it has proved surprisingly time consuming to include these. We hope it is worth our efforts.

	Crystal	Pink	Green
Bowl, 5¼", 2-handled	10.00	30.00	33.00
Bowl, 6", footed relish	9.00	28.00	30.00
Bowl, 7", 1-handle preserve	8.00	28.00	28.00
Bowl, 7½", salad	13.00	50.00	72.00
Bowl, 8", 2-handled, oval	12.00	30.00	35.00
Bowl, 9½", 3¼", deep	25.00	150.00	180.00
‡Creamer, footed	12.00	35.00	35.00
Cup, footed, 2 styles		35.00	38.00

	Crystal	Pink	Green
*Pitcher, 64 ounce	350.00	1,000.00	1,500.00
13 ▸ ‡Plate, 6⅜", sherbet	5.00	14.00	16.00
12 ▸ **Plate, 8¼", luncheon	7.00	17.00	22.00
8 ▸ Plate, 10¼", 2-handled, cake	14.00	50.00	60.00
5 ▸ Saucer, 6⅜"		22.00	24.00
11 ▸ ‡Sherbet		55.00	70.00
3 ▸ ‡Sugar, footed	12.00	35.00	35.00
9 ▸ *Tumbler	35.00	210.00	335.00

* Caution on pink. The orange-pink is new. White: Pitcher $300.00; Tumbler $35.00.
** Apple design $15.00. Amber has been newly made.
‡ Remade in dark shade of green.

BEADED BLOCK, #710, IMPERIAL GLASS COMPANY, 1927 – 1930s; Late 1970s – Early 1980s

Colors: pink, green, crystal, ice blue, Canary, iridescent, amber, red, opalescent colors, and milk white

You should know that true connoisseurs of this pattern make a distinction between plain Beaded Block and the frosted, stippled pieces. They refer to the latter as "Frosted Block."

Beaded Block plates are mostly found in square shapes; round plates are in short supply. Most 8¾" – 9" round "plates" were transformed into bowls and even these bowls are sparse in the collecting landscape. There are size variances in this pattern as pointed out in the round plate which varies a ¼". The sizes listed here were all obtained from actual measurements of the pieces and not those cataloged by Imperial. The two-handled jelly, so called by Imperial, was termed a cream soup by most companies and varies from 4¾" to 5". Neither size seems to be common. Be sure to read the section on measurements on page 2. I have found early company catalog size listings were more nearly approximations than precise calculations.

The red lily bowl remains one of the rarer items today and was made during that 30s thirst for red. We have never found out why they were distributed around Vandalia, Ohio, but most of the ones known were found there. They are actually selling in the $500 ball park even though one once brought over $1,200 on an Internet auction. That is why books using Internet auction prices should make you a bit cautious. Prices are not consistent at auction whether on the Internet or down the street. There are too many factors depending upon who is observing at any particular time and how much money is available to them at that one moment.

Beaded Block pitchers are scarce; however crystal and green can be found with some searching. Pink and white pitchers are a different matter as few of these have turned up over the years. Beaded Block was one of the patterns that had only inconsistent recognition until the Internet auctions came along. For some reason, new collectors seemed to be impressed with Beaded Block's color and style. They adopted it and prices were soaring. That too, has passed; but some upward price adjustments linger.

Six inch vases sold as Beaded Block usually are not. The true vase has a scalloped top as shown on other pieces. There is a 6" vase/parfait with a straight top and no beading that was called a footed jelly by Imperial. These level edged ones were premium items found with a product inside at grocery stores. Most commonly found are ones with labels and tops from "Frank Tea & Spice Co., Cin., O." Dry mustard and pepper were most often packed in these. Just know these are "go-with" pieces and not truly Beaded Block pattern.

Neophyte dealers and sellers on the Internet like to categorize Beaded Block as pricey, older Sandwich glass, which is either an accolade to it or an insult to Sandwich glass. It was sold at Woolworth's. We have also seen at least one source crediting the 1930s Sea Foam decoration (white edges) to about 40 years before it was cataloged by Imperial.

Imperial reissued pink and iridized pink (pink carnival) in the late 1970s and early 1980s. These pieces are plainly marked IG on the bottom. Visiting the factory in 1981, information was gleaned that the white was made in the early 1950s and the IG mark (for Imperial Glass) was first used around 1951. Few marked pieces of Beaded Block are found but they include the white covered pear. This two-part candy in the shape of a large pear dates from the mid-50s. Pears have been found in yellow, green, pink, and amber. Amber seems to be the more easily found color and for some unknown reason are usually found on the West Coast. Still, this item is coveted by Beaded Block collectors.

		*Crystal, Pink, Green, Amber	Opalescent colors
3 ▸	Bowl, 4⅞" – 5", 2-handled jelly	20.00	45.00
12 ▸**	Bowl, 4½", round, lily	20.00	45.00
5 ▸	Bowl, 5½", square	20.00	35.00
14 ▸	Bowl, 5½", 1-handle	20.00	35.00
8 ▸	Bowl, 6", deep, round	25.00	40.00
11 ▸	Bowl, 6¼", round, flared	25.00	40.00
	Bowl, 6½", round	25.00	40.00
4 ▸	Bowl, 6½", 2-handled pickle	30.00	50.00
10 ▸	Bowl, 6¾", round, unflared	25.00	40.00
9 ▸	Bowl, 7¼", round, flared	30.00	45.00
7 ▸	Bowl, 7½", round, fluted edges	30.00	45.00
	Bowl, 7½", round, plain edge	30.00	45.00
	Bowl, 8¼", celery	38.00	60.00
6 ▸	Candy, pear shaped	395.00	
1 ▸	Creamer	22.00	55.00
‡	Pitcher, 5¼", pint jug	110.00	
15 ▸	Plate, 7¾", square	20.00	40.00
16 ▸	Plate, 8¾", round	30.00	50.00
13 ▸	Stemmed jelly, 4½"	28.00	45.00
	Stemmed jelly, 4½", flared top	28.00	45.00
2 ▸	Sugar	22.00	55.00
14 ▸	Vase, 6", bouquet	22.00	55.00

*All pieces 25% to 40% lower   ** Red $495.00   ‡ White $195.00, pink $175.00, crystal $85.00

6

14   15   9   16   12   15   13

9   5   3

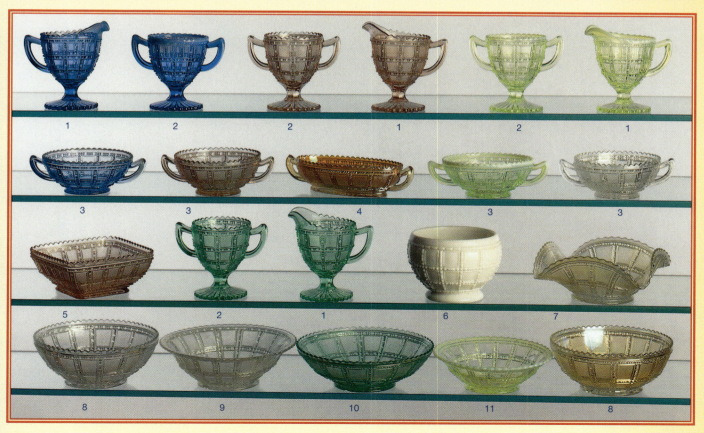

1   2   2   1   2   1

3   3   4   3   3

5   2   1   6   7

8   9   10   11   8

"BERLIN," "REEDED WAFFLE," LINE #124, WESTMORELAND SPECIALTY COMPANY, c. 1924

Colors: blue, crystal, green, pink; ruby, c. 1980s

Westmoreland's Line #124 has been called "Berlin" and "Reeded Waffle" due to its similarity to a pattern glass design primarily produced in the 1870s. The older ware is found with colored stains of ruby or amber. Westmoreland made at least 15 pieces of their #124 pattern in established Depression era colors; so it was added to this book.

There has been some confusion between this pattern and one known as "Plaid" or "Open Plaid," which is similar at first glance. Plaid has a definite basketweave design and was only created in crystal.

Pattern glass books report that the older "Berlin" design produced tumblers, wines, cracker jars, cruets, cups, butter dishes, etc. Consequently, an abundance of items occur in this design, but were ascribed to other companies.

We have been informed that Westmoreland made a ruby colored pitcher sometime in the 1980s, just before going out of business, but we have been unable to find one offered for sale to show you.

		*Crystal
7 ▸	Basket	27.50
	Bowl, bonbon, 1 handle	16.00
	Bowl, 6½", round	15.00
	Bowl, square	20.00
8 ▸	Bowl, 2-handle cream soup	20.00
1 ▸	Bowl, 7", round	22.00
9 ▸	Bowl, 7½", round	25.00
	Bowl, oval, pickle	22.50
2 ▸	Creamer	18.00

		*Crystal
6 ▸	Mayonnaise	25.00
4 ▸	Pitcher	55.00
5 ▸	Plate, 7"	12.00
	Plate, 9", lunch	15.00
3 ▸	Sugar	18.00
	Tray, 2- handle, celery	30.00
10 ▸	Vase, footed	35.00

*Double price of crystal for colors.

Colors: green, pink, yellow, crystal, and some amber, blue, and clambroth green

The Block Optic layout in the last edition showing variations of pitchers, tumblers, cups, creamers, and sugars was a big winner with readers. Showing these again along with a "legend" of pieces pictured should solve myriad identification problems.

Hocking's Block Optic pattern approval rates high with collectors. Several reasons come to mind: its availability due to length of production, its simplicity of design and variety of colors, and its history of being inexpensive to collect. There are a few costly items, but, in general, most collectors can afford to assemble this pattern. Many beginners started with Block and went on to collect additional patterns when time and money permitted. Also, today, when things Deco are prized, this pattern fits right in.

Large sets of green Block can be gathered with a multitude of stems and tumblers. However collecting pink is more difficult due to its limited production. Additionally, not all pieces were produced in pink. Only a very few were made in crystal and yellow; so collecting those colors exclusively is a chore. However that should not stifle you if you like those colors because small sets can be put together with work and patience. In addition, at recent shows, a few people have been asking for the black footed stems. Around the 1928 – 1932 period, glass companies started to make bi-colored wares, either by decorating that way, or by actually fusing two (or three) colors. Hocking's effort gave us a more Deco look by their firing black over the stems and foot of regular green sherbets and goblets. See the high sherbet pictured with stems on page 27 for an example.

Greenhorns to collecting should be aware that Block Optic has five variations of sugars and creamers, due to their variety of handles, their being footed or flat, or their having rayed or non-rayed bottoms. Individual pictures should help you differentiate styles.

Some Block was satinized or frosted, also a big push of that era. Items were dipped in camphoric acid which gave the items a softer look. In fact, I understand that today's crafters are etching things much the same way. In the early days of collecting, no one wanted anything to do with the satinized wares unless hand painted with flowers, birds, or other colorful decorations. However, that, too, is changing.

Block stems are difficult to find now. Many people liked their shape and capacity whether they collected much glass or not. Both yellow and green fluoresce in black light, a display technique being used more and more often. Do not fall for the tale that this guarantees glass to be old, however; it simply means there's uranium oxide among the mix, something still being used to produce glassware by some factories today.

Both sizes of water goblets hold nine ounces and are often used more for wine than water.

25

BLOCK OPTIC

	Green	Yellow	Pink
Bowl, 4¼" diam., 1⅜" tall	8.00		12.00
Bowl, 4½" diam., 1½" tall	27.00		45.00
Bowl, 5¼", cereal	15.00		30.00
Bowl, 7¼", salad	140.00		160.00
Bowl, 8½", large berry	40.00		35.00
5 ▸ *Bowl, 11¾", rolled-edge console	70.00		70.00
**Butter dish and cover, 3" x 5"	50.00		
Butter dish bottom	30.00		
Butter dish top	20.00		
4 ▸ ‡Candlesticks, 1¾", pr.	110.00		70.00
8 ▸ Candy jar & cover, 2¼" tall	60.00	75.00	60.00
7 ▸ Candy jar & cover, 6¼" tall	65.00		165.00
Comport, 5⅜" wide, mayonnaise	90.00		95.00
Creamer, 3 styles: cone shaped, round, rayed-foot & flat (5 kinds)	13.00	15.00	15.00
Cup, four styles	7.00	8.00	10.00
Goblet, 3½", short wine	525.00		525.00
Goblet, 4", cocktail	40.00		40.00
Goblet, 4½", wine	45.00		45.00
Goblet, 5¾", 9 ounce	27.50		30.00
Goblet, 7¼", 9 ounce, thin		40.00	
6 ▸ Ice bucket	42.50		95.00
1 ▸ Ice tub or butter tub, open	65.00		125.00
Mug	40.00		
2 ▸ Pitcher, 7⅝", 54 ounce, bulbous	95.00		495.00
3 ▸ Pitcher, 8½", 54 ounce	65.00		55.00
9 ▸ Pitcher, 8", 80 ounce	100.00		165.00
Plate, 6", sherbet	2.50	3.00	3.00
Plate, 8", luncheon	7.00	8.00	8.00
Plate, 9", dinner	25.00	50.00	38.00

	Green	Yellow	Pink
Plate, 9", grill	150.00	125.00	
Plate, 10¼", sandwich	25.00		25.00
Plate, 12¾"	35.00		
Salt and pepper, footed, pair	45.00	95.00	90.00
Salt and pepper, squatty, pair	120.00		
Sandwich server, center handle	75.00		75.00
Saucer, 5¾", with cup ring	8.00		7.00
Saucer, 6⅛", with cup ring	8.00		7.00
Sherbet, non-stemmed (cone)	3.50		
Sherbet, 3¼", 5½ ounce	6.00	10.00	7.50
Sherbet, 4¾", 6 ounce	18.00	21.00	18.00
Sugar, 3 styles: as creamer	12.50	15.00	12.50
Tumbler, 3 ounce, 2⅝"	25.00		30.00
Tumbler, 5 ounce, 3½", flat	25.00		28.00
Tumbler, 9½ ounce, 3¹³⁄₁₆", flat	15.00		17.00
Tumbler, 10 or 11 oz., 5", flat	20.00		18.00
Tumbler, 12 ounce, 4⅞", flat	30.00		26.00
Tumbler, 15 ounce, 5¼", flat	55.00		55.00
Tumbler, 3 ounce, 3¼", footed	30.00		30.00
Tumbler, 9 ounce, footed	22.00	27.50	17.00
Tumbler, 6", 10 ounce, footed	35.00		38.00
Tumble-up night set	90.00		
Tumbler, 3" only	70.00		
Bottle only	20.00		
Vase, 5¾", blown	365.00		
Whiskey, 1⅝", 1 ounce	45.00		50.00
Whiskey, 2¼", 2 ounce	32.00		35.00

*Amber $45.00
**Green clambroth $295.00, blue $695.00, crystal $195.00
‡Amber $50.00

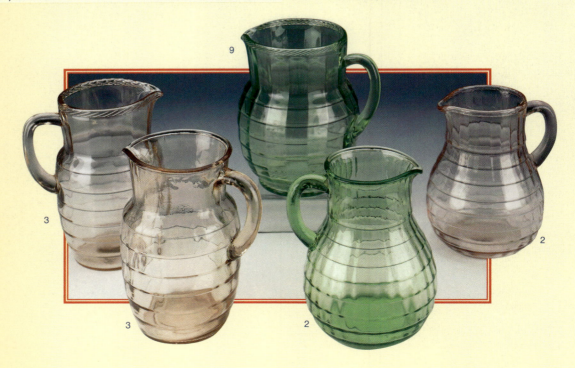

Tumblers, left to right: 15 ounce, 5¼"; 12 ounce, 4⅞"; 9½ ounce, 3¹³⁄₁₆"; 5 ounce, 3½"; 3 ounce, 2⅝"; 2 ounce, 2¼"; 1 ounce, 1⅝".

Bowls: 4½", 5¼", 7¼".

Left, heavy moulded sherbet; right, thin blown sherbet.

Left to right: 9 ounce, 7¼" goblet; 6 ounce, 4¾" sherbet; 9 ounce, 5¾" water; 3 ounce, 3½" short wine; 3½ ounce, 4½" wine; 3 ounce, 4" cocktail.

Cups, bottom row, left to right: rounded plain handle; mug; angled handle. Top row: rounded fancy handle; cone-shaped; pointed handle.

Creamers and sugars, left to right: rounded plain handle; cone-shaped pointed handle; flat; cone-shaped plain handle; round fancy handle.

"BOWKNOT," ATTRIBUTED TO BELMONT TUMBLER COMPANY, Probably late 1920s

Color: green

Depression glass beginners should realize that many dealers do not proffer smaller patterns such as "Bowknot" at glass shows because they take up the same valuable space as more costly items or patterns having many collectors. Space is at a premium in a show booth and ever escalating expenses (gas, food, motel, and booth rent) eat into profits before the first customer arrives. As a result, smaller patterns are often left behind and you will probably have to inquire if the dealers have any pieces in inventory which are not displayed.

We have found that "Bowknot" pieces sell well, when you can find them. Since this ware was heavily used, it is very necessary to check them for inner rim roughness (irr), particularly on the bowls and sherbets. Cereal bowls and tumblers are on many collectors' wish lists; and there are two styles of tumblers, a footed and a flat version.

No saucer has turned up for the cup, but that is not too surprising. It was a practice back then to produce custard cups alone. People don't drink custard much these days, but judging from the pages of these found in older company catalogs, it seems to have been a very popular beverage back then, equivalent to our ice cream consumption today. Back in the early 70s, we sold a cup to a beginning collector in Georgia for $3. He was collecting 54 sets and needed cups in "Bowknot." We became great friends. Years later when he sold his glass collection, he joked that the "Bowknot" cup was the only piece of glass he ever bought and sold for a loss. Today, they fetch a better price, but collectors keep asking, "Where's the saucer?"

5 ▸	Bowl, 4½", berry		28.00	4 ▸	Sherbet, low footed	23.00
	Bowl, 5½", cereal		38.00		Tumbler, 5", 10 ounce	28.00
2 ▸	Cup		10.00	1 ▸	Tumbler, 5", 10 ounce, footed	25.00
3 ▸	Plate, 6¾", salad		16.00			

CAMEO, "BALLERINA," or "DANCING GIRL," HOCKING GLASS COMPANY, 1930 – 1934

Colors: green, yellow, pink, and crystal w/platinum rim (See Reproduction Section.)

We get more letters and e-mails about undiscovered pieces of Cameo turning up than any other pattern in this book. Not only that, but newly discovered children's pieces are appearing. We need to call attention to the fact that all miniature pieces with the Cameo design have been made in the last 20 years by Mosser Glass Company in Cambridge, Ohio. These were never made originally by Hocking. The so-called undiscovered pieces such as salt dips or miniature bowls are also items from this children's set production. I've now seen the miniature comport peddled as a rare item and as a salt dip. If you see a small piece that looks like a miniature of a normally found Cameo item, it is likely a piece from a "Jennifer" set as these children's pieces were called. See the Reproduction Section (page 242) regarding these "Jennifer" sets. I have noticed that these sometime command fantastic sums from the unaware on Internet auctions.

While we are discussing what isn't Cameo, I should remind you of the imported, weakly patterned shakers that appeared a few years ago in pink, and a darker green and cobalt blue color that were never made originally. Don't pay more than $12.00 for these fakes and if no one buys them, maybe they will stop producing them.

Cameo moulds integrated a pattern design called Springtime from Monongah Glass Company (bought by Hocking). Several of Monongah's patterns were altered or continued by Hocking. Monongah's glass was plate etched, made in crystal, and usually was gold trimmed. Hocking took the plate etchings and converted them into their moulds. Collectors now are seeking Springtime (see page 212) which is extremely scarce in comparison to Cameo.

The Cameo centered-handled sandwich server and short, 3½" wines are choice Cameo collectibles. A few pink wines have surfaced in the last three years, but lately no more green ones. An unlisted, yellow, 15 ounce Cameo tumbler did cause awe last year. Twelve of these were sold by a dealer in the Midwest. One is pictured beside the 11 ounce tumbler to illustrate the differences in their sizes. How did these remain in hiding all these years? Cameo yellow butter dishes and milk pitchers are rare. However, there are more cups, saucer/sherbet plates, footed waters, and dinner and grill plates than there are collectors searching for them.

Again the rare Cameo saucer has a recessed, "well" type, 1¾" diameter cup ring. Due to the price, collectors now are generally buying one only. Hocking ordinarily made a smooth center, dual-purpose saucer/sherbet plate for their patterns, which will accommodate the foot of a sherbet. No recessed ring, yellow Cameo saucers have ever been confirmed even though I get a dozen or so letters a year from people not understanding what a recessed indentation is. It's like a 1¾" hole or pond in the smooth surface of the piece that the foot of the cup fits down into exactly.

You can still assemble a large set of green Cameo, the most collected color, without investing an enormous amount of money if you stay away from buying the rarer pieces and purchase only one or two sizes of stems or tumblers when found.

Cameo has two styles of grill ("T" shape divider bars) plates. One has tab handles and one does not. Both styles are common in yellow. However, the green grill with the tab or closed handles is harder to find and priced accordingly. The 10½" rare, rimmed dinner or flat cake plate is like the heavy edged (no tabs) grill plate without the dividers. The regular dinner plate has a large center as opposed to the small centered sandwich plate. These are pictured in the order listed so you can see the difference.

The less expensive sandwich plate (small center) is often priced as the more expensive dinner plate (large center). Some collectors are beginning to buy those sandwich plates to use as dinners. They are a little cheaper and larger.

Darker green bottles with the Cameo design are marked on the bottom "Whitehouse Vinegar." These were sold with a cork. Plain green glass stoppers top water bottles.

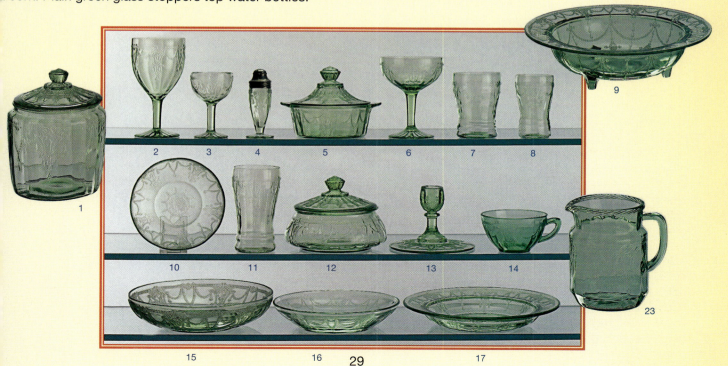

29

CAMEO

	Green	Yellow	Pink	Crystal w/Plat.
Bowl, 4¼", sauce				8.00
31 ▸ Bowl, 4¾", cream soup	205.00			
10 ▸ Bowl, 5½", cereal	40.00	35.00	150.00	8.00
16 ▸ Bowl, 7¼", salad	70.00			
15 ▸ Bowl, 8¼", large berry	45.00		175.00	
17 ▸ Bowl, 9", rimmed soup	90.00		225.00	
32 ▸ Bowl, 10", oval vegetable	38.00	45.00		
9 ▸ Bowl, 11", 3-legged console	90.00	125.00	80.00	
27 ▸ Butter dish and cover	235.00	1,500.00		
Butter dish bottom	140.00	500.00		
Butter dish top	95.00	1,000.00		
34 ▸ Cake plate, 10", 3 legs	20.00			
Cake plate, 10½", flat	130.00		195.00	
13 ▸ Candlesticks, 4", pair	130.00			
12 ▸ Candy jar, 4", low, and cover	90.00	115.00	595.00	
Candy jar, 6½", tall, and cover	205.00			
Cocktail shaker (metal lid) appears in crystal only				995.00
29 ▸ Comport, 5⅜" wide, mayonnaise	45.00		225.00	
1 ▸ Cookie jar and cover	65.00			
24 ▸ Creamer, 3¼"	25.00	20.00		
Creamer, 4¼"	32.00		125.00	
14 ▸ Cup, 2 styles	15.00	9.00	85.00	5.50
41 ▸ Decanter, 10", with stopper	215.00			300.00
36 ▸ Decanter, 10", with stopper, frosted (stopper represents ⅓ value of decanter)	40.00			
Domino tray, 7", with 3" indentation	225.00			
Domino tray, 7", with no indentation			275.00	175.00
43 ▸ Goblet, 3½", wine	1,000.00		500.00	
3 ▸ Goblet, 4", wine	80.00		250.00	
2 ▸ Goblet, 6", water	70.00		195.00	
42 ▸ Ice bowl or open butter, 3" tall x 5½" wide	210.00		750.00	395.00

	Green	Yellow	Pink	Crystal w/Plat.
5 ▸ Jam jar, 2", and cover	265.00			175.00
Pitcher, 5¾", 20 ounce, syrup or milk	335.00	2,000.00		
23 ▸ Pitcher, 6", 36 oz., juice	75.00			
22 ▸ Pitcher, 8½", 56 oz., water	70.00		1,500.00	500.00
28 ▸ Plate, 6", sherbet	4.00	3.00	90.00	2.00
Plate, 7", salad				3.50
37 ▸ Plate, 8", luncheon	12.00	10.00	35.00	4.00
39 ▸ Plate, 8½", square	65.00	250.00		
35 ▸ Plate, 9½", dinner	23.00	12.00	85.00	
40 ▸ Plate, 10", sandwich	20.00		55.00	
47 ▸ ‡Plate, 10½", rimmed, dinner	130.00		195.00	
Plate, 10½", grill	15.00	10.00	50.00	
Plate, 10½", grill with closed handles	75.00	6.00		
48 ▸ Plate, 10½", with closed handles	22.00	14.00		
Platter, 12", closed handles	28.00	40.00		
33 ▸ Relish, 7½", footed, 3 part	30.00			195.00
4 ▸ *Salt and pepper, ftd., pr.	75.00		900.00	
44 ▸ Sandwich server, center handle	7,000.00			
Saucer with cup ring	250.00			
28 ▸ Saucer, 6" (sherbet plate)	4.00	3.00	90.00	2.00
Sherbet, 3⅛", molded	16.00	40.00	75.00	
30 ▸ Sherbet, 3⅛", blown	18.00		75.00	
6 ▸ Sherbet, 4⅞"	32.00	90.00	125.00	
25 ▸ Sugar, 3¼"	21.00	20.00		
26 ▸ Sugar, 4¼"	30.00		125.00	
8 ▸ Tumbler, 3¾", 5 oz., juice	35.00		90.00	
7 ▸ Tumbler, 4", 9 oz., water	30.00		80.00	10.00
11 ▸ Tumbler, 4¾", 10 oz., flat	30.00		95.00	
46 ▸ Tumbler, 5", 11 oz., flat	35.00	90.00	110.00	
45 ▸ Tumbler, 5¼", 15 oz.	80.00	350.00	135.00	
Tumbler, 3 oz., footed, juice	80.00		135.00	
20 ▸ Tumbler, 5", 9 oz., footed	30.00	18.00	115.00	
21 ▸ Tumbler, 5¾", 11 oz., ftd.	75.00		135.00	
Tumbler, 6⅜", 15 oz., ftd.	595.00			
Vase, 5¾"	310.00			
19 ▸ Vase, 8"	65.00			
38 ▸ Water bottle (dark green), Whitehouse vinegar	30.00			

*Beware reproductions
‡Same as flat cake plate

19 20 21 22 23

24 25 26 5 27

14/28 14/28 29 30 31

32 33 34

35 36 37 38 39 41 40

42

Experimental item

43

27

45

46

44

CHERRYBERRY, U.S. GLASS COMPANY, Early 1930s

Colors: pink, green, crystal; some iridized

Cherryberry pattern has a few admirers. It was first noticed by Strawberry collectors who thought their pattern was unique until close examination revealed cherries instead of strawberries. Since there was a Cherry Blossom already being sought, the Cherryberry name was coined to coincide with the already popular Strawberry.

Cherryberry is another U.S. Glass pattern that has no cup or saucer and a plain butter base. If all these Depression era U.S. Glass patterns are "sister" patterns, then Strawberry and Cherryberry are twins. You can only differentiate by fruit inspection.

Despite the fact that U.S. Glass patterns have comparatively few pieces, there are other collectors competing for some of those items. Carnival glass followers look for iridized pitchers, tumblers, and butters which are the most precious pieces in their world. Then, there are "item" collectors for butter dishes and pitchers who acquire those, too. That makes for quite a bit of contention for the few pieces of Cherryberry uncovered.

Crystal is the uncommon "color"; however, only a few endeavor to find it. As with other U.S. Glass Company patterns, many pieces have uneven mould seams.

Color discrepancies remain the greatest obstacle to overcome. Green coloration can be found from a very yellow tint to a bluish one. There is not as much color difference with the pink, but there are some pieces that are noticeably lighter than others. If you are a collector who is concerned about matching color hues, this may not be the pattern for you.

However, if you can factor in that this old glassware was made under less controlled conditions than those today and that the resulting burned out or poor quality color matches were part and parcel of this glass genre, then there should be no problem.

	Crystal, Iridescent	Pink, Green		Crystal, Iridescent	Pink, Green
7 ▸ Bowl, 4", berry	6.50	15.00	4 ▸ Pickle dish, 8¼", oval	9.00	20.00
Bowl, 6¼", 2" deep	50.00	165.00	Pitcher, 7¾"	185.00	195.00
5 ▸ Bowl, 6½", deep, salad	20.00	25.00	6 ▸ Plate, 6", sherbet	6.00	12.00
Butter dish and cover	150.00	190.00	Plate, 7½", salad	7.50	16.00
Butter dish bottom	80.00	90.00	9 ▸ Sherbet	6.50	10.00
Butter dish top	70.00	100.00	Sugar, small, open	11.00	22.00
▸ Comport, 5¾"	18.00	28.00	2 ▸ Sugar, large	15.00	20.00
Creamer, small	11.00	22.00	3 ▸ Sugar cover	30.00	50.00
8 ▸ Creamer, 4⅝", large	16.00	40.00	Tumbler, 3⅝", 9 ounce	22.00	38.00
▸ Olive dish, 5", one-handled	9.00	20.00			

CHERRY BLOSSOM, JEANNETTE GLASS COMPANY, 1930 – 1939

Colors: pink, green, Delphite (opaque blue), crystal, Jadite (opaque green), and red
(See Reproduction Section.)

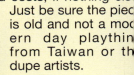

Cherry Blossom prices are cyclic. For a while you can't give it away and all of a sudden you cannot keep it in stock. It has been that way since the 70s when reproductions first appeared. Collectors are fickle and Cherry Blossom seems to emphasize their quirks. Prices began softening about three years ago on the basic dinnerware items, but not the harder to find pieces. That trend has continued and cup and saucers can now be purchased at prices of ten years ago. The supply out weighs the demand and eventually, that will change and prices will move upward as the rarer items are still doing.

That 9" platter remains the most difficult piece to find (after genuine pink shakers). Only one green 9" platter has been seen. (Measure this platter outside edge to outside edge.) We have calls for verification if we really mean outside edge. We do. The common 11" platter measures 9" from the inside to inside rim. The pink mug is the next rarely found item, but even green ones have disappeared into collections.

Cherry Blossom is prone to inner rim chips, nicks, or those famous "chigger bites" as auctioneers like to call chips. Inner rim roughness (irr) was caused as much from stacking glass together as from using it. Of 1_ berry bowls in a set bought not long ago, only one was mint. You can carefully store dishes (bowls or plates) with pape_ plates/bowls between them. This is particularly true at glass shows where stacks of items are banged and clanged regularly.

Other Cherry Blossom items that are hard to attain include the flat iced teas, soup or cereal bowls, and the 10" gree_ grill plate. That larger grill plate has never even been found in pink. Mint condition grill plates are a prize. Mint is the ope_ ative word as damaged ones are available.

The reproduction pessimism does not seem to bother anyone today as educated collectors treat it as just an annoy_ ing part of all collecting. If you are a beginner, turn to the Reproduction Section in the back of the book and educat_ yourself on Cherry Blossom reproductions. (See page 244 – 245.)

Remember that only two pairs of original pink Cherry Blossom shakers were ever documented and as far as I know these have never resurfaced for sale after being sold into collections. Therefore, that price has remained constant. (Orig_ nal ones are pictured on page 35.) We have lost count, but around 30 times we've received calls about that third pa_ being "found." None of these were *real*. The country has been absolutely flooded with reproduction Cherry shakers wit_ their squared, jut wing collars. The odds are not on your side for finding genuine pink Cherry shakers today.

The letters AOP in listings and advertisements stand for "all over pattern" on the footed tumblers and rounded pitch_ er. The large, footed tumblers and the AOP pitcher come in two styles. One style has a scalloped or indented foot whil_ the other is merely round with no indentations. Sherbets are also found like that. The letters PAT stand for "pattern at th_ top," illustrated by the flat-bottomed tumblers and pitchers.

I used to list two sizes of flat PAT pitchers in my earlier books, and somehow between third and fourth edition the 3_ oz. pitcher was omitted. This time I am presenting them side by side so you can see there is a difference in shape. Als_ note the experimental pink pitcher, which looks like Jeannette first started to make a footed, round, PAT pitcher.

There are some known experimental pieces of Cherry Blossom such as a pink cookie jar, pink five-part relish dishe_ orange with green trim slag bowls, and amber children's pieces. Note the opaque red bowl with yellow rim pictured._ few red (both opaque and transparent) and yellow pieces have surfaced, but the reproduction transparent red wiped ou_ most collectors' desire to own red. The original red was glossy and quite beautiful. You can see most of these piece_ pictured in past *Very Rare Glassware of the Depression Era* books and my *Treasure of Very Rare Glassware*.

Pricing on experimental items or colors is particularly tricky to establish; but d_ not pass them up if the price is right — for you. The latest rarity being circulated _ Cherry Blossom is a green covered casserole dish. Most experimental pieces had _ small run of a couple of dozen or more pieces to justify mould costs, if nothing els_ Just be sure the piec_ is old and not a mod_ ern day plaything_ from Taiwan or th_ dupe artists.

Experimental
pitcher

1   2

	Pink	Green	Delphite
Bowl, 4¾", berry	20.00	20.00	20.00
Bowl, 5¾", cereal	55.00	50.00	
Bowl, 7¾", flat soup	110.00	95.00	
10▸* Bowl, 8½", round berry	48.00	50.00	50.00
Bowl, 9", oval vegetable	55.00	50.00	50.00
6▸ Bowl, 9", 2-handled	50.00	75.00	28.00
** Bowl, 10½", 3-leg, fruit	90.00	100.00	
11▸ Butter dish and cover	100.00	125.00	
Butter dish bottom	25.00	25.00	
Butter dish top	75.00	100.00	
13▸ Cake plate (3 legs), 10¼"	35.00	40.00	
17▸ Coaster	12.00	13.00	
Creamer	25.00	25.00	20.00
Cup	20.00	20.00	20.00
15▸ Mug, 7 oz.	450.00	395.00	
19▸‡ Pitcher, 6¾", AOP, 36 ounce scalloped or round bottom	75.00	65.00	80.00
2▸ Pitcher, 7¼", PAT, 42 ounce, flat	80.00	80.00	
Pitcher, 7¾", PAT, 36 ounce, footed	75.00	75.00	
1▸ Pitcher, PAT, 36 ounce, flat			
Plate, 6", sherbet	8.00	10.00	10.00
Plate, 7", salad	27.00	23.00	
‡‡ Plate, 9", dinner	24.00	24.00	20.00
3▸§ Plate, 9", grill	30.00	30.00	

	Pink	Green	Delphite
Plate, 10", grill		125.00	
Platter, 9", oval	950.00	1,100.00	
16▸ Platter, 11", oval	50.00	55.00	45.00
9▸ Platter, 13"			
7▸ Platter, 13", divided	75.00	80.00	
4▸ Salt and pepper (scalloped bottom)	1,300.00	1,100.00	
Saucer	4.00	5.00	5.00
Sherbet	19.00	20.00	17.00
Sugar	14.00	15.00	18.00
Sugar cover	20.00	20.00	
14▸ Tray, 10½", sandwich	32.00	35.00	22.00
18▸ Tumbler, 3¾", 4 ounce, footed, AOP	18.00	23.00	25.00
Tumbler, 4½", 9 ounce, round, footed, AOP	38.00	38.00	20.00
5▸ Tumbler, 4½", 8 ounce, scalloped, footed, AOP	38.00	38.00	20.00
Tumbler, 3½", 4 ounce, flat, PAT	21.00	31.00	
Tumbler, 4¼", 9 ounce, flat, PAT	20.00	25.00	
Tumbler, 5", 12 ounce, flat, PAT	75.00	85.00	

* Yellow $395.00
** Jadite $325.00
‡ Jadite $325.00

‡‡ Translucent green $225.00
§ Jadite $85.00

CHERRY BLOSSOM — CHILD'S JUNIOR DINNER SET

	Pink	Delphite
Creamer	50.00	45.00
Sugar	50.00	45.00
Plate, 6"	10.00	10.00
(design on bottom)		
Cup	40.00	40.00
Saucer	5.00	5.00
14 piece set	320.00	310.00

Original box sells for $35.00 extra with pink sets.

7

3

9

10

11

6

13

14

5

15

16

17

18

19

Chinex Classic collectors are keeping their accumulating talents hidden. They quietly collect as bargains appear, but are not running up prices on Internet auctions as some have done for other patterns in the past. There are not the thousands seeking Chinex so they can be choosy about their purchases. There are different decorations on Chinex. If you can find one that draws your attention, start with that.

It will be an adventure to match the different florals found on this ivory tint and affiliated Cremax ware. It is enough to even find the scroll decorated Chinex Classic pattern; but locating a piece you do not have, only to have it decorated with a decal other than the one you seek, could be disappointing.

Windsor castle decals are the most captivating decoration to collectors; darker blue trims appear to be more popular than the lighter blue or brown, but they are, also, more difficult to uncover. The brown Windsor castle comes with or without a brown trim. We see more brown decorated, but that is comparatively speaking as only a dozen or so pieces are displayed at shows each year.

Mostly, we see Chinex in the Michigan area when we shop there.

Have you noticed that separate tops and bottoms of butters are becoming scarcer as more collectors are involved in buying glassware? Matching Chinex top and bottom is a serious chore if you are lucky enough to spot a Chinex butter part. The butter bottom looks like the Cremax pattern on the edge rather than Chinex. The butter tops have the scroll-like design that distinguishes Chinex, but this scroll design is missing from the butter bottoms. The bottom has a plain "pie crust" edge (like Cremax). The floral or castle designs will be inside the base of the butter, and seemingly surrounding the knob of the top if the top is floral decorated.

Chinex is also found in the Pittsburgh and eastern Pennsylvania area since MacBeth Evans was located near there. Owing to the Internet, the latest discoveries have been made in Canada where Corning was a mainstay in glass fabrication. Chinex was made to challenge chinaware that crazed and chipped. It was promoted as resistant to crazing and chipping which helps explain its comparatively excellent condition, today. That was a good marketing point.

Few collect plain, undecorated ivory pieces; so if you like that color, you could purchase a small useable set as inexpensively as buying currently made dinnerware.

		Browntone or Plain Ivory	Decal Decorated	Castle Decal
1 ▸	Bowl, 5¾", cereal	5.50	8.00	18.00
11 ▸	Bowl, 6¾", salad	12.00	20.00	40.00
	Bowl, 7", vegetable	14.00	25.00	40.00
	Bowl, 7¾", soup	12.50	20.00	40.00
6 ▸	Bowl, 9", vegetable	11.00	25.00	40.00
	Bowl, 11"	17.00	35.00	45.00
	Butter dish	55.00	75.00	150.00
8 ▸	Butter dish bottom	12.50	27.50	50.00
7 ▸	Butter dish top	42.50	47.50	100.00
9 ▸	Creamer	5.00	10.00	20.00
12 ▸	Cup	4.50	6.00	12.00
4 ▸	Plate, 6¼", sherbet	2.50	4.00	7.50
10 ▸	Plate, 9¾", dinner	4.00	9.00	15.00
5 ▸	Plate, 11½", sandwich or cake	7.50	14.00	25.00
13 ▸	Saucer	2.00	3.00	4.00
2 ▸	Sherbet, low footed	7.00	11.00	25.00
3 ▸	Sugar	5.00	10.00	20.00

CHINEX CLASSIC

CIRCLE, HOCKING GLASS COMPANY, 1930s

Colors: green, pink, and crystal

Green is the only color in Circle that can be collected in sets with time and patience. However finding bowls in each style may take more luck than patience. Notice that the bowls have jumped in price due to demand being placed on small supply. Demand is always the driving factor in prices; rarity helps fuel that fire in this case. From time to time a piece is too rare to generate any market interest whatsoever, but that is not the case with Circle.

Excluding those bowls, Circle is reasonably priced, but not so easily found. Pink apparently crops up only as a luncheon set. We are having little luck getting our hands on it. Many pieces thought to be common in the early days of collecting are not. If you have a piece of pink not in the listing, please let us know.

Crystal occurs in stems; and some crystal stems come with green tops. Green stems with crystal tops are more easily found than all green stems. In many Elegant patterns, two-toned stems are more expensive and avidly sought. This has not yet proved true for Circle. The good news is that you can buy these inexpensively.

There are three different small bowls pictured so you can see the differences. They range from 4½" to 5¼" with the flared one measuring 5", but it is clearly a darker shade of green when compared with the other pieces.

Both the 9⅜" and 5¼" green bowls shown have ground bottoms. With Hocking patterns, ground bottoms usually suggest early production or experimental pieces.

The idiosyncrasies of Circle include two different styles of cups. The flat-bottomed style fits a saucer/sherbet plate while the rounded cup takes an indented saucer. Pink is found in both styles, but not easily.

Kitchenware collectors (specifically reamer collectors) are aware of Circle. They treasure that 80-ounce pitcher which is found with a reamer top. Color variations between the pitcher and reamers make buying them separately, "iffy" at best. That 80-ounce pitcher shown here is a darker green (similar to the flared bowl) than the other green items pictured.

	Green	Pink			Green	Pink
5 ▸ Bowl, 4½", deep	17.50			Plate, 8¼", luncheon	6.00	10.00
3 ▸ Bowl, 5¼"	25.00			Plate, 9½"	12.00	
▸ Bowl, 5", flared, 1¾" deep	30.00		6 ▸	Plate, 10", sandwich	14.00	
2 ▸ Bowl, 8"	35.00		4 ▸	Saucer w/cup ring	2.50	3.00
Bowl, 9⅜"	40.00		13 ▸	Sherbet, 3⅛"	6.00	10.00
Creamer	9.00	25.00	1 ▸	Sherbet, 4¾"	8.00	
8 ▸ Cup (2 styles)	6.00	10.00		Sugar	7.00	25.00
▸ Goblet, 4½", wine	15.00		7 ▸	Tumbler, 3½", 4 ounce, juice	9.00	
4 ▸ Goblet, 8 ounce, water	11.00		2 ▸	Tumbler, 4", 8 ounce, water	10.00	
Pitcher, 60 ounce	75.00			Tumbler, 5", 10 ounce, tea	20.00	
6 ▸ Pitcher, 80 ounce	40.00			Tumbler, 15 ounce, flat	30.00	
▸ Plate, 6", sherbet/saucer	3.00	5.00				

CLOVERLEAF, HAZEL-ATLAS GLASS COMPANY, 1930 – 1936

Colors: pink, green, yellow, crystal, and black

Recognition of Cloverleaf may be its biggest asset. Even the non-collecting public notices the "good luck" symbol and may even call it shamrocks, but they at least recognize the symbol. You might need the "luck of the Irish" to find some of the pieces in this pattern regardless of the color you choose.

Collectors of green Cloverleaf have an extensive array of pieces to gather. It is the color most sought. The 8" bowl and tumblers sell quickly but are rarely offered. All bowls, in any color, as well as grill plates and tumblers are becoming more difficult to garner. Of the three styles of tumblers pictured, it is the flat, straight-sided one, obtainable only in green, which is as rarely seen as a four-leaf clover.

The grill plate (three-part) must serve as a dinner-sized plate if you wish one, since the luncheon plate is only 8¼". The candy dish, shakers, and bowls are all difficult to find in yellow. We have seen only one yellow cereal bowl in our travel and none of the other size bowls.

There appear to be similar numbers of collectors for black or yellow Cloverleaf. Few pursue pink or crystal. Besides luncheon pieces in pink, a berry bowl and a flared, 10 ounce tumbler exist. That pink tumbler was scantily distributed and has never been found in crystal.

Black Cloverleaf prices have been relatively stable over the last few years with just a little rise on a few pieces. Small ashtrays are often ignored while the larger ones sell occasionally. We need to point out that the black sherbet plate and saucer are the same size. The saucer has no Cloverleaf design in the center, but the sherbet plate does. Observe the price difference. These sherbet plates still turn up in stacks of saucers occasionally, so keep your eyes open.

We repeatedly receive questions concerning Cloverleaf pattern being found on both sides of the pieces, inside or outside. In order for the black to show the pattern, moulds had to be designed with the pattern on the top side of pieces; otherwise, it looked like unadorned black. On transparent pieces, the pattern could be on the bottom or the inside and would still show. Over the years, transparent pieces were made using the moulds designed for the black; so, you now find these pieces with pattern on either top or bottom. This does not make a difference in value or collectibility.

		Pink	Green	Yellow	Black
18 ▸	Ashtray, 4", match holder in center				65.00
19 ▸	Ashtray, 5¾", match holder in center				90.00
3 ▸	Bowl, 4", dessert	40.00	50.00	40.00	
2 ▸	Bowl, 5", cereal		58.00	60.00	
4 ▸	Bowl, 7", deep salad		100.00	110.00	
8 ▸	Bowl, 8"		125.00		
1 ▸	Candy dish and cover		85.00	125.00	
12 ▸	Creamer, 3⅝", footed		15.00	22.00	16.00
10 ▸	Cup	9.00	9.00	11.00	16.00
6 ▸	Plate, 6", sherbet		15.00	10.00	40.00
5 ▸	Plate, 8", luncheon	11.00	10.00	14.00	15.00
7 ▸	Plate, 10¼", grill		30.00	30.00	
13 ▸	Salt and pepper, pair		42.00	135.00	100.00
11 ▸	Saucer	3.00	3.00	4.00	5.00
17 ▸	Sherbet, 3", footed	10.00	12.00	15.00	20.00
9 ▸	Sugar, 3⅝", footed		10.00	22.00	16.00
16 ▸	Tumbler, 4", 9 ounce, flat		70.00		
15 ▸	Tumbler, 3¾", 10 ounce, flat, flared	30.00	60.00		
14 ▸	Tumbler, 5¾", 10 ounce, footed		35.00	45.00	

COLONIAL, "KNIFE AND FORK," HOCKING GLASS COMPANY, 1934 – 1936

Colors: pink, green, crystal, and Vitrock (white)

Collecting Colonial has remained steady over the last few years. A few new collectors start and some older ones sell their collections; so a supply continues to come onto the marketplace. Rarer pieces are quickly snapped up by long-time collectors. The higher prices of these rare items may shock beginners, but today's high price may turn out to be tomorrow's bargain.

Colonial in green is still the color of choice. All rare and hard to find items are increasing in price regardless of color. Prices for pink are similar to those of green because of rarity more than for any other reason. If pink were as sought as green, there is no telling to what height prices would ascend. A crystal Colonial collection can still be started, but it is no longer easy on the pocket. In crystal, Colonial looks incredibly like older pattern glass which probably explains Hocking's "Colonial" name — meaning it had its foundation in an older glass design.

To date, only one of the beaded top Colonial pitchers in each color has been spotted — though I doubt only one of each was made. Both of these have been pictured in previous books.

Colonial soup bowls (both cream and flat), cereals, mint shakers, and unmarred dinner plates are still difficult to obtain in any color. The vertical ridges on Colonial pieces have a tendency to flake or chip; so while examining a piece, look at those ridges first. Always take the top off any shaker to check for damage. There may be a big surprise of missing glass under that top if you do not check before buying. Been there, done that!

Coveted Colonial mugs are seldom seen today. The 11-ounce Colonial tumbler measures 2¾" across the top while the 12 ounce measures exactly 3". These two tumblers are frequently confused and there is quite a price distinction if you buy the 11 ounce for a 12 ounce price. Vice versa works in your favor, so you need to know the difference. It is easier to measure across the top than to measure the contents if you are out shopping. The spooner is 5½" tall, while the sugar without a lid is only 4½" high. That inch makes a huge difference in price.

The cheese dish consists of a wooden board with an indented groove upon which the glass lid rests.

Quite a number of white pieces of Colonial are beginning to show up with so many people becoming aware of Depression glass. As of now, the following pieces have been uncovered: cream soup and liner, water pitcher, cups, saucers (two styles), luncheon plates, creamers, and sugar bowls. No top has been spotted for that sugar. White has been largely overlooked due to the small number of pieces originally found, but it's beginning to look like a small set might be possible if one wanted to set about that arduous task. There was supposition once that this white was Corning manufactured, but it still looks like Hocking's Vitrock to us.

There are three sizes of footed tumblers and five sizes of stems in Colonial. Because it was brought to my attention at a show, I realize that another book pictures and identifies the tumblers as stems.

COLONIAL

	Pink	Green	Crystal
7▸ * Bowl, 3¾", berry	65.00		
8▸ * Bowl, 4½", berry	20.00	14.00	10.00
6▸ * Bowl, 5½", cereal	65.00	100.00	35.00
1▸ Bowl, 4½", cream soup, white $60	75.00	85.00	65.00
Bowl, 7", low soup	75.00	78.00	35.00
3▸ Bowl, 9", large berry	30.00	32.00	25.00
1▸ * Bowl, 10", oval vegetable	42.00	40.00	22.00
4▸ Butter dish and cover	750.00	60.00	42.00
* Butter dish bottom	475.00	35.00	25.00
Butter dish top	275.00	25.00	17.00
7▸ * Cheese dish		250.00	
9▸ * Cream/milk pitcher, 5", 16 oz.	70.00	28.00	20.00
Cup, white $8	10.00	14.00	7.00
Mug, 4½", 12 oz.	600.00	800.00	
5▸ + Pitcher, 7", 54 oz.	50.00	55.00	35.00
0▸ *+Pitcher, 7¾", 68 oz., white $300	70.00	80.00	45.00
Plate, 6", sherbet	7.00	8.00	3.00
7▸ Plate, 8½", luncheon	10.00	11.00	6.00
28▸ * Plate, 10", dinner	60.00	65.00	30.00
26▸ * Plate, 10", grill	25.00	25.00	15.00
12▸ * Platter, 12", oval	35.00	25.00	20.00
6▸ Salt and pepper, pair	150.00	130.00	65.00
33▸ Saucer/sherbet plate, white $3	7.00	8.00	3.00
Sherbet, 3"	28.00		
2▸ Sherbet, 3⅜"	12.00	16.00	8.00
25▸ * Spoon holder or celery, 5½"	135.00	130.00	90.00
10▸ * Stem, 3¾", 1 oz., cordial		30.00	18.00
15▸ * Stem, 4", 3 oz., cocktail		25.00	14.00
32▸ * Stem, 4½", 2½ oz., wine		24.00	14.00
21▸ * Stem, 5¼", 4 oz., claret		24.00	20.00
34▸ * Stem, 5¾", 8½ oz., water		30.00	25.00
30▸ * Sugar, 4½"	25.00	18.00	8.00
31▸ * Sugar cover	65.00	27.00	16.00
9▸ Tumbler, 3", 5 oz., juice	22.00	25.00	15.00
4▸ ** Tumbler, 4", 9 oz., water	20.00	22.00	15.00
8▸ Tumbler, 5⅛" high, 11 oz.	35.00	42.00	22.00
Tumbler, 12 oz., iced tea	52.00	52.00	24.00
19▸ * Tumbler, 15 oz., lemonade	65.00	75.00	45.00
13▸ * Tumbler, 3¼", 3 oz., footed	20.00	25.00	10.00
Tumbler, 4", 5 oz., footed	40.00	45.00	20.00
14▸ ‡ Tumbler, 5¼", 10 oz., footed	50.00	50.00	27.50
23▸ * Whiskey, 2½", 1½ oz.	16.00	16.00	12.00

*Beaded top $1,250.00 **Royal ruby $125.00
‡Royal ruby $175.00 +With or without ice lip

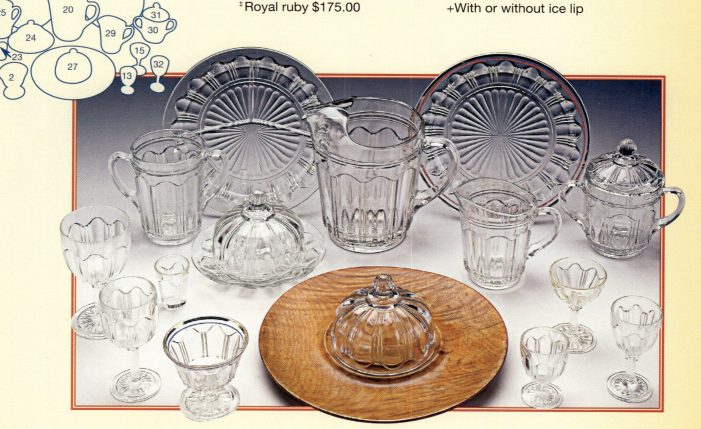

"COLONIAL BLOCK," MODERNISTIC, HAZEL-ATLAS GLASS COMPANY, Early 1930s

Colors: green, crystal, black, pink, and rare in cobalt blue; white in 1950s

"Colonial Block" is the name most collectors have used for this pattern for almost 40 years, but the name it wa advertised under was Modernistic. We found numerous little tidbits like this while researching for our Hazel-Atlas book. you want to find out more about Hazel-Atlas productions besides dinnerware patterns — we have a book for you!

Green "Colonial Block" is the color most often sought. You will find an occasional crystal piece or white creamer an sugar sets. A few black and frosted green "Colonial Block" powder jars are being found. A cobalt blue "Colonial Block creamer is shown in our Hazel-Atlas book as well as a creamer with Shirley Temple's image in white. (Hazel-Atlas als made a different creamer, a mug, and cereal bowl with that same Shirley image. These have now been reproduced.) Th Modernistic style however, is so rare, the copycat artists probably couldn't find one to reproduce.

Most pieces of "Colonial Block" are marked HA, but not all. The H is on top of the A, which confuses some peop who assume that this is the symbol for Anchor Hocking. The anchor was a symbol used by Anchor Hocking and that wa not used until after the 1930s.

U.S. Glass made a pitcher similar in style (shown) to Hazel-Atlas's "Colonial Block." There is little difference in ther except most Hazel-Atlas pitchers are marked; the one in the photo is not so marked. The handle on the actual Haze Atlas pitcher is shaped like those of the creamer and sugar. Collectors today are not as inflexible in their collecting princ ples as they previously were. Many collectors will buy either pitcher to go with their set. That is why items that are simila to a pattern, but not actually a part of it, are referred to as "go-with" or "look-alike" pieces. In general, these items ar more reasonably priced.

Green 4" and 7" bowls, sherbets, butter tub, and the pitcher are the pieces most often lacking in "Colonial Block collections. The recently discovered 5-ounce footed juice is the rarest piece in this set. How does a small pattern like thi have so many hard to find pieces? "Colonial Block" was most likely limited in distribution; and some of those hard-to find pieces might have been premiums for some marketed product that did not sell well.

More green sherbets are now finding their way into collections. These were exposed about ten years ago and subse quently, the market was saturated with them.

		Crystal	Pink, Green	White			Crystal	Pink, Green	White
1 ▸	Bowl, 4"	4.00	11.00		7 ▸	Goblet	6.00	15.00	
6 ▸	Bowl, 7"	12.00	22.00		8 ▸	Pitcher	25.00	50.00	
10 ▸	Butter dish	30.00	40.00			*Powder jar w/lid	12.00	17.50	
	Butter dish bottom	5.00	10.00		9 ▸	Sherbet	4.00	7.00	
	Butter dish top	25.00	30.00		2 ▸	Sugar	7.00	10.00	8.00
4 ▸	Butter tub	25.00	45.00		3 ▸	Sugar lid	8.00	15.00	7.50
5 ▸	Candy jar w/cover	25.00	42.00			Tumbler, 5¼", 5 oz., footed		75.00	
11 ▸	Creamer	6.00	12.00	8.00					

COLONIAL FLUTED, "ROPE," FEDERAL GLASS COMPANY, 1928 – 1933

Colors: green and crystal

Most Colonial Fluted items display a "F" in a shield, usually in the center of pieces. This symbol was used by the Federal Glass Company but is not found on every item. That "F" does not stand for Fire-King as I am often asked. Many white Federal kitchenware items are similar to Fire-King wares. More Federal Glass is shown in *Florences' Ovenware from the 1920s to the Present*.

There has not been a new discovery in Colonial Fluted pattern since we started writing in 1972. That makes it a difficult pattern to write about for the seventeenth time.

Colonial Fluted used to be a basic set for beginning collectors who wanted an inexpensive green pattern. Now, quantities are so inadequate that new collectors become discouraged looking for it. Bowls are very scarce. Notice that all bowls have increased in price. Evidently, these were not sold with basic luncheon sets and today their paucity is apparent.

Colonial Fluted was a functional pattern that was regularly used. You will find most flat pieces have heavy wear. Knife cuttings erode the surface of glassware and Colonial Fluted scratched plates are evidence of that. When you find Colonial Fluted, usually is priced moderately enough to use; so, if you like it, do so. Treat this older glass with respect, but enjoy using it.

A few collectors find it an ideal bridge set. Indeed, much of the original advertising for this pattern was centered on bridge parties, which are not as in vogue now as they were in the 1930s. Crystal decorated pieces with hearts, spades, diamonds, and clubs are very collectible — but infrequently spotted.

There is no dinner plate in the Colonial Fluted pattern, but there is a dinner-sized plate made by Federal (#3 below) that goes very well. It has the roping around the outside of the plate, but not the fluting. There is also a grill plate (#5 below) that goes well with the pattern. It has no roping, but flutes. Both of these pieces can expand the number of items in your set and give you larger serving pieces to use. Federal made those items mentioned, so they match in color and most are also marked Federal.

	Green			Green
Bowl, 4", berry	15.00	10 ▸ Saucer		2.00
▸ Bowl, 6", cereal	18.00	12 ▸ Sherbet		8.00
Bowl, 6½", deep (2½") salad	38.00	7 ▸ Sugar		10.00
▸ Bowl, 7½", large berry	28.00	6 ▸ Sugar cover		20.00
▸ Creamer	10.00			
▸ Cup	9.00			
▸ Plate, 6", sherbet	4.00			
▸ Plate, 8", luncheon	9.00			

COLUMBIA, FEDERAL GLASS COMPANY, 1938 – 1942

Colors: crystal, some pink

If you have ever noticed the Columbia pattern before, you probably saw it as a butter dish. This Federal product wa copiously distributed as dairy premiums in the Midwest in various styles. Butters were fashioned with flashed colors an floral decal decorations. Others were satinized (frosted); some were flashed with color after the satin finish was applied Most other Columbia items are less frequently encountered.

Pink Columbia sells exceptionally well for a pattern that exhibits only four pieces. Prices have decelerated for th moment after some leaps a few years ago when pink Columbia could not be found fast enough to keep up with demand

Columbia tumblers were never easy to find; but, currently, there are other complexities to deal with. Tumblers (no corroborated) are a 2⅞" four-ounce juice and nine-ounce water. An "analogous" water tumbler has materialized which labeled "France" on the bottom. Collectors of Columbia need to be conscious of this before paying for foreign-mac look-alikes. We emphasize that any glassware marked France is not Depression glass.

You may well find Columbia water tumblers with advertisements for dairy products printed on them. These wer mostly used as containers for cottage cheese.

The formerly elusive (except in Colorado) snack tray has begun to turn up more frequently, causing the price to dro somewhat. I just picked up four last weekend for $10.00. That dealer did not recognize them. Many collectors have n known what to look for, since it is an unusual piece and shaped differently from most Columbia. The pictures in rece editions have shown the tray so well that collectors are finding these to the point that supply is overrunning demand rig now. These snack plates were found with Columbia cups in a boxed set over 30 years ago in northern Ohio. Feder Glass Company labeled the box "Snack Sets," with no other label. Snack trays are also being found with Federal cup other than the Columbia pattern, which is probably why so many are being located after all these years. I should menti that there are bowls and snack sets that are designed like the Columbia snack tray. They do not have the center desig but do have the "winged" tab handles. These are being found in original Federal boxes labeled "Homestead."

Satinized, pastel-banded, and floral-decaled luncheon sets in Columbia have been seen. These sets are scarce ar are selling better since mixing and matching colors is more popular among collectors.

		Crystal	Pink
5▶	Bowl, 5", cereal	17.00	
1▶	Bowl, 8", low soup	22.00	
10▶	Bowl, 8½", salad	20.00	
4▶	Bowl, 10½", ruffled edge	20.00	
3▶	Butter dish and cover	18.00	
	Ruby flashed	22.00	
	Other flashed	21.00	
	Butter dish bottom	5.00	

		Crystal	Pink
	Butter dish top	13.00	
12▶	Cup	8.00	25.00
6▶	Plate, 6", bread & butter	4.00	15.00
9▶	Plate, 9½", luncheon	10.00	35.00
8▶	Plate, 11", chop	18.00	
11▶	Saucer	2.00	10.00
13▶	Snack plate	25.00	
2▶	Tumbler, 2⅞", 4 ounce, juice	30.00	
7▶	Tumbler, 9 ounce, water	32.00	

Colors: pink, green, crystal, and Royal Ruby

Coronation was introduced in 1936 and most likely so named as a result of the coronation going on in England at that point in time. It was definitely headline news.

Most collectors first become aware of Coronation because of its tumbler's similarity to rarely found Old Colony ("Lace Edge") tumblers. Coronation's tumblers were perpetually offered for sale as Old Colony. Please note the row of fine ribs above the middle of the Coronation tumbler. These ribs are missing on the Old Colony footed tumbler. Look at the bottom of page 156 to see the differences with those shown on page 48. Some collectors intentionally buy Coronation tumblers to use with Old Colony since they can buy three Coronation tumblers for the asking price of one Old Colony. Both are the same shape and color and made by the same manufacturer. Just don't accidentally confuse the two since there is quite a price disparity. Of course, if you see Old Colony tumblers priced as Coronation, which sometimes happen, you just smile as you purchase those.

Royal Ruby Coronation cups were sold with crystal, non-indented saucers. Those crystal saucer/sherbet plates are common crystal pieces found in Coronation. However, we can now report that crystal saucers with an indented cup ring have recently been discovered. A few other crystal pieces are turning up, but there is little demand for them (save for the crescent salads). No Royal Ruby Coronation saucer or sherbet plates have ever been seen. Royal Ruby is the name of the red glass that was made by Hocking beginning in 1938 and only their red glassware can be called Royal Ruby.

Coronation pitchers are rarely seen in person or offered for sale, but I have provided a photo so you will know what to look for in your explorations.

The handles on Royal Ruby Coronation bowls are open; handles on the pink are closed. Two newly discovered bowls in pink have surfaced without handles. They measure 4¼" and 8", just like the previously discovered green ones. The items pictured in green Coronation are shown compliments of Anchor Hocking. Additional green pieces have been found including the luncheon plate, and large and small berry bowls. The larger green tumbler is 5⁷⁄₁₆" tall and holds 14½ ounces and has never been seen outside the factory. That green crescent salad plate is a rather interesting item for Depression glass. Crescent salads are more prevalent in elegant patterns. A few of these have also been uncovered in crystal and pink.

Some dealers often price those commonly found red handled Coronation berry bowls extraordinarily high. We have seen them priced as high as $22.00. They have always been abundant.

Please note that Anchor Hocking, in the late 1990s, made pattern called Annapolis in pink and crystal that is based upon the Coronation design. Some pieces are shown above. We bought two pink iced teas a couple of years ago as Coronation; but something did not seem right. We put them aside and decided to see what we could find out. On a trip last year we saw several crystal pieces and one was marked with Anchor Hocking's anchor symbol. Since then we have seen catalog information, bowls and plates besides several sizes of tumblers, both footed and flat. Not all pieces are marked.

		Pink	Royal Ruby	Green
8▸	Bowl, 4¼", berry, handled	8.00	8.00	
9▸	Bowl, 4¼", no handles	95.00		65.00
2▸	Bowl, 6½", nappy, handled	8.00	18.00	
3▸	Bowl, 8", large berry, handled	16.00	18.00	
	Bowl, 8", no handles	225.00		225.00
6▸	*Cup	5.00	6.50	
12▸	Pitcher, 7¾", 68 ounce	695.00		
7▸	Plate, 6", sherbet/saucer	3.00		
5▸	Plate, 8½", luncheon	5.00		75.00
10▸	Plate, crescent salad	95.00		150.00
	Saucer w/indent (crystal only)		3.00	
1▸	Sherbet	10.00		100.00
4▸	Tumbler, 5", 10 ounce, footed	31.00		195.00
11▸	Tumbler, 5⁷⁄₁₆", 14½ ounce, experimental	N/A	N/A	N/A

*Crystal $4.00

CORONATION

CRACKLE, VARIOUS COMPANIES (L.E. SMITH, MCKEE GLASS, MacBETH-EVANS, FEDERAL GLASS, U.S. GLASS, ET. AL.), c. 1924

Colors: amber, amethyst, blue, canary, crystal, green, pink, satin (frosted) colors, crystal with color trims

In the past, collectors have asked us from time to time why we did not include crackle in our books. We were finally convinced to add it after talking to some passionate collectors. One lady when asked which company's wares she collected said, "Oh, it makes no difference. If it's crackled, that's all I need to know!" When asked what form of crackle she collected, the genuinely cold water, reheated crackle, or the moulded type, she said. "Oh, I'm only interested in the moulded type. But," she added, "It would be nice to know what all is available and what kind of prices I should be paying."

We decided that if we were to lump every moulded piece we could find into a listing, then that could serve the objective of getting it out there before collectors. Shown here is what we've been able to find. Feel free to contribute what you turn up. Again, we're only dealing with the moulded, crackled appearing wares that were advertised throughout the late twenties and early thirties as making drink liquids "look like cracked ice" or putting you in "refreshing anticipation of a cool summer's drink."

Not everybody had ice available to them at that time, so many companies hopped onto this "suggestion of ice" effect in their glassware lines, particularly in beverage sets; and judging by the available pieces found in markets today, so did the buying public. We wonder if the crackle effect really made the drink seem cooler.

We are not listing various finely stippled and crinkled effect wares that attempted to mimic the same idea. We're trying to include only the moulded items with the large veins making that cracked ice look. For now, we're pricing only crystal, using prices observed in the market. Colored crackle will fetch 20 – 25% more, except for canary, which will cost up to 50% more.

	*Crystal			*Crystal			*Crystal
Bottle, water	20.00	6 ▸	Candle, sq. base	15.00	1 ▸	Plate, cloverleaf, snack	14.00
10 ▸ Bowl, 6", ruffled	12.00		Candy box, hexagonal lid	28.00		Plate, cracker w/center rim	17.00
Bowl, console	20.00	8 ▸	Candy, footed, round, dome lid	25.00		Plate, server, 2-handle	20.00
Bowl, flare rim on black base	35.00	15 ▸	Compote, cheese (for cracker)	12.50		Sherbet, octagon rim	10.00
7 ▸ Bowl, footed, small vegetable	20.00	14 ▸	Compote, 6", candy	15.00	12 ▸	Sherbet, round rim	8.00
Bowl, ruffled, vegetable	20.00		Cup	10.00		Tray, 3-footed, flat	22.50
Bowl, hexagon, cereal	12.00		Jar, screw threads	22.00		Tumbler, 4¾", footed cone	8.00
Butter, small (powder jar style)	25.00	3 ▸	Pitcher, bulbous middle, water,			Tumbler, 5 oz., bowed middle, juice	10.00
Caddy, center handle, 6 holder	12.00		no lid	28.00	2 ▸	Tumbler, 9 oz., bowed middle, water	8.00
Caddy, center handle, 4 holder	10.00		Pitcher, 64 oz., bulbous, w/lid	45.00		Tumbler, 12 oz., bowed middle, tea	9.00
9 ▸ Candle, 1¾"	9.00		Pitcher, 9", cone, footed	48.00		Tumbler, juice, straight side	8.00
Candle, cone	22.00		Pitcher, water, slant edge, flat			Tumbler, tea, straight side	6.00
			bottom, optic, no lid	30.00		Tumbler, water, straight side	8.00
		11 ▸	Plate, dessert, round or octagon	8.00	4 ▸	Vase, 8", bulbous w/ruffled rim	25.00
			Plate, salad, round or octagon	9.00	13 ▸	Vase, squat, bulbous w/flat rim	12.50
		5 ▸	Plate, 8", round or octagon	10.00			

*Colors add 20 – 25%, except canary, add 50%

49

CREMAX, MacBETH-EVANS DIVISION OF CORNING GLASS WORKS, Late 1930s – Early 1940s

Colors: Cremax, Cremax with fired-on colored trim or decals

Cremax pattern is often called "pie crust" design; it is also a general idiom for tableware patterns that were produced in the light ivory glass coloring (called Cremax). These patterns relate to the color itself as well as being part of the pattern name. For instance, there was Cremax Bordette line, with pink, yellow, blue, and green borders; Cremax Rainbow line with pastel pink and green borders; the Cremax Windsor line, with Windsor brown, blue, and green castle decals; and a plain ware simply called Cremax. A hexagon-sided center floral ware was called Princess Pattern and one with a floral spray was known as Flora.

The blue or pink-bordered roses have more admirers than do the non-colored border items. You can also find "Mountain Flowers" which is usually found as a Petalware decoration. Plain Cremax sets could be acquired very reasonably (and still can). Cremax was competing for china dinnerware dollars and was advertised as resistant to chips and guaranteed to be in service for years. Most of what you find today is in good shape, except for worn decaled pieces.

Blue Cremax (in two distinctly different shades) has lured the most collectors to this pattern. Blue is commonly found in Canada and some bordering states; few other collectors realized that there were so many pieces of blue to gather. You can find pictures of both shades of blue in our new *Florence's Ovenware from the 1920s to the Present* book. The Internet has made blue more available to those wishing to collect it. I have found out that the lighter robin's egg blue was distributed by Corning almost exclusively in Canada. That darker blue shade is not as commonly found in Canada. However, most of what I have found has been in northern states, especially Michigan and New York. At this time, price both shades of blue about the same as the pieces with decals. Assembling a set of the light blue will take time.

Cremax Bordette demitasse sets were advertised in sets of eight. Some sets have been found on a wire rack. The usual make-up of these sets has been two sets each of four colors: pink, yellow, blue, and green.

	Cremax	*Blue, decal decorated			Cremax	*Blue, decal decorated
Bowl, 5¾", cereal	4.00	12.00		7 ▸ Plate, 11½", sandwich	5.50	18.00
1 ▸ Bowl, 7¾", soup	7.50	25.00		3 ▸ Saucer	1.00	3.50
Bowl, 9", vegetable	12.00	22.00		8 ▸ Saucer, demitasse	4.00	
Creamer	4.50	10.00		10 ▸ Sugar, open	4.50	10.00
2 ▸ Cup	4.00	5.00				
9 ▸ Cup, demitasse	11.00			*Add 50% for castle decal		
5 ▸ Egg cup, 2¼"	10.00					
4 ▸ Plate, 6¼", bread and butter	2.00	4.00				
6 ▸ Plate, 9¾", dinner	4.50	12.00				

50

"CROW'S FOOT," LINE 412 & LINE 890, PADEN CITY GLASS COMPANY, 1930s

Colors: Ritz blue, Ruby red, amber, amethyst, black, pink, crystal, white, and yellow

Paden City's "Crow's Foot" blanks were used for many of their well known etchings, but the blanks themselves are grabbed up in unadorned Ruby and Ritz blue. Line #412 is a squared mould shape, and Line #890 is the round one. When "Crow's Foot" is offered for sale at shows, it never fails to attract new admirers. Price is a significant factor for collecting "Crow's Foot" since not everyone can meet the expense of paying for popular Paden City etched patterns like "Cupid," "Orchid," or "Peacock & Wild Rose."

This new collecting awareness has made red and cobalt blue "Crow's Foot" tricky for dealers to keep in stock. Inexperienced collectors are being drawn to many Paden City patterns through the Internet; and this publicity seems to be infectious as more and more people are requesting this smaller company's glassware. Often, the initial lure is the color rather than the pattern. Some are searching for only round or square items; but others are mixing them. Fewer collectors are acquiring amber, crystal, or yellow; but small sets can be found in these colors. Black is not ordinarily found, but white is especially limited. You may not admire white glass, but this is one pattern you need to consider purchasing if you find it reasonably priced in white.

Many Paden City Ruby red pieces are inclined to run toward an amberina color (especially tumblers). Amberina is a collector's term for the yellowish tint of pieces that were supposed to be red. It was originally an improperly heated glass mistake and not a color that glass manufacturers tried to make. Over the years, amberina has attracted a following of collectors who now seek it for that particular bi-color effect.

You may find silver decorated designs on cobalt added by some other company and even non-"Crow's Foot" collectors often find them attractive. The candy dish and plate on page 52 have nicely decorated silver embellishments. That squared bowl to the right of those pieces has yellow decorated flowers in each corner. We have never before seen that decoration.

	Ruby Red	Black, Ritz Blue	Other colors
Bowl, 4⅞", square	25.00	30.00	12.50
Bowl, 8¾", square	50.00	55.00	25.00
Bowl, 6", deep	40.00	35.00	15.00
Bowl, 6½", rd., 2½" high, 3½" base	45.00	50.00	22.50
Bowl, 8½", square, 2-handle	50.00	60.00	27.50
Bowl, 10", footed	75.00	75.00	32.50
Bowl, 10", square, 2-handle	75.00	75.00	32.50
Bowl, 11", oval	35.00	40.00	20.00
Bowl, 11", square	60.00	70.00	30.00
Bowl, 11", square, rolled edge	65.00	75.00	32.50
Bowl, 11½", 3 footed, round console	85.00	100.00	42.50
Bowl, 11½", console	75.00	85.00	37.50
Bowl, cream soup, footed/flat	22.00	26.00	10.00
Bowl, Nasturtium, 3 footed	185.00	210.00	90.00
Bowl, whipped cream, 3 footed	55.00	65.00	27.50
Cake plate, square, 2", pedestal foot	85.00	95.00	42.50
Cake stand, 4½" high	100.00	100.00	50.00
Candle, round base, tall	80.00	90.00	37.50
Candle, square, mushroom	37.50	42.50	20.00
Candlestick, 5¾", sq. based	28.00	30.00	12.50
Candy w/cover, 6½", 3 part (2 styles)	85.00	95.00	40.00
Candy, 3 footed, rd., 6⅛" wide, 3¼" high	150.00	185.00	75.00
Cheese stand, 5"	35.00	30.00	12.50
Comport, 3¼" tall, 6¼" wide	35.00	38.00	15.00
Comport 4¾" tall, 7⅜" wide	50.00	60.00	35.00
Comport, 6⅝" tall, 7" wide	60.00	75.00	30.00
Creamer, flat	14.00	16.00	8.00
Creamer, footed	14.00	16.00	8.00
Cup, footed or flat	12.00	16.00	8.00
Gravy boat, flat, 2 spout	95.00	100.00	50.00
Gravy boat, pedestal	135.00	150.00	65.00
Mayonnaise, 3 footed	55.00	65.00	30.00
Plate, 5¾"	5.00	6.00	1.50
Plate, 8", round	11.00	13.00	4.50
Plate, 8½", square	12.00	14.00	3.50
Plate, 9¼", round, small dinner	30.00	30.00	12.50

	Ruby Red	Black, Ritz Blue	Other colors
Plate, 9½", round, 2-handle	65.00	75.00	32.50
Plate, 10⅜", round, 2-handle	50.00	60.00	25.00
Plate, 10⅜", square, 2-handle	40.00	50.00	20.00
Plate, 10½", dinner	90.00	100.00	40.00
4 ▶ Plate, 11", cracker	45.00	50.00	22.50
Platter, 12"	30.00	35.00	15.00
Relish, 11", 3 part	95.00	100.00	45.00
Sandwich server, round, center-handle	65.00	75.00	32.50
15 ▶ Sandwich server, square, center-handle	45.00	50.00	17.50
Saucer, 6", round	4.00	5.00	1.00
Saucer, 6", square	4.50	6.00	1.50
Sugar, flat	12.00	15.00	5.50
Sugar, footed	12.00	15.00	5.50
3 ▶ Tumbler, 4¼"	75.00	85.00	37.50
Vase, 4⅝" tall, 4⅛" wide	75.00	80.00	40.00
Vase, 10¼", cupped	110.00	129.00	45.00
Vase, 10¼", flared	100.00	115.00	32.50
Vase, 11¾", flared	175.00	195.00	65.00

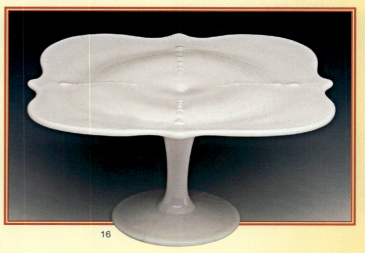

16

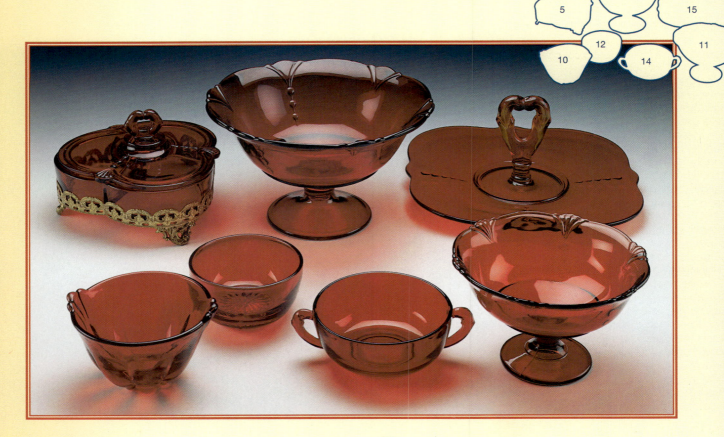

Cube was Jeannette's geometric pattern probably designed to attract Fostoria American buyers looking for some color for their dishes. American was primarily made in crystal with only a few pieces in color; so for all practical purposes, any green or pink Cube you find will not be Fostoria. Novices often confuse Cube 2⅝" creamer and 2⁹⁄₁₆" sugar on the 7½" round tray. Only those three Cube pieces were produced in crystal and there is no 7½" Fostoria round tray. Crystal Cube is less bright or sparkling in appearance when compared to the brilliant, clearer quality of Fostoria's American pattern. I need to point out that the amber and white sugar and creamers pictured were made by Hazel-Atlas and are not Jeannette's Cube.

The major confusion lies with Indiana's Whitehall pattern that was produced in the 1980s and 1990s. Their colored cube-like pitchers are shaped differently than the ones pictured here. If not shaped like the pink or green pitchers on page 54, then they are not Jeannette's Cube. We constantly get e-mail photos about these pitchers thought to be Cube or rare Fostoria. Unfortunately, these have been advertised and auctioned on the Internet as "rare" Cube. They are neither Cube nor rare.

Speaking of Internet auctions, notice whether the seller will guarantee his merchandise. That is usually a strong indication as to whether he is legitimate and reliable. Some make honest mistakes; but others want you to make the mistake. (Other than pitchers, pink Whitehall tumblers were marketed, as well as a darker {avocado} shade of green, not Cube's original green.) Cube tumblers are always flat, and were made in only one size, as pictured. If you see colored, footed tumblers, they are Whitehall, not Jeannette or Fostoria.

Original Cube tumblers are difficult to find in either color. Even though pitchers are infrequently found, most collectors find the pitcher before latching onto four, six, or eight tumblers. Inspect the pointed cubes on the sides of the tumblers and pitchers since they frequently were damaged before the heavy rims.

Cube powder jars are three-footed. A few experimental colors have turned up such as canary yellow and two shades of blue. Occasionally, these jars are found with celluloid or plastic lids. Powder jars were made with glass lids from the factory. These may have been sold as replacements when tops were broken. Another possibility is that left-over powder bottoms were sold to someone who made celluloid lids to match brush, mirror, or comb handles for sets they sold. In any case, prices below are for intact, original glass lids. The powder jars with other types of lids sell for half or less. A celluloid lid is better than no lid at all — and for collectors of celluloid items, it's probably better than a glass one.

Cube is another pattern where varying shades of pink or green occur. That is another problem when buying on the Internet that is solved by attending a Depression glass show and examining what you are buying. You might actually be willing to pay a little more for that satisfaction.

	Pink	Green
‣ Bowl, 4½", dessert, pointed edge	13.00	13.00
‣ *Bowl, 4½", deep	9.00	
‣ Bowl, 5", tab hdld.	75.00	
‣**Bowl, 6½", salad	14.00	15.00
‣ *Bowl, 7¼", pointed edge	20.00	22.00
‣ *Butter dish and cover	70.00	65.00
Butter dish bottom	20.00	20.00
Butter dish top	45.00	45.00
‣ Candy jar and cover, 6½"	30.00	30.00
‣ Coaster, 3¼"	7.50	10.00
‣*‡Creamer, 2⅝"	3.00	
‣ Creamer, 3⁹⁄₁₆"	12.00	14.00
‣ Cup	7.50	9.00
‣ Pitcher, 8¾", 45 ounce	235.00	255.00
‣ *Plate, 6", sherbet	3.00	3.00
‣ *Plate, 8", luncheon	8.00	9.00
‣ Powder jar and cover, 3 legs	30.00	35.00
‣ Salt and pepper, pair	35.00	38.00
‣ Saucer	2.50	2.50
‣ *Sherbet, footed	9.00	10.00
‣ ‡Sugar, 2⅜"	3.00	
‣ *Sugar, 3"	7.00	8.00
‣ *Sugar/candy cover	15.00	15.00
Tray for 3⁹⁄₁₆" creamer and sugar, 7½" (crystal only)	4.00	
‣ *Tumbler, 4", 9 ounce	78.00	85.00

19

*Ultra Marine $50.00   **Ultra Marine $90.00
‡Amber or white (Hazel-Atlas) $3.00; crystal $1.00

"CUPID," PADEN CITY GLASS COMPANY, 1930s

Colors: pink, green, light blue, peacock blue, black, canary yellow, amber, and crystal

"Cupid" was introduced to an entirely new group of buyers via the Internet. Many people there found it as exciting as we collectors did when we started buying it in the 1970s. However, prices 30 years ago were quite a bit less than those of today; wild prices reigned for a time on the 'Net, but did not last long. There were many eyes watching and a number of long-time collectors cashed in on the surge of new money. As a result, prices for Cupid really spiraled and buying was brisk. Then came the economic downturn and more pieces were being offered than were being bought. Prices tend to run in cycles; and demand causes prices to fluctuate. Most Paden City etchings have increased at least 20% to 30% in the last few years with rare items doubling or nearly so. Have you followed the stock market in that time?

Some outrageous prices are still being asked, but there seem to be few buyers for now. These prices may well seem very tame in the future, but not at present.

Prices are the most difficult part of writing this book. Even with all the help from other dealers around the country, prices never please everyone. If you own a piece, you want it to be highly priced; if you want to buy the same piece, you want the price to be low. Keep in mind that one sale at a high price (think Internet) does not mean that everyone would be willing to pay that. That is especially true of rare glass and any outrageous sums obtained at auctions. If two people want something and have the money (or if one person simply does not want the other to get the item cheaply), then there may be any price paid. That does not mean that that identical item will sell for that price the next time — or ever again. Only you can determine what a piece of glass is worth to you. If a price is more than you wish to pay, walk away. There will be other pieces you want, and maybe at a price you like.

Cupid cups and saucers are still in demand. They have only been found in pink. A bottom to a tumble-up has been seen, but there have been no reports of a tumbler surfacing. Several pink and green casseroles have been found, but only two casseroles in black with silver overlay (pictured in earlier books).

Samovars are found occasionally and are a magnet of attention when they are displayed. To be a "Cupid" samovar, the "Cupid" pattern has to be etched on it. Mould shape alone does not make the pattern. I once had a beautiful, expensive, but plain, samovar shipped to me as "Cupid"; so I speak of this from experience. Yes, the etch does makes a difference.

Reports of "Cupid" design found on silver overlay vases marked "Made in Germany" keep coming. These vases have been found in cobalt, orange, and lavender. The last report involves a silver overlay vase marked "Made in Czechoslovakia," which may help date these, at least.

"CUPID"

		Green, Pink	Blue
2 ▶	Bowl, 8½", oval, footed	275.00	
14 ▶	Bowl, 9¼", footed fruit	295.00	
17 ▶	Bowl, 9¼", center-handled	275.00	
18 ▶	Bowl, 10¼", fruit	230.00	
13 ▶	Bowl, 10½", rolled edge	200.00	
	Bowl, 11", console	200.00	
	Cake plate, 11¾"	200.00	
	Cake stand, 2" high, footed	200.00	
8 ▶	Candlestick, 5" wide, pair	210.00	395.00
16 ▶	Candy w/lid, footed, 5¼" high	395.00	
1 ▶	Candy w/lid, 3 part, flat	295.00	
	*Casserole, covered	795.00	
12 ▶	Comport, 6¼"	195.00	250.00
	Creamer, flat	195.00	
6 ▶	Creamer, 4½", footed	135.00	
	Creamer, 5", footed	135.00	
	Cup	195.00	
3 ▶	Ice bucket, 6"	275.00	
9 ▶	Ice tub, 4¾"	295.00	
	**Lamp, silver overlay	495.00	
7 ▶	Mayonnaise, 6" diameter, fits on 8" plate, spoon, 3 pc.	210.00	295.00

		Green, Pink	Blue
	Plate, 10½"	150.00	225.00
15 ▶	Samovar	1,100.00	
	Saucer	35.00	
	Sugar, flat	195.00	
5 ▶	Sugar, 4¼", footed	130.00	
	Sugar, 5", footed	130.00	
10 ▶	Tray, 10¾", center-handled	200.00	
11 ▶	Tray, 10⅞", oval-footed	250.00	
4 ▶	Vase, 8¼", elliptical	695.00	
	Vase, fan-shaped	525.00	
	Vase, 10"	335.00	
	Water bottle w/tumbler	750.00	

*Black (silver overlay) $75.00   **Possibly German

56

DAISY AND BUTTON W/NARCISSUS, LINE 124, INDIANA GLASS COMPANY, c. 1920s

Colors: crystal and with colored stains; Sunset (amberina) and Ruby for Tiara Exclusives

Pattern glass books assign Line 124 to the 1890s, so we never gave it much thought. However, in doing research for the Pattern ID books, we ran across a *Glass Review* article written in 1980 by Barbara Shaeffer and Vel Hinchliffe that intrigued us. They stated they found Daisy and Button w/Narcissus in a 1932 Indiana Glass catalog. That would certainly make the pattern Depression era. Hence, we are including the pattern here. Another author is said to have found a piece of this advertised in a 1918 Sears catalog. We're certain there are more items to be found than those in our listing and we would appreciate your letting us know what you uncover, particularly if you have a collection of it.

Indiana reintroduced a decanter and tray with six wines in crystal and their amberina (Sunset) and Ruby color for Tiara Exclusives home party ware division after Tiara's opening in the 1970s. The original tray was scalloped. Indiana's newer version has paneled edging and a flat rim. All amberina and ruby colored wares were made in the last 30 years. Be aware that they are newer versions. Cathy spotted a wine set with faint amethyst staining and that would've been done originally. Staining techniques were used in the early part of the twentieth century to enhance plain crystal wares. Many of these stains have weakened over the years and finding one without wear is unusual.

		*Crystal				*Crystal
	Bowl, 4⅛", salad (their call)	8.00			Creamer	12.50
	Bowl, 4⅛", 3-toed fruit	12.50	1 ▸	Decanter w/stop, 12½"	38.00
	Bowl, 5½", ftd. bonbon	15.00		Goblet, water	12.50
	Bowl, round vegetable	25.00	6 ▸	Goblet, 4⅝", wine	12.50
	Bowl, 9½", oval, ftd.	28.00		Pitcher	65.00
	Butter w/cover	38.00		Sugar	12.50
	Compote, 4½", ftd. jelly	15.00	3 ▸	Tray, 10⅜"	25.00
	Cup, custard	8.00	5 ▸	Tumbler, 4⅜", water	13.00

DELLA ROBBIA, #1058, WESTMORELAND GLASS COMPANY, Late 1920s – 1940s

Colors: crystal, crystal w/applied lustre colors, milk glass, pink, purple slag, and opaque blue

Note that Della Robbia is pattern #1058. I previously have shown catalog pages that had some other lines show along with Della Robbia items. If not shown as #1058, then it is not Della Robbia.

You will find Della Robbia in crystal, crystal with applied lustre colors, pink, opaque blue, green, and milk glass. Tha is an interesting color on the plate pictured on page 59. Notice that the fruit on each piece consists of apple, pear, an grape. Two dissimilar color variations occur in the fruit decorations on crystal. All apples are red; pears, yellow; an grapes, purple; but the luster of the colors applied is diverse. Those darker colored fruits are most sought. The quandar with this darker color is that the applied lustre abrades easily. Scratches are prominent on the darker hue. Most collec tors prefer not to mix the two colored wares. However, I have never seen a punch set in the darker version.

There are a couple of other patterns similar to Della Robbia, but both include a banana in the design. If there is banana in the design, it most likely is an Indiana pattern. Be sure to see Indiana's #301 in our 8th edition of *Collectib Glassware from the 40s, 50s, 60s....*

If you have ever tried to carry around an 18" plate for that punch set, you will understand why you see don't se many for sale at shows. Special boxes have to be designed to hold it.

Della Robbia dinner plate prices have finally slowed down their ever ascending spiral, if you can find one at ar price. All serving pieces need to be carefully scrutinized for wear. Keep in mind the prices listed are for mint conditio pieces and not ones that are worn or scuffed. One of the reasons prices for mint condition pieces are high is that the are many worn pieces found but few perfect ones.

Della Robbia pitcher and tumbler moulds were used to make some carnival colored water sets. These were made fo Levay just as were pieces of red English Hobnail. They appear in light blue and amethyst carnival. I am told that Wes moreland collectors seek them; but no collector of Della Robbia has ever asked us about them.

	Crystal w/ lustre colors		Crystal w lustre col
Basket, 9"	210.00	11 ▸ Pitcher, 32 ounce	275.00
15 ▸ Basket, 12"	310.00	5 ▸ Plate, 6", finger liner	10.00
Bowl, 4½", nappy	30.00	14 ▸ Plate, 6⅛", bread & butter	12.00
Bowl, 5", finger	35.00	Plate, 7¼", salad	22.00
2 ▸ Bowl, 6", one-handle heart	37.50	10 ▸ Plate, 9", luncheon	40.00
8 ▸ Bowl, 6", nappy, bell	35.00	16 ▸ Plate, 10½", dinner	150.00
1 ▸ Bowl, 6½", one-handle nappy	35.00	*Plate, 14", torte	110.00
Bowl, 7½", nappy	45.00	Plate, 18"	235.00
Bowl, 8", nappy, bell	65.00	Plate, 18", upturned edge, punch bowl liner	210.00
Bowl, 8", bell, handle	85.00	Platter, 14", oval	205.00
Bowl, 8", heart, handle	125.00	Punch bowl set, 15 piece	995.00
6 ▸ Bowl, 9", nappy	115.00	Salt and pepper, pair	80.00
Bowl, 12", footed	165.00	Salver, 14", footed, cake	150.00
Bowl, 13", rolled edge	160.00	Saucer	10.00
7 ▸ Bowl, 14", oval, flange	275.00	Stem, 3 ounce, wine	30.00
Bowl, 14", punch	335.00	12 ▸ Stem, 3¼ ounce, cocktail	25.00
Bowl, 15", bell	225.00	Stem, 5 ounce, 4¾", sherbet, high foot	22.00
Candle, 4"	33.00	13 ▸ Stem, 5 ounce, sherbet, low foot	20.00
Candle, 4", 2-lite	135.00	Stem, 6 ounce, champagne	25.00
Candy jar w/cover, scalloped edge	125.00	Stem, 8 ounce, 6", water	33.00
9 ▸ Candy, round, flat, chocolate	110.00	Sugar, footed	23.00
3 ▸ Comport, 6½", 3⅝" high, mint, footed	40.00	Tumbler, 5 ounce, ginger ale	25.00
Comport, 8", sweetmeat, bell	110.00	Tumbler, 8 ounce, footed	28.00
Comport, 12", footed, bell	130.00	Tumbler, 8 ounce, water	22.00
Comport, 13", flanged	135.00	Tumbler, 11 ounce, iced tea, footed	35.00
Creamer, footed	23.00	Tumbler, 12 ounce, iced tea, bell	40.00
Cup, coffee	20.00	4 ▸ Tumbler, 12 ounce, iced tea, bell, footed	40.00
Cup, punch	15.00	Tumbler, 12 ounce, 5³⁄₁₆", iced tea, straight	42.00

*Pink $150.00

58

DIAMOND QUILTED, "FLAT DIAMOND," IMPERIAL GLASS COMPANY, Late 1920s – Early 1930s

Colors: pink, blue, green, crystal, black; some red and amber

Imperial's Diamond Quilted does not get as much recognition in the glass collecting world as do some of Imperial's other wares, namely Beaded Block, Candlewick, and Cape Cod. It can be collected in sets of pink or green with time and patience. Some pieces are available in other colors of red and amber. Red is purchased by more collectors of red glass than by Diamond Quilted collectors since only a few pieces were made. It is a shame since it is a strong red color unlike the amberina colored pieces found in their famous Candlewick and Cape Cod lines.

Diamond Quilted in black may take a long time to accumulate a luncheon set. Flat black pieces have the design on the bottom. Thus, the design on the plate or saucer can only be seen if it is turned over. Intermittently, items in blue can be located, but it will take more than a little luck to get your hands on very much. There is a similar Fenton pattern found more frequently in both blue and black. If you are willing to blend these, you might serve your guests more quickly.

16

The pink cake salver pictured here is the first one we have ever found. We photographed it, took it to a show and excited a dealer-collector from North Carolina.

Punch bowl sets remain difficult to locate. Those punch bowls in green are a different shade of green than most other pieces. Therefore finding cups to match the punch is a major chore. Of course, you have to find the bowl first. Since the regular cup mold was also used to make the punch cup that causes some havoc in finding green cups and saucers in matching hues. I saw several cups at a recent show that cried out for a punch bowl; they were a mismatched color for the saucers on which they were displayed.

There is no dinner-sized plate in Diamond Quilted. Lack of a dinner plate used to be a detriment. We've noticed that some actually prefer the smaller luncheon plates for use for appetizers when entertaining.

Hazel-Atlas made a quilted diamond pitcher and four sizes of flat tumblers in crystal, pink, green, and cobalt blue. They are often confused with Imperial's Diamond Quilted. The quilting on Hazel-Atlas pieces ends in a straight line around the top of each piece. Notice Imperial's Diamond Quilted pattern ends unevenly in points. You may also notice that the diamond designs on Hazel-Atlas pieces are flat as opposed to those Imperial ones that are curved. The Hazel-Atlas pitcher itself is flat and shaped like the straight-sided pitcher so commonly seen in Royal Lace.

Note the original sales catalog depiction below. Console sets at 65¢ and a dozen candy dishes in assorted colors for $6.95 would be quite a bargain today. No, I do not have any for sale at that price. This ad is from 1930.

	Pink, Green	Amber, Blue, Black
10 ▸ Bowl, 4¾", cream soup	15.00	25.00
Bowl, 5", cereal	10.00	15.00
15 ▸ Bowl, 5½", one handle	9.00	22.00
3 ▸ Bowl, 7", crimped edge	12.00	25.00
8 ▸ Bowl, 7", straight	16.00	20.00
Bowl, 10½", rolled edge console	35.00	60.00
16 ▸ Cake salver, tall, 10" diameter	95.00	
9 ▸ Candlesticks (2 styles), pair	30.00	40.00
4 ▸ Candy jar and cover, footed	75.00	
14 ▸ Compote, 6" tall, 7¼" wide	45.00	
Compote and cover, 11½"	95.00	125.00
1 ▸ Creamer	12.00	15.00

	Pink, Green	Amber, Blue, Black
6 ▸ Cup	9.50	17.50
Goblet, 1 ounce, cordial	15.00	
Goblet, 2 ounce, wine	14.00	
Goblet, 3 ounce, wine	14.00	
Goblet, 6", 9 ounce, champagne	12.00	
13 ▸ Ice bucket	55.00	85.00
12 ▸ Mayonnaise set:		
ladle, plate, comport	40.00	60.00
Pitcher, 64 ounce	55.00	
Plate, 6", sherbet	4.00	8.00
Plate, 7", salad	6.00	11.00
5 ▸ Plate, 8", luncheon	10.00	15.00
Punch bowl and stand	650.00	
Plate, 14", sandwich	15.00	
Sandwich server, center handle	25.00	50.00
7 ▸ Saucer	4.00	6.00
11 ▸ Sherbet	10.00	16.00
2 ▸ Sugar	12.00	15.00
Tumbler, 9 ounce, water	9.00	
Tumbler, 12 ounce, iced tea	9.00	
Tumbler, 6 ounce, footed	8.50	
Tumbler, 9 ounce, footed	12.50	
Tumbler, 12 ounce, footed	15.00	
Vase, fan, dolphin handles	55.00	75.00
Whiskey, 1½ ounce	10.00	

Covered Bowl—6⅜ in. diam., deep round shape with 3 artistic feet, dome cover, fine quality brilliant finish **pot glass**, allover block diamond design, transparent Rose Marie and emerald green. I C5603—Asstd. ½ doz. in carton, 20 lbs. **Doz $6.95**

I C989—3 piece set, 2 transparent colors (rose and green), good quality, 10⅜ in. rolled rim bowl, TWO 3½ in. wide base candlesticks. Asstd. 6 sets in case, 30 lbs............ **SET (3 pcs) 65c**

DIANA, FEDERAL GLASS COMPANY, 1937 – 1941

Colors: pink, amber, and crystal

16

Crystal Diana is not as available as it once was, and collectors have been paying more to finish sets. Those crystal tumblers may be as rare as their pink counterparts. Amber and crystal are not as sought by collectors, a good thing since there is a dearth of these colors.

Pink Diana continues to be the color to collect. Price advances are not as frenzied as they were in the late 1990s, but prices for candy jars, shakers, and tumblers have increased in each color. For a few years, prices doubled on some items, but that is not happening today. There has been a price correction for many Depression glass patterns in the market.

Below is a crystal, gold trimmed cake set which begs to be used, and above is a red stained children's set. Flashed red demitasses are selling for $10.00 to $12.00 each. Pink demitasse cup and saucer sets are being found occasionally, but the demand for these has slowed causing prices to slip a bit. We have encountered at least one demitasse collector who told us the Diana pattern is what got her started on those.

Prices listed are actual selling prices for Diana and not advertised or wished-for prices. There is a major difference between an advertised price and the price being accepted by both buyer and seller. Rarely have I heard of something selling for more than advertised, but often I have heard of less. Today, dealers coast to coast are sharing information on prices. That's been a tremendous help to me as I work to keep pricing current in these books. The Internet, though a new tool for pricing, has to be approached carefully and not taken too literally. I attend as many Depression glass shows as possible and spend many hours checking prices and talking to dealers about what is, and what is not selling, and for what price.

Frosted or satinized pieces of Diana that have shown up in crystal and pink have a few admirers. Some of the larger bowls were frosted and drilled for ceiling globes.

There is a propensity for new collectors to mistake Diana with other swirled patterns such as Swirl and Twisted Optic. The centers of Diana pieces are swirled where the centers of the other swirled patterns are plain.

17

13 (all)

		Crystal	Pink	Amber
	* Ashtray, 3½"	2.50	3.50	
5 ▸	Bowl, 5", cereal	6.00	8.00	14.00
2 ▸	Bowl, 5½", cream soup	12.00	30.00	20.00
	Bowl, 9", salad	12.00	20.00	18.00
9 ▸	Bowl, 11", console fruit	16.00	35.00	18.00
	Bowl, 12", scalloped edge	16.00	30.00	20.00
6 ▸	Candy jar and cover, round	16.00	52.00	50.00
11 ▸	Coaster, 3½"	2.50	8.00	10.00
3 ▸	Creamer, oval	9.00	16.00	9.00
14 ▸	Cup	6.00	18.00	9.00
	Cup, 2 ounce demitasse and 4½" saucer set	13.00	42.00	
13 ▸	Plate, 6", bread & butter	2.00	4.00	2.00
4 ▸	Plate, 9½"	6.00	16.00	9.00
17 ▸	Plate, 11¾", sandwich	9.00	25.00	12.50
8 ▸	Platter, 12", oval	12.00	33.00	15.00
10 ▸	Salt and pepper, pair	40.00	95.00	100.00
15 ▸	Saucer	1.50	5.00	2.00
12 ▸	Sherbet	3.00	10.00	12.00
1 ▸	Sugar, open oval	9.00	16.00	8.00
7 ▸	Tumbler, 4⅛", 9 ounce	35.00	55.00	30.00
16 ▸	Junior set: 6 demitasse cups & saucers with round rack	100.00	275.00	

* Green $3.00

DOGWOOD, "APPLE BLOSSOM," "WILD ROSE," MacBETH-EVANS GLASS COMPANY

1929 – 1932

Colors: pink, green, some crystal, Monax, Cremax, and yellow

Dogwood remains one of the top ten collectible Depression patterns, but it is rapidly approaching being among the top five. Pink is the color most desired, which is fortuitous since pink is most frequently found. Green is obtainable in small quantities. Pink luncheon plates are bountiful and any-one who likes this pattern will probably see these first, last, and always. The larger dinner plates are hard to find especially without scratches or scuffs; and the large fruit bowl and platter are almost non-existent for today's collectors. They were infrequently found over the years and usually enter the market now only through collections being sold or split among family members. Dealers in antique malls do make mistakes at times. On our way out to Texas last year we found six dinners priced as luncheon plates in one booth. The next booth over had dinners $10.00 over my book price. Sometimes it might pay to look around in "your" mall where you sell

Large fruit bowls are so scarce because they were marketed to some company that satinized the bowls, bored a hol in the center, and made ceiling fixtures out of them. These sell in the $125.00 range whether pink or green. Notice this i considerably less than prices for normal bowls.

Green pitchers and water tumblers are seldom found and are costly. Iced teas are scarce and the pink juice tumbler truly rare. That juice price has escalated so that few collectors buy more than one. One thing that has become apparen over the last year is the abundance of pink Dogwood pitchers. In three shows we did, there were six or more for sale. I se a price adjustment coming shortly as supply has seemingly out paced demand.

Tumblers and pitchers which have the same shape as Dogwood, but are not silk screened with Dogwood pattern, ar not Dogwood. They are merely the mould blanks made by MacBeth-Evans to go with the plain, no design tumblers tha they sold separately with various pink sets such as "S" pattern and even American Sweetheart. The Dogwood design ha to be silk screened onto the tumbler or pitcher for it to be considered Dogwood and to com-mand those prices shown below. Some collectors buy the plain blanks to use with their sets, and that's perfectly fine as long as they understand that they are not the costly Dogwood.

The thick, footed-style Dogwood sugar and creamer are illustrated in pink. There is a thin, flat style creamer and sugar, also. Pink sugar/creamer sets are found in both styles, but green is only found in the thin version. There are thick and thin pink cups, but saucers for both styles are the same. Green cups were only made in thin.

Pink grill plates occur in two styles. Some have the Dogwood pattern all over the plate, and others have the pattern only around the rim. Dogwood sherbets are found with either a Dogwood blossom etched on the bottom or plain. It makes no difference in price since they are only from different moulds.

	Pink	Green	Monax, Cremax		Pink	Green	Monax, Crema
13 ▸ * Bowl, 5½", cereal	30.00	35.00	15.00	Plate, 9¼", dinner	33.00		
1 ▸ * Bowl, 8½", berry	60.00	135.00	40.00	2 ▸ * Plate, 10½", grill, AOP or			
6 ▸ ** Bowl, 10¼", fruit	625.00	295.00	125.00	border design only	23.00	28.00	
Cake plate, 11", heavy				19 ▸ Plate, 12", salver	35.00		15.0
solid foot	1,295.00			Platter, 12", oval	695.00		
7 ▸ * Cake plate, 13", heavy				5 ▸ * Saucer	5.00	7.00	20.0
solid foot	165.00	145.00	235.00	11 ▸ * Sherbet, low footed	30.00	125.00	
Coaster, 3¼"	695.00			12 ▸ * Sugar, 2½", thin, flat	18.00	45.00	
10 ▸ * Creamer, 2½", thin, flat	18.00	47.50		14 ▸ * Sugar, 3¼", thick, footed	16.00		
15 ▸ * Creamer, 3¼", thick, footed	23.00			Tumbler, 3½", 5 oz.,			
18 ▸ * Cup, thick	17.00		45.00	decorated	210.00		
4 ▸ * Cup, thin	16.00	42.00		16 ▸ * Tumbler, 4", 10 oz., decorated	50.00	105.00	
9 ▸ * Pitcher, 8", 80 oz., decorated	225.00	575.00		3 ▸ * Tumbler, 4¾", 11 oz.,			
Pitcher, 8", 80 oz. (American				decorated	50.00	110.00	
Sweetheart Style)	650.00			17 ▸ * Tumbler, 5", 12 oz., decorated	80.00	135.00	
8 ▸ * Plate, 6", bread and butter	9.00	9.00	22.00	Tumbler, moulded band	22.50		
* Plate, 8", luncheon	8.00	11.00					

* Yellow $75.00   **Lampshade $150.00

DORIC, JEANNETTE GLASS COMPANY, 1935 – 1938

Colors: pink, green, some Delphite, Ultra Marine, and yellow

Collectors of green Doric are tormented by the shortage of pitchers and cream soups. The green, 48-ounce pitcher, with or without ice lip, is nearly a fantasy for collectors to own. Green cereal bowls and all tumblers are only spotted infrequently. Those pieces in pink are not commonly seen either, but they can all be located with determined searching, save for the cream soup, never yet found in pink. Cream soups, or consommés as some companies called them, have two handles. Cereal bowls have no handles but are often offered for sale as cream soups.

Green Doric is found in Florida, but is often cloudy ("sick") glass. Apparently, well water created mineral deposits that react with the glass. You could make a fortune if you could figure out a way to easily remove these deposits. I know have heard of everything from Zud® to Efferdent® tablets. As far as I know, this cloudiness cannot be expunged short of professionally polishing it out over a span of time. Do not be hoodwinked into buying cloudy glass unless it is inexpensive, you plan to use and wash it in your dishwasher regularly, or you have that elusive magic cure. Harsh dishwater detergents will also cloud your glass over time.

Doric has become an enjoyable challenge to collectors, and may require years to finish a set. Collectors tell us they do not care how difficult a pattern is to acquire because the "hunt" fascinates them almost as much as the glass itself. In addition, some collectors aren't even trying for complete sets in today's market. They're blending patterns and colors into "rainbow" settings.

Mould seam roughness is the norm on Doric, especially on those hard to find footed tumblers or cereals. This discourages fussy collectors who look for perfection. Factory irregularities shouldn't stop you from owning these pieces if you see them for sale. Keep in mind that Depression glass was relatively inexpensive or give-away glass. Mint condition, though desirable in glass collecting, can be carried to ludicrous extremes. Magnifying glasses to look for flaws and black (ultraviolet) lights to check for repairs are seen at shows today. At least glass collecting doesn't have people being paid to determine quality and "grades" for glass as in other collecting fields — or at least, not yet.

Only one yellow Doric pitcher is known to exist; but it is improbable that the factory made only one. Former workers have advised me that even experimental color runs commonly consisted of 30 to 50 items.

The 48-ounce Doric pitchers come with or without an ice lip, but the 32-ounce flat pitcher is only found without a lip. Oddly, candy and sugar lids in this Jeannette pattern are not interchangeable as is true for most of their wares. The candy lid is taller and more domed.

Sherbet and cloverleaf candies are commonly found in Delphite. All other Delphite pieces are rare in Doric and the price is still inexpensive for that rare color. Only the Delphite pitcher creates much of a pricing disturbance and that is not too great considering its scarcity. Jeannette made mostly kitchenware items in Delphite, rather than dinnerware.

An iridescent, three-part candy was made in the 1970s and sold for 79¢ in our local dish barn. Sometimes an Ultra Marine candy is found within a piece of hammered aluminum hollowed for the candy to fit. I recently saw a 1950s ad showing that the company Everlast Metal Products Corp. made that 12" piece of aluminum. I pass that along for whatever worth it may be to the growing number of collectors for 50s aluminum wares.

		Pink	Green	Delphite			Pink	Green	Delphite
10 ▸	Bowl, 4½", berry	13.00	14.00	55.00		Plate, 6", sherbet	6.00	7.00	
	Bowl, 5", cream soup, 2 hdld.		595.00			Plate, 7", salad	25.00	25.00	
14 ▸	Bowl, 5½", cereal	80.00	95.00		6 ▸	Plate, 9", dinner,			
13 ▸	Bowl, 8¼", large berry	33.00	38.00	150.00		serrated 195.00	20.00	20.00	
2 ▸	Bowl, 9", 2-handled	30.00	42.00		5 ▸	Plate, 9", grill	26.00	26.00	
18 ▸	Bowl, 9", oval vegetable	42.00	55.00			Platter, 12", oval	33.00	35.00	
	Butter dish and cover	80.00	100.00			Relish tray, 4" x 4"	16.00	14.00	
	Butter dish bottom	25.00	30.00		17 ▸	Relish tray, 4" x 8"	25.00	20.00	
	Butter dish top	55.00	70.00		9 ▸	Salt and pepper, pair	32.00	40.00	
	Cake plate, 10", 3 legs	30.00	32.00		12 ▸	Saucer	5.00	6.00	
7 ▸	Candy dish and cover, 8"	40.00	45.00		8 ▸	Sherbet, footed	14.00	17.00	10.00
1 ▸*	Candy dish, 3-part	12.00	12.00	12.00		Sugar	15.00	15.00	
15 ▸	Coaster, 3"	20.00	20.00			Sugar cover	20.00	30.00	
16 ▸	Creamer, 4"	17.50	15.00			Tray, 10", handled	28.00	30.00	
11 ▸	Cup	11.00	14.00		3 ▸	Tray, 8" x 8", serving	40.00	40.00	
	Pitcher, 5½", 32 oz., flat	50.00	55.00	1,500.00		Tumbler, 4½", 9 oz.	75.00	115.00	
	Pitcher, 7½", 48 oz.,				4 ▸	Tumbler, 4", 10 oz., footed	85.00	100.00	
	footed, yellow at $2,000.00	750.00	1,350.00			Tumbler, 5", 12 oz., footed	95.00	140.00	

*Candy in metal holder $40.00, Iridescent made in the 70s, Ultra Marine $18.00

DORIC AND PANSY, JEANNETTE GLASS COMPANY, 1937 – 1938

Colors: Ultra Marine; some crystal and pink

Today, a set of Doric and Pansy can be purchased even more effortlessly and economically than it could 20 years ago. We thought the teal butter, sugar, creamer, salt, and pepper were rare in those early collecting days of the 1970s. They were; but apparently, only within our original collecting sphere of the United States. We were not looking outside our boundaries for our American-made glassware. We have discovered that much Depression era glassware was shipped overseas. Rarely found items of yesteryear in Ultra Marine Doric and Pansy are no longer rare today. They keep coming into America from England and Canada from container importers and via sales on the Internet.

We have a booth in an antique mall where the owner regularly imports from England and I cannot compete with his prices on Doric and Pansy, as well as some other patterns he receives on a regular basis such as pink and green Royal Lace and green Floral. Australia and New Zealand dealers are adding their Depression wares by selling on the Internet. The major problem of buying glassware from overseas is the cost of having it delivered to the States. If it were not for shipping costs, I suspect there would be a lot more coming "home."

Tumblers and berry bowls are not being found in the hoards abroad; so prices are holding up well on them. There are two tumblers pictured. The common one (shaped like the flat Doric tumbler) has a flared out top. Only two of the straight-sided, heavy and darker in color, 4¼", ten-ounce tumblers have been unearthed. Both turned up in California years ago and no others have since surfaced. Be wary of inadequately patterned shakers. These should be priced less (25% to 40%). If color and shape are the only indications of a Doric and Pansy patterned shaker, then leave it alone unless it is seriously under valued. Weak patterns and cloudiness ruin many shakers. Hazy shakers are not worth mint prices. Cloudiness is caused by a chemical reaction between the glass and its contents of salt or pepper. Salt often corrodes original metal shaker tops and while those are desirable, new lids are adequate and available to collectors. To my knowledge, there is nothing on the market that will take out this dullness. The only way a shaker will shine again is to have it tumbled/cleaned by a professional.

Color dissimilarities plague every collector buying Jeannette's Ultra Marine. Some pieces have a distinctly green hue instead of blue. Notice variations in my picture. Few collectors currently collect the green shade of Ultra Marine, but it is rarer and maybe it too will be in vogue down the road.

Berry bowls and children's sets are found in pink. Strangely, there have been no reports of children's sets or pink Doric and Pansy found in England or Canada.

Luncheon sets in crystal can be gathered and a few collectors are beginning to notice. That has driven up the prices on these rarely seen pieces. Sugar and creamer collectors compete for these.

		Green, Ultra Marine	Pink, Crystal			Green, Ultra Marine	Pink, Crystal
1 ▸	Bowl, 4½", berry	23.00	15.00		Plate, 7", salad	45.00	
	Bowl, 8", large berry	100.00	30.00	11 ▸ Plate, 9", dinner	40.00	25.00
	Bowl, 9", handled	45.00	25.00	6 ▸ Salt and pepper, pr.	425.00	
13 ▸	Butter dish and cover	395.00		16 ▸ Saucer	5.00	5.00
	Butter dish bottom	45.00		7 ▸ Sugar, open	100.00	110.00
	Butter dish top	350.00		8 ▸ Tray, 10", handled	38.00	
2 ▸	Cup	18.00	20.00	9 ▸ Tumbler, 4½", 9 ounce	100.00	
12 ▸	Creamer	100.00	110.00	10 ▸ Tumbler, 4¼", 10 ounce	595.00	
5 ▸	Plate, 6", sherbet	12.00	7.50			

DORIC AND PANSY
"PRETTY POLLY PARTY DISHES"

		Teal	Pink			Teal	Pink
3 ▸	Cup	45.00	35.00	15 ▸ Creamer	55.00	35.00
4 ▸	Saucer	9.00	7.00	14 ▸ Sugar	55.00	35.00
5 ▸	Plate	12.00	8.00	14-piece set	375.00	275.00

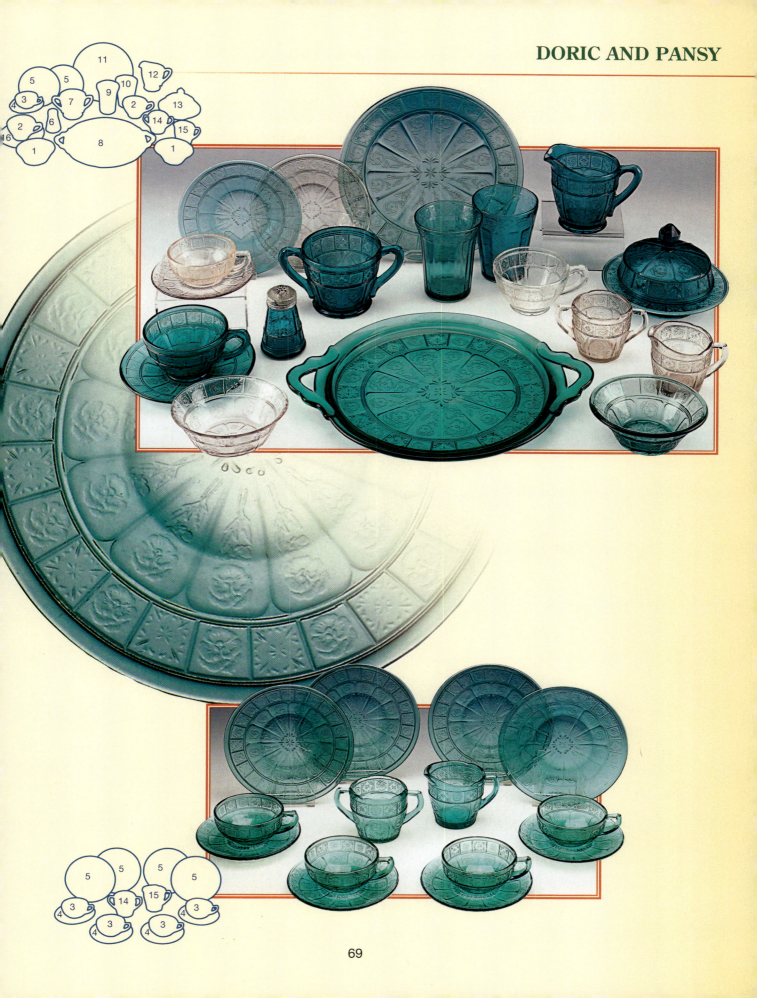

"ELLIPSE," "SHERATON," "TWITCH," LINE NO. 92, BARTLETT-COLLINS, c. Late 1930s

Colors: crystal, and with applied primary colors (yellow, red, blue, and green) and patterns; green

We see Ellipse when we travel to Midwestern cities near its maker. Since the catalog information didn't list some items or colors we are showing, we assume you can help add to these listings. Cathy was so excited by finding several colored pieces in a mall recently that she missed seeing a rarely found item sitting near them. I was hanging back to see if she'd notice it. For some reason, we seem to find more cups than saucers. Is that true for you, as well? Usually it's the other way around.

		All colors
	Bowl, 4½", hdld.	12.00
6 ▸	Bowl, 8", vegetable, hdld.	30.00
5 ▸	Creamer	12.50
1 ▸	Cup	12.00
7 ▸	Goblet, 14 oz,. ftd. tea	20.00
	Jug, 24 oz.	42.00
	Jug, 61 oz., 7½"	55.00
	Plate, 8½"	9.00
	Salt shakers, 3", pr.	35.00
2 ▸	Saucer	2.00
8 ▸	Sherbet	10.00

		All colors
4 ▸	Sugar, open	12.50
	Tumbler, 5 oz., juice	10.00
3 ▸	Tumbler, 9 oz., water	12.00
	Tumbler, 12 oz., tea	15.00

ENGLISH HOBNAIL, LINE #555, WESTMORELAND GLASS COMPANY, 1917 – 1940s; few items through 1980s

Colors: pink, turquoise/ice blue, cobalt blue, green, lilac, red, opal trimmed blue, red flashed, black, blue, amber, and milk

Line #555, English Hobnail, was produced irregularly by Westmoreland for over 70 years. It was originally called Early American and was by far Westmoreland's most extensive line. The primary manufacturing years ran from 1926 through the early 1940s. During that time, it was advertised as English Hobnail. Two separate shapes occur in the pattern, round and square. These shapes extend to the bases on stems so that round based pieces match round plates and bowls, etc. Black footed (c.1929), flashed red, and gold-trimmed items are occasionally found today, but are mostly thought of as novelties except by a few avid collectors.

English Hobnail is often confused with Hocking's Miss America, which was a similar design. English Hobnail pieces have rays of varying distances in the center of the piece. Notice the photographs for this six-point star effect. In Miss America, shown on page 132, the center rays all end equidistant from the center. The hobs on English Hobnail are more rounded and feel smoother to the touch; goblets flare and the hobs go directly into a plain rim area. Miss America's hobs are sharper to touch and the goblets do not flare at the rim. All goblets and tumblers of Miss America have three sets of rings above the hobs before entering a plain glass rim. If you have a candy jar that measures more or less than Miss America's 11½" including the cover, then it is most likely English Hobnail which is found in several sizes, both smaller and larger.

Due to space limitations, we have grouped crystal, amber, Westmoreland's 1960s "Golden Sunset" color, and others into the *Collectible Glassware of the 40s, 50s, 60s...* and are pricing only the most collected colors in this book. I am conscious that crystal was made from the early teens and darker amber in the late 1920s; but crystal was a major impetus by the company in the WWII years, when chemicals for color production were unavailable in quantity. We have shown quite a few catalog pages from Westmoreland's later years in earlier editions of *Collectible Glassware of the 40s, 50s, 60s...* if you should be interested in those.

Pricing has been broken into pink or green and turquoise/ice blue. A piece in the very sparse cobalt blue or black will bring 40% to 50% more than the turquoise prices listed. It took me four years to gather enough turquoise/ice blue items for the photo below. Very little cobalt English Hobnail is being unveiled and even fewer pieces in black. The black pieces are totally black and not crystal trimmed in black.

Additional turquoise items were produced in the 1970s. These later items appear to be an inferior quality and have a deeper color when put side by side with the older pieces.

Shakers are usually found footed. Most of the ones found in color have round feet instead of square. Flat shakers are rarely seen; turquoise blue ones are a prize.

Collections of pink or green English Hobnail can be put together with time and perseverance. This pattern does have major color inconsistencies, doubt- the most abundant shades. There yellow-green less due to various times of manufacture. Pink is color to find, but it is found in two dissimilar are three different greens, from a light, to a deep, dark green.

ENGLISH HOBNAIL

	Pink, Green	Turquoise, *Ice Blue
12 ▸ Ashtray, 3"	20.00	
Ashtray, 4½"		22.50
Ashtray, 4½", square	25.00	
Bonbon, 6½", handled	25.00	40.00
18 ▸ Bottle, toilet, 5 ounce	35.00	50.00
13 ▸ Bowl, 3", cranberry	20.00	
Bowl, 4", rose	50.00	
15 ▸ Bowl, 4½", finger	15.00	
20 ▸ Bowl, 4½", round nappy	13.00	30.00
Bowl, 4½", square footed, finger	15.00	35.00
Bowl, 5", round nappy	15.00	40.00
8 ▸ Bowl, 6", crimped dish	18.00	
1 ▸ Bowl, 6", round nappy	16.00	
14 ▸ Bowl, 6", square nappy	16.00	
Bowl, 6½", grapefruit	22.00	
Bowl, 6½", round nappy	20.00	
Bowl, 7", round nappy	22.00	
Bowl, 8", cupped, nappy	30.00	
Bowl, 8", footed	60.00	

	Pink, Green	Turquoise, *Ice Blue
Bowl, 8", hexagonal footed, 2-handled	95.00	165.00
Bowl, 8", pickle	30.00	
16 ▸ Bowl, 8", round nappy	35.00	
Bowl, 9", celery	32.00	
Bowl, 10", flared	40.00	
27 ▸ Bowl, 11", rolled edge	50.00	80.00
Bowl, 12", celery	40.00	
Bowl, 12", flange or console	50.00	
Candlestick, 3½", round base	25.00	35.00
Candlestick, 9", round base	45.00	55.00
Candy dish, 3 footed	65.00	
17 ▸ Candy, ½ lb. and cover, cone shaped	55.00	100.00
Cigarette box and cover, 4½" x 2½"	35.00	55.00
21 ▸ Cigarette jar w/cover, round	50.00	60.00
Compote, 5", round, footed	25.00	
Compote, 6", honey, round, footed	30.00	
Compote, 8", ball stem, sweetmeat	60.00	

	Pink, Green	Turquoise, *Ice Blue
7 ▸ Creamer, hexagonal footed	22.50	45.00
Creamer, square footed	42.50	
2 ▸ Cup	18.00	25.00
9 ▸ Cup, demitasse	55.00	
4 ▸ Ice tub, 4"	50.00	100.00
Ice tub, 5½"	75.00	135.00
Lamp, 6¼", electric	75.00	
Lamp, 9¼", electric	150.00	
Marmalade w/cover	60.00	85.00
Mayonnaise, 6"	20.00	
9 ▸ Nut, individual, footed	20.00	
Pitcher, 23 ounce, rounded	150.00	
Pitcher, 32 ounce, straight side	185.00	
Pitcher, 38 ounce, rounded	225.00	
Pitcher, 60 ounce, rounded	295.00	
1 ▸ Pitcher, 64 ounce, straight side	300.00	
Plate, 5½", round	9.50	
Plate, 6", square finger bowl liner	9.00	
5 ▸ Plate, 6½", round	10.00	
Plate, 6½, round finger bowl liner	9.50	
5 ▸ Plate, 8", round	12.50	
Plate, 8½", round	15.00	25.00
4 ▸ Plate, 10", round	37.00	85.00
Plate, 14", round torte	60.00	

	Pink, Green	Turquoise, *Ice Blue
Puff box, w/ cover, 6", round	50.00	77.50
28 ▸ Saucer, demitasse, round	15.00	
3 ▸ Saucer, round	4.00	5.00
Shaker, pair, flat	150.00	250.00
10 ▸ Shaker, pair, round footed	75.00	
Stem, 2 oz., square footed, wine	30.00	60.00
26 ▸ Stem, 3 oz., round footed, cocktail	20.00	40.00
Stem, 5 oz., sq. footed, oyster cocktail	16.00	
Stem, 8 oz., sq. footed, water goblet	30.00	50.00
Stem, sherbet, round foot, low		12.00
Stem, sherbet, square footed, low	12.00	
30 ▸ Stem, sherbet, round high foot	15.00	30.00
Stem, sherbet, square footed, high	15.00	35.00
22 ▸ Stem, water, round foot		30.00
6 ▸ Sugar, hexagonal footed	22.50	45.00
Sugar, square footed	45.00	
Tidbit, 2 tier	45.00	85.00
19 ▸ Tumbler, 5 ounce, ginger ale	18.00	
Tumbler, 8 ounce, water	22.00	
Tumbler, 10 ounce, ice tea	25.00	
23 ▸ Tumbler, 12 ounce, ice tea	30.00	
Urn, 11", w/cover (15")	395.00	
Vase, 7½", flip	90.00	
Vase, 7½", flip jar w/cover	135.00	
27 ▸ Vase, 8½", flared top	145.00	250.00
Vase, 10" (straw jar)	125.00	

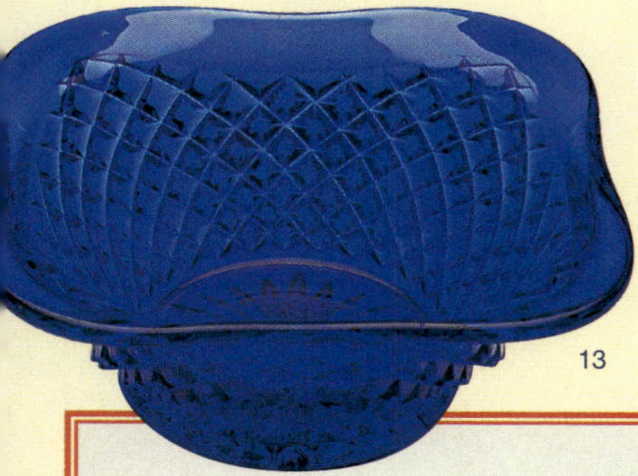

13

29

28

22

5

30

26

FANCY COLONIAL, #582, IMPERIAL GLASS COMPANY, c. 1914

Colors: crystal, pink, green, teal, some iridized Rubigold and Ice (rainbow washed crystal)

We have sold many pieces of Fancy Colonial in our shop over the years, never taking into consideration we would eventually war to include it in our book. Collecting trends change and we have always tried to keep up with those to make our books current.

Were we anticipating the future properly, we could have easily had twice the number of pieces pictured here. However, it is costly t store a multitude of glass for future use, so the Fancy Colonial pieces acquired from time to time were sold to buy other glass to show.

Fancy Colonial was one of the most copious, open stock patterns that Imperial ever produced. When we first began searching fo glass almost 40 years ago, Fancy Colonial was regularly found, possibly due to some reintroduction of pieces at the time. Cathy kep asking me if I wanted to gather this line, which people in the field were calling "Button and Flute" and "Pillar & Optic." I felt that glas currently being made was a waste of time. Well, collectors weren't buying then; but now that Imperial is out of business, we're bein asked for it at shows. Consequently, we're being forced to catch up since I didn't listen to her prompting.

Fancy Colonial was in production, off and on, throughout the company's history, a few items being made in whatever colors an for whatever promotions they were running at the time. Moulds were expensive to make. Sheer economics mandated companies us them for as long as they possibly could. Reissues by the company itself have always been a hassle for collectors since original mould are used and determining old items from new is a problem. Sometimes a short run is made in an odd color, which turns out to be co lectible, and other times they inundate the market with the same colors made originally.

	All colors*			All colors*			All col
Bonbon, 5½", handle	25.00	4 ▸ Cup, punch, straight edge	15.00	Stem, 3 oz., port, deep	30.00
Bottle, water, no stop	75.00	Goblet, egg cup, low foot, deep	28.00	6 ▸ Stem, 4½ oz., cocktail, shallow	20.00
Bowl, 3½", nappy	12.00	Goblet, low foot, café parfait	28.00	Stem, 4 oz., burgundy, deep	30.00
Bowl, 4½", nappy	15.00	9 ▸ Mayo w/liner, flat	50.00	Stem, 5 oz., claret, deep	30.00
Bowl, 4½", rim foot berry	15.00	Oil bottle w/stopper, 6¼ oz.	65.00	Stem, 6 oz., champagne, deep	21.00
Bowl, 5", nappy or olive	15.00	Oil bottle, 5½ ounce, bulbous,		Stem, 6 oz., saucer/	
Bowl, 5", footed, 2 handle	20.00	w/stopper	75.00	champagne, shallow	20.00
Bowl, 5", nut or lily (cupped rim)	22.00	10 ▸ Pickle, 8", oval	30.00	Stem, 8 oz., goblet, deep	25.00
Bowl, 5", rim foot berry	20.00	Pitcher, 3 pint	150.00	Stem, 10 oz., goblet, deep	25.00
12 ▸ Bowl, 6", nappy	20.00	Plate, 5¾"	12.00	14 ▸ Sugar w/lid	35.00
Bowl, 7", nappy or rim foot berry	35.00	7 ▸ Plate, 7½", salad	22.00	Tumbler, 2 oz., whiskey	22.00
Bowl, 7", lily	42.00	Plate, 10½", cake	45.00	Tumbler, 4 oz.	15.00
2 ▸ Bowl, 8", 2-handle berry	65.00	Plate, mayonnaise liner	15.00	Tumbler, 5 oz., belled rim or not	15.00
Bowl, 8", nappy or salad	38.00	Salt & pepper, pair	75.00	Tumbler, 6 oz.	15.00
Bowl, 8", spoon tray (hump edge)	38.00	3 ▸ Salt, table or footed almond,		Tumbler, 8 oz.	18.00
13 ▸ Bowl, 8", lily (cupped)	45.00	handled	20.00	Tumbler, 10 oz.	18.00
Bowl, 8", rim foot berry	38.00	Saucer	8.00	Tumbler, 12 oz., iced tea	20.00
1 ▸ Bowl, 9", rim foot berry	40.00	Sherbet, 3¼", low ft., flare rim		Tumbler, 14 oz., iced tea	25.00
Butter & cover	80.00	or not	22.50	Vase, 8", low foot, flare	65.00
Celery,12", oval	50.00	Sherbet, 4¼", low foot	22.50	Vase, 10"flat, bead base,	
Comport, 4", footed	25.00	Sherbet, 4¾", footed jelly	25.00	ruffled rim	85.00
5 ▸ Comport, 5½", footed	30.00	Spoon (flat open sugar)	20.00	Vase, 12" flat, bead base,	
Comport, 6¼", footed	35.00	11 ▸ Stem, 1 oz., cordial, deep	40.00	ruffled rim	110.00
8 ▸ Creamer, footed	25.00	Stem, 2 oz., wine, deep	30.00	*Crystal subtract 25%; teal add 25%	
Cup, custard, flare edge	17.50	Stem, 3 oz., cocktail, shallow	20.00		

FIRE-KING DINNERWARE "PHILBE," HOCKING GLASS COMPANY, 1937 – 1938

Colors: blue, green, pink, and crystal

Fire-King Dinnerware has always been a challenge to collect. Finding heretofore undiscovered pieces has not been as much a problem as finding quantities of items that we already know exist. As it is, most collectors would settle for any piece of this elusive pattern.

After including this pattern in our *Anchor Hocking's Fire-King & More*, collectors who had never seen my Depression glass book were captivated by it. The question repeatedly asked was, "Where do I find a piece?" Finding it is like mining gold with pick and shovel. If you're very lucky, you might see a piece once in a while. Everybody gets lucky sometime. You wouldn't want to miss your opportunity.

In 1972, on my first research trip to Anchor Hocking there was a large set of this blue dinnerware displayed in an outer office window. I was just beginning writing and didn't know what I was seeing and neither did anyone else I talked to at the factory. All anyone knew was it was from the morgue and a pattern they made in the 1930s. All I knew was that it was the same color as blue Mayfair which we were collecting at the time. Years later, when I was visited the morgue again, I found that few pieces were left, and I have often wondered where it all went.

Many blue pieces have a platinum trim that can be seen in the photograph, but I have never seen any blue Mayfair rimmed in platinum. This seems strange since these patterns were made about the same time. Mayfair was finishing up as Fire-King was being introduced. Was this a special order production, which would account for its scarcity?

The easiest to find blue items are the footed tumblers that are extremely rare in other colors. The tea seems twice as available as the water, so the water is priced higher. Blue seems to be the color seen if anything is found at all. It is also the most desired color, but most collectors will buy any color found. As many different pieces as were made, there should be a bigger supply out there waiting to be salvaged.

The pink oval vegetable bowls and the 10½" salver are items most found in that color. Oval bowls are available in green and crystal. The green grill or luncheon plates will be the next easiest pieces to obtain. All colored 6" saucer/sherbet plates are rarely seen. Why should you care if you don't collect this pattern? If you actually find a piece, it's guaranteed that someone wants it. Sell or trade it for something you want.

A non-stemmed sherbet has been found to go along with the high sherbet/champagne previously known. Customarily, Fire-King dinnerware is found on Cameo shaped blanks; but some pieces, including footed tumblers, nine-ounce water goblets, and the high sherbets are on a Mayfair shaped blank. Additional stems should be found.

FIRE-KING DINNERWARE

	Crystal	Pink, Green	Blue
Bowl, 5½", cereal	35.00	50.00	75.00
10 ▶ Bowl, 7¼", salad	50.00	80.00	115.00
6 ▶ Bowl, 10", oval vegetable	85.00	95.00	195.00
Candy jar, 4", low, with cover	300.00	750.00	850.00
11 ▶ Cookie jar with cover	600.00	995.00	1,500.00
Creamer, 3¼", footed	75.00	135.00	150.00
Cup	60.00		195.00
Goblet, 7¼", 9 ounce, thin	115.00	195.00	250.00
12 ▶ Pitcher, 6", 36 oz., juice	495.00	695.00	895.00
Pitcher, 8½", 56 oz.	495.00	995.00	1,250.00
3 ▶ Plate, 6", sherbet	40.00	65.00	95.00
1 ▶ Plate, 8", luncheon	20.00	37.50	47.50
Plate, 10", heavy sandwich	40.00	95.00	125.00

	Crystal	Pink, Green	Blue
Plate, 10½", salver	65.00	95.00	110.00
4 ▶ Plate, 10½", grill	40.00	75.00	95.00
5 ▶ Plate, 11⅝", salver	50.00	62.50	95.00
13 ▶ Platter, 12", closed handles	75.00	150.00	195.00
Saucer, 6" (same as sherbet plate)	40.00	65.00	95.00
8 ▶ Sherbet, 3¾", no stem	75.00		550.00
Sherbet, 4¾", stemmed		300.00	350.00
2 ▶ Sugar, 3¼", footed	75.00	135.00	150.00
Tumbler, 4", 9 oz., flat water	40.00	105.00	130.00
Tumbler, 3½", footed, juice	40.00	150.00	175.00
9 ▶ Tumbler, 5¼", 10 oz., footed	40.00	80.00	110.00
7 ▶ Tumbler, 6½", 15 oz., footed, iced tea	50.00	100.00	110.00

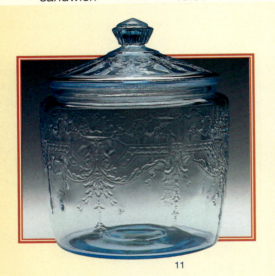

11

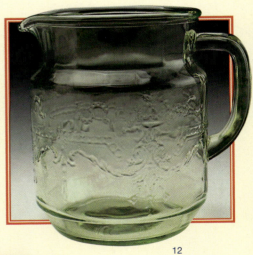

12

13

FLORAL, "POINSETTIA," JEANNETTE GLASS COMPANY, 1931 – 1935

Colors: pink, green, Delphite, Jadite, crystal, amber, red, black, custard, and yellow

Floral was the dubbed name for this pattern years before we started writing. Most collectors think it looks like poinsettia leaves, but one letter we received from someone who knew the plant better than we did suggested it had to be hemp! After that, a botanist weighed in with documentation this is a passion flower (Passiflora), not a poinsettia or hemp. Passion flower might have been an apt name since collectors for this pattern are definitely passionate in their regard for it.

Several green Floral pieces, rarely found in the United States, are being discovered in England and Canada. These include the vases, rose bowls, flat pitcher, and flat tumblers. Minor variations of color and design exist in these items. They are frequently a lighter green color, slightly paneled, and have ground bottoms. A ground bottom often indicates an earlier production run of the pattern. The green cups found in England have ground bottoms and are slightly footed. The base of the cup is larger than the normally found saucer indentation. There may have been an English customer for these items, but so far no records have been forthcoming to show this pattern was advertised there as there have been for Fostoria's American pattern.

Today, some dealers have buyers in England hunting for American-made glassware along with those fine European antiques. I ship more and more books to England as well as Australia and New Zealand. Prices remain steady on green Floral, flat-bottomed pitchers and tumblers since there are enough being found so that everyone wanting one can own them. The lemonade pitchers are rarely found; but I heard of a green one turning up in a market here yesterday for about 10% of its value. The seller must have had an old book.

We bought a set of pink Floral last summer and found that there is still quite a demand for some of the harder to find pieces but especially lemonade tumblers. We displayed them at a show and sold them to a lady who was very excited to get them. About thirty minutes later, another customer almost had a heart attack in the booth when she returned to buy them and they were gone. If you see an item you have been looking for, the time to buy it is now. On the other hand from that same purchased set, some of the common pieces are still in our inventory because most pink Floral collectors already have them. Do not assume you cannot get a basic set of Depression glass any more. You can. It's mostly just rarely found items that may elude you.

Floral sugar and candy lids are interchangeable, as are most Jeannette lids. Floral designs can be found on the under side of lids and on the base of square Jadite kitchenware/refrigerator storage containers made by Jeannette in the mid-1930s. As with other Jadite items, there is a demand for these.

On a sour note, the smaller, footed Floral shakers have been reproduced in pink, cobalt blue, red, and a very dark green color. The last three colors are of little concern since they were never made originally. The darker green will not glow under a black (ultraviolet) light, as does the old. The new pink shakers, however, are a good copy of pattern and color. The best way to tell the Floral reproduction is to look at the threads where the lid screws onto the shaker. On the old, two parallel threads end right before the side mould seams. The new Floral has one continuous line thread that starts on one side and continues around the shaker until it ends above the beginning line on the other side. There is approximately one inch of overlapped thread making two lines for that inch; but the whole thread is one continuous line and not two separate ones as on the old. To my knowledge, no other Floral reproductions have been made as of May 2005.

23

24

FLORAL

	Pink	Green	Delphite	Jadite
1 ▸ Bowl, 4", berry	22.00	23.00	50.00	
23 ▸ Bowl, 4", berry, ruffled	75.00			
Bowl, 5½", cream soup	750.00	750.00		
14 ▸ * Bowl, 7½", salad, ruffled $150.00	30.00	30.00	60.00	
21 ▸ Bowl, 8", covered vegetable	55.00	70.00	75.00 (no cover)	
10 ▸ Bowl, 9", oval vegetable	25.00	30.00		
22 ▸ Butter dish and cover	105.00	105.00		
Butter dish bottom	30.00	30.00		
Butter dish top	75.00	75.00		
Canister set: coffee, tea, cereal, sugar, 5¼" tall, each				95.00
Candlesticks, 4", pair	105.00	100.00		
4 ▸ Candy jar and cover	45.00	47.50		
2 ▸ Creamer, flat, Cremax $160.00	18.00	20.00	77.50	
18 ▸ Coaster, 3¼"	12.00	14.00		
3 ▸ Comport, 9", ruffled or plain rim	1,000.00	1,025.00		
15 ▸ ‡ Cup	16.00	13.00		
Dresser set		1,250.00		
Frog for vase, also crystal $500.00		725.00		
Ice tub, 3½", high, oval	950.00	995.00		
Lamp	325.00	325.00		
Pitcher, 5½", 23 or 24 ounce		500.00		
Pitcher, 8", 32 ounce, footed, cone	42.00	48.00		
Pitcher, 10¼", 48 ounce, lemonade	295.00	295.00		
11 ▸ Plate, 6", sherbet	7.00	8.00		
Plate, 8", salad	14.00	15.00		
20 ▸ ** Plate, 9", dinner	18.00	22.00	150.00	
Plate, 9", grill		325.00		
8 ▸ Platter, 10¾", oval	22.50	27.50	150.00	
Platter, 11" (like Cherry Blossom)	95.00			
17 ▸ Refrigerator dish and cover, 5" square		75.00	95.00	50.00
‡ Relish dish, 2-part oval	20.00	22.00	160.00	
‡‡ Salt and pepper, 4", footed, pair	52.00	55.00		
Salt and pepper, 6", flat	55.00			
6 ▸ ‡ Saucer	10.00	10.00		
9 ▸ Sherbet	18.00	20.00	85.00	
24 ▸ Sherbet, ruffled	100.00			
5 ▸ Sugar, Cremax $160.00	12.00	14.00	72.50 (open)	
16 ▸ Sugar/candy cover	17.50	20.00		
12 ▸ Tray, 6", square, closed handles	27.50	27.50		
Tray, 9¼", oval for dresser set		195.00		
Tumbler, 3½", 3 ounce, footed		175.00		
13 ▸ Tumbler, 4", 5 ounce, footed, juice	20.00	24.00		
Tumbler, 4½", 9 ounce, flat		185.00		
19 ▸ Tumbler, 4¾", 7 ounce, footed, water	24.00	25.00	195.00	
7 ▸ Tumbler, 5¼", 9 ounce, footed, lemonade	55.00	60.00		
Vase, 3 legged rose bowl		525.00		
Vase, 3 legged, flared (also in crystal)		495.00		
Vase, 6⅞" tall (8 sided), crystal $275.00		425.00		

* Cremax $125.00

** These have now been found in amber and red.

‡ This has been found in yellow.

‡‡ Beware reproductions.

FLORAL AND DIAMOND BAND, U.S. GLASS COMPANY, Late 1920s

Colors: pink, green; some iridescent, black, and crystal

Floral and Diamond is the name we inherited for this pattern when we first started writing in 1972. Notice that the 1928 ad below called it the reverse - Diamond and Floral.

Typical U. S. Glass rough mould seams are found on many Floral and Diamond Band pieces. This thick, seamed pattern was not as refined as later patterns. This roughness is routine for Floral and Diamond Band and not considered to be damage by long-time collectors who have come to ignore it. Difficulty in gathering Floral and Diamond Band is finding it in varying hues of green and pink. Some green has a distinctive blue tint and some pink tends to be very light or lean toward a slight hint of orange. You need to decide how accommodating you are willing to be about color matching.

Finding luncheon plates, sugar lids, pitchers, and iced tea tumblers (in both pink and green) is an arduous task. Six tumblers were advertised in that '28 catalog for 85 cents. The pitcher and six tumblers were $1.15; that pitcher added only 30 cents to your bill. Today, finding a pitcher for less than $100.00 would be quite a bargain.

Many Floral and Diamond Band butter bottoms have been "borrowed" over the years to be used with tops from more expensive U.S. Glass patterns such as Strawberry and Cherryberry. This ha taken place because these U.S. Glass butter bottoms are plain and, thus, compatible, since the pattern designs are situated on the top only. We used to buy all the Floral and Diamond Band butters we could find just for those plain bottom Today, there is a dearth of bottoms for this pattern possibly due to that universal practice of dealers. Small Floral and Diamond Band creamers and sugars have been found in black with ground bottoms; no other pieces have been spotted in th color. That small sugar and creamer, in various colors, is often found with a cut flower over the top of the customary mould ed flower. That duplicated idea of cut over moulded seems odd today; but early century glass cuttings were very much in vogue. Thus, the cutting may have made it more marketable at a time when moulded glass wasn't as valued.

Floral and Diamond Band pitchers with brilliant iridescent color bring premium prices from carnival glass collectors as a pattern called "Mayflower." Regrettably, most iridescent pitchers are generally blandly colored and rejected by carnival buyers. Sometimes glassware overlaps collecting categories and, occasionally, it receives more respect (higher prices) from one group of collectors than it does the other.

	Pink	Green			Pink	Greer
Bowl, 4½", berry	10.00	12.00	11▸ *Pitcher, 8", 42 ounce	115.00	125.00
Bowl, 5¾", handled, nappy	15.00	15.00	9▸ Plate, 8", luncheon	40.00	40.00
Bowl, 8", large berry	20.00	20.00	8▸ Sherbet	7.00	8.00
*Butter dish and cover	125.00	115.00	Sugar, small	11.00	11.00
4▸ Butter dish bottom	90.00	90.00	1▸ Sugar, 5¼"	15.00	15.00
3▸ Butter dish top	35.00	25.00	2▸ Sugar lid	55.00	65.00
7▸ Compote, 5½", tall	20.00	25.00	10▸ Tumbler, 4", water	22.00	24.00
5▸ Creamer, small	11.00	11.00	Tumbler, 5", iced tea	45.00	53.00
6▸ Creamer, 4¾"	18.00	20.00	*Iridescent $275.00; Crystal $125.00		

FLORENTINE NO. 1, OLD FLORENTINE, "POPPY NO. 1,"
HAZEL-ATLAS GLASS COMPANY, 1932 – 1935
Colors: pink, green, crystal, yellow, and cobalt blue (See Reproduction Section.)

Some collector/sellers and new dealers on the Internet have difficulty separating Florentine No. 1 and Florentine No. 2. Scrutinize the shapes since the jagged edged pieces are hexagonal (six sided) on all flat pieces of Florentine No. 1. Footed pieces (such as tumblers, shakers, or pitchers) also have that serrated edge on the foot. On Florentine No. 2, all pieces have plain edging as can be seen on the following pages. Florentine No. 1 was even advertised as "Hexagonal" and Florentine No. 2 was advertised as "Round." On the other hand, both patterns were promoted and put up for sale in mixed pattern sets. Many collectors follow that lead now because these combined sets blend well.

The 48 ounce, flat-bottomed pitcher was sold with both Florentine No. 1 and No. 2 sets. It was cataloged as 54 ounces, but ordinarily measures six ounces less. It varies owing to the shape of the hand-formed lip as to how many ounces it will hold before liquid runs out. My inclination is to list this pitcher only with Florentine No. 1 using the handle shape as the significant factor. However, this pitcher is continually found with flat-bottomed Florentine No. 2 tumblers which compel us to list it with both.

Flat tumblers with paneled interiors are found in sets with Florentine No. 1 pitchers. These paneled tumblers should be accepted as Florentine No. 1 rather than Florentine No. 2. That suggestion is for diehard collectors only. Paneled flat tumblers are tough to find; but only a few collectors seem concerned about the panels.

Pink Florentine No. 1 is the most difficult color to find. Pink footed tumblers, covered oval vegetable bowls, and butter dishes are virtually unobtainable in mint condition. Used, chipped, and damaged pieces abound, but most collectors pursue mint items only. Those irregular edges are easily blemished; look beneath and on top when you pick up a piece to buy. More chips are found underneath the edge than on top. Sets can still be gathered in green, crystal, or yellow with time and effort, but pink is "iffy" unless you have lots of time and are tenacious.

Fired-on colors have appeared in luncheon sets, but there is little collector zeal for them now. Item collectors are more interested in these. Sugars, creamers, cups, and saucers are snatched up in unusual colors. You can find all sorts of colors and colored bands on crystal. A disadvantage to these banded colors is finding enough to put a set together, although they do add color appeal to regular crystal sets.

Collectible cobalt blue Florentine No. 1 pitchers have appeared on the scene from time to time. Do not mix up one of these with the cone shaped, reproduction cobalt No. 2 pitcher found all over the place.

Florentine No. 1 shakers have been imitated in pink and cobalt blue, but other colors could be available. No real cobalt blue Florentine No. 1 shakers have ever been discovered, so those are easy to ignore. The reproduction pink shaker is somewhat problematic to differentiate from old. When comparing a reproduction shaker to several old pairs from our inventory, the old shakers have a major open flower on each side. There is a top circle on this blossom with three smaller circles down each side. The seven circles form the outside of the blossom. The reproduction blossom looks more like a strawberry with no circles forming the outside of the blossom. Do not use the threading test mentioned under Floral for the Florentine No. 1 shakers, however. It will not work for Florentine although the same company out of Georgia makes these. The threads are correct on this reproduction pattern. The reproductions we have seen as of May 2005 have been badly formed, but that is not to say it will not be rectified.

	* Green	Yellow	Pink	Cobalt Blue			* Green	Yellow	Pink	Cobalt Blue
15 ▸ Ashtray, 5½"	22.00	30.00	30.00		5 ▸ Plate, 8½", salad	10.00	14.00	12.00	
19 ▸ Bowl, 5", berry	14.00	18.00	18.00	25.00	Plate, 10", dinner	23.00	28.00	30.00	
11 ▸ Bowl, 5", cream					6 ▸ Plate, 10", grill	14.00	20.00	22.00	
soup or ruffled nut	28.00		16.00	60.00	16 ▸ Platter, 11½", oval	28.00	32.00	28.00	
Bowl, 6", cereal	25.00	32.00	50.00		10 ▸ ‡ Salt and pepper, footed	40.00	55.00	55.00	
19 ▸ Bowl, 8½", large berry	30.00	35.00	40.00		8 ▸ Saucer	3.00	14.00	5.00	17.00
12 ▸ Bowl, 9½", oval vegetable					13 ▸ Sherbet, 3 ounce, footed	12.00	15.00	15.00	
and cover	65.00	85.00	85.00		1 ▸ Sugar	9.50	12.00	12.00	
17 ▸ Butter dish and cover	125.00	180.00	160.00		2 ▸ Sugar cover	18.00	30.00	30.00	
Butter dish bottom	50.00	85.00	85.00		4 ▸ Sugar, ruffled	40.00		45.00	65.00
Butter dish top	75.00	95.00	75.00		Tumbler, 3¼", 4 oz., footed	16.00			
Coaster/ashtray, 3¾"	20.00	22.00	30.00		22 ▸ Tumbler, 3¾", 5 oz.,				
Comport, 3½", ruffled	40.00		16.00	65.00	footed, juice	16.00	28.00	28.00	
21 ▸ Creamer	11.00	22.00	20.00		Tumbler, 4", 9 oz., ribbed	16.00		22.00	
3 ▸ Creamer, ruffled	45.00		45.00	65.00	14 ▸ Tumbler, 4¾", 10 oz.,				
7 ▸ Cup	9.00	13.00	10.00	85.00	footed, water	22.00	26.00	26.00	
8 ▸ Pitcher, 6½", 36 oz., footed	40.00	60.00	50.00	895.00	Tumbler, 5¼", 12 oz.,				
Pitcher, 7½", 48 oz.,					footed, iced tea	28.00	33.00	33.00	
flat, ice lip or none	75.00	135.00	265.00		Tumbler, 5¼", 9 oz.,				
7 ▸ Plate, 6", sherbet	6.00	7.00	7.00		lemonade (like Floral)			150.00	

Crystal 20 to 30% less   ‡Beware reproductions

FLORENTINE NO. 2, "POPPY NO. 2," HAZEL-ATLAS GLASS COMPANY, 1932 – 1935

Colors: pink, green, yellow, crystal, some cobalt, amber, and ice blue (See Reproduction Section.)

Pay particular attention to the distinctions mentioned between the two Florentines in the first paragraph of the Florentine No. 1 pattern. If you are a new or advanced Florentine collector running out of pieces to find, try mixing the Florentines together, a practice the company itself engaged in since boxed sets have turned up over the years including both patterns.

An ambiguity in this pattern is illustrated by the ruffled nut/cream soup, similar to the normally found cream soup. This piece meets the standards as Florentine No. 1 because it matches the other ruffled pieces (comport, creamer, and sugar) in that pattern. The frustration here is the handle shape on the bowl matches items in Florentine No. 2. Thus, we have characteristics common to either pattern on a small piece.

The more costly footed, 6¼", 24-ounce cone-shaped Florentine No. 2 pitcher is not as frequently confused with the regularly found footed pitcher that stands 7½" tall. That is mainly due to the fact that few of the smaller pitchers are being found. To measure the height of a pitcher, stretch a ruler perpendicular from the base to the top of the spout. There is over an inch difference and this will not fluctuate as greatly as ounce capacities often do in pitchers with handmade spouts.

That 7½" pitcher and footed water tumbler have been reproduced in an extremely dark cobalt blue, amber, pink, and a dark green. This pitcher was never originally made in those colors; therefore, no one should presume these reproductions to be old, although you would not believe the letters and e-mails we receive about those colors. Everyone has found the amber pitcher that we don't price. We often see these presented as old in antique malls and flea markets. Note the name antique mall does not mean everything in it is antique. We have visited a few where the only antique present was the owner.

Custard cups remain the most elusive piece in Florentine No. 2. The custard plate is flat with a larger indentation than the bottom of a regular cup while the saucer curves up on the edges. Green custard cup liners are found, but where are the custards?

The 10" relish dish comes in three styles. The most commonly found "Y" style is pictured in green and yellow. The unusual style has two curved, divisions, one on each side and is shown as an insert photo. The undivided is the most difficult to attain. Grill plates with a round indent for the cream soup have been found in green, crystal and, now, yellow. These look like they should hold a cup, but the indent fits the bottom of the cream soup and is too large for the cup. Normally, these are referred to as snack plates with cup, but the designation with cream soup remains a mystery — perhaps a soup set?

Green Florentine is more requested than crystal, but crystal is scarce; hence, prices are comparable. Some amber, shown in earlier editions, is the rarest Florentine color; but only a few items have been discovered.

The candy lid measures 4¾" in diameter, the butter lid 5".

27   27

		Green	Pink	Yellow	Cobalt Blue
2 ▶	Bowl, 4½", berry	*16.00	17.00	22.00	
3 ▶	Bowl, 4¾", cream soup	17.00	16.00	22.00	
	Bowl, 5½"	35.00		45.00	
1 ▶	Bowl, 6", cereal	33.00		42.00	
	Bowl, 7½", shallow			100.00	
	Bowl, 8", large berry	30.00	32.00	40.00	
	Bowl, 9", oval vegetable	30.00		40.00	
	with cover			85.00	
	Bowl, 9", flat	27.50			
	Butter dish and cover	110.00		160.00	
	Butter dish bottom	25.00		70.00	
	Butter dish top	75.00		85.00	
7 ▶	Candlesticks, 2¾", pair	50.00		70.00	
	Candy dish and cover	100.00	145.00	160.00	
6 ▶	Coaster, 3¼"	13.00	16.00	25.00	
5 ▶	Coaster/ashtray, 3¾"	17.50		32.00	
	Coaster/ashtray, 5½"	20.00		35.00	
7 ▶	Comport, 3½", ruffled	40.00	45.00		65.00
8 ▶	Creamer	9.00		12.00	
9 ▶	Cup, amber 50.00	9.00		10.00	
	Custard cup or jello	60.00		85.00	
9 ▶	Gravy boat			55.00	
	Pitcher, 6¼", 24 ounce,				
	cone-footed			165.00	
3 ▶	**Pitcher, 7½", 28 ounce,				
	cone-footed	38.00		38.00	
	Pitcher, 7½", 48 ounce	75.00	135.00	275.00	
	Pitcher, 8¼", 76 ounce	110.00	225.00	495.00	

		Green	Pink	Yellow	Cobalt Blue
24 ▶	Plate, 6", sherbet	4.00		6.00	
	Plate, 6¼", with indent	22.00		30.00	
6 ▶	Plate, 8½", salad	9.00	8.50	8.00	
	Plate, 10", dinner	16.00		15.00	
12 ▶	Plate, 10¼", grill	16.00		18.00	
	Plate, 10¼", grill				
	w/cream soup ring	45.00			
22 ▶	Platter, 11", oval	16.00	16.00	25.00	
20 ▶	Platter, 11½", for				
	gravy boat			60.00	
26 ▶	Relish dish, 10", 3-part				
	or plain	28.00	30.00	35.00	
8 ▶ ‡	Salt and pepper, pair	45.00		45.00	
10 ▶	Saucer, amber $15.00	3.00		4.00	
	Sherbet, ftd., amber $40.00	10.00		10.00	
27 ▶	Sugar	10.00		12.00	
	Sugar cover	15.00		28.00	
	Tray, round, condiment for				
	shakers, creamer/sugar			80.00	
3 ▶	Tumbler, 3⅜", 5 oz., juice	14.00	12.00	22.00	
1 ▶	Tumbler, 3⁹⁄₁₆", 6 oz., blown	18.00			
14 ▶ ‡‡	Tumbler, 4", 9 oz., water	14.00	16.00	20.00	70.00
15 ▶	Tumbler, 5", 12 oz., blown	20.00			
‡‡	Tumbler, 5", 12 oz., tea	38.00		55.00	
18 ▶	Tumbler, 3¼", 5 oz., footed	16.00		20.00	
11 ▶	Tumbler, 4", 5 oz., footed	15.00		16.00	
4 ▶	Tumbler, 5", 9 oz., footed	32.00		32.00	
5 ▶	Vase or parfait, 6"	30.00		60.00	

*Crystal 20 to 30% less   **Ice Blue $595.00   ‡ Fired-on Red, Orange, or Blue, Pr. $42.50   ‡‡ Amber $75.00

26

FLOWER GARDEN WITH BUTTERFLIES, "BUTTERFLIES AND ROSES," BROCADE
U.S. GLASS COMPANY, FACTORY "R," TIFFIN PLANT, c. 1924

Colors: pink, green, blue-green, canary yellow, crystal, amber, blue, and black

After collecting Flower Garden with Butterflies for over 20 years, in a moment of madness, we sold our set. Earlier editions showed a much larger grouping because of our collection. Now, we are having trouble finding pieces and can better identify with people who search for it.

Tiffin catalog pages continue to be unearthed from all over the country, so we are fortunate to learn things about our glassware that pioneer authors didn't know. The original name for this pattern was Brocade. It is understood to have been in production for about a 10-year period, though evidently not continuously considering the deficiency of items available today.

This pattern is found so rarely that few new collectors are attempting it. Over the years, Brocade collections have been assembled and today, only materialize on the market when complete sets are sold. Yet, this is one pattern that lends itself extremely well for a one-piece display. Please know that even one piece of any pattern you like can give you visual pleasure with every glance.

There are three styles of powder jars, which may explain why oval and rectangular dresser trays are easily found. Dresser trays and luncheon plates are the only consistently found items in the pattern. Two different footed powders exist. One is 6½" high; but the taller stands 7½". Luckily the lids for these footed powders are the same. The flat powder jar is 3½" in diameter. We never found a blue, flat powder while we were collecting, though we feel certain there must be some out there.

The search for butterflies on each piece is entertaining. Sometimes they are prominently displayed, but often not. We owned a black candlestick that only had the end of a butterfly antenna on it. You really had to search to find that little piece of butterfly. The other candlestick of the pair had half a butterfly. Will an item turn up where the butterfly flew away entirely?

A crystal cologne with black stopper turned up for us after we had earlier photographed a black cologne sans stopper. We missed the opportunity to photograph them together. Possibly the black one had a crystal stopper originally, but we are not sure. Check the dauber in the perfumes. Many of them are broken off or ground down to hide the broken end. Daubers are much harder to find than the bottles themselves; take that into consideration when buying only the bottle. That is true for any perfume/cologne in any pattern. The piece handled most often usually suffered the damage and was tossed away. However, if the lone bottle gives you pleasure, corks are available.

There is a semi-circular, footed glass dresser box which holds five wedge (pie shaped) bottles that is often advertised as Flower Garden because it has flower designs on it. Labels found intact on bottles promoted the New York/Paris affiliation of "Charme Volupte". One bottle contained cold cream, another vanishing cream, and three others once held perfumes. There are dancing girls at either end of the box, and flowers abound on the semi-circle. There are no dancing girls on Flower Garden. Other not-to-be-mistaken-for Flower Garden pieces include the 7" and 10" trivets with flowers all over them made by U.S. Glass. They were also used as mixing bowl covers and they do not have butterflies.

	Amber, Crystal	Pink, Green, Blue-Green	Blue, Canary
Ashtray, match-pack holders	150.00	175.00	195.00
Candlesticks, 4", pair	42.50	55.00	95.00
Candlesticks, 8", pair	77.50	135.00	150.00
Candy w/cover, 6", flat		130.00	155.00
Candy w/cover, 7½", cone-shaped	80.00	130.00	175.00
9 ▸ Candy w/cover, heart-shaped		1,250.00	1,400.00
* Cologne bottle w/stopper, 7½"		225.00	350.00
Comport, 2⅞" h.		23.00	28.00
Comport, 3" h., fits 10" plate	20.00	23.00	28.00
Comport, 4¼" h. x 4¾" w.			50.00
6 ▸ Comport, 4¾" h. x 10¼" w.	48.00	65.00	85.00
Comport, 5⅞" h. x 11" w.	55.00		95.00
5 ▸ Comport, 7¼" h. x 8¼" w.	60.00	80.00	
Creamer		70.00	
1 ▸ Cup		70.00	

	Amber, Crystal	Pink, Green, Blue-Green	Blue, Canary
Mayonnaise, footed, 4¾" h. x 6¼" w., w/7" plate & spoon	75.00	95.00	135.00
Plate, 7"	15.00	20.00	30.00
Plate, 8", two styles	15.00	16.00	22.00
Plate, 10"		42.50	48.00
Plate, 10", indent for 3" comport	32.00	40.00	45.00
Powder jar, 3½", flat		75.00	
4 ▸ Powder jar, footed, 6¼" h.	75.00	145.00	185.00
7 ▸ Powder jar, footed, 7½" h.	75.00	145.00	195.00
3 ▸ Sandwich server, center handle	55.00	70.00	100.00
2 ▸ Saucer		25.00	
Sugar		70.00	
Tray, 5½" x 10", oval	55.00	60.00	
Tray, 11¾" x 7¾", rectangular	60.00	75.00	90.00
Tumbler, 7½"	175.00		
8 ▸ Vase, 6¼"	75.00	100.00	175.00
Vase, 10½"		135.00	235.00
* Stopper, if not broken off, ½ price of bottle			

85

FLOWER GARDEN WITH BUTTERFLIES

Bonbon w/cover, 6⅝" diameter	250.00
Bowl, 7¼", w/cover, "flying saucer"	395.00
Bowl, 8½", console, w/base	150.00
Bowl, 9", rolled edge, w/base	200.00
Bowl, 11", footed orange	200.00
Bowl, 12", rolled edge console w/base	195.00
Candlestick 6" w/6½" candle, pair	495.00
Candlestick, 8", pair	295.00
Cheese and cracker, footed, 5⅜" h. x 10" w.	250.00
Comport and cover, 2¾" h. (fits 10" indented plate)	200.00
Cigarette box & cover, 4⅜" long	150.00
Comport, tureen, 4¼" h. x 10" w.	225.00
Comport, footed, 5⅝" h. x 10" w.	225.00
Comport, footed, 7" h.	175.00
Plate, 10", indented	100.00
Sandwich server, center-handled	120.00
Vase, 6¼", Dahlia, cupped	145.00
Vase, 8", Dahlia, cupped	195.00
Vase, 9", wallhanging	395.00
Vase, 10", 2-handled	195.00
Vase, 10½", Dahlia, cupped	250.00

"FLUTE & CANE," "SUNBURST & CANE," "CANE," "HUCKABEE," SEMI-COLONIAL,
NO. 666 & 666½, IMPERIAL GLASS COMPANY, c. 1921

Colors: crystal, pink, green, Rubigold (marigold), Caramel slag

Since the last book came out, I have not had one communication on this pattern, so I will repeat from the last book how this pattern came to be listed. My wife talked me into including this pattern with the unfortunate "Devil's" line number. She finds the cane look intriguing. In an aside, we were standing in line at a license bureau in officialdom once, when a lady came in and pitched a license at the clerk and said very loudly, "I'm not having this Devil's number on my car." Sure enough, she'd been issued "666" something. Bible belt people know this association. It appears whoever assigned the numbers at Imperial did not. (Neither did the state.) I was told that the half number beside Imperial's line numbers indicated the less expensively made glassware sold in places like F.W. Woolworth, Sears, Montgomery Wards, et. al.

I suspect there are additional pieces and had hoped for confirmation from collectors, but that has not happened. I imagine there are even pieces out there in blue, which was being run in this period; but I can't confirm that right now. I am certain I've seen some; but since I wasn't paying specific attention to this pattern until recent years, I can't be 100 percent sure of it. I do remember seeing a sugar and creamer in slag when I was at the factory in the 80s, though it is not in any of the catalogs they presented me then. As was Imperial's (and other) glass companies' wont, they launched a few items from older moulds into their wares from time to time, and in whatever colors they were running. Since my catalog information doesn't encompass Imperial's entire history, I can't be positive what other colors you'll find in "Flute and Cane." If you'll be kind enough to let me know what you turn up, I'd be most appreciative and will make an effort to pass it along to collectors.

Many of the marigold pieces are quite rare and highly prized by carnival glass collectors. The tall, slender pitcher, tumblers, cups, 6" plates, and goblets are considered very desirable items to own. However, various bowls are what are usually seen, today. The 6" plate was marketed with the sherbet as an ice cream set, with the molasses as an underliner, and with the custard cup as a saucer. There ought to be quite a few of those available; but, alas, not so. Sorry, but there is a very cane-appearing candle in the picture that officially belongs with the Amelia #671 line, shown on page 10. You cannot always trust what you see in an author's photo, so one does actually need to read the text from time to time.

		Crystal*			Crystal*			Crystal*
8 ▸	Bowl, 4½", fruit	10.00		Celery, 8½", oval	22.00	3 ▸	Pitcher, tall/slender	75.00
	Bowl, 6½", oval, pickle	16.00		Celery, tall, 2 handle	40.00		Plate, 6"	20.00
	Bowl, 6½", square	15.00		Compote, 6½", oval, ftd., 2-hdl.	30.00		Salt & pepper	45.00
1 ▸	Bowl, 7½", ruffled	28.00		Compote, 7½", stem w/bowl	25.00	6 ▸	Sherbet, 3½", stem	12.00
5 ▸	Bowl, 7½", salad	25.00		Compote, 7½", stem, flat	25.00		Spooner (open sm. sug)	15.00
	Bowl, 8½", large fruit	30.00	2 ▸	Compote, ruffled top	25.00		Stem, 1 ounce, cordial	25.00
4 ▸	Bowl, crème soup, 5½", ftd.	22.00		Creamer	15.00		Stem, 3 ounce, wine	18.00
	Butter w/lid, small			Cup, custard	12.00		Stem, 6 ounce, champagne	15.00
	(powder box look)	35.00		Molasses, nickel top	70.00		Stem, 9 ounce, water	18.00
	Butter, dome lid	55.00		Oil bottle w/stopper, 6 ounce	45.00	7 ▸	Sugar w/lid	20.00
	Candle, 8"	22.00		Pitcher, 22 ounce, 5¼"	45.00		Tumbler, 9 ounce	25.00
9 ▸	Candlestick (Amelia)	25.00		Pitcher, 51 ounce	65.00	10 ▸	Vase, 6"	37.50

*Add 50% for colors

87

FORTUNE, HOCKING GLASS COMPANY, 1937 – 1938

Colors: pink and crystal

The Fortune covered candy is a useful item. It makes a wonderful gift for beginning collectors and is one of the most economically priced pink candy dishes in Depression glass.

Fortune is a small pattern where luncheon plates are valuable and you normally find them only one at a time. An expense of time and a little luck can help assemble a set of Fortune.

Over the years, both Fortune tumblers have been garnered by collectors of Queen Mary and Old Colony to use with those sets because they were inexpensive and complemented them. Seeing as Hocking made all three patterns, the colors do match. Now the prices of Fortune tumblers have reached heights similar to those other patterns and it is not as realistic to use them with other sets. We see tumblers and small berry bowls when we spot Fortune. Other items are not so easily found.

There is a pitcher whose pattern is similar to Fortune that is surfacing sporadically and some collectors are buying them for use with their sets since no true Fortune pitcher has yet been found. These "go-with" juice pitchers are selling in the $30.00 to $40.00 range.

	Pink, Crystal			Pink, Crystal
1 ▸ Bowl, 4", berry	10.00		6 ▸ Cup	13.00
Bowl, 4½", dessert	10.00		4 ▸ Plate, 6", sherbet	8.00
Bowl, 4½", handled	10.00		Plate, 8", luncheon	28.00
5 ▸ Bowl, 5¼", rolled edge	20.00		7 ▸ Saucer	5.00
Bowl, 7¾", salad or large berry	28.00		3 ▸ Tumbler, 3½", 5 ounce, juice	12.50
Candy dish and cover, flat	28.00		2 ▸ Tumbler, 4", 9 ounce, water	15.00

FRANCES, CENTRAL GLASS WORKS, Late 1920s – Early 1930s

Colors: amber, black, blue, crystal, green, pink

Frances pattern from Central Glass Works has been collected by a few for years, but has been noticed by more collectors recently. Predominately found items include bowls, sandwich servers, and vases.

We accumulated a few duplicate pieces over the years while searching for Frances for photography. After the photo session, we priced the extras for sale. Now, six months later, we only have a green vase left. The last pink bowl we placed in our booth in a mall only sat three days before it was sold.

Blue and black items are rarely seen which makes that blue powder/candy special. When we bought it several years ago, we first thought it was Hocking's Gem. Upon proper study, we were happy to determine it was a piece of Frances that we did not know existed at that time.

	*All colors			*All colors
Ashtray, 5", 2-piece	75.00		Celery, 7½" high, 2-hdld., ftd.	40.00
Bowl, 6", round	20.00		Celery, 10¼" 4-ftd	35.00
Bowl, 8", round	40.00		Comport, 5¼" high	30.00
4▶ Bowl, 9½" round	45.00	7▶	Creamer, ftd.	30.00
3▶ Bowl, 10", 3-ftd. two-sided, fluted	50.00		Plate, 6¼"	10.00
Bowl, 10", 3-ftd., round	50.00	3▶	Powder/candy jar w/tab knobbed lid	85.00
Bowl, 10", 3-ftd., triangular, fluted	50.00	2▶	Sugar, ftd.	30.00
1▶ Bowl, 12", console	50.00		Tray, 10¼", center handled server	45.00
6▶ Cake plate, 12", 3-ftd.	65.00		Tumbler, 10 oz.	40.00
Candle stick, 3½"	35.00	5▶	Vase, 8½" to 10½" high	75.00

*Crystal 30 – 35% less, black or blue 50% more

89

FRUITS, HAZEL-ATLAS AND OTHER GLASS COMPANIES, 1931 – 1935

Colors: pink, green, some crystal, and iridized

Fruits pitchers have only cherries in the pattern. Sometimes they are mislabeled as Cherry Blossom, flat-bottome pitchers. Notice that the handle is shaped like that of flat Florentine pitchers (Hazel-Atlas Company) and not like Cher Blossom (Jeannette Glass Company) flat pitchers. Crystal Fruits pitchers sell for less than half the price of green ar other crystal pieces are hardly noticed. Both pitchers and tumblers are available should you want an economically price beverage set.

The Fruits water tumblers (4") are the pieces regularly found. Iridescent "Pears" tumblers are bountiful. Federal Glas Company probably made these carnival-colored tumblers at the same time they were making iridescent Normandie ar a few pieces in Madrid in the late 1930s. Water tumblers with cherries or a combination of fruits are found in pink.

Fruits green water tumblers are found occasionally; but the 3½" (5 ounce) juice and 5" (12 ounce) iced tea tumble have joined the large and small berry bowls as the choice pieces of green to obtain.

Fruits berry bowls in both sizes are among the hardest to locate in all Depression glass patterns. Since this is n one of the most collected patterns with thousands of admirers, the meagerness of both sizes of bowls has only bee perceived in recent years. I have only owned one iced tea and no juice tumblers. The Cherry Blossom flat juice tum bler is sometimes mistaken as a Fruits juice. Cherry Blossom juices have blossoms along the top edge whereas Frui has cherries.

Given that so many collectors are pursuing green iced teas, juice tumblers, and bowls, their prices have continued rise for years. Currently, prices are steady since many collectors have settled for sets without these rare pieces. They a still rarely seen, but not as in demand as they once were.

I have never found a pink pitcher or juice and tea tumblers, though we once inadvertently listed them. In the ve beginning, we only showed one price for all Fruits colors. The price of green rose faster than pink due to more collectir demand. When we split prices into two colors no one realized that the seemingly non-existent pink juice and tea tum blers were cloaked under that "all colors" label. It took a while for us to realize that no one was finding those in pink.

		Green	Pink
7 ▸	Bowl, 4½", berry	40.00	30.00
3 ▸	Bowl, 8", berry	95.00	55.00
1 ▸	Cup	9.00	9.00
6 ▸	Pitcher, 7", flat bottom	125.00	
4 ▸	Plate, 8", luncheon	12.00	12.00
2 ▸	Saucer	5.50	4.00
5 ▸	Sherbet	12.00	13.00
	Tumbler, 3½", juice	80.00	

		Green	Pink
9 ▸	*Tumbler, 4" (1 fruit)	20.00	18.00
10 ▸	Tumbler, 4" (combination of fruits)	30.00	22.00
8 ▸	Tumbler, 5", 12 ounce	165.00	

*Iridized $8.00

90

GEM, "KALEIDOSCOPE," HOCKING GLASS COMPANY, c. 1933

Colors: "Mayfair" blue, crystal, green, and pink

"Kaleidoscope" was our name for this ware when we added it to our book four years ago. As later reported, a former Anchor-Hocking employee's wife gave him our book for Christmas. He found our new listing for "Kaleidoscope" and sent the credentials to show this was definitely a Hocking pattern and he owned a labeled piece designating it as Gem. It is not a plentiful pattern, but there are enough basic pieces to gather a nice table setting if you wish.

Blue seems to be the most plentiful color; but pieces in pink, green, and even crystal can be unearthed. Crystal and cobalt blue are pictured for the first time. Of note is a blue coaster with raised rays like those on Hocking's Miss America coaster. We have only found the divided relish in crystal, but the undivided celery has been found in every color.

The cobalt plate with its divider may have been a snack plate. Several sets of blue were spotted years ago when we were not looking for photography items. Some items were made for Woolworth's, which should make those more available. Let me know what you find.

	Blue	*Green, Pink			Blue	*Green, Pink
Bowl, 5", berry	20.00	15.00	6 ▸ Cup		75.00	60.00
1 ▸ Bowl, flat soup	50.00	35.00	Plate, 6", bread		12.00	10.00
Bowl, oval vegetable w/tab hdls.	65.00	55.00	5 ▸ Plate, 8" salad w/indent		60.00	
8 ▸ Celery, tab handles	60.00	50.00	4 ▸ Plate, 9½", dinner		35.00	25.00
11 ▸ Coaster	30.00		10 ▸ Plate, 9½", grill		30.00	20.00
9 ▸ Creamer	50.00	35.00	Platter, oval w/tab handles		75.00	60.00
			2 ▸ Relish, 11½", divided, tab hdls.			45.00
			7 ▸ Saucer		20.00	15.00
			Stem, 6 ounce, sherbet		25.00	20.00
			3 ▸ Stem, 10 ounce, water		40.00	30.00
			Sugar		50.00	35.00

91

GEORGIAN, "LOVEBIRDS," FEDERAL GLASS COMPANY, 1931 – 1936
Colors: green, crystal, and amber

Federal Glass Company's Georgian pattern shows two lovebirds (or parakeets, as one ornithologist reader informe us) perched side by side. Georgian is easily identified by these birds; however, there are a few pieces of the pattern with out birds. Both sizes of tumblers, the hot plate, and a few dinner plates have only baskets. Few collectors seek dinne plates without birds; that non-bird style plate sells for less. Baskets alternate with birds in the design on all other pieces.

We received what I thought was an astonishing phone call from a dealer friend a couple of weeks ago. He said ther were two iced tea tumblers at an auction that looked like Georgian, but there were no birds on them. In 30+ years of buy ing and selling, he never knew Georgian tumblers have no birds. So, we're not getting the message out there that Geor gian tumblers do not show the birds. You can occasionally find a good buy on tumblers if the owner does not recogniz that Georgian tumblers have no birds.

Fundamental pieces of Georgian are easily found. Berry bowls, cups, saucers, sherbets, sherbet plates, and lun cheon plates can be found. Georgian tumblers (no birds) are challenging to acquire. Several boxed sets of 36 water tum blers were found in the Chicago area, where a newspaper gave the tumblers away to subscribers in the 1930s. We als heard that an antique mall recently opened in Ohio and six water tumblers were purchased there for around $30.00. Tha was quite a find; but amazingly, upon returning a couple of days later, those tumblers had been replaced with six mor for the same price. That supply was then exhausted; but it was fun while it lasted.

Prices for iced teas have more than doubled the price of water tumblers. Supplies of waters keep turning up, but no so the iced teas. I have owned at least a dozen Georgian waters for every iced tea to give you an idea of how difficu teas are to locate. (Remember, these tumblers have no birds.)

Few new collectors are searching for Georgian which has caused some reduction on the prices of items offered fo less than $50.00. Rarely seen items usually hold their own when it comes to prices. Georgian serving pieces were great utilized; so be cautious of mint pricing for pieces that are often scratched and worn from use. You will pay a premium fo mint condition. Keep in mind that all prices listed in this book are for mint condition pieces. Damaged or scratched an worn pieces should go for less depending upon the degree of damage and deterioration. If you are gathering this glas to use, some defects may not make as much difference as collecting for eventual reselling. Mint condition glass will se faster and for a much better price if you ever decide to part with your collection.

Georgian Lazy Susans (cold cuts servers as shown below) are more rarely seen than the Madrid ones that turn up infrequently, at best. Walnut trays have surfaced in southern Ohio and northern Kentucky with original decal labels read ing "Kalter Aufschain Cold Cuts Server Schirmer Cincy." These wooden Lazy Susans are made of walnut and are 18½ across with seven 5" openings for holding the so-called hot plates. Somehow, I believe these 5" hot plates are misident fied since they are found on a cold cuts server. These cold/hot plates have only the center motif design and can also b found in crystal.

There is a round, thin plate made by Indiana Glass having two large parakeets as its center design, covering near the whole plate. This is not Georgian, but can be found in green as well as amber and canary. All Georgian plates ar thick and have baskets around the edge as well as the birds.

15

	Green			Green
Bowl, 4½", berry	10.00	7 ▸ *Hot plate, 5", center design		80.00
▸ Bowl, 5¾", cereal	25.00	**Plate, 6", sherbet		7.00
▸ Bowl, 6½", deep	65.00	6 ▸ Plate, 8", luncheon		10.00
Bowl, 7½", large berry	60.00	12 ▸ Plate, 9¼", dinner		25.00
Bowl, 9", oval vegetable	60.00	5 ▸ Plate, 9¼", center design only		20.00
Butter dish and cover	85.00	Platter, 11½", closed-handled		65.00
Butter dish bottom	50.00	10 ▸ Saucer		3.00
Butter dish top	35.00	11 ▸ Sherbet		11.00
▸ Cold cuts server, 18½", wood with		3 ▸ Sugar, 3", footed		10.00
seven 5" openings for 5" coasters	995.00	Sugar, 4", footed		18.00
▸ Creamer, 3", footed	12.00	4 ▸ Sugar cover for 3"		50.00
Creamer, 4", footed	18.00	14 ▸ Tumbler, 4", 9 ounce, flat		70.00
▸ Cup	10.00	13 ▸ Tumbler, 5¼", 12 ounce, flat		120.00

*Crystal $30.00   ** Amber $40.00

93

GLADES, LINE #215, NEW MARTINSVILLE, c. 1930s

Colors: amethyst, crystal and w/etches, cobalt, ruby, green, blue, black

Glades, Line #215 is a Paden City pattern showing the wonderful linear influence that was so strong in the early to mid 1930s. It is very "Deco" and collectible. We recently acquired an amber two-lite candlestick with Oriental Garden etching which will now be included in our second candlestick book due out next year. Its two arms and trunk are all ribbed.

The amethyst items pictured have ground bottoms, which is indicative of earlier, hand-finished glassware. Canton Glass was still making Glades as late as 1954 from Paden City moulds. You will doubtless find additional pieces than those listed

		*Crystal
	Bowl, 4½", tab hdld., fruit	10.00
6 ▸	Bowl, 4¾", cream soup	12.50
	Bowl, 5", tab hdld., flare rim, cereal	12.50
	Bowl, 6", tab hdld., shallow	15.00
	Bowl, 6", tab hdld., bonbon	15.00
	Bowl, 7"	12.50
	Bowl, 7¼", gravy	30.00
1 ▸	Bowl, 10", tab hdld., oval	50.00
	Bowl, 3 toe, 12½", flat rim, console	45.00
	Candle, 5", double light	35.00
	Cocktail, 8", 30 oz.; w/metal lid, 11"	45.00
	Cocktail, double cone shape, 3 oz.	13.00
	Comport, 3½" high	27.50
	Comport, 7⅝" high, indented top	37.50
	Creamer, 7 oz.	12.50
8 ▸	Cup	13.00
	Decanter, 6½", 12 oz., tilt w/handle, cordial	55.00
	Ice tub, 4" high x 6⅜" diameter	75.00
	Plate, 6½", tab hdld.	5.00
2 ▸	Plate, 7"	6.00

		*Cryst
4 ▸	Plate, 8"	7.50
3 ▸	Plate, 10"	15.00
	Plate, 11½" serving	20.00
	Relish, 4 part, tab hdld	32.50
	Relish tray, 12¾", 2 hdld., 2 part	40.00
	Server, center-hdle. w/round, lined center knob	35.00
7 ▸	Saucer	2.50
	Shaker, 2⅛", round, pr.	30.00
5 ▸	Sugar, 7 oz.	12.50
	Tray, 11", oval celery	20.00
	Tumbler, 3 oz., flat whiskey	12.50
	Tumbler, 3½ oz.	17.50
9 ▸	Tumbler, 4", 8 oz.	17.50
	Tumbler, 5¼", 12 oz., tea	20.00

* Double price for
  color; add 10 –
  15% with etching

GOTHIC GARDEN, PADEN CITY GLASS COMPANY, 1930s

Colors: amber, pink, green, black, yellow, and crystal

Gothic Garden is a fairly extensive Paden City etched pattern that is found mostly on Paden City's Line #411 (square shapes with the corners cut off), which is also referred to as "Mrs. B" line. It does occur on other Paden City blanks, however.

A lack of cups and saucers has not hurt collecting other Paden City patterns. Cups and saucers are rare in all etched patterns of this company. Did the etching department not like to work on smaller pieces? For now, I am only listing one price; add 25% for black and subtract 25% or more for crystal. What little crystal I have seen has been gold trimmed which, with good gold, will fetch nearly the price of colored ware if the right collector can be found. We see Gothic Garden at glass and antique shows, some pieces with exorbitant prices. However, since I keep seeing those same pieces, I think for some reason Gothic Garden etch has not caught on with collectors to the magnitude of those prices.

All the fundamental designs of 1930s glassware decoration (including birds, flowers, scrolls, garlands, and urns) are found in Gothic Garden. It should be the most sought-after etch ever made in that period, but, alas, it is not. There is an awkward pose by the bird in the design. The bird's body faces outward on either side of the designed medallion, but its head turns backward toward the center floral motif. It is reminiscent of a Phoenix bird, that mythological bird that rose from the ashes.

Measurements may vary up to an inch due to the degree of the turned up edges on bowls; do not take our listings as absolute gospel. All measurements listed are ones from the pieces we owned.

We bought a black bowl like the one pictured in pink and saw a flat, yellow candy like the one pictured in "Peacock Reverse" on page 171. Since it was prized more highly by the seller than by us, he still owns it.

	All colors			All colors
Bowl, 9", 2-handle	65.00	6 ▸ Creamer		40.00
Bowl, 10", footed	85.00	10 ▸ Ice bucket		125.00
Bowl, 10⅛", handle	95.00	Plate, 11", tab handle		60.00
Bowl, 10½", oval, handle	110.00	5 ▸ Server, 9¾", center handled		85.00
Cake stand, 8½", footed	75.00	7 ▸ Sugar		40.00
Cake stand, 10½", footed	90.00	Vase, 6½"		130.00
Candy, flat	130.00	3 ▸ Vase, 8"		175.00
Comport, tall, deep top	65.00	4 ▸ Vase, 9½"		135.00

GRAPE, CUT #6, STANDARD GLASS MANUFACTURING COMPANY, 1932 – 1936

Colors: crystal, green, pink, and topaz

For over twenty years, inquires have been made about when we were going to add this Grape Cut to our book. After all, most of the pieces are shaped like Cameo or Mayfair. There were always a few collectors for Grape Cut, but with supplies of many popular patterns drying up, more are turning to some of the less noticed 1930s patterns such as this. Gathering a set of Grape Cut is certainly trying due to lack of mass production that popular mould etched patterns enjoyed. Rewards of finding pieces are just as satisfying, however.

Grape Cut was made at the Standard glass plant even after they were bought out by Hocking. Orders for cut patterns were sent to the Standard plant for years. The mid-1930 Hocking catalogs have pages dedicated to cut patterns with Standard Glass Company's name still shown at the bottom of the page.

Grape Cut was made primarily in green and pink, but some Topaz (yellow) can occasionally be found. We find a few pieces in crystal, but mostly stems. Pitchers and tumblers were heavily promoted in the 1936 catalog and they sure sold well as they are the pieces easiest to find today. Few cup and saucer sets are located. The handles on the cup, creamer, and sugar are the ones found on Cameo and Block Optic known as "fancy" handles.

Our listing is from Hocking catalogs. There are two older terminologies listed. In one catalog, the 57 oz. jug is listed but in later ones jugs are listed as pitchers. The 4¾, 7 ounce goblet is listed as sundae in one and high sherbet in another. Neither place is it called a saucer champagne as in White Band which is a new pattern shown later in this book.

		All colors			All colors
4▶	Creamer	17.50		Sherbet, 6 oz.	8.00
	Cup	12.50	3▶	Sugar	17.50
	Goblet, 3 oz., cocktail	15.00		Tumbler, 3½ oz., ftd., juice	15.00
1▶	Goblet, 7 oz., sundae or high sherbet	10.00	7▶	Tumbler, 5 oz., juice	8.00
2▶	Goblet, 9 oz., water	20.00		Tumbler, 9 oz., barrel	20.00
	Pitcher, jug, 57 oz.	40.00		Tumbler, 9 oz., table	10.00
	Pitcher, 80 oz., ice lip	45.00		Tumbler, 10 oz., ftd., water	12.50
5▶	Pitcher, 80 oz., no lip	50.00		Tumbler, 10 oz., shell	10.00
	Plate, 6", sherbet	3.00		Tumbler, 10 oz., table	10.00
	Plate, 8", luncheon	8.00		Tumbler, 10 oz., water	10.00
	Salt and pepper, pr.	40.00	6▶	Tumbler, 12 oz., iced tea	12.50
	Saucer	2.50		Tumbler, 15 oz., ftd tea	18.00

* 25% less for crystal

HEX OPTIC, "HONEYCOMB," JEANNETTE GLASS COMPANY, 1928 – 1932

Colors: pink, green, Ultra Marine (late 1930s), and iridescent in 1950s

Jeannette's Hex Optic was one of the earliest Depression glass patterns. Introduced in 1928 and made in new brilliant green and wild rose colors, Hex Optic made an impact on the consumers of that time. It was a historic glass design, fabricated in one of the first fully automated glassmaking systems of the time. Hex Optic was utilized as everyday kitchen and dinnerware; so few pieces found today are without scratches or damage. Hex Optic provided a homemaker's total glass needs as it could be assembled in matching wares. It was novel and striking in a trade just moving from making glass by hand into an age of mechanization.

Today, Hex Optic is more scrutinized by kitchenware collectors than any other pattern of Depression glass because of the numerous kitchenware pieces it includes. Sugar shakers, bucket reamers, mixing bowls, refrigerator stacking sets, and butter dishes were designed in green and pink. Actually, were it not for kitchenware collectors becoming zealous about Hex Optic, it might still be ignored in the glass-collecting sphere.

Cups, sugars, and creamers in this pattern have innovative solid handles which make them dangerous to pick up with wet fingers. You might note that some creamer and sugars have a floral cutting. Someone outside of Jeannette would have cut that. Some early pieces of Jeannette's glass were embossed with a J in a triangle trademark.

There are two styles of pitchers in Hexagon Optic, one being footed and having the Deco cone shaped look and the other, a flat-bottomed, cylindrical shape. This 8" tall, 70-ounce, flat-bottomed version is being found in both colors, although green is not as abundant. They turn up in Minnesota and Wisconsin where they were dairy premiums according to one reader. The footed pitcher is hard to find now, having quietly disappeared into collections. Price does not reflect how hard it is to find as demand is rather quiet for now. Note that Jeannette's Hex Optic pitcher is thick. Other companies' honeycomb pitchers are thin; so keep that in mind when you see an inexpensive thin one.

Iridescent oil lamps, both style pitchers, and tumblers were all made during Jeannette's iridized obsession of the late 1950s. The Ultra Marine tumblers were probably a product of the late 1930s when the company was making Doric and Pansy.

		Pink, Green				Pink, Green
▸	Bowl, 4¼", ruffled berry	10.00	8 ▸	Plate, 8", luncheon		5.50
▸	Bowl, 7½", ruffled large berry	16.00		Platter, 11", round		15.00
	Bowl, 7¼", mixing	18.00		Refrigerator dish, 4" x 4"		18.00
	Bowl, 8¼", mixing	25.00	4 ▸	Refrigerator stack set, 4 piece		85.00
	Bowl, 9", mixing	28.00		Salt and pepper, pair		40.00
	Bowl, 10", mixing	30.00	1 ▸	Saucer		3.00
	Bucket reamer	70.00	13 ▸	Sugar, 2 styles of handles		7.00
	Butter dish and cover, rectangular, 1 pound size	100.00		Sugar shaker		250.00
▸	Creamer, 2 style handles	7.00		Sherbet, 5 ounce, footed		7.00
▸	Cup, 2 style handles	10.00	5 ▸	Tumbler, 3¾", 9 ounce		4.50
	Ice bucket, metal handle	32.00	3 ▸	Tumbler, 5", 12 ounce		7.00
	Pitcher, 5", 32 ounce, sunflower motif in bottom	25.00	9 ▸	Tumbler, 4¾", 7 ounce, footed		7.50
▸	Pitcher, 9", 48 ounce, footed	45.00	12 ▸	Tumbler, 5¾", footed		9.00
	Pitcher, 8", 70 ounce, flat	140.00		Tumbler, 7", footed		10.00
	Plate, 6", sherbet	2.50		Whiskey, 2", 1 ounce		9.00

HOBNAIL, HOCKING GLASS COMPANY, 1934 – 1936

Colors: crystal, crystal w/red trim, and pink

Hocking's Hobnail is recognized by experienced collectors as a consequence of its pieces being moulded like those found in Miss America or Moonstone. Actually, the 1940s Moonstone pattern is essentially Hocking's Hobnail design with an added white emphasis to the hobs and edges. Most Depression-era glass companies made some variety of hobnail and this was Hockings'. They went one step further and continued during the war years with Moonstone.

Crystal Hobnail serving pieces are not easy to find, but beverage and decanter sets are plentiful. You can gather a set economically if you can find it for sale. This is another pattern that many dealers do no carry to shows. You might need to ask if they have inventory on hand that is not being shown.

Hobnail displays beautifully. Collectors have been captivated by the red trim that is found predominantly on the Wes Coast. The decanter and footed juices/wines are the only red-trimmed pieces we see in my travels in the eastern half of the country. An occasional piece is found in the Ohio area, but rarely are sets found there. It always sells well when w put it out for sale, particularly if red trimmed.

Hocking made only four pieces in pink. Another pink Hobnail pattern, such as one made by MacBeth-Evans, ca coexist with this Hocking pattern; that way, you can add a pitcher and tumblers, something unavailable in Hocking ware. Many other companies' Hobnail patterns will mingle with Hocking's Hobnail.

Footed juice tumblers were sold with the decanter as a wine set; thus, it was also a wine glass until the preache dropped in. Terminology had a lot to do with tumblers and stems during this era. During Prohibition, wine glasses were so as juices and the champagnes as high sherbets. Wine glasses during that era routinely held around three ounces. Now, peo ple believe the 8 – 10 ounce water goblets from the Depression era are wine goblets; today's wine drinkers want larger glass es. Dealers should verify size with customers when they ask for wines since they may really be asking for water goblets.

	Pink	*Crystal
1 ▶ Bowl, 5½", cereal		5.00
15 ▶ Bowl, 6½", crimped, hdld.		17.50
5 ▶ Bowl, 7", salad		5.50
9 ▶ Cup	6.00	4.50
17 ▶ Creamer, footed		9.00
11 ▶ Decanter and stopper, 32 ounce		35.00
2 ▶ Goblet, 10 ounce, water		8.00
Goblet, 13 ounce, iced tea		10.00
14 ▶ Pitcher, 18 ounce, milk		20.00

	Pink	*Crysta
12 ▶ Pitcher, 67 ounce		27.50
Plate, 6", sherbet	5.00	1.50
4 ▶ Plate, 8½", luncheon	8.00	5.00
8 ▶ Saucer/sherbet plate	4.00	1.50
18 ▶ Sherbet	7.00	3.00
6 ▶ Sugar, footed		9.00
Tumbler, 5 ounce, juice		4.00
13 ▶ Tumbler, 9 ounce, 10 ounce, water		5.00
3 ▶ Tumbler, 5¼",15 ounce, iced tea		15.00
10 ▶ Tumbler, 3 ounce, footed, wine/juice		5.00
7 ▶ Tumbler, 5 ounce, footed, cordial		6.00
16 ▶ Whiskey, 1½ ounce		7.00

*Add 20 – 25% for re
trimmed pieces

Experiment
item

98

HOMESPUN, "FINE RIB," JEANNETTE GLASS COMPANY, 1939 – 1949

Colors: pink and crystal, fired-on colors

Homespun bowls have tab handles which have a tendency to get nicks and chips. Sherbets often suffer from inner rim roughness (irr), but are hard to pin down. Buy them when you see them.

There is no true Homespun sugar lid. The lid occasionally presented on the sugar is a Fine Rib powder jar top.

Homespun has nine tumblers, which is surprising for a pattern so small that it does not include a pitcher. A large Fine Rib pitcher, made by Hazel-Atlas was originally packaged by some unknown company for use with Homespun tumblers with 13½ ounce, band-at-top iced teas. The pitcher has similar narrow bands around the neck and matches in color, but has no waffling design. Band-at-top tumblers are harder to find; but most collectors seek the ribbed.

Pictured on the right are the flat, 13½ ounce (band at top) tea and the 12½ ounce (no band) tea. In front of them is the 9 ounce (band above ribs, waffle bottomed) tumbler. Confusion reigns with the three tumblers on the left in front of the footed teas. There is little difference in height; but the 7 ounce (ribs to top, straight, concentric ring bottom) and 9 ounce (ribs to top, straight, waffle bottomed) are similar. Although there is a two ounce difference in capacity, there is only ³⁄₁₆" difference in height. Notice the small 8 ounce (ribs to top, flared, plain bottomed) tumbler on the right of those. This style is challenging to find. Also, the two footed teas hold 15 ounces but there is only ⅛" difference in height. Collectors sometimes refer to them as "skinny" and "fat bottomed." There is a slight stem on the taller one and no stem on the other. It only makes a difference when ordering by mail or off the Internet. You need to specify no stem or slight stem and hope the seller knows enough to differentiate.

There is no child's teapot in crystal and there are no sugars and creamers in this child's tea set.

	Pink, Crystal
4 ▸ Bowl, 4½", closed handles	17.00
6 ▸ Bowl, 5", cereal, closed handles	35.00
2 ▸ Bowl, 8¼", large berry, closed handles	32.00
0 ▸ Butter dish and cover	60.00
Coaster/ashtray	6.50
1 ▸ Creamer, footed	12.50
8 ▸ Cup	11.00
Plate, 6", sherbet	7.00
7 ▸ Plate, 9¼", dinner	20.00
3 ▸ Platter, 13", closed handles	22.00
9 ▸ Saucer	7.00

	Pink, Crystal
15 ▸ Sherbet, low flat	20.00
17 ▸ Sugar, footed	12.00
2 ▸ Tumbler, 3⅞", 7 ounce, straight	20.00
4 ▸ Tumbler, 4⅛", 8 ounce, water, flared top	20.00
19 ▸ Tumbler, 4¼", 9 ounce, band at top	20.00
3 ▸ Tumbler, 4⁵⁄₁₆", 9 ounce, no band	20.00
18 ▸ Tumbler, 5⅜", 12½ ounce, iced tea	30.00
20 ▸ Tumbler, 5⅞", 13½ ounce, iced tea, band at top	30.00
11 ▸ Tumbler, 4", 5 ounce, footed	8.00
5 ▸ Tumbler, 6¼", 15 ounce, footed	30.00
6 ▸ Tumbler, 6⅜", 15 ounce, footed	30.00

HOMESPUN CHILD'S TEA SET

	Pink	Crystal		Pink	Crystal
Cup	35.00	25.00	Teapot cover	100.00	
Saucer	11.00	8.00	Set: 14-pieces	395.00	
Plate	13.00	10.00	Set: 12-pieces		175.00
Teapot	60.00				

INDIANA CUSTARD, "FLOWER AND LEAF BAND," INDIANA GLASS COMPANY, 1930s; 1950s

Colors: ivory or custard, early 1930s; white, 1950s

Indiana Custard attracts a few new admirers every year, but most cannot find sufficient pieces unless they live in central Indiana. On the other hand, at a recent antique show, a dealer had a significant set displayed. There were no sherbets, but most everything else was there. Shading on the cups and saucers varied, which is a small problem with Indiana Custard. Some of the pieces are more yellow and translucent than the beige of others.

This set was being marketed as a whole, with an extra premium for its being a set — something that seldom works with glass. Sets are not worth more than the sum of the pieces. Few people buy complete sets unless they are dealers buying wholesale. Collectors generally buy a piece or two at a time. Granted, obtaining an entire set a piece or two at a time is a formidable task. However, most people enjoy chasing glass patterns. They tell me repeatedly at shows how much fun they've had doing it — often for years. In my experience, individual pricing of items will often see an entire set sell in a much smaller amount of time than trying to market the entire set.

Indiana Custard is the only Depression-era pattern where cups and sherbets are the most elusive items to find. Some collectors consider the sherbet overrated; but those who have searched for years without owning one would contradict that. In all honesty, they are likely a good acquisition at today's price. Cups have been more difficult for me to find than the sherbets, but usually have found the sherbets in groups of six or eight and the cups one or two at a time. Both sell, even at these prices.

Indiana made this pattern in white in the 1950s under the name Orange Blossom. So far, there is only minor demand for this color, though it is a lovely, pristine white. Orange Blossom can now be found in my *Collectible Glassware from the 40s, 50s, 60s....*

I have been unable to establish if there is a full set of yellow floral decorated pieces available. I have seen a set of Indiana Custard decorated like the saucer with the colored flowers in the center. After 60 years, a problem with collecting the florals might be that the decorations flake.

		French Ivory			French Ivory
13 ▸	Bowl, 5½", berry	12.00	Plate, 7½", salad		15.00
11 ▸	Bowl, 6½", cereal	30.00	Plate, 8⅞", luncheon		17.00
2 ▸	Bowl, 7½", flat soup	32.00	Plate, 9¾", dinner		28.00
	Bowl, 9", 1¾" deep, large berry	35.00	5 ▸ Platter, 11½", oval		35.00
1 ▸	Bowl, 9½", oval vegetable	32.00	4 ▸ Saucer		6.00
8 ▸	Butter dish and cover	65.00	10 ▸ Sherbet		90.00
12 ▸	Cup	33.00	7 ▸ Sugar		10.00
9 ▸	Creamer	15.00	6 ▸ Sugar cover		25.00
3 ▸	Plate, 5¾", bread and butter	7.00			

INDIANA SILVER, INDIANA GLASS COMPANY, c. 1918

Color: crystal w/sterling silver overlay

Indiana Silver was able to combine the look of the past Art Nouveau (flowered scrolls) era and the upcoming simple, linear Deco era. Applying silver to the glass also blended with the silver craze of that era. Much of the glass we find today is missing the silver; but the superb design is still present. If you choose to collect this, worry about silver condition after you find the pieces, and then replace them as you can. Please note that the plate was designated as a calling card tray. Of all pieces, sherbets and footed vases seem to turn up regularly.

We were doing a book signing last year in an antique mall and during a slow time Cathy went exploring. She found 15 sherbets with great silver priced for $15.00. The owner of the mall came back to ask what the pattern was and we told her. After she looked it up in our book, she came back and told us she thought we might have found a bargain.

Two assorted lists of Indiana Silver were offered to dealers of the time, a 130-pound 13 dozen-piece "Sensation" assortment and a 100-pound "Sterling dining assortment." The dining assortment selling prices were to be $1.25 – $1.50 each — which was pricey at that time, considering most wares in their other lines were designed to be sold for 10¢ to 25¢.

	Bowl, 4½", dessert	10.00		Goblet, wine	16.00
2 ▸	Bowl, 5½", ftd., bonbon	15.00	4 ▸	Plate, 7½", card tray	10.00
6 ▸	Bowl, 8½", berry	25.00		Pitcher, ½ gal.	45.00
	Butter w/cover	40.00	3 ▸	Sherbet, ftd.	10.00
7 ▸	Cup, custard	12.50		Spoon	10.00
	Compote, ftd., jelly	15.00		Sugar w/cover, large	20.00
9 ▸	Creamer, small berry	10.00	8 ▸	Sugar, open, small, berry	10.00
	Creamer, large	15.00	1 ▸	Tumbler	20.00
	Goblet, water	25.00	5 ▸	Vase, 6½", ftd.	40.00

IRIS, "IRIS AND HERRINGBONE," JEANNETTE GLASS COMPANY, 1928 – 1932; 1950s; 1970s

Colors: crystal, iridescent; some pink and green; recently bi-colored red/yellow and blue/green combinations, and white (See Reproduction Section.)

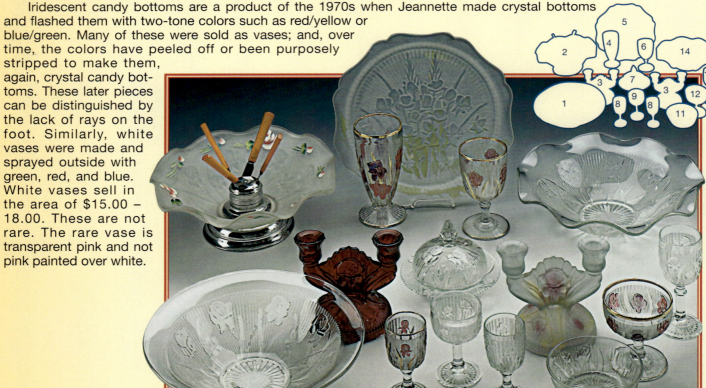

Iris pattern is widely collected and greatly beloved. However, reproduction Iris has been the dominate Iris news for the past few years. We are constantly asked what is being made now or what do I do about my collection? The latest rip off is the cocktail which joins the dinner plates, iced teas, flat tumblers, and coasters that have previously been dumped into the market. Be sure to see the Reproduction section in the back of this book for easy telltale signs to differentiate old from new.

Do not panic; this has happened with other patterns, and this, too, shall pass, albeit slowly. All the new crystal is exceedingly clear. If you place old crystal Iris on a white table-cloth or paper, it will look gray or even slightly yellow. The new is very crystal without a tinge of color of any sort. The flat tumblers have no herringbone on the bottom — just Iris. The coaster is more than half-full of glass when you look from the side. Turn to page 247 for details.

Sellers on the Internet auctions have exploded sales of these reproductions. Jeannette is often used as a "creden-tial" in the wording of these auctions. Sometimes the ploy is that I bought these at an estate or auction and don't know how old they are. Reproduced items get on the Internet first as "old" and unsuspecting bidders pay high prices before word gets out in the collecting world. Most of these sellers know their products are new, so if bidding, ask about return policy before you bid. Reputable sellers will offer refunds or returns.

The bright yellow Iris sugar bowl pictured on the cover has now been joined by pink, green, and blue. All of these are being found in Australia. Were these shipped "down under" or decorated there? That has not been determined, but they do add color to Iris collecting. The originally found pink and green are transparent — not fired-on.

Crystal Iris prices continue to soften a bit, especially for iced teas and dinner plates. Prices for coasters and flat water tumblers have been socked hard. Several large collections are having a tough time finding buyers right now because owners want pre-reproduction prices. We have been through this with other patterns numerous times in the past and it will take a while for collectors to feel comfortable buying. Know your dealer and buy from established and reputable ones.

Original crystal production for Iris began in 1928. Some was made in the late 1940s and 1950s; candy bottoms and vases appeared as late as the 1970s. The crystal Iris decorated with red and gold that keeps turning up was called Cor-sage and styled by Century in 1946. This information was on a card attached to a 1946 wedding gift. The satinized (frost-ed) plates and bowls usually had hand-colored or painted irises on them. It wears off easily and does not sell well unless the original decoration is still bright. Those rarely seen 8" luncheon plates may be scarce because many more of them were frosted than were not. In any case, the frosted ones are a tough sell at $35.00.

Iridescent candy bottoms are a product of the 1970s when Jeannette made crystal bottoms and flashed them with two-tone colors such as red/yellow or blue/green. Many of these were sold as vases; and, over time, the colors have peeled off or been purposely stripped to make them, again, crystal candy bottoms. These later pieces can be distinguished by the lack of rays on the foot. Similarly, white vases were made and sprayed outside with green, red, and blue. White vases sell in the area of $15.00 – 18.00. These are not rare. The rare vase is transparent pink and not pink painted over white.

102

		Crystal	Iridescent	Green, Pink
18 ▸	Bowl, 4½", berry, beaded edge	42.00	7.00	
28 ▸	Bowl, 5", ruffled sauce	10.00	24.00	
11 ▸	Bowl, 5", cereal	115.00		
22 ▸	Bowl, 7½", soup	155.00	65.00	
	Bowl, 8", berry, beaded edge	80.00	25.00	
14 ▸	Bowl, 9½", ruffled salad	15.00	10.00	200.00
23 ▸	Bowl, 11½", ruffled fruit	15.00	14.00	
1 ▸	Bowl, 11", fruit, straight edge	62.00		
7 ▸	Butter dish and cover	47.50	45.00	
	Butter dish bottom	12.50	12.50	
	Butter dish top	35.00	32.50	
3 ▸	Candlesticks, pair	40.00	45.00	
30 ▸	Candy jar and cover	180.00		
24 ▸	‡Coaster	75.00		
15 ▸	Creamer, footed	13.00	12.00	150.00
31 ▸	Cup	16.00	14.00	
16 ▸	*Demitasse cup	45.00	150.00	
17 ▸	*Demitasse saucer	145.00	250.00	
2 ▸	Fruit or nut set	100.00	150.00	
	Goblet, 4", wine		26.00	

		Crystal	Iridescent	Green, Pink
9 ▸	‡Goblet, 4½", 4 oz., cocktail	22.00		
8 ▸	Goblet, 4½", 3 oz., wine	15.00		
13 ▸	Goblet, 5½", 4 oz.	23.00	495.00	
6 ▸	Goblet, 5½", 8 oz.	25.00	295.00	
	**Lamp shade, 11½"	90.00		
27 ▸	Pitcher, 9½", footed	42.50	42.50	
20 ▸	Plate, 5½", sherbet	14.00	11.00	
19 ▸	Plate, 8", luncheon	100.00		
25 ▸	‡Plate, 9", dinner	50.00	45.00	
5 ▸	Plate, 11¾", sandwich	38.00	32.00	
32 ▸	Saucer	9.00	9.00	
21 ▸	Sherbet, 2½", footed	28.00	14.00	
12 ▸	Sherbet, 4", footed	26.00	295.00	
33 ▸	‡‡Sugar	12.00	11.00	150.00
	Sugar cover	14.00	12.00	
29 ▸	‡Tumbler, 4", flat	110.00		
26 ▸	Tumbler, 6", footed	17.00	17.00	
4 ▸	‡Tumbler, 6½", footed	25.00		
	Vase, 9"	30.00	25.00	225.00

* Ruby, Blue, Amethyst priced as iridescent
** Colors, $85.00

‡ Has been reproduced
‡‡ Yellow, $195.00

JUBILEE, LANCASTER GLASS COMPANY, Early 1930s

Colors: yellow, crystal, and pink

The accepted Jubilee cut (#1200) on Lancaster blanks has a 12 petal, open centered flower. We bring that up fc readers who are asking if any ware with an open center, 12-petal flower is Jubilee. No, it is not. We also need to point ou that the cut design has to be on the Lancaster blank. Plain, uncut, exactly the same blanks are not Jubilee — merely th blanks employed for the cutting.

The confusion with Jubilee occurs when you find Standard Glass Company's paneled blanks with a #1200 cut. . previous author gave these the name "Tat"; but people seeing these pieces over the years said, "Ah! Jubilee!" and gath ered them with their pattern. This practice developed into the Standard items being accepted as "Jubilee" pattern. Add tional perplexity arises when people find Standard Glass Company's closed center, 12-petal flower cut (#89) on panele blanks, which Standard sold as Martha Washington pattern. Basic pieces of Lancaster's Jubilee were presented o smooth blanks (no optic panels). Standard's #1200 was presented on optic paneled blanks. Martha Washington came o optic paneled blanks, with rayed foot tumblers and fancy handled cups. Both of these sister companies showed con panion-serving wares for these patterns using the same petal edged, fancy handled blanks. To further confuse things Standard had a #200 and a #28 cut, very like #1200, which had the same flower with more cut branches. These wer presented on those same type serving pieces, with some petal blank, three-toed bowls and trays thrown in for goo measure. Other like cuts include a mayo bowl with 16 petals and a cutting with 12 petals, but having a smaller petal i between the larger ones. Frankly, most collectors are happy to buy any of these pieces as Jubilee pattern to enhanc their sets. Ultimately, you have to decide how much of a purist you wish to be.

Notice the four pink pieces pictured on 105. The petal blank, three-toed bowl is Standard's #200 cut. The cup, sauce and plate are Lancaster #1200. Probably all the pulled (no ball) stems are Standard lines; but there are ball-stemmed, opti panel goblets like the smooth ones found in Jubilee. Therefore, these ball types cannot only belong to Lancaster.

After all the detailed information above, I must point out that two pieces of Jubilee only have 11 petals, the 3", ounce, non-stemmed sherbet and the three-footed covered candy. Having only 11 petals on the candy and sherbe apparently came from cutting problems experienced when using the typical 6" cutting wheel. The foot of the sherbet an the knob on the candy were in the way when a petal of the 12 design was cut directly up and down. The glasscutter ha to move over to the side in order to cut a petal. Because of this placement, only an 11-petal flower resulted on thes pieces. Yes, those two 11 petal pieces are Jubilee and both are hard to find.

The #889 liner plate for the #890 mayo does have a raised rim, making that liner plate scarcer than the mayo. Som mayonnaise sets have 16 petals on bowl and plate.

Jubilee luncheon sets remain bountiful and prices reflect that. However, there is a decided lack of serving pieces fc #1200 Jubilee. Prices indicate seldom-found items.

JUBILEE

		Pink	Yellow
	Bowl, 8", 3-footed, 5⅛" high	225.00	195.00
	Bowl, 9", handled fruit		125.00
	Bowl, 11½", flat fruit	175.00	150.00
6 ▸	Bowl, 11½", 3-footed	210.00	205.00
12 ▸	Bowl, 11½", 3-footed, curved in		195.00
	Bowl, 13", 3-footed	225.00	195.00
16 ▸	Candlestick, pair	185.00	185.00
	Candy jar, w/lid, 3-footed	295.00	295.00
	Cheese & cracker set	195.00	195.00
1 ▸	Creamer	32.00	17.00
10 ▸	Cup	28.00	12.00
	Mayonnaise & plate	195.00	175.00
	w/original ladle	215.00	195.00
15 ▸	Plate, 7", salad	18.00	11.00
5 ▸	Plate, 8¾", luncheon	22.50	10.00
	Plate, 13½", sandwich, handled	65.00	45.00
	Plate, 14", 3-footed		175.00
11 ▸	Saucer, two styles	8.00	4.00
	Sherbet, 3", 8 oz.		65.00
	Stem, 4", 1 oz., cordial		250.00
	Stem, 4¾", 4 oz., oyster cocktail		75.00
9 ▸	Stem, 4⅞", 3 oz., cocktail		110.00
8 ▸	Stem, 5½", 7 oz., sherbet/champagne		65.00
13 ▸	Stem, 7½", 11 oz.		160.00
2 ▸	Sugar	35.00	16.00
14 ▸	Tray, 11", 2-handled cake	65.00	40.00
7 ▸	Tumbler, 5", 6 oz., footed, juice		95.00

		Pink	Yellow
4 ▸	Tumbler, 6", 10 oz., water	65.00	32.00
3 ▸	Tumbler, 6⅛", 12½ oz., iced tea		135.00
17 ▸	Tray, 11", center-handled sandwich	150.00	160.00
	Vase, 12"	195.00	250.00

LACED EDGE, "KATY BLUE," IMPERIAL GLASS COMPANY, Early 1930s

Colors: blue w/opalescent edge and green w/opalescent edge, et al.

Imperial's Laced Edge pattern was produced a little at a time in an array of colors, although only their opalescent blue and green dinnerware contributions are being dealt with in this book since that is where collector interest lies. Most of the colors without the white edge were made into the 1950s and later; so, they exited the time constraint (pre-1940) for this book. Imperial christened this white decoration "Sea Foam." Sea Foam treatment varies from narrowly coating the edge of pieces to others having an ½" of prominent, opalescent edging.

Old-timers in the business call opalescent blue "Katy Blue." Some have called the green, "Katy Green." Blue and green pieces without the white edge sell for about half of the prices listed if a buyer can be found, since few collectors seek those. There appears to be little demand for crystal pieces, which are often spotted in malls with big prices. I have never seen Sea Foam edging on crystal.

Some collectors do not accept the 12" cake plate (luncheon plate in Imperial catalog) or the 9" vegetable bowl (salad in ad on next page) as Laced Edge because the edges are more open than those of the other items. They are shown with all the other accepted pieces. A Laced Edge collector from Illinois let us borrow an original ad (page 107) showing an inflated retail price along with the cost in coupons (product) for Laced Edge pieces.

Spouts for creamers often have different shapes due to them being individually formed using a wooden tool. Cereal bowls vary from 4⅞" to 5⅝", soup bowls from 6⅞" to 7¼", and berry bowls from 4⅜" to 4¾". Turning out the edge of the bowl while still hot caused size differences. Some edges go straight up while others are horizontally correct. Collectors will accept these minor discrepancies in order to have enough bowls. Stacking these bowls is sometimes perplexing.

The rarely glimpsed, undivided, oval vegetable bowl is absent from that ad and most collections today. Notice the divided bowl and the platter were the most expensive pieces to earn with coupons.

		Opalescent				Opalescent
	Basket bowl	235.00		2 ▸	Mayonnaise, 3-piece	135.00
9 ▸	Bowl, 4⅜"– 4¾", fruit	25.00			Plate, 6½", bread & butter	13.00
17 ▸	Bowl, 5"	33.00		3 ▸	Plate, 8", salad	28.00
	Bowl, 5½"	33.00		4 ▸	Plate, 10", dinner	65.00
	Bowl, 5⅞"	33.00		14 ▸	Plate, 12", luncheon	
13 ▸	Bowl, 7", soup	75.00			(per catalog description)	75.00
12 ▸	Bowl, 9", vegetable	100.00		5 ▸	Platter, 13"	165.00
1 ▸	Bowl, 11", divided oval	115.00		11 ▸	Saucer	10.00
6 ▸	Bowl, 11", oval	150.00		8 ▸	Sugar	35.00
15 ▸	Candlestick, double, pair	175.00			Tidbit, 2-tiered, 8" & 10" plates	110.00
10 ▸	Cup	30.00		7 ▸	Tumbler, 9 ounce	46.00
16 ▸	Creamer	35.00				

6 FOOTED TUMBLERS
27 COUPONS
Retail Value $1.20

SALAD BOWL
13 COUPONS
Retail Value 60c

3 SAUCE DISHES
14 COUPONS
Retail Value 60c

3 CUPS AND SAUCERS
25 COUPONS
Retail Value $1.20

3 PIECE MAYONNAISE SET
15 COUPONS
Retail Value 60c

3 SALAD PLATES
20 COUPONS
Retail Value 90c

PLATTER
(13 INCH)
30 COUPONS
Retail Value $1.25

3 BREAD AND BUTTERS
14 COUPONS
Retail Value 75c

3 SOUP DISHES
20 COUPONS
Retail Value 90c

3 CEREAL DISHES
14 COUPONS
Retail Value 75c

SUGAR AND CREAMER
14 COUPONS
Retail Value 50c

DIVIDED VEGETABLE DISH
30 COUPONS Retail Value $1.25

CAKE PLATE (12 INCH)
18 COUPONS Retail Value 75c

3 DINNER PLATES
33 COUPONS Retail Value $1.50

LAKE COMO, HOCKING GLASS COMPANY, 1934 – 1937

Color: Vitrock with blue scene; some with red scene

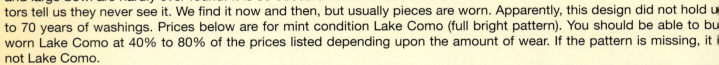

The red Lake Como creamer and sugar finally drew a comment from a sugar and creamer collector looking for a set. Other than that, no one seemed to notice! These are the only red decorated pieces we have seen.

There are only 13 different pieces of Lake Como and all but the shakers and large bowl are hardly ever found. It is so obscure now that some collectors tell us they never see it. We find it now and then, but usually pieces are worn. Apparently, this design did not hold u to 70 years of washings. Prices below are for mint condition Lake Como (full bright pattern). You should be able to bu worn Lake Como at 40% to 80% of the prices listed depending upon the amount of wear. If the pattern is missing, it i not Lake Como.

One couple told us that they were buying less than mint Lake Como in order to have some of the harder-to-fin pieces. Unlike many patterns, we have never found anyone who uses Lake Como regularly. It is displayed, but not cur rently being used for serving. When offered for sale, "like new" Lake Como sells very swiftly.

The flat soup has a floral embossed decoration on the edge (like the normally found Vitrock soup) instead of bein painted in blue. Only the center of the soup has the design and if ever used, the design has usually gone AWOL. You w find platters almost as difficult to find as soup bowls; but most collectors are looking for only one platter, which is smaller problem than finding more than one soup.

Small supplies of vegetable bowls have been found in the last few years; thus, the price has softened somewhat o them. Finding either style cup in mint condition will be a headache. If you are willing to buy them worn, then no problem

4 ▸	Bowl, 6", cereal	25.00	7 ▸	Plate, 9¼", dinner	35.00
6 ▸	Bowl, 9¾", vegetable	50.00	2 ▸	Platter, 11"	85.00
5 ▸	Bowl, flat soup	105.00	3 ▸	Salt & pepper, pair	45.00
11 ▸	Creamer, footed	25.00	9 ▸	Saucer	10.00
8 ▸	Cup, regular	25.00	13 ▸	Saucer, St. Denis	10.00
12 ▸	Cup, St. Denis	30.00	10 ▸	Sugar, footed	30.00
1 ▸	Plate, 7¼", salad	20.00			

LARGO, LINE #220, PADEN CITY GLASS COMPANY, Late 1937 – 1951; CANTON GLASS COMPANY, 1950s

Colors: amber, amethyst, cobalt blue, crystal, crystal w/ruby flash, light blue, red

11

Paden City's Largo is sometimes confused with Cambridge's Caprice pattern due to similarities in color and design. Some of our first pieces of this pattern were actually identified as Caprice, but thankfully not priced as such. Paden City's Largo was not as widely dispersed as Cambridge's Caprice, something which causes us to look high and low for Largo today. Our experiences have shown us that the three-toed candy dish lid and the two-lipped comport are relatively scarce. We have found several divided candy bottoms in our travels, but never a Largo top though they do exist.

Sugar and creamer collectors put a dent in that meager supply. There are few four-footed sugar and creamers in other collectible patterns; so these stand out. We, personally, have found several Paden City etchings on Largo items.

We finally found a saucer in amber but no cup. All blue cups have been found with the non-indented 6⅝" plates. Now we wonder about the existence of blue saucers.

You have to be observant to discern the Largo pattern line atop the single candle cup. Indeed, I passed one at a show; but following behind me, Cathy spotted it.

Please note that Largo pieces have four half circle ridged lines while its sister pattern, Maya (#221) has a bristle haired thistle ball design. Because of like colors and similar items, these patterns are sometimes mistaken for each other.

	Amber, Crystal	Blue, Red			Amber, Crystal	Blue, Red
Ashtray, 3", rectangle	16.00	30.00	9 ▸	Comport, double spout, pedestal	35.00	75.00
Bowl, 5"	15.00	25.00		Comport, fluted rim, pedestal	35.00	75.00
Bowl, 6", deep	18.00	35.00		Comport, 6½" x 10", plain rim,		
Bowl, 7½"	20.00	37.50		pedestal	32.50	70.00
▸ Bowl, 7½", crimped	22.50	45.00	4 ▸	Creamer, footed	25.00	40.00
▸ Bowl, 9", tab-handled	30.00	70.00	3 ▸	Cup	15.00	30.00
Bowl, 11⅝", 3½" deep, tri-footed,				Mayonnaise, toed	25.00	55.00
flared rim	35.00	80.00		Plate, 6⅝"	8.00	15.00
Bowl, 12¾", 4¾" deep, tri-footed,			7 ▸	Plate, 8"	10.00	20.00
flat rim	45.00	80.00		Plate, 10¾", cheese w/indent	20.00	40.00
▸ Cake plate, pedestal	35.00	95.00	2 ▸	Saucer	5.00	12.50
Candleholder	30.00	55.00	5 ▸	Sugar, footed	25.00	45.00
Candy, flat w/lid, 3-part	35.00	95.00		Tray, 13¾", tri-footed, serving	25.00	75.00
Cigarette box, 4" x 3¼" x 1½"	30.00	65.00	11 ▸	Tray, 14", five-part, relish	50.00	
▸ Comport, cracker	15.00	25.00				

LAUREL, McKEE GLASS COMPANY, 1930s

Colors: French Ivory, Jade Green, White Opal, Poudre Blue, and various colors of decorated rims

McKee's Laurel has been avidly sought for years in Poudre (powder) Blue and to some extent in French Ivory. There was an abundance of Jade Green around, but few early collectors noticed it. That has changed. The popularity of Fire-King's Jade-ite on the Internet and Jadite colors in particular, bled over into Laurel's Jade Green. Prices nearly doubled on every piece and shortages of some items were exposed. Luckily, Jade Laurel was the color most often seen, followed closely by French Ivory (beige) and then Poudre Blue, (not Delphite blue as called by some collectors). French Ivory stimulates few collectors at this time; prices there have remained stable. I have moved the White Opal pricing into the same column as French Ivory since those prices are more typical of its worth, now, than that of the Jade.

The short sugar and creamer have finally been found in Poudre Blue; and thanks to an Ohio dealer, you can see them pictured. We rarely see blue in our travels or at shows. Early collectors grabbed it as it became available and it has not been brought back to the marketplace.

Serving pieces in all colors are insufficient for the demand. That trend is gradually raising its ugly head in many patterns from this era. Serving pieces, priced separately, were not in basic sets. They were too large to pack in products as premiums, so few people were willing to spend the extra money for serving items to match what they received free, or bought as a basic set.

Laurel children's tea sets are abiding in long-time collections. The Scottie dog decorated sets were produced in Jade Green or French Ivory colors. Collectors of Scottie items have spiked the prices on these sets to levels where few collectors try to buy full sets. They are thrilled just to acquire one piece. Other Laurel children's sets are found with edged trims of red, green, or orange. Watch for wear on these colored trims; it appears many children did, in fact, play with these dishes.

Laurel has two styles of candlesticks. The 4" style is available, but the three-footed variety is rare. The footed style has only been spotted in green.

	Jade or Decorated Rims	White Opal, French Ivory	Poudre Blue		Jade or Decorated Rims	White Opal, French Ivory	Poudre Blue
14 ▸ Bowl, 4¾", berry	15.00	9.00	15.00	Plate, 6", sherbet	16.00	10.00	10.0
2 ▸ Bowl, 5½"	35.00			Plate, 7½", salad	20.00	10.00	16.0
15 ▸ Bowl, 6", cereal	28.00	14.00	28.00	4 ▸ Plate, 9⅛", dinner, 2 styles	25.00	15.00	30.0
Bowl, 6", three legs	28.00	15.00		8 ▸ Plate, 9⅛", grill, round or			
1 ▸ Bowl, 7⅞", soup, 2 styles	45.00	35.00	85.00	scalloped	25.00	15.00	
3 ▸ Bowl, 9", large berry	45.00	30.00	55.00	Platter, 10¾", oval	55.00	30.00	60.0
Bowl, 9¾", oval vegetable	55.00	30.00	55.00	Salt and pepper	90.00	50.00	
Bowl, 10½", three legs	60.00	40.00	70.00	17 ▸ Saucer	4.50	3.00	7.5
Bowl, 11"	60.00	40.00	85.00	11 ▸ Sherbet	20.00	12.00	
Candlestick, 4", pair	65.00	30.00		Sherbet/champagne, 5"	80.00	50.00	
6 ▸ Candlestick, 3 footed	150.00			5 ▸ Sugar, short	25.00	10.00	50.0
9 ▸ Cheese dish and cover	110.00	55.00		Sugar, tall	25.00	11.00	35.0
23 ▸ Creamer, short	25.00	12.00	50.00	Tumbler, 3⅜", 7 ounce, flat		35.00	
7 ▸ Creamer, tall	25.00	15.00	40.00	Tumbler, 4½", 9 ounce, flat	75.00	40.00	
16 ▸ Cup	15.00	8.00	22.50	Tumbler, 5", 12 ounce, flat		55.00	

CHILDREN'S LAUREL TEA SET

	French Ivory	Jade or Decorated Rims	Scottie Dog Jade	Scottie Dog Ivory
21 ▸ Creamer	30.00	100.00	260.00	130.00
19 ▸ Cup	25.00	50.00	100.00	50.00
22 ▸ Plate	10.00	20.00	80.00	40.00
18 ▸ Saucer	8.00	12.50	75.00	37.50
20 ▸ Sugar	30.00	100.00	260.00	130.00
14-piece set	235.00	530.00	1,550.00	775.00

LINCOLN INN, LINE NO. 1700, FENTON GLASS COMPANY, Late 1920s

Colors: amber, amethyst, black, cobalt, crystal, green, green opalescent, jade (opaque), light blue, pink, and red

Lincoln Inn plates are shown in a 1930s catalog with a fruit design (intaglio) in the center. Besides the plates we have seen a 9" and 7½" crystal bowl with the fruit center. There may be additional pieces of intaglio, but that is all we can confirm. There have never been any reports of this design in colored wares.

Tumblers are a little more difficult to find than the omnipresent stems, but acquiring an old pitcher in any color is a challenge. Fenton made an iridized, dark carnival colored pitcher and tumblers in the 1980s. Any other iridescent piece you might see in this pattern is of recent production. All original light blue pitchers surfaced in the South, but none that we've heard of in recent years.

Stems appear to be the only pieces of the pattern you can glimpse with regularity and the champagne/sherbet is the stem of note. If someone asks us for Lincoln Inn, it is usually prefaced with, "I don't need stems, but…." A small collection of stems could be made in a multitude of colors. Stemware was sold to accompany china. Today, you might possibly collect a setting in crystal, but colors are less certain, even using the Internet. In spite of the fact that tableware was advertised in at least eight of the above listed colors in 1929, little color other than red and the several shades of blue are accumulated today. Serving pieces are scarce. This pattern absolutely fits rainbow-collecting trends that are flourishing in the Depression world.

Lincoln Inn shakers are inadequate for the demand. Even crystal shakers are proficient at hiding. Collectors of shakers tell us that Lincoln Inn ones may not be the most expensive ones in our book, but they are among the most difficult to find. Red and black shakers are favored colors; but do not sidestep any in your travels. Years ago a red pair were found sitting with Royal Ruby in a dark corner of a shop. They were priced as red shakers and not Lincoln Inn. You need to check in every little corner when you shop.

Red Lincoln Inn pieces are often amberina in color. For novices, amberina is red glass that has some yellow hue in it. Some old timers in glass collecting reject amberina pieces for their collections as unfit to own. However, there are some devotees actually searching for amberina glass. There is a growing fascination for all two-toned glassware; and amberina color certainly fits that bill.

	Cobalt Blue, Red	**All other colors
Ashtray	17.50	12.00
Bonbon, handled, square	15.00	12.00
Bonbon, handled, oval	16.00	12.00
Bowl, 5", fruit	15.00	9.00
10 ▸ Bowl, 5¾", footed	30.00	
8 ▸ Bowl, 6	28.00	
Bowl, 6", cereal	25.00	10.00
Bowl, 6", crimped	18.00	8.50
Bowl, 9", shallow		23.00
Bowl, 9¼", footed	80.00	30.00
16 ▸ Bowl, 9½", crimped	45.00	35.00
Bowl, 10½", footed	80.00	35.00
Bowl, handled olive	18.00	9.50
9 ▸ Bowl, finger	22.00	12.50
Candy dish, footed, oval	45.00	20.00
Comport	30.00	14.50
15 ▸ Creamer	22.50	14.50
5 ▸ Cup	12.00	12.00
1 ▸ Goblet, water	30.00	15.50
2 ▸ Goblet, wine	32.00	16.50
Nut dish, footed	25.00	12.00

	Cobalt Blue, Red	**All other colors
Pitcher, 7¼", 46 ounce	800.00	700.00
Plate, 6"	9.00	4.50
14 ▸ Plate, 8"	15.00	10.00
4 ▸ Plate, 9¼"	45.00	11.50
Plate, 12"	65.00	15.50
*Salt/pepper, pair	225.00	150.00
Sandwich server, center handle	175.00	110.00
6 ▸ Saucer	5.00	3.50
Sherbet, 4½", cone shape	22.00	11.50
12 ▸ Sherbet, 4¾"	22.00	12.50
Sugar	22.50	14.00
Tumbler, 4 ounce, flat, juice	30.00	9.50
Tumbler, 9 ounce, flat, water		19.50
7 ▸ Tumbler, 5 ounce, footed	32.00	11.00
Tumbler, 9 ounce, footed	30.00	14.00
3 ▸ Tumbler, 12 ounce, footed	55.00	19.00
Vase, 9¾"	165.00	85.00
11 ▸ Vase, 12", footed	250.00	125.00

*Black $300.00
**w/fruits, add 20 – 25%

1   2   3   5, 6   7   7   1

8   9   9   10

11   12   5, 6   15

4

14

LINE #555, PADEN CITY GLASS COMPANY, Late 1930s – 1951; CANTON GLASS COMPANY, 1950s

Colors: crystal, light blue, red

Line #555 mould shape was used for several different Paden City etches and cuttings. The Gazebo pattern illustrated in our *Elegant Glassware of the Depression Era* is the etching most seen. Additional pieces of Line #555 are pictured there with the Gazebo etching. Heart-shaped candy bottoms are divided into three sections and the lids need to be checked carefully as many have been damaged over the years. They have a tendency to slip from your grasp when you try to pick them up. Some of these candy lids have etchings or cuttings on them possibly from other companies who decorated the lids. The candles, both single and double, appear in many candlestick collections since they are a striking design and stand out.

The tray pictured was used for the creamer and sugar, but was also listed separately. Canton Glass bought Paden City moulds and continued many of the pieces of Line #555 during the early 1950s. They regularly made crystal, but color could be special ordered.

Though a couple of "names" which never caught on have been ascribed to the line by other authors, the best we've heard recently was from a little geriatric lady dealer who told us "Oh, that's the 'Pearls and Teardrops' pattern."

	*Crystal			*Crystal
Bowl, 6", 2-part nappy	12.00		Plate, 6"	5.00
Bowl, 6", nappy	13.00		Plate, 8"	10.00
Bowl, 9", 2-handled	22.00		Plate, 12½", 2-handled	22.50
Bowl, 14", shallow	25.00		Plate, 16", salad or punch liner	40.00
Cake stand, pedestal foot	30.00		Punch bowl	65.00
5 ▸ Candlestick, 1-light	25.00		Punch cup	7.00
Candlestick, 2-light	28.00		Relish, 7½", square, 2-part	14.00
1 ▸ Candy, w/lid, "heart"	60.00		Relish, 9¾", rectangular, 3-part	20.00
Candy, w/lid, 10¼", pedestal foot	35.00		6 ▸ Relish, 10½", round, 5-part	26.00
Candy, w/lid, 11", pedestal foot	40.00		Relish, 11", round, 3-part	25.00
7 ▸ Comport, 7"	25.00		Saucer	3.00
3 ▸ Creamer	10.00		2 ▸ Sugar	10.00
Cup	8.00		4 ▸ Tray, creamer/sugar	12.00
Mayonnaise liner	7.50		Tray, 9"	15.00
Mayonnaise	15.00		Tray, 11", center handle	28.00

* Double price for colors

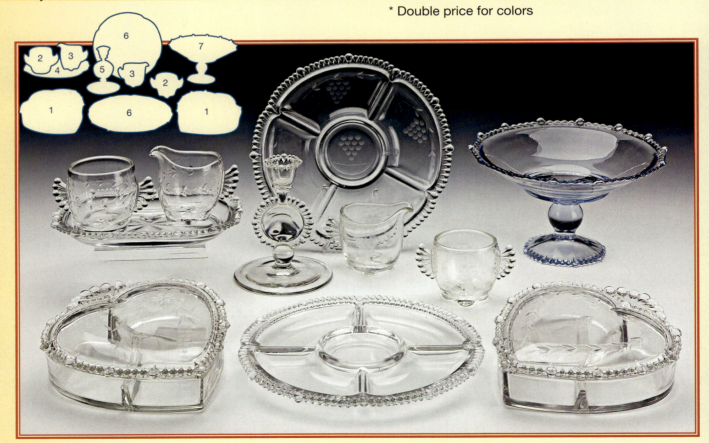

114

"LITTLE JEWEL," DIAMOND BLOCK, LINE #330, IMPERIAL GLASS COMPANY, Late 1920s – Early 1930s

Colors: black, crystal, green, iridescent, pink, red, white, yellow

Diamond Block or Line #330 as Imperial called it was advertised for sale in a 1920s catalog under the "Little Jewel" label. This name stuck rather than the Diamond Block given by Imperial. Colored items are the most popular, but not a lot of color is being found. Red, black, and yellow are rarely seen, but blue is the color mostly snatched by collectors. Yet, even crystal with this delightful design can make an excellent display.

"Little Jewel" is a diminutive Imperial pattern that is attracting people, in general, not just collectors. Seldom do customers recognize it as Depression-era glass. They are only buying it because it appeals to them. This appreciation for the pattern makes owning a piece or two desirable rather than acquiring it as a set. "Little Jewel" does not cause sticker shock, another appealing aspect.

Blue and black items are the fastest selling colors for us when we display them at shows. Keep that in mind when you see "Little Jewel" for sale.

	Crystal	Colors*			Crystal	Colors*
5 ▸ Bowl, 5½", square, honey dish	10.00	18.00	7 ▸ Jelly, 4½", handle		8.00	15.00
9 ▸ Bowl, 5", lily	10.00	15.00	Jelly, 5", footed		10.00	15.00
3 ▸ Bowl, 6½"	10.00	15.00	Jug, pint tankard		22.50	45.00
4 ▸ Bowl, 7½", berry	15.00	20.00	1 ▸ Pickle dish, 6½", 2 handles		15.00	22.50
6 ▸ Celery, 8½", tray	18.00	22.50	2 ▸ Sugar		8.00	15.00
8 ▸ Creamer	8.00	15.00	10 ▸ Vase, 6", bouquet		12.00	20.00

"LOIS," LINE #345 et al., UNITED STATES GLASS COMPANY, c. 1920s

Colors: crystal, green, and pink

"Lois" was a pattern that we kept getting pictures and questions about, so it seemed time to add it to the book. Not long ago we had an e-mail picture from a lady who had inherited a set of pink glass which she could not find in any book. After we identified it as "Lois," she happily bought the book it was in and later wrote back to say she had over $2,000.00 worth of "Lois." It was a lucky inheritance which more than paid for her book.

"Lois" was etched for the most part on Line #345, which is made-up of octagonal shaped pieces. It was first offered to merchants as a selection package. "Assortments," as they were labeled, normally contained 6 to 15 items, and in the case of etchings, they could be on several different mould lines. Sometimes assortment packages were assembled around a theme, such as table settings or bridge sets or serving items; but, often as not, they were just various wares put in a grouping. Sometimes it took several assortments to stock the entire line. Doubtless some pieces are lacking today because stores did not stock all assortments. These were early promotional schemes used by companies to vend their wares; and we know "Lois" was thus advertised from old catalogs.

You should find other items than those in the listing and some of them will be on other than octagon shape #345. Let us know what else you find.

		All colors			All colors
4 ▸	Bowl, 10", fruit, pedestal foot	50.00	Creamer, footed		25.00
	Bowl, 10", salad, flat rim	40.00	Mayonnaise or whipped cream w/ladle		45.00
	Bowl, 12", console, rolled edge	50.00	Pitcher, milk		55.00
	Cake, salver, pedestal foot	55.00	Plate, cheese liner		25.00
2 ▸	Candle, short, single	30.00	6 ▸ Plate, dinner		40.00
	Candy box, octagonal lid	70.00	Server, center handled		50.00
	Candy jar w/lid, cone shape	60.00	1 ▸ Stem, cocktail		25.00
	Comport, cheese	22.00	3 ▸ Stem wine		30.00
			Sugar, footed		25.00
			5 ▸ Tumbler, footed		35.00
			Vase, 10"		85.00

116

LORAIN, "BASKET," NO. 615, INDIANA GLASS COMPANY, 1929 – 1932

Colors: green, yellow, and some crystal

Periodically, rarer pieces of Indiana's Lorain skyrocket in price. Usually that means several collectors are searching for the same piece at about the same time. Collectors are starting to buy green Lorain because of price and availability. Green is less expensive and more easily found. A few pieces are found in crystal, but I am not sure a set is possible. A few items could augment your colored wares, however.

Yellow Lorain, much-admired by early collectors, is in short supply today. When you do locate it, you almost certainly will have to settle for mould roughness on the seams of the pieces. If you are determined about totally mint condition glassware, then you should focus on some other non-Indiana pattern.

Having bought and sold several collections of Lorain over the years, certain conclusions evolve. First, you should buy any cereal bowls you can find. Inspect inner rims closely; they chip and flake. The 8" deep berry is the rarest piece. Most collectors only want one, but they often wait years to find it. Dinner plates are almost as scarce as cereals, but scratches are standard for these. After all, these were every day dishes. Have you looked at your daily dishes for scratches recently? Few people know how to polish these scratches away, now; so, if the plates are reasonably priced or you are planning on using them, scratches may be acceptable. Oval vegetable bowls are uncommon in all colors. Saucers are harder to track down than cups because of mould roughness and wear and tear on them over the years. Collecting has turned upside-down. Dealers used to decline to buy saucers unless there were cups with them. Today, many of these once ignored saucers are eagerly bought even without cups. There are several patterns of Depression glass where saucers are more difficult to find than cups, and this is one of them.

Some crystal snack trays are found with fired-on colored borders of red, yellow, green, and blue. This tray is made from the platter mould that had a ring added for a cup. These trimmed in yellow or green do not seem to be offered at any price. Collectors of yellow or green used to add these to their sets. Crystal cups are found trimmed in the four colors to match the snack trays; but sometimes, they are just crystal, lacking the trim.

New collectors, please note that the white and green avocado-colored sherbets (which have an open lace border) are a mid-1950s (or later) issue made by Anchor Hocking. They were sold to florists for small floral arrangements and many are found with a tacky, clay-like substance in the bottom that was used to secure flowers. Recently someone also reported these were an Indiana Glass product. The more research we do, the more we find out about wares starting with one company and being subsequently made by others. However, several of these have been found with Anchor Hocking paper stickers, a practice of theirs in the late 1950s and early 1960s.

We have had a couple of letters regarding goblets with a basket design like that of Lorain. These are probably an early Tiffin product. If you want to use them with Lorain, do so. There is also a heavy Hazel-Atlas green goblet similar in shape to Colonial Block that has a basket etching. Basket designs were prolific in the 1920s and 1930s. There are no Lorain goblets per se; so, if you want goblets, then mix these with your set. These are known in the trade as "go-with" items.

LORAN

	Crystal, Green	Yellow
2 ▸ Bowl, 6", cereal	60.00	95.00
1 ▸ Bowl, 7¼", salad	65.00	95.00
10 ▸ Bowl, 8", deep berry	140.00	210.00
16 ▸ Bowl, 9¾", oval vegetable	55.00	60.00
4 ▸ Creamer, footed	20.00	25.00
11 ▸ Cup	12.00	14.00
13 ▸ Plate, 5½", sherbet	9.00	11.00
Plate, 7¾", salad	14.00	14.00
15 ▸ Plate, 8⅜", luncheon	20.00	25.00
6 ▸ Plate, 10¼", dinner	55.00	75.00
3 ▸ Platter, 11½"	30.00	45.00
9 ▸ Relish, 8", 4-part	23.00	38.00
12 ▸ Saucer	4.50	6.00
8 ▸ Sherbet, footed	25.00	30.00
14 ▸ Snack tray, crystal/trim	35.00	
5 ▸ Sugar, footed	20.00	25.00
7 ▸ Tumbler, 4¾", 9 ounce, footed	26.00	30.00

LOTUS, PATTERN #1921, WESTMORELAND GLASS COMPANY, 1921 – 1980

Colors: amber, amethyst, black, blue, crystal, green, milk, pink, red, and various applied color trims; satinized colors

Lotus, pattern #1921, like Westmoreland's English Hobnail, was in production off and on for over 60 years. Numerous companies had their own versions of a Lotus design on their glassware and china during this era. We've met at least one collector for anything with a lotus flower or name. Pictures of her collection were impressive.

We searched and purchased every different piece and color of Westmoreland's Lotus we could find over a ten year period. After our last photo session, we decided to eliminate pieces not being used in decorating our home. We packed three boxes of Lotus for sale and took it to our next show. We had less than a box left at show's end. Colors and shapes attracted buyers, some of whom even had to ask what that pattern was. They were captivated with these fascinating flower shaped pieces just as Cathy had been when she first noticed it. The longevity of the pattern should have clued us to its appeal. One piece was all most admirers wanted, but some bought multiples.

Purportedly, candles with a domed foot are more recently made than those with the foot flattened which is an indication of an earlier mould. Red is a newer color and most of it tends to be amberina (yellow tint in the red) which is just fine with collectors of amberina glass, but upsets some collectors of red.

Rarely seen pieces of Lotus include a lamp, tumbler, cologne bottle, and puff box, although most colognes found are of later manufacture. They are still desirable. The elusive tumbler is crystal with a colored petal foot. The only one we have seen had a green foot.

	Satinized Colors, Amber, Crystal, White	Blue, Green, Pink	Cased colors
Bowl, 6", lily (flat mayonnaise)	15.00	25.00	40.00
5 ▶ Bowl, 9", cupped	50.00	85.00	110.00
Bowl, 11", belled	60.00	95.00	125.00
Bowl, oval vegetable	45.00	85.00	110.00
3 ▶ Candle, 4", single	20.00	35.00	40.00
9 ▶ Candle, 9" high, twist stem	55.00	75.00	100.00
10 ▶ Candle, triple	40.00	55.00	
16 ▶ Candy jar w/lid, ½ pound	65.00	100.00	135.00
Coaster	12.00	15.00	20.00
Cologne, ½ ounce	85.00	110.00	145.00
22 ▶ Comport, 2½", mint, twist stem	30.00		
Comport, 6½", honey	20.00	30.00	45.00
14 ▶ Comport, 5" high, twist stem	30.00	40.00	50.00
17 ▶ Comport, 8½" high, twist stem	58.00	88.00	110.00
7 ▶ Creamer	22.00	30.00	40.00

	Satinized Colors, Amber, Crystal, White	Blue, Green, Pink	Cased colors
19 ▶ Lamp	195.00	295.00	
23 ▶ Lamp with metal rod	35.00		
21 ▶ Mayonnaise, 4", ftd., flared rim	15.00	25.00	30.00
1 ▶ Mayonnaise, 5", footed, bell rim	27.50	52.50	72.50
2 ▶ Plate, 6", mayonnaise	8.00	12.00	15.00
15 ▶ Plate, 8½", salad	10.00	35.00	40.00
Plate, 8¾", mayonnaise	12.50	17.50	22.50
6 ▶ Plate, 13", flared	35.00	50.00	65.00
11 ▶ Puff box, 5", w/cover	110.00	145.00	
12 ▶ Salt, individual	15.00	20.00	25.00
18 ▶ Shaker	30.00	45.00	
4 ▶ Sherbet, tulip bell	22.00	35.00	40.00
8 ▶ Sugar	22.00	30.00	40.00
13 ▶ Tray, lemon, 6", handle	30.00	43.00	53.00
20 ▶ Tumbler, 10 ounce		50.00	

LUCY, #895 PADEN CITY GLASS COMPANY, c. 1935

Colors: crystal, amber, Cheriglo, Royal Blue, Ruby

Paden City's Lucy was first listed in a 1935 trade journal according to Jerry Barnett who wrote a Paden City book in 1978. We see amber and crystal, the latter usually with an etching. Ruby and Royal Blue are the colors making collectors drool, but you should see eyes light up when Cheriglo (pink) appears. We have only found some footed bowls in pink, but other pieces should turn up. Cheriglo seems to be the rarest color and is priced with the Ruby and Royal Blue due to its scarcity. One of the first pieces we bought was a crystal center handled bowl with an etching and silver overlay around the etch. Today, we still haven't found a name for that etch.

There is a double candle that stands 5⅛" high and is almost 6" wide which belongs to this line, according to the recent consensus. It has been identified with several different patterns over the years which may have been the intent of Paden City.

	Amber Crystal	Pink/Ruby Royal Blue		Amber Crystal	Pink/Ruby Royal Blue
Bowl, 6¾"	8.00	18.00	9 ▸ Compote, 2⅞", cheese	9.50	17.50
2 ▸ Bowl, 9", 2-hdld.	30.00	67.50	Compote, 5", low foot	30.00	65.00
4 ▸ Bowl, 9½", ftd., crimped	45.00	95.00	Compote, 7", high ft.	25.00	50.00
3 ▸ Bowl, 9½", ftd.	40.00	90.00	Gravy, 5"x7¼"	35.00	60.00
1 ▸ Bowl, 9¾", center hdld.	35.00	75.00	Ice tub, 5⅝"	50.00	90.00
6 ▸ Bowl, 9⅞", flared	30.00	67.50	8 ▸ Mayonnaise, 3⅞" w/liner	30.00	55.00
Bowl, 10", 3-ftd., crimped	45.00	95.00	Plate, 6¼"	8.00	16.00
7 ▸ Bowl, 11½", 3-ftd.	40.00	90.00	Plate, 10½", cracker	17.50	37.50
5 ▸ Cake salver, 11¾" x 2⅛" high	45.00	90.00	Plate, 13¾", 2-hdld.	25.00	50.00
Candlestick, 5"	40.00		Relish 10¾"x7¼", 3-part	45.00	90.00
Candlestick, 5⅛", double	35.00	65.00	Server, 10⅝", center hdld.	35.00	65.00

Colors: green, pink, amber, crystal, and "Madonna" blue (See Reproduction Section.)

Madrid was one of the easiest found and most collected Depression glass patterns in the early 1970s. Blue was prized foremost although green and amber were found more regularly. You could not visit a show without seeing it on dealers' tables. Today, you rarely see a piece of the old, soft "Madonna" blue Madrid. It has all vanished into collections. What you see outside of shows from malls to the internet are blue reproductions. New collectors are avoiding the blue today since so little of the old is available. Green was never reproduced but is not found with regularity, so it is difficult to gather a large green set. Amber, however, is still very available in today's marketplace, and is still being collected even though there have been tons of the newer amber Madrid dumped on the market since 1976. Prices have remained inexpensive on all but the rare pieces, so if you like amber colored ware, this pattern may be for you.

Madrid has been subject of discussion and cussing since 1976 when the Federal Glass Company reintroduced this pattern for the Bicentennial under a new name "Recollection" glassware. Many companies resurrected wares from past lines during this period, not just Federal. Each piece of this reissued Federal ware was embossed '76 in the design. The flaw, here, was that it was remade in an amber color comparable to the original which caused concern with collectors of the older amber Madrid. Collectors were informed about the products, and many purchased these sets presuming they would someday be collectible as Bicentennial products. Unfortunately, Indiana Glass bought the Madrid moulds when Federal went out of business, removed the '76 date and made crystal and amber without the '76 mark. The older crystal butter was selling for several hundred dollars and the new one sold for $2.99. Prices nose-dived. Next, they made pink; and even though it was a lighter pink than the original, prices dipped in the collectibles market for the old pink. Later, Indiana made blue; it was a brighter, harsher blue than the beautiful, soft blue of the original Madrid; still, it had a detrimental effect on the prices of the 1930s blue. All pieces made in pink have now been made in several shades of blue and teal. All original blue pieces are priced in our listings and if you find something not priced, then it is new. Today, that is all water under the bridge and knowledgeable collectors are now buying the beautiful older Madrid with confidence at Depression glass shows.

I keep noticing the later-made, lightly colored pink Madrid sugar and creamers with high prices at flea markets and antique malls. Originally, there were no pink sugars and creamers made. Check my list for pieces made in pink. If no price is listed, then it was not made in the 1930s. (See the new pink in the Reproduction Section in the back.)

The rarely seen Madrid gravy boats and platters have usually been found in Iowa. They must have been premiums for some product sold there.

Mint condition sugar lids in any color Madrid are a treasure. Footed tumblers are harder to find than flat ones, with juice tumblers making a surge in price. Amber footed shakers are harder to find than flat ones. Footed shakers are the only style you can find in blue. Any heavy, flat shakers you spot are new.

The wooden Lazy Susan is like the Georgian one pictured on page 92 only with Madrid inserts. Those Madrid inserts have seen a big jump in price in the last two years.

MADRID

	Amber	Pink	Green	Blue
6 ▸ Ashtray, 6", square	450.00		450.00	
26 ▸ Bowl, 4¾", cream soup	15.00			
Bowl, 5", sauce	9.00	10.00	9.00	30.00
16 ▸ Bowl, 7", soup	16.00		16.00	
9 ▸ Bowl, 8", salad	14.00		17.50	50.00
Bowl, 9⅜", large berry	20.00	20.00		
21 ▸ Bowl, 9½", deep salad	35.00			
2 ▸ Bowl, 10", oval veg.	20.00	15.00	22.50	40.00
*Bowl, 11", low console	14.00	12.00		
10 ▸ Butter dish w/lid	72.50		90.00	
Butter dish bottom	25.00		40.00	
Butter dish top	47.50		50.00	
18 ▸ *Candlesticks, pr., 2¼"	22.00	20.00		
Cookie jar w/lid	50.00	30.00		
3 ▸ Creamer, footed	10.00		12.50	20.00
4 ▸ Cup	7.00	9.00	9.00	16.00
20 ▸ Gravy boat	1,000.00			
19 ▸ Gravy platter	1,000.00			
11 ▸ Hot dish coaster	120.00		100.00	
Hot dish coaster w/indent	120.00		100.00	
12 ▸ Jam dish, 7"	27.50		20.00	40.00
25 ▸ Jello mold, 2⅛", tall	10.00			
Pitcher, 5½", 36 oz., juice	42.00			
**Pitcher, 8", sq., 60 oz.	50.00	35.00	140.00	195.00

	Amber	Pink	Green	Blue
Pitcher, 8½", 80 oz.	60.00		200.00	
23 ▸ Pitcher, 8½", 80 oz., ice lip	60.00		225.00	
13 ▸ Plate, 6", sherbet	4.00	3.50	4.00	8.00
Plate, 7½", salad	9.00	9.00	9.00	22.00
8 ▸ Plate, 8⅞", luncheon	9.00	7.00	9.00	18.00
Plate, 10½", dinner	68.00		55.00	80.00
22 ▸ Plate, 10½", grill	9.50		20.00	
Plate, 10¼", relish	15.00	14.00	16.00	
Plate, 11¼", round cake	20.00	12.00		
17 ▸ Platter, 11½", oval	18.00	14.00	16.00	24.00
Salt/pepper, 3½", footed, pair	125.00		110.00	165.00
Salt/pepper, 3½", flat, pair	50.00		65.00	
5 ▸ Saucer	3.00	5.00	5.00	10.00
1 ▸ Sherbet, two styles	7.00		11.00	17.50
15 ▸ Sugar	7.00		14.00	15.00
14 ▸ Sugar cover	50.00		60.00	225.00
Tumbler, 3⅞", 5 oz.	15.00		32.00	42.00
7 ▸ Tumbler, 4¼", 9 oz.	16.00	17.00	20.00	35.00
24 ▸ Tumbler, 5½", 12 oz., 2 styles	20.00		30.00	55.00
Tumbler, 4", 5 oz., footed	45.00		40.00	
Tumbler, 5½", 10 oz., footed	30.00		45.00	
Wooden Lazy Susan, cold cuts coasters	1,225.00			

* Iridescent priced slightly higher   ** Crystal $150.00

Colors: crystal, pink; some green, ruby, and iridized

If you find a piece of Manhattan that does not match the measurements in the list below, then you may have a piece of Anchor Hocking's newer line, Park Avenue. You can see this more recent pattern and listings for it in our book *Anchor Hocking's Fire-King & More, Second Edition.*

Park Avenue was introduced by Anchor Hocking in 1987 to "re-create the Glamour Era of 1938 when Anchor Hocking first introduced a classic" according to the Inspiration '87 catalog issued by the company. Anchor Hocking went to the trouble to preserve the integrity of their older glassware, however. None of the pieces in this line are precisely like the old Manhattan. They are only similar and Manhattan was never made in blue as this line has been. Some collectors of Manhattan bought this new pattern to augment their Manhattan or for use. One Park Avenue piece is generating a problem. A Park Avenue martini glass has been designed for the beverage market which is so similar to the old comport that it took us a while to figure out a difference that can easily be seen. The old comport has four wafers on the stem while the new one has five. That is not much difference, but it was only made in crystal to our knowledge.

Comport price hikes in Manhattan can be directly attributed to margarita and/or martini drinkers. These were intended for candy or mints at inception, but you cannot persuade an avid drinker that these were not designed for mixed drinks as the new Park Avenue piece is.

Manhattan's collectibility has not been affected by the making of Park Avenue; however, the new line has caused some chaos with Manhattan cereal bowls. The older 5¼" cereals are rarely seen, particularly in mint condition; Park Avenue line lists a small bowl at 6" and the height is a hair over 2" The original cereal only measures 1¹⁵⁄₁₆" high. You need an accurate ruler to check this. Once you have seen the new, it will be easily recognized because that silly ¹⁄₁₆" looks so much bigger that you'll wonder why you were worried. Be particularly cautious if the bowl is mint as old ones rarely are. Manhattan cereals do not have handles. The handled berry measures 5⅜". I mention the measurements because there is an immense price difference. In fact, the reason the 5⅜" handled berry has increased in price so much is from people selling them as cereals to uninformed customers.

Pink Manhattan cups, saucers, and dinner plates do exist, but are rarely found. The saucer/sherbet plates of Manhattan are like many of Hocking's saucers; they have no cup ring. The juice pitcher has been found in Royal Ruby and four or five large pitchers have been seen in Jade-ite.

Manhattan sherbets have a beaded bottom like the tumblers, but the center insert to the relish tray does not have these beads, but vertical ribs. Sherbets are often "misplaced" as center inserts. Other relish tray inserts can be found in crystal, pink, and Royal Ruby, but the center insert is always crystal on these relish trays.

Manhattan is one pattern that is bolstered by the many look-alike pieces that can be added to it. Some collectors buy Hazel-Atlas shakers to use with Manhattan since they are round rather than the original squared ones that Hocking made. There are additional pieces including the candy in the listing. One piece that is often labeled Manhattan is the "eared" flat piece shown at right. It may come from an older ware that Manhattan was designed from, but it is not a Hocking piece from the late 1930s.

MANHATTAN

	Crystal	Pink
1 ▸ *Ashtray, 4", round	9.00	
10 ▸ Ashtray, 4½", square	14.00	
7 ▸ Bowl, 4½", sauce, closed handles	9.00	
11 ▸ Bowl, 5⅜", berry w/closed handles	18.00	20.00
Bowl, 5¼", cereal, no handles	110.00	225.00
Bowl, 7½", large berry	22.00	
3 ▸ Bowl, 8", closed handles	25.00	28.00
Bowl, 9", salad	30.00	
Bowl, 9½", fruit, open handle	35.00	45.00
12 ▸ Candlesticks, 4½", square, pair	18.00	
Candy dish, 3 legs, 6¼"		15.00
**Candy dish and cover	37.50	
Coaster, 3½"	15.00	
Comport, 5¾"	35.00	42.00
21 ▸ Creamer, oval	11.00	15.00
16 ▸ Cup	16.00	295.00
8 ▸ ‡‡Pitcher, 24 ounce	35.00	75.00

	Crystal	Pink
13 ▸ Pitcher, 80 ounce, tilted	48.00	70.00
17 ▸ Plate, 6", sherbet or saucer	5.00	75.00
20 ▸ Plate, 8½", salad	17.00	
14 ▸ Plate, 10¼", dinner	20.00	250.00
Plate, 14", sandwich	28.00	
18 ▸ Relish tray, 14", 5-part	20.00	
5 ▸ Relish tray, 14", with inserts	75.00	85.00
2 ▸ Relish tray, center	10.00	14.00
6 ▸ ‡Relish tray insert	5.50	9.00
Salt & pepper, 2", square, pair	30.00	50.00
17 ▸ Saucer/sherbet plate	5.00	75.00
4 ▸ Sherbet	12.50	18.00
15 ▸ Sugar, oval	11.00	15.00
9 ▸ §Tumbler, 10 ounce, footed	18.00	25.00
19 ▸ Vase, 8"	25.00	
**Wine, 3½"	6.00	

*Add for Hocking $15.00; add for others $12.50 **Look-Alike
‡Ruby $5.00   ‡‡Ruby $695.00   §Green or iridized $20.00

MAYA, LINE #221, PADEN CITY GLASS COMPANY, Late 1930s – 1951; CANTON GLASS COMPANY, 1950s

Colors: crystal, light blue, red

Please note that Maya (#221) pieces can be distinguished from Largo (#220) by the thistle (ball) design. That same intriguing pointed thistle/ball element is designed into the knobs of the candy and butter dishes as well as the center handled server. The cheese dish with its plain rim top seems to be the most sought piece of Maya to own.

Maya's sugars and creamers materialize even less than those of Largo. Sugar and creamer collectors also prize them. They are flat and not four-footed like those of Largo. We have finally found a pair, but they didn't make it to the Maya photography box in time.

The Maya candy is flat rather than footed like Largo's.

Cuttings and etchings can be found on Maya's light blue and crystal. Red Maya is generally found plain.

	Crystal	Colors			Crystal	Colors
Bowl, 7", flared rim	18.00	35.00	8 ▸	Comport, 6½" x 10", plain rim, pedestal	32.50	75.00
3 ▸ Bowl, 9½", flared, tri-footed	30.00	60.00		Creamer, flat	20.00	55.00
Bowl, 11⅝", 3½" deep, tri-footed, flared rim	35.00	80.00		Mayonnaise, tri-footed	15.00	40.00
2 ▸ Bowl, 12¾", 4¾" deep, tri-footed, flat rim	35.00	80.00	6 ▸	Mayonnaise, tri-footed, crimped	20.00	45.00
				Plate, 6⅝"	8.00	15.00
Cake plate, pedestal	35.00	80.00		Plate, 7", mayonnaise	10.00	20.00
Candleholder	30.00	55.00		Sugar, flat	20.00	55.00
▸ Candy, footed w/lid, 3-part	42.50	145.00	4 ▸	Tray, 13¾", tri-footed, serving	25.00	70.00
▸ Cheese dish w/lid	75.00	175.00		Tray, tab-handled	25.00	60.00
▸ Comport, fluted rim, pedestal	35.00	75.00				

MAYFAIR, FEDERAL GLASS COMPANY, 1934

Colors: crystal, amber, and green

Federal redesigned their Mayfair glass moulds into what finally became known as the Rosemary pattern becaus[e]
Hocking had copyrighted the name Mayfair several years before. We have shown only the old Federal Mayfair patter[n]
before it was altered. You will have to refer to a previous book to see the transitional period glassware made between th[e]
old Federal Mayfair pattern and what was to become known as the Rosemary pattern. These transitional pieces hav[e]
arching in the bottom of each piece rather than the waffle design, and there is no waffling between the top arches. If yo[u]
turn to the Rosemary (page 197) for reference, you will see that the design under the arches is entirely plain. Collector[s]
regard the transitional pieces a part of Federal Mayfair rather than Rosemary and that is why they are priced here.

Federal's Mayfair was an extremely limited production (before limited productions were the fashion of selling mer[-]
chandise). Maybe that is a hint that you ought to start looking at Mayfair as another possible set to collect. Amber an[d]
crystal are the colors that can be collected (in the true pattern form). Amber cream soups have been found in small num[-]
bers and platters in even fewer. Federal's crystal Mayfair can be collected as a set and it will be reasonably priced whe[n]
and if you find it. We had a letter about a large set of eight selling for less than $100.00 on the Internet. Green can on[ly]
be bought in transitional and the prices here are for that style and not truly Mayfair.

Generally, you will find several pieces of Mayfair together, rather than a piece here and there. You can get a quick sta[rt]
to a collection that way. We used to see sets here in Florida, but in recent years, it has been sets of amber Rosemar[y]
instead.

		Transitional					Transitional		
		Green	Amber	Crystal			Green	Amber	Cryst[al]
6 ▸	Bowl, 5", sauce	12.00	9.00	6.50		Plate, 9½", dinner	15.00	16.00	12.00
	Bowl, 5", cream soup	25.00	22.00	15.00		Plate, 9½", grill	15.00	18.00	8.50
2 ▸	Bowl, 6", cereal	25.00	18.00	10.00	9 ▸	Platter, 12", oval	40.00	30.00	20.00
3 ▸	Bowl, 10", oval vegetable	40.00	30.00	18.00	8 ▸	Saucer	4.00	4.00	2.50
5 ▸	Creamer, footed	20.00	13.00	10.50	4 ▸	Sugar, footed	20.00	13.00	11.00
7 ▸	Cup	12.00	10.00	5.00	1 ▸	Tumbler, 4½", 9 ounce	40.00	35.00	18.00
	Plate, 6¾", salad	9.00	7.00	4.50					

MAYFAIR, "OPEN ROSE," LINE NO. 2000, HOCKING GLASS COMPANY, 1931 – 1937

Colors: ice blue, pink; some green, yellow, and crystal (See Reproduction Section.)

Hocking's Mayfair is likely the most popular Depression glass pattern in the country, due somewhat to its major distribution throughout the1930s. Many families still have pieces left in their possession. The cookie jar is one the most recognized pieces of Depression glass. Cookie jars were premiums with "bought" cookies and soaps. (Remember, this was during a time when people still made their own cookies and soap at home!) Buying them, you received the container as a bonus. Over the years, more than any other item we have been asked if we have a spare Mayfair cookie jar lid for sale. They were used and the lids were damaged or broken. Unfortunately, lids are rarely offered for sale by themselves. We have always suggested that customers buy a complete cookie and use the old bottom for some other purpose that doesn't need a lid. Blue tops are even more difficult to find than pink as their distribution was more limited than those of pink. We should note that the Mayfair cookie jar has been reproduced, so check the Reproduction section (page 249) for information on these.

Pink Mayfair has a large selection of pieces. There are numerous stems and tumblers possible. A setting for four with all the serving pieces is costly. However, if you do not buy everything made, you can put a small set together for about the same money as most other patterns. Price depends upon how many diverse stems or tumblers you wish as well as whether you want a sugar lid or the elusive three-footed bowl.

A 1937 distributor's catalog lists ten items of No. 2000 line pink Mayfair "exquisitely etched (painted) with rose floral design" that could be bought by the dozen for under $1.75. The least expensive item was the cereal bowl for 37¢ a dozen. The most expensive was the 80-ounce pitcher for $1.75 a dozen. This illustrates how inexpensively a shop owner could obtain this ware to help sell his product or lure people to his store. This particular advertised ware was satinized using camphoric acid and hand painted. Most collectors ignored satin pieces in the past; but a few, today, try to find mint examples of this hand-painted pattern. Note the deep fruit bowl pictured which has been satinized and a hole drilled in it to use as a lamp or ceiling fixture.

All yellow Mayfair is rare and all green except for five large pieces which sell in the ballpark of $50.00. You can tell rarity by the prices listed. If no price is listed, it means that that piece has not been found in that color. Pieces in these colors are rarely seen and very expensive in mint condition; most collectors strive to own only one piece of yellow or green. A set would be a dream on today's market, but a nightmare to find and a fortune to own. However, we've met four collector/owners of yellow Mayfair sets.

A few crystal creamers and a covered sugar are known but few collectors search for crystal Mayfair. The juice pitcher, shakers, butter bottom (only), and the divided platter are commonly found. The platter is often found in a fitted metal holder and a reader wrote that the divided platter was given as a premium with the purchase of coffee or spices in late 1930s. Although some crystal items are rare, with little demand, they do not presently command big prices.

Blue Mayfair is strikingly beautiful and regrettably, nearly all gone from the market today. In the early days of collecting, a large set could be assembled. Today, you might have to settle for a smaller set as few accumulations are being found in basements or attics. Now, already collected sets being sold have to satisfy demands and that seldom happens. Thus, availability of blue Mayfair in the market is currently preventing its rise in price. This blue has always been my favorite color. We collected a set, but sold it in 1972 to have money to buy other patterns for the first book. That was a pure financial risk which we don't regret today, as we work on this seventeenth book. However, then it was a heart-wrenching decision!

There are a few fine points about Mayfair that you need to know. Some stems have a plain foot while others are rayed. The 10" celery measures 11½" handle to handle and the 9" one measures 10½" handle to handle. (The measurements in this book do not include handles unless so noted.) Footed iced teas vary in height. Some teas have a short stem above the foot and others have almost none. This causes the heights to vary to some extent. It is just a mould variation, which may account for capacity differences, too. Note under measurements on page 2 the listings of tumblers that I have taken from old Hocking catalogs.

	*Pink	Blue	Green	Yellow
Bowl, 5", cream soup	60.00			
Bowl, 5½", cereal	30.00	55.00	85.00	85.00
Bowl, 7", vegetable	30.00	60.00	175.00	175.00
Bowl, 9", 3⅛ high, 3-leg console	5,995.00		5,500.00	
Bowl, 9½", oval vegetable	38.00	80.00	125.00	135.00
Bowl, 10", vegetable	33.00	75.00		135.00

*Frosted or satin finish items slightly lower if paint is worn or missing

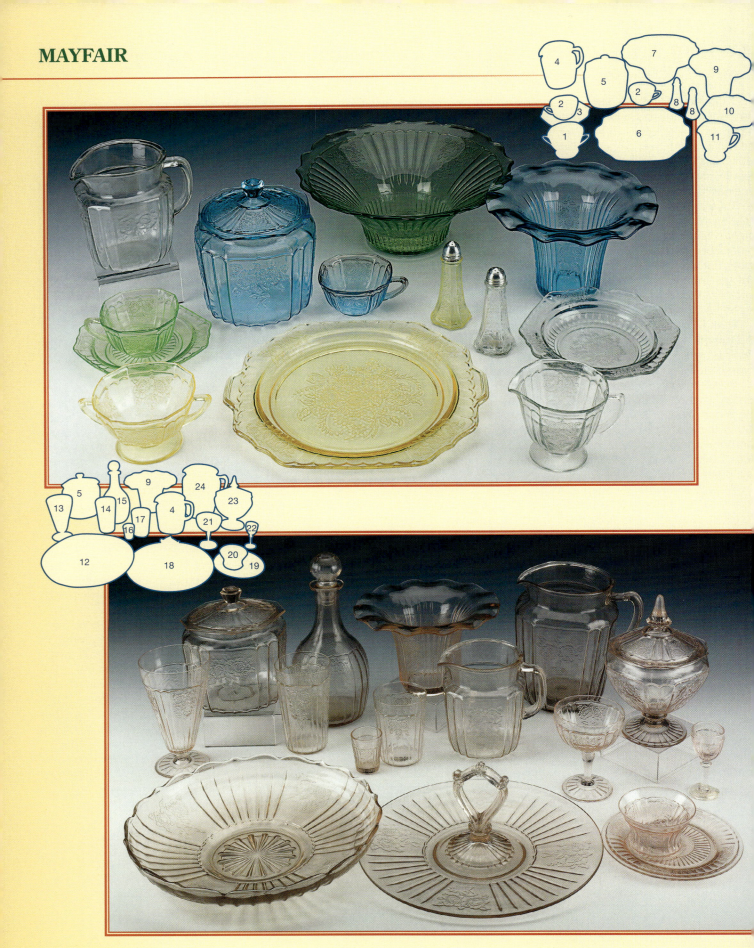

	*Pink	Blue	Green	Yellow
Bowl, 10", same covered	145.00	150.00		995.00
12 ▸ Bowl, 11¾", low flat	65.00	72.50	50.00	225.00
7 ▸ Bowl, 12", deep, scalloped fruit	65.00	105.00	50.00	255.00
Butter dish and cover or 7", covered vegetable	78.00	325.00	1,300.00	1,300.00
10 ▸ Butter bottom with indent				300.00
Butter dish top	45.00	265.00	1,150.00	1,150.00
Cake plate, 10", footed	33.00	70.00	150.00	
23 ▸ Candy dish and cover	60.00	310.00	595.00	495.00
Celery dish, 9", divided			195.00	195.00
Celery dish, 10"	48.00	75.00	125.00	125.00
Celery dish, 10", divided	295.00	70.00		
5 ▸ Cookie jar and lid	60.00	295.00	595.00	895.00
11 ▸ Creamer, footed	32.50	85.00	225.00	225.00
2 ▸ Cup	18.00	60.00	155.00	155.00
Cup, round	350.00			
15 ▸ Decanter and stopper, 32 ounce	215.00			
22 ▸ Goblet, 3¾", 1 ounce cordial	1,200.00		995.00	
Goblet, 4⅛", 2½ ounce	995.00		950.00	
Goblet, 4", 3 ounce, cocktail	115.00		395.00	
Goblet, 4½", 3 ounce, wine	120.00		450.00	
Goblet, 5¼", 4½ ounce, claret	1,000.00		950.00	
Goblet, 5¾", 9 ounce, water	80.00		495.00	
Goblet, 7¼", 9 ounce, thin	325.00	275.00		
4 ▸ ** Pitcher, 6", 37 ounce	65.00	165.00	600.00	600.00
Pitcher, 8", 60 ounce	70.00	195.00	650.00	500.00
24 ▸ Pitcher, 8½", 80 ounce	125.00	240.00	800.00	850.00
3 ▸ Plate, 5¾" (often substituted as saucer)	15.00	23.00	90.00	90.00
Plate, 6½", round sherbet	15.00			
19 ▸ Plate, 6½", round, off-center indent	25.00	30.00	135.00	135.00
Plate, 8½", luncheon	28.00	55.00	85.00	85.00
Plate, 9½", dinner	60.00	85.00	150.00	150.00
Plate, 9½", grill	50.00	55.00	85.00	125.00
Plate, 11½", handled grill				125.00
Plate, 12", cake w/handles	45.00	75.00	40.00	
6 ▸ Plate, 12" with tab handles				150.00
‡ Platter, 12", oval, open handles	35.00	75.00	175.00	
Platter, 12½", oval, 8" wide, closed handles			235.00	235.00
Relish, 8⅜", 4-part	38.00	75.00	165.00	165.00
Relish, 8⅜", non-partitioned	225.00		295.00	295.00
8 ▸ ‡‡ Salt and pepper, flat, pair	65.00	325.00	1,100.00	875.00
Salt and pepper, footed	10,000.00			
18 ▸ Sandwich server, center handle	55.00	85.00	40.00	135.00
Saucer (cup ring)	32.00			150.00
3 ▸ Saucer (same as 5¾" plate)	14.00	25.00	90.00	90.00
20 ▸ Sherbet, 2¼", flat	210.00	195.00		
Sherbet, 3", footed	17.50			
21 ▸ Sherbet, 4¾", footed	85.00	90.00	165.00	165.00
1 ▸ Sugar, footed	32.50	85.00	210.00	210.00
Sugar lid	2,995.00		1,500.00	1,500.00
Tumbler, 3½", 5 ounce, juice	55.00	125.00		
17 ▸ Tumbler, 4¼", 9 ounce, water	38.00	115.00		
Tumbler, 4¾", 11 ounce, water	225.00	155.00	225.00	225.00
14 ▸ Tumbler, 5¼", 13½ ounce, iced tea	70.00	275.00		
Tumbler, 3¼", 3 ounce, footed, juice	95.00			
Tumbler, 5¼", 10 ounce, footed	46.00	160.00		225.00
13 ▸ Tumbler, 6½", 15 ounce, footed, iced tea	45.00	300.00	300.00	
9 ▸ Vase (sweet pea)	195.00	125.00	325.00	
16 ▸ Whiskey, 2¼", 1½ ounce (w/split stem)	130.00			

*Frosted or satin finish items slightly lower if paint is worn or missing   ** Crystal $15.00
‡ Divided Crystal $12.50   ‡‡ Crystal $17.50 pair — Beware reproductions.

MISS AMERICA (DIAMOND PATTERN), LINE #2500, HOCKING GLASS COMPANY, 1935 – 1938

Colors: crystal, pink; some green, ice blue, Jade-ite, and Royal Ruby (See Reproduction Section.)

The Miss America name brings more to mind than Depression glass; however it is another one of the glass beauties that is sought at shows and is often seen at flea markets. Novices need to know to check the points carefully on the design, particularly the pointed edges. Often, the tip of these points is missing, particularly underneath where most damage occurs. You need also to inspect candy jar knobs to make certain they have not been glued back on.

Miss America tumblers and stems all have three parallel lines before going into a plain glass rim. Westmoreland's English Hobnail pattern, which was made earlier and continued production past that of Miss America, is often incorrectly labeled as Miss America. Check the differences by reading the comparison of the two under that pattern on page 71. Because of marketing schemes promoting Hocking's inexpensive wares, Miss America exceeded English Hobnail's popularity with the public during the late 1930s. The last Miss America color made was Royal Ruby (c. 1938).

We have pictured a Royal Ruby set in the previous editions. This particular set went home with a factory worker and we later bought it from his heirs. A few pieces turn up occasionally in the market.

A reproduced butter dish surfaced in several colors in the late 1970s; but the red ones were an amberina red. No original red, blue, or green butter has been discovered and those you may find are reproductions. Additional reproductions have appeared in Miss America pattern since the early 1970s. Please refer to page 251 for a listing and facts regarding these aggravations. Today, informed collectors have learned how to tell old from new; so, it hardly causes a ripple in collector circles.

Some pieces of Miss America are found with metal lids. The relish (four-part dish) and cereal bowl are often found that way. These glass pieces were sold to some company who made lids to fit. They are not original factory lids. The cereal is the butter bottom; so, a metal lid on that does not make it a butter dish, although it could serve as such. The metal lid adds around $10 to the price of the cereal and not hundreds of dollars as some Internet sellers might have you believe.

Any time a glass pattern was made for several years, it will be possible to find pieces that deviate in size. In talking to former Anchor Hocking mould makers, I learned that moulds were "cut down" when they wore. Therefore, some pieces deviated a little each time the moulds were reworked and cut away to sharpen the design. If the mould were reworked several times, the sizes of a piece could vary up to $1/16$" or more.

There are two styles of Miss America shakers. Shakers that are fatter toward the foot are the best ones to buy, since that style has not been reproduced. Narrow, thinner bottomed reproduction shakers are everywhere. Read how to tell the difference on page 251.

A few odd-colored or flashed pieces of Miss America surface infrequently as well as a piece or two in Jade-ite. We have pictured some of these in previous editions. Flashed-on red, green, or amethyst are not plentiful enough to collect a set, but they make interesting additions to your collection when found.

		Crystal	Pink	Green	Royal Ruby
18 ▸	Bowl, 4½", berry			17.50	
17 ▸	Bowl, 6¼", cereal	11.00	30.00	20.00	
6 ▸	Bowl, 8", curved in at top	40.00	100.00		695.00
	Bowl, 8¾", straight, deep fruit	35.00	90.00		
7 ▸	Bowl, 10", oval vegetable	16.00	45.00		
	Bowl, 11", shallow				950.00
12 ▸	*Butter dish and cover	210.00	650.00		
	Butter dish bottom	10.00	30.00		
	Butter dish top	200.00	620.00		
1 ▸	Cake plate, 12", footed	28.00	65.00		
	Candy jar and cover, 11½"	65.00	150.00		
13 ▸	‡Celery dish, 10½", oblong	16.00	40.00		
2 ▸	Coaster, 5¾"	16.00	35.00		
20 ▸	Comport, 5"	17.50	35.00		
	Creamer, footed	11.00	23.00		250.00
14 ▸	Cup	9.00	23.00	15.00	325.00
	Goblet, 3¾", 3 oz., wine	22.00	120.00		325.00

		Crystal	Pink	Green	Royal Ruby
24 ▸	Goblet, 4¾", 5 oz., juice	25.00	115.00		325.00
	Goblet, 5½", 10 oz., water	18.00	57.50		295.00
	Pitcher, 8", 65 ounce	50.00	175.00		
	Pitcher, 8½", 65 ounce, w/ice lip	70.00	225.00		
3 ▸	**Plate, 5¾", sherbet	6.00	12.00	8.00	60.00
19 ▸	Plate, 6¾"			14.00	
4 ▸	Plate, 8½", salad	7.50	28.00		175.00
5 ▸	‡Plate, 10¼", dinner	16.00	42.00		
11 ▸	Plate, 10¼", grill	11.00	30.00		
	Platter, 12¼", oval	15.00	45.00		
21 ▸	Relish, 8¾", 4-part	11.00	22.50		
22 ▸	Relish, 11¾", round, divided, 5-part	25.00	6,750.00		
23 ▸	Salt and pepper, pair	35.00	67.50		
15 ▸	Saucer	3.00	8.00		75.00
16 ▸	**Sherbet	8.00	16.00		165.00
	Sugar	9.00	25.00		250.00
10 ▸	‡Tumbler, 4", 5 oz., juice	16.00	85.00		235.00
9 ▸	Tumbler, 4½", 10 oz., water	14.00	42.00	25.00	
8 ▸	Tumbler, 5¾", 14 oz., iced tea	28.00	120.00		

*Absolute mint price   **Also in Ice Blue $50.00   ‡Also in Ice Blue $225.00

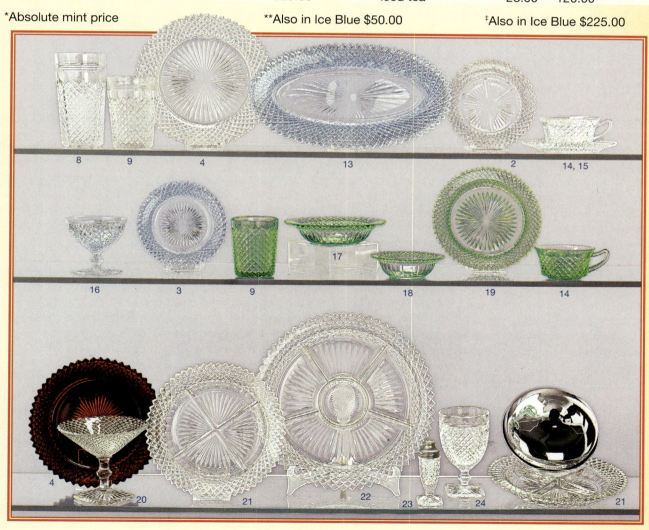

MODERNTONE, HAZEL-ATLAS GLASS COMPANY, 1934 – 1942; Late 1940s – Early 1950s

Colors: amethyst, cobalt blue; some crystal, pink, and Platonite fired-on colors

Moderntone is admired first for its rich colorings of blue and amethyst and for its down-to-earth style. It is more moderately priced today than many of its rival patterns made in cobalt or amethyst. It originally was priced about the same as those other patterns. In the 1930s, a 36-piece set of cobalt Moderntone could be bought for $1.69 plus freight costs for 24 pounds as long as you sent two or four coupons from flour. That was not difficult since baking was an everyday thing at that time. You need to remember that $1.69 was a goodly sum then, more than a day's wages for workers making 20 cents to a dollar a day.

Moderntone did not specifically make a tumbler for the set. Tumblers sold, today, as Moderntone were just marketed together with this pattern, but they were never sold as a component of the set. There are two unlike style tumblers that have been accepted for this set. Some water and juice tumblers are paneled and have a rayed bottom, while another juice is not paneled and has a plain bottom and is marked H over top A, the Hazel-Atlas trademark. Either tumbler is acceptable, but most collectors choose the circled, paneled one. All sizes of these tumblers are hard to find in cobalt or amethyst except for the water. Green, pink, or crystal tumblers were produced, but there is little demand for these except for the tiny shot glass that is also gathered by a growing crowd of collectors buying any shot glass that can be found.

The butter bottom and sugar were apparently marketed to another company who made metal tops. Lids appear with black, red, or blue knobs, but red materializes most often. No one knows which is original, so all colored knobs are accepted. By attaching a metal notched lid and adding a spoon, mustards were made from the handle-less custard. Speaking of that custard, there is a punch set being sold as Moderntone, which uses a Hazel-Atlas mixing bowl and either the plain, cobalt, roly-poly cups found with the Royal Lace toddy set or Moderntone custard cups. This was not Hazel-Atlas assembled; but some embrace it to "go-with" Moderntone. Our thinking is that you should at least have a set with the handle-less cups rather than roly-poly cups to be accepted as Moderntone.

In past editions, we have shown a boxed child's set with crystal Moderntone shot glasses in a metal holder that came with a Colonial Block creamer. (You can see a set in our new book on Hazel-Atlas.) These boxed children's sets sell in the $100.00 range. There are a few collectors chasing crystal Moderntone. It brings about half the price of amethyst. Flat soups are rare in any color except crystal. They are hard to find, but not in comparison to the colored ones. Today's collectors combine colors; so, crystal soups may become popular in place of the rarer and more costly colored ones.

Ruffled cream soups have surpassed the sandwich plates in price. Sandwich plates can be acquired, but finding one not heavily scraped or worn, is a problem. When you pick up a blue plate that looks white in the center from years of use, it is not a good indication for ownership. A collector gleefully related that she bought nearly a dozen of these sandwich trays on a table in a used furniture store for $18. We forgot to ask if for each or all.

The cheese dish remains the highest priced piece of Moderntone. This cheese dish is fundamentally a salad plate with a metal cover and wooden cutting board inside the lid. Evidently, the cutting boards were tossed and few are found today.

Green, crystal, and pink ashtrays are around, but there is limited demand for them by Moderntone collectors. Collectors of ashtrays are now appearing, so that could change. Blue ashtrays still command a hefty price for an ashtray.

Finding any Moderntone bowl without inner rim roughness (irr) is a difficult task. Bowls, themselves, are not rare; mint condition bowls are. Prices are for mint condition pieces. That is why bowls are so highly priced. Used, nicked, and bruised bowls are the norm and should be priced half or less.

Platonite Moderntone has been switched to the *Collectible Glassware from the 40s, 50s, 60s...* since it better fits the period covered by that book.

		Cobalt	Amethyst
	*Ashtray, 7¾", match holder in center	175.00	
9 ▸	Bowl, 4¾", cream soup	23.00	22.00
21 ▸	Bowl, 5", berry	29.00	25.00
15 ▸	Bowl, 5", cream soup, ruffled	65.00	
12 ▸	Bowl, 6½", cereal	97.50	75.00
1 ▸	Bowl, 7½", soup	165.00	100.00
16 ▸	Bowl, 8¾", large berry	55.00	40.00
	Butter dish with metal cover	110.00	
	Cheese dish, 7", with metal lid	350.00	
4 ▸	Creamer	13.50	11.00
7 ▸	Cup	12.00	10.00
3 ▸	Cup (handle-less) or custard	20.00	15.00
3 ▸	Plate, 5⅞", sherbet	6.00	5.00
	Plate, 6¾", salad	11.00	10.00

* Pink $50.00; green $75.00
** Pink or green $17.50

		Cobalt	Amethyst
17 ▸	Plate, 7¾", luncheon	12.00	11.00
6 ▸	Plate, 8⅞", dinner	17.00	13.00
18 ▸	Plate, 10½", sandwich	52.00	40.00
20 ▸	Platter, 11", oval	48.00	37.50
5 ▸	Platter, 12", oval	90.00	45.00
19 ▸	Salt and pepper, pair	45.00	40.00
8 ▸	Saucer	4.00	3.00
11 ▸	Sherbet	14.00	12.00
2 ▸	Sugar	13.50	10.00
	Sugar lid (metal)	37.50	
22 ▸	Tumbler, 5 ounce	75.00	40.00
10 ▸	Tumbler, 9 ounce	40.00	30.00
	Tumbler, 12 ounce	135.00	90.00
14 ▸	**Whiskey, 1½ ounce	42.00	

MONTICELLO, Later WAFFLE, #698, IMPERIAL GLASS COMPANY, c. 1920 – 1960s

Colors: crystal, Rubigold, milk, clambroth, teal

Monticello was introduced in the early 1920s in crystal and Rubigold which was Imperial's name for their marigold (iridescent) colored carnival glass.

Monticello was a successful pattern for Imperial. Over sixty pieces were produced in the forty plus years they were fabricated. We see mostly crystal pieces, but Carnival collectors search for the Rubigold.

Monticello was renamed Waffle by Imperial, which is what it was being called at markets in the late 1960s and 1970s when we first started buying glassware.

Imperial reissued an assortment of items from this line throughout their production years in whatever colors were foremost at that moment. So, it's to be expected you may find other, later colors than those listed above. I am pricing crystal only for now. Colors will add to the listed prices, with teal and clambroth bringing the most. Pricing for Rubigold will add up to double on choice items.

	Crystal		Crystal		Crystal		Crystal
4 ▸ Basket, 10"	22.00	Bowl, 8½", belled	17.50	Compote, 5¾", belled		5 ▸ Punch cup	8.00
Bonbon, 5½", 1 handle	12.00	Bowl, 8", lily (cupped)	40.00	rim	15.00	Relish, 8¼", divided	18.00
Bowl, 4½", finger	10.00	Bowl, 8", round veg.	25.00	1 ▸ Creamer	12.50	Salt & pepper w/glass	
Bowl, 4½", fruit, 2 styles	8.00	Bowl, 8", round	17.00	Cup	10.00	tops	20.00
Bowl, 5½", crème soup	12.50	Bowl, 8", shallow	17.00	Cuspidor	65.00	Saucer	4.00
2 ▸ Bowl, 5", lily	20.00	Bowl, 9", round	20.00	Mayo set, 3-piece	35.00	8 ▸ Sherbet	10.00
Bowl, 5", fruit	10.00	Bowl, 9", shallow	17.50	7 ▸ Pickle, 6", oval	17.00	Stem, cocktail	12.50
Bowl, 6½", belled	12.50	Bowl, 10", belled	25.00	Pitcher, 52 oz., ice lip	65.00	Stem, water	15.00
Bowl, 6", lily	22.50	Bowl, 10", shallow	25.00	Plate, 6", bread	5.00	3 ▸ Sugar, open	12.50
Bowl, 6", round	10.00	Bowl, 12", deep	30.00	Plate, 8", salad	9.00	Tidbit, 2-tier	
Bowl, 7½", square	17.50	Buffet set, 3-pc. (mayo,		Plate, 9", dinner	20.00	(7½" & 10½")	45.00
Bowl, 7½", belled	15.00	spoon, 16½" rnd. plate)	90.00	6 ▸ Plate, 10½", square	25.00	Tumbler, 9 oz., water	15.00
Bowl, 7", flower		Butter tub, 5½"	35.00	Plate, 12", round	35.00	Tumbler, 12 oz., tea	18.00
(w/flower grid)	45.00	Celery, 9", oval	20.00	Plate, 16", cupped	55.00	Vase, 6"	22.00
Bowl, 7", lily	30.00	Cheese dish and cover	75.00	Plate, 16½", round	55.00	Vase, 10½", flat	40.00
Bowl, 7", nappy	12.50	Coaster, 3¼"	8.00	Plate, 17", flat	55.00		
Bowl, 7", round	12.50	9 ▸ Compote, 5¼"	12.50	Punch bowl, belled rim	65.00		

MOONDROPS, NEW MARTINSVILLE GLASS COMPANY, 1932 – 1940

Colors: amber, pink, green, cobalt, ice blue, red, amethyst, crystal, dark green, light green, Jadite, smoke, and black

Moondrops collectors find red and cobalt blue the irresistible colors; and these are selling briskly on Internet auctions, though red is dominant. Every antique dealer knows that red and cobalt blue glass are expensive colors; consequently, prices are generally high even if they are not acquainted with Moondrops. On the other hand, other colors escape unappreciated; you might find a deal if you know what to look for. Pink and light green cordial prices have amazed me on Internet auctions. So, other colors of Moondrops are being accredited in collecting circles but only in rarely found items. Amber was the least chosen color for a while, but even that is changing, not only in Moondrops, but in other patterns as well. Perfume bottles, powder jars, mugs, gravy boats, and triple candlesticks are symbols of more elegant glassware than most of its contemporaries, so those items are swept off the market quickly. Bud vases, decanters, and popular "rocket style" stems present an arcade of unusual pieces. A number of "rocket style" decanters are pictured in my *Very Rare Glassware* series.

Apparently, New Martinsville or one of their glass distributors mismatched some of their Moondrops colors. I have found two powder jars with crystal bottoms and cobalt blue tops in antique malls in Ohio and Florida, so they were probably marketed that way. I have seen one complete cobalt perfume. They can be found that way, too.

The butter has to have a matching glass top to obtain the prices listed below. The metal top with a bird finial found on some butter bottoms sells for about $35.00. However, a metal top with a fan finial sells for approximately $65.00. Those fan finials are not easily found. Collectors have a propensity to want glass tops on their butter dishes.

	Blue, Red	Other colors			Blue, Red	Other colors
Ashtray	30.00	17.00	8 ▸	Bowl, 12", round, 3-footed console	75.00	32.00
5 ▸ Bowl, 4¼", cream soup	100.00	40.00	22 ▸	Bowl, 13", console with "wings"	120.00	42.00
Bowl, 5¼", berry	25.00	12.00		Butter dish and cover	485.00	250.00
Bowl, 5⅜", 3-footed, tab handle	75.00	40.00		Butter dish bottom	60.00	40.00
6 ▸ Bowl, 6¾", soup	95.00			Butter dish top (glass)	425.00	210.00
Bowl, 7½", pickle	35.00	20.00		Candles, 2", ruffled, pair	45.00	25.00
Bowl, 8⅜", footed, concave top	45.00	25.00	7 ▸	Candles, 4½", sherbet style, pair	30.00	20.00
Bowl, 8½", 3-footed divided relish	40.00	20.00		Candlesticks, 5", ruffled, pair	40.00	25.00
9 ▸ Bowl, 9½", 3-legged, ruffled	70.00		3 ▸	Candlesticks, 5", "wings," pair	110.00	60.00
Bowl, 9¾", oval vegetable	75.00	45.00		Candlesticks, 5¼", triple light, pair	150.00	95.00
6 ▸ Bowl, 9¾", covered casserole	250.00	145.00		Candlesticks, 8½", metal stem, pair	50.00	33.00
7 ▸ Bowl, 9¾", handled, oval	52.50	36.00		Candy dish, 8", ruffled	40.00	20.00
Bowl, 11", boat-shaped celery	32.00	23.00		Cocktail shaker with or without		
				handle, metal top	60.00	35.00

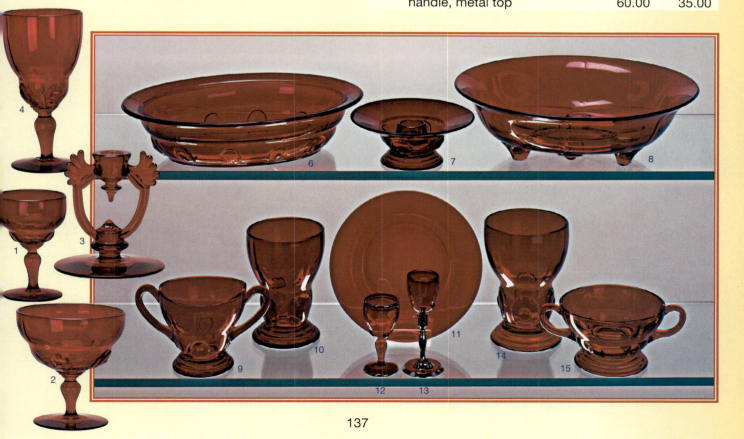

MOONDROPS

	Blue, Red	Other colors
Comport, 4"	27.50	18.00
Comport, 11½"	95.00	55.00
Creamer, 2¾", miniature	18.00	11.00
Creamer, 3¾", regular	18.00	10.00
17 ▸ Cup	18.00	8.00
Decanter, 7¾", small	67.50	38.00
Decanter, 8½", medium	70.00	42.00
Decanter, 11¼", large	100.00	50.00
Decanter, 10¼", "rocket"	595.00	425.00
12 ▸ Goblet, 2⅞", ¾ oz., cordial	35.00	23.00
13 ▸ Goblet, 3¾", ¾ oz., metal stem cordial	65.00	40.00
1 ▸ Goblet, 4", 4 oz., cocktail	18.00	12.00
20 ▸ Goblet, 4½", 3 oz., wine	22.00	18.00
21 ▸ Goblet, 4¾", "rocket," wine	65.00	35.00
Goblet, 4¾", 5 oz.	24.00	15.00
4 ▸ Goblet, 5¾" 8 oz.	40.00	20.00
Goblet, 5⅛", 3 oz., metal stem, wine	16.00	11.00
5 ▸ Goblet, 5½", 4 oz., metal stem, wine	20.00	11.00
Goblet, 6¼", 9 oz., metal stem, water	23.00	16.00
Goblet, 6½", 9 oz.	60.00	30.00
2 ▸ Grapefruit, 4¾"	60.00	35.00
Gravy boat	195.00	100.00
Mayonnaise, 5¼"	65.00	40.00
Mug, 5⅛", 12 oz.	40.00	23.00
Perfume bottle, "rocket"	295.00	195.00
Pitcher, 6⅞", 22 oz., small	165.00	90.00
Pitcher, 8⅛", 32 oz., medium	185.00	115.00
Pitcher, 8", 50 oz., large, with lip	195.00	115.00
19 ▸ Pitcher, 8⅛", 53 oz., large, no lip	185.00	125.00
Plate, 5⅞"	11.00	8.00
11 ▸ Plate, 6⅛", sherbet	8.00	5.00

	Blue, Red	Other colors
Plate, 6", round, off-center sherbet indent	12.00	9.00
Plate, 7⅛", salad	14.00	10.00
Plate, 8½", luncheon	17.00	12.00
Plate, 9½", dinner	30.00	20.00
23 ▸ Plate, 14", round sandwich	45.00	20.00
Plate, 14", 2-handled sandwich	60.00	25.00
Platter, 12", oval	45.00	25.00
28 ▸ Powder jar, 3-footed	295.00	160.00
18 ▸ Saucer	4.00	3.00
Sherbet, 2⅝"	16.00	11.00
Sherbet, 4½"	28.00	16.00
Sugar, 2¾"	15.00	10.00
9 ▸ Sugar, 3½"	18.00	11.00
Tumbler, 2¾", 2 oz., shot	22.00	10.00
Tumbler, 2¾", 2 oz., handled shot	16.00	12.00
24 ▸ Tumbler, 3¼", 3 oz., footed juice	18.00	11.00
26 ▸ Tumbler, 3⅝", 5 oz.	18.00	10.00
Tumbler, 4⅜", 7 oz.	16.00	10.00
25 ▸ Tumbler, 4⅜", 8 oz.	22.00	11.00
Tumbler, 4⅞", 9 oz., handled	30.00	16.00
10 ▸ Tumbler, 4⅞", 9 oz.	20.00	15.00
14 ▸ Tumbler, 5⅛", 12 oz.	30.00	14.00
Tray, 7½", for mini sugar/creamer	37.50	19.00
Vase, 7¾", flat, ruffled top	60.00	57.00
Vase, 8½", "rocket" bud	295.00	195.00
Vase, 9¼", "rocket" style	295.00	165.00

MT. PLEASANT, "DOUBLE SHIELD," L. E. SMITH GLASS COMPANY, 1920s – 1934

Colors: black amethyst, amethyst, cobalt blue, crystal, pink, green, and white

Mt. Pleasant prices are faintly edging higher. Mt. Pleasant is frequently purchased for its cobalt blue or black colors more than for its being Depression glass.

Not long ago, we had to explain that "double shield" on a piece to a novice collector, because you cannot really see that moulded "double shield" design in our photos without carefully scrutinizing them. Sorry about that.

The picture on page 140 portrays a few of many decorations found on Mt. Pleasant. Plain pieces of white Mt. Pleasant are known, but the black stripes and handles dress it up from stark white. Crystal with striped colors is rarely seen. We have had sporadic reports of pink and green items, generally, sugars and creamers. We recently found a green double candle for our second candlestick book due out next year. A few pink plates turn up intermittently, suggesting a luncheon set might be possible.

Cobalt blue Mt. Pleasant was prevalent in the Midwest and in northern New York. We understand that Mt. Pleasant was displayed and awarded as premiums in hardware stores in those areas. Black overshadows in other areas of the country, but we have not found anyone who can provide evidence that color was also used as premiums.

Pieces of both colors are found with a platinum (silver) band. This decorated band disappears with use. Prices should be less for worn decorated wares. This brings to mind the fact that gold and silver trims deteriorate quickly with dishwasher/lemon soap exposure; so, you should hand wash items with those trims in non-lemon soap, if you care to preserve them.

Speaking of that, we should warn that one collector was dismayed to learn her decal vanished when she put one such decorated item in the dishwasher. In the 40s and 50s you could buy hand-applied decals at the five and dime. You wet the backing and applied the decal to anything you wished to adorn. However, submerging the piece in water again would cause the decal to flake and peel. That is what occurred with the canister jar this woman had put in her dishwasher. You can generally feel or see the edges of this type of temporary decal. Wash it with care and little water to preserve it.

	Pink, Green	Amethyst, Black, Cobalt			Pink, Green	Amethyst, Black, Cobalt
Bonbon, 7", rolled-up, handle	16.00	23.00		Leaf, 11¼"		30.00
Bowl, 4" opening, rose	18.00	24.00	12 ▸ Mayonnaise, 5½", 3-footed, 2 styles	18.00	25.00
▸ Bowl, 4⅞", square, footed, fruit	13.00	22.00		Mint, 6", center handle	16.00	25.00
▸ Bowl, 6", 2-handle, square	13.00	18.00		Plate, 7", 2-handle, scalloped	9.00	14.00
Bowl, 7", 3-footed, rolled out edge	16.00	25.00	9 ▸ Plate, 8", scalloped or square	10.00	12.00
Bowl, 8", scalloped, 2-handle	19.00	35.00		Plate, 8", 2-handle	11.00	20.00
▸ Bowl, 8", square, 2-handle	19.00	35.00	18 ▸ Plate 8¼", square w/indent for cup		16.00
▸ Bowl, 9", scalloped, 1¾" deep, ftd.		35.00		Plate, 9", grill		20.00
Bowl, 9¼", square, footed, fruit	19.00	35.00	5 ▸ Plate, 10½", cake, 2-handle, 2 styles	16.00	25.00
▸ Bowl, 10", scalloped fruit		45.00		Plate, 10½", 1¼" high, cake		45.00
Bowl, 10", 2-handle turned-up edge		35.00		Plate, 12", 2-handle	20.00	35.00
Cake plate, 10½", footed, 1¼" high		37.50		Salt and pepper, 2 styles	25.00	45.00
▸ Candlestick, single, pair	20.00	30.00		Sandwich server, center-handle		35.00
▸ Candlestick, double, pair	50.00	45.00	3 ▸ Saucer	2.50	6.00
▸ Creamer	18.00	17.00	8 ▸ Sherbet, 2 styles	10.00	15.00
▸ Cup (waffle-like crystal)	4.50		1 ▸ Sugar	18.00	17.00
▸ Cup	9.50	13.00		Tumbler, footed		25.00
▸ Leaf, 8"		15.00		Vase, 7¼"		33.00

MT. VERNON, Later WASHINGTON, #699, IMPERIAL GLASS COMPANY, Late 1920s – 1970s

Colors: crystal, red, green, yellow, milk, iridized, red flash

Mt. Vernon is an Imperial pattern often confused with Tiffin's Williamsburg made in the late 20s in crystal and in the 50s in colors. Williamsburg has a rayed star bottom design; Mt. Vernon's pattern shows a waffle type design in the bottom and extended tip handle protrusions.

Mt. Vernon was a popular, prismatic design, attuned to its modernistic roots that can be found today due to its being made as late as the 1970s. The design adopts square, round, triangle, cubist forms, along with innovative handle protrusions and waferred stems.

The name celebrated the George Washington bicentennial event that was a big hoopla in 1932. Mt. Vernon appears mostly in crystal; limited pieces in color surface from time to time, as is usual with Imperial moulds that were occasionally reintroduced throughout production. Cobalt and emerald items were made in a last ditch effort to raise money to "save Imperial Glass." You should be able to gather a set now without breaking the bank. The tall celery becomes a pickle by adding a lid; both styles of sugar bowls, the 5¾" two-handled bowl, and the 69-ounce pitcher were sold with or without lids.

	Crystal
► Bonbon, 5¾", one-handle	10.00
Bowl, 5", finger	12.00
Bowl, 5¾", two-handle	10.00
Bowl, 5¾", two-handle, w/cover	22.00
► Bowl, 6", lily	15.00
Bowl, 7", lily	18.00
Bowl, 8", lily	20.00
Bowl, 10", console	25.00
Bowl, 10", 3-footed	25.00
Bowl, punch	35.00
Butter dish, 5"	30.00
Butter dish, dome top	35.00
Butter tub, 5"	15.00
Candlestick, 9"	30.00
Celery, 10½"	22.00
► Compote, 5½"	$
Compote, tri-stem knob	30.00
Creamer, individual	8.00

	Crystal
Creamer, large	12.00
Cup, coffee	8.00
Cup, custard or punch	5.00
Decanter	38.00
11 ► Oil bottle, 6 ounce	30.00
Pickle jar, w/cover	35.00
Pickle, tall, two-handle	22.00
Pickle, 6", two-handle	15.00
Pitcher top, for 69 ounce	35.00
Pitcher, 54 ounce	35.00
Pitcher, 69 ounce, straight edge	40.00
5 ► Plate, 6", bread and butter	5.00
8 ► Plate, 8", round	10.00
12 ► Plate, 8", square	10.00
6 ► Plate, 11", cake	20.00
Plate, 12½", sandwich	25.00
Plate, 13¼", torte	27.00
Plate, 18", liner for punch	28.00

	Crystal
Saucer	2.00
Shaker, pair	22.00
Spooner	22.00
3 ► Stem, 2 ounce, wine	12.00
4 ► Stem, 3 ounce, cocktail	8.00
2 ► Stem, 5 ounce, sherbet	6.00
9 ► Stem, 9 ounce, water goblet	10.00
Sugar lid, for individual	8.00
Sugar lid, for large	12.00
Sugar, individual	8.00
7 ► Sugar, large	12.00
Syrup, 8½ ounce, w/cover	45.00
Tidbit, two-tier	30.00
Tumbler, 7 ounce, old fashioned	10.00
Tumbler, 9 ounce, water	8.00
Tumbler, 12 ounce, iced tea	12.50
Vase, 10", orange bowl	50.00

NEW CENTURY, HAZEL-ATLAS GLASS COMPANY, 1930 – 1935

Colors: green; some crystal, pink, amethyst, and cobalt

New Century has lured collectors for years, but not in the hordes of other Hazel-Atlas's patterns like Royal Lace o the Florentines. Sets of green are the only color that can be snared. A few pieces are found in crystal, but not enough t assemble a set. Crystal prices are similar to green due to rarity. Were there more crystal available, the prices might lea over green. You can find crystal powder jars made from a sugar lid set atop a sherbet. The knob of the sherbet usuall has decorative glass marbles or beads attached by a wire. One of these is pictured on the next page. I believe thes were a legitimate product of the 30s. Realize powder jars in most patterns could be assembled in this fashion.

Pink, cobalt, and amethyst New Century have only appeared as water sets and an occasional cup or saucer. Onl flat tumblers have been found in those colors. Incidentally, in doing some other research, we found that most beverag sets in the 30s were priced around a $1.00 and were often used as sales promotions. If you shopped the sales at a stor you could buy a seven-piece beverage set for 79 cents to a $1.00.

This classic "pillow optic" design, as it was promoted in a Butler Brothers catalog, has definitely withstood the test of time

New Century bowls are all but impossible to find. We haven't found a 4½" berry bowl in years. That Butler Brother ad mentioned above sold them for 37¢ a dozen, and they were packed three dozen to a carton. So, where are the today? The larger 8" bowl can be found occasionally, but that too, is missing from many collections.

Casseroles, whiskeys, wines, decanters, grill plates, and cocktails are rarely seen. Cream soups are showing u but not regularly enough for all collectors. As in Adam, the casserole bottom is more challenging to find than the top We recently examined a badly chipped casserole lid sticker priced for $10.00. When returned to the display table, th seller informed us that any Depression glass lid was worth way more than that. Well, not really; and particularly n badly damaged ones.

	Green, Crystal	Pink, Cobalt, Amethyst
5 ▸ Ashtray/coaster, 5⅜"	30.00	
1 ▸ Bowl, 4½", berry	35.00	
12 ▸ Bowl, 4¾", cream soup	22.00	
21 ▸ Bowl, 8", large berry	30.00	
2 ▸ Bowl, 9", covered casserole	95.00	
Butter dish and cover	65.00	
13 ▸ Cup	10.00	20.00
25 ▸ Creamer	15.00	
3 ▸ Decanter and stopper	75.00	

	Green, Crystal	Pink, Cobalt, Amethyst
Goblet, 2½ ounce, wine	35.00	
20 ▸ Goblet, 3¼ ounce, cocktail	35.00	
19 ▸ Pitcher, 7¾", 60 ounce, with or without ice lip	35.00	35.00
15 ▸ Pitcher, 8", 80 ounce, with or without ice lip	40.00	42.00
Plate, 6", sherbet	8.00	
7 ▸ Plate, 7⅛", breakfast	12.00	
Plate, 8½", salad	14.00	
8 ▸ Plate, 10", dinner	20.00	
23 ▸ Plate, 10", grill	20.00	
6 ▸ Platter, 11", oval	25.00	
22 ▸ Salt and pepper, pair	42.00	
14 ▸ Saucer	3.00	7.50
11 ▸ Sherbet, 3"	12.00	
24 ▸ Sugar	10.00	
10 ▸ Sugar cover	18.00	
17 ▸ Tumbler, 3½", 5 ounce	18.00	15.00
Tumbler, 3½", 8 ounce	30.00	
18 ▸ Tumbler, 4¼", 9 ounce	22.00	18.00
9 ▸ Tumbler, 5", 10 ounce	22.00	22.00
16 ▸ Tumbler, 5¼", 12 ounce	33.00	30.00
Tumbler, 4", 5 ounce, footed	22.00	
4 ▸ Tumbler, 4⅞", 9 ounce, footed	25.00	
Whiskey, 2½", 1½ ounce	22.00	

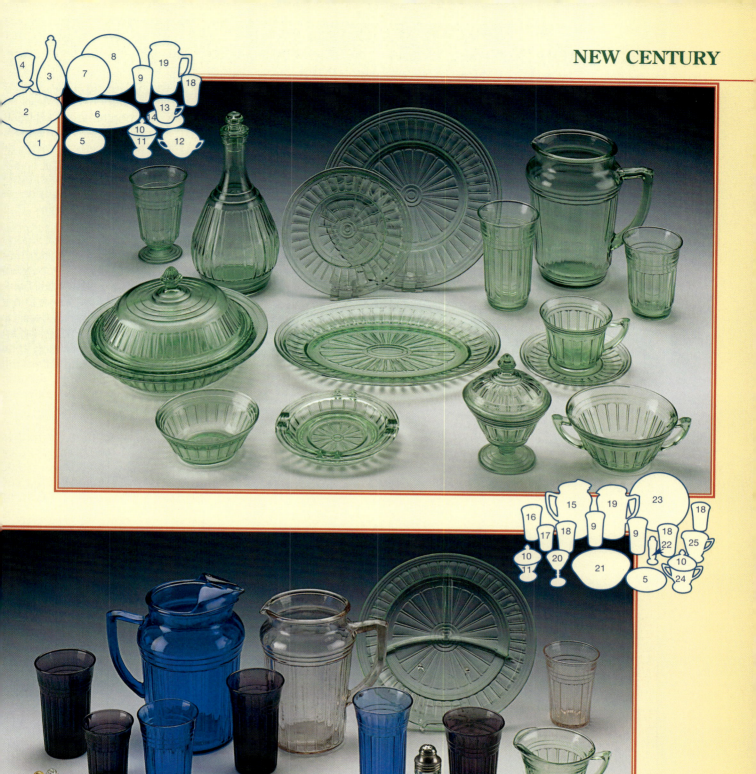

NEWPORT, "HAIRPIN," HAZEL-ATLAS GLASS COMPANY, 1936 – 1940

Colors: cobalt blue, amethyst; some pink, Platonite white, and fired-on colors

Collectors prefer cobalt blue in this Newport pattern. Let's face it; cobalt blue is popular in any pattern. We rarely see amethyst for sale in quantity, but last weekend at a market in Florida, there were four dealers offering large sets for sale. While checking prices, one dealer approached and told us he could give us a great deal if interested. Many pieces were chipped and worn; so he offered it at half his prices. Were we going to be using it, that might have been tempting, but not for resale.

Little pink Newport is found today; so the 32-piece set shown below that was free but with collect shipping charges may not have increased seed sales much. That seems like a good deal today for only ordering a $4.00 packet of seeds. That was a lot of seeds and $4.00 was a tidy sum in those days. We usually see berry bowls and little else in pink. Price pink ½ to ⅓ of amethyst prices due to less demand.

Cereal bowls, sandwich plates, large berry bowls, and tumblers are nowhere to be found unless an old collection is sold into the market. I finally bought a large amethyst berry bowl; but I have not replaced the large cobalt berry bowl that was shattered years ago in an accidentally dropped box of Newport. We have seen several since, but not at an acceptable price for storage in photography. One dealer offered one with a large piece missing for only $20.00. He probably still has it.

There is a ⁵⁄₁₆" difference between a so-called "larger" dinner and a luncheon plate. At any rate, the larger dinner plate measures 8¹³⁄₁₆" while the luncheon plate measures 8½"; and, truthfully, after that first flurry over the difference being pointed out, few collectors really seem to care. It was originally mentioned because of problems mail order and Internet dealers were having. ("The plates you sent me were smaller than the ones I have!") The only official listing I have states plates of 6", 8½", and 11½". However, after obtaining these plates, I found actual measurements quite different as you can see from our listing below. One of the problems with catalog measurements is that they are not always accurate. Measurements were rounded off or sometimes seem to have been estimated instead of measured. Maybe the difference occurred when worn moulds were "cut down" to re-use.

		Cobalt	Amethyst			Cobalt	Amethyst
2 ▸	Bowl, 4¾", berry	20.00	17.00	12 ▸ Plate, 8¹³⁄₁₆", dinner		30.00	22.00
1 ▸	Bowl, 4¾", cream soup	20.00	24.00	Plate, 11¾", sandwich		45.00	40.00
4 ▸	Bowl, 5¼", cereal	45.00	35.00	7 ▸ Platter, 11¾", oval		52.00	43.00
8 ▸	Bowl, 8¼", large berry	45.00	45.00	11 ▸ Salt and pepper		45.00	40.00
10 ▸	Cup	14.00	12.00	9 ▸ Saucer		5.00	5.00
13 ▸	Creamer	17.50	14.00	15 ▸ Sherbet		15.00	15.00
16 ▸	Plate, 5⅞", sherbet	8.00	8.00	14 ▸ Sugar		17.50	16.00
5 ▸	Plate, 8½", luncheon	16.00	15.00	6 ▸ Tumbler, 4½", 9 ounce		45.00	40.00

No. 200. LADIES! Here's a gorgeous Dinner Set in that new shade Rose Crystal. It consists of 6 large plates, 6 small plates, 6 cups, 6 saucers, 6 cereal dishes, vegetable dish and large meat platter. This sparkling set, more beautiful than you can imagine, is given for one $4.00 order of Seeds. Weight 22 lbs. Sent Express collect.

32-Piece Rose Crystal Dinner Set

NEWPORT, NEW MARTINSVILLE, c. 1930s

Colors: cobalt, red, green, amber

In our travels, the New Martinsville Newport we stumble upon is usually priced out of sight due to the colors in which it's seen and not necessarily for any knowledge of the pattern or manufacturer. We have added amber to the listing after finding a small luncheon set in that color. Amber is not as avidly sought today; so, the prices below need to be reduced to half of those listed to be more in line with its selling price.

Red seems to be the color most sold in Florida although some green occasionally appears. We have not run into cobalt, but several collectors tell us this pattern is equally charming in that color.

		Amber, Green	Red, Cobalt
4 ▸	Creamer	15.00	25.00
1 ▸	Cup	15.00	25.00
5 ▸	Plate, 8"	12.00	15.00
2 ▸	Saucer	4.00	5.00
3 ▸	Sugar	15.00	25.00
6 ▸	Tray, 13½", round torte	35.00	45.00

NORMANDIE, "BOUQUET AND LATTICE," FEDERAL GLASS COMPANY, 1933 – 1940

Colors: Sunburst (iridescent), amber, pink, and crystal

Normandie was called "Bouquet and Lattice" by early carnival collectors before the real designation was found. Pink is the most preferred color as many Depression glass collectors bought anything pink when they started and that tendency stuck through the years. Normandie was also made in amber and Sunburst (iridescent), which you will have a better chance of collecting today. The color was achieved by spraying color over crystal and re-firing the wares. We once met a collector who told us he bought every piece of Sunburst Normandie he found, so someday when it was hard to find, he would be rich. He came to a show a few years ago and said he had over 5,000 pieces and was fast on his way to poverty instead of riches.

Always buy any hard-to-find Normandie items first, or anytime you see them. That recommendation goes for collecting any pattern. Rarer, harder-to-find items have always increased in price quicker than commonly found ones. Also, if you unearth pieces of pink, grab them; someone will want them.

Pink Normandie has been difficult to get for several years; but amber tumblers, sugar lids, and dinner-sized plates have scant supply too. Should you discover any pink Normandie tumblers, prices are rapidly approaching those of American Sweetheart. Normandie collectors are extremely outnumbered by those buying American Sweetheart; so, it is probably a good thing there are fewer searching for Normandie tumblers. Were they available to buy, pink Normandie pitchers are reasonably priced when compared to those in American Sweetheart; but most are already tucked away in collections. We have owned at least 20 American Sweetheart pitchers, but only two pink Normandie to put those supplies into perspective.

All rare pieces of pink continue to rise in value, but we have not seen a pink dinner plate for sale in over four years. Actually, we have only owned one of those in over 30 years of selling.

Some Sunburst Normandie is still being offered for sale at Depression glass shows. There are enough buyers to raise the prices slightly. Sunburst is realistically priced in comparison to pink and amber and is actually rather striking in this particular pattern.

A console bowl and candlesticks (frequently found with sets of Sunburst Normandie) are Madrid pattern. These were sold about the same time as Normandie and evidently sold with Normandie in sets. That does not make them Normandie; they are still Madrid. The design on the glass determines pattern, not the color. We have received a letter and an e-mail recently asking why we did not list Normandie candles as they had bought candles in a set of iridescent Normandie. See Madrid for pricing of these console sets.

	Amber	Pink	Iridescent
8 ▸ Bowl, 5", berry	9.00	9.00	5.00
3 ▸ *Bowl, 6½", cereal	25.00	60.00	10.00
Bowl, 8½", large berry	30.00	40.00	15.00
Bowl, 10", oval vegetable	20.00	45.00	18.00
6 ▸ Creamer, footed	8.00	14.00	10.00
7 ▸ Cup	7.50	9.00	6.00
12 ▸ Pitcher, 8", 80 ounce	85.00	215.00	
▸ Plate, 6", sherbet	4.50	7.00	3.00
Plate, 7¾", salad	11.00	15.00	
Plate, 9¼", luncheon	8.50	17.00	15.00
Plate, 11", dinner	33.00	150.00	11.50

	Amber	Pink	Iridescent
11 ▸ Plate, 11", grill	15.00	25.00	9.00
Platter, 11¾"	22.00	50.00	12.00
Salt and pepper, pair	50.00	100.00	
1 ▸ Saucer	2.00	3.00	2.00
7 ▸ Sherbet	6.50	11.00	6.00
10 ▸ Sugar	8.00	12.00	6.00
9 ▸ Sugar lid	105.00	210.00	
Tumbler, 4", 5 ounce, juice	28.00	95.00	
4 ▸ Tumbler, 4¼", 9 ounce, water	22.00	65.00	
Tumbler, 5", 12 ounce, iced tea	42.00	125.00	

*Mistaken by many as butter bottom

No. 610, "PYRAMID," INDIANA GLASS COMPANY, 1926 – 1932

Colors: green, pink, yellow, white, crystal, blue, or black in 1974 – 1975 by Tiara

"Pyramid," as Indiana's pattern No. 610 is called by collectors, has finally slowed its price ascent for the first time in years. Two reasons have caused this slow down. First, little of this deco looking pattern is being found in the market; and secondly, pricing heights have discouraged new admirers from seeking it. Art Deco devotees as well as Depression glass collectors have pushed prices for years, but supplies are needed to stimulate sales.

Mint condition "Pyramid" is bringing premium prices when it does appear. Chips do downgrade the price — even more on rare items. The prices below are for mint condition glassware; any with a "ding" or two should market for less. No. 610 was, and still is, easily damaged on its points. Be sure to examine all the ridged panels and corners on each piece. You will be amazed how often a chipped or cracked piece of "Pyramid" is offered as mint.

We haven't found much to buy save a pink beverage set, several years ago. There was a price of $500 firm for a set placed on two tumblers on a table at a flea market. When asked about the set, the owner produced a pitcher and two more tumblers making the set price a little more palpable. It was a pretty expensive price for a set of two, but not bad for a set of five. Sometimes you have to ask about prices.

You should know that Indiana made blue and black pieces of "Pyramid" for Tiara during the 1970s. You will see two sizes of black tumblers, blue and black berry bowls, small and large, and the four-part center-handled relish in either color. It was advertised as their Art Deco collection. If you like these colors, it is fine to buy them as a reissue from the original company. Just realize that they are not Depression era. Do not pay antique glass prices for them. That handled four-part relish is occasionally mistaken for Tea Room; but it is not.

The bona fide sugar/creamer stand (tray) has squared indentations on each side to fit the squared bottoms of the sugar and creamer. Stands were common in an assortment of patterns, but it takes one with square indentations for it to truly be "Pyramid."

Crystal pitchers and tumblers in "Pyramid" are priced higher than all but yellow, even though yellow ones are seen more often. There are so many collectors of yellow No. 610 that prices have kept steady. Ice buckets turn up often, even in yellow. However, it is the yellow lid to the ice bucket that is nearly unattainable. No lids have yet been found for any other colors.

"Pyramid" oval bowls and pickle dishes are intermittently confused because both measure 9½". The oval bowl has pointed edges; the pickle dish has rounded edges and is handled.

	Crystal	Pink	Green	Yellow
11 ▸ Bowl, 4¾", berry	20.00	25.00	25.00	40.00
8 ▸ Bowl, 8½", master berry	30.00	55.00	60.00	75.00
6 ▸ Bowl, 9½", oval	30.00	40.00	45.00	65.00
3 ▸ Bowl, 9½", pickle, 5¾" wide, handled	30.00	35.00	35.00	55.00
7 ▸ Creamer	20.00	35.00	30.00	40.00
Ice tub	125.00	135.00	125.00	225.00
Ice tub lid				700.00
5 ▸ Pitcher	495.00	395.00	265.00	595.00
1 ▸ Relish tray, 4-part, handle	35.00	60.00	65.00	67.50
9 ▸ Sugar	17.50	35.00	30.00	40.00
10 ▸ Tray for creamer and sugar	25.00	30.00	30.00	55.00
2 ▸ Tumbler, 8 ounce, footed, 2 styles	55.00	55.00	55.00	80.00
4 ▸ Tumbler, 11 ounce, footed	80.00	70.00	90.00	100.00

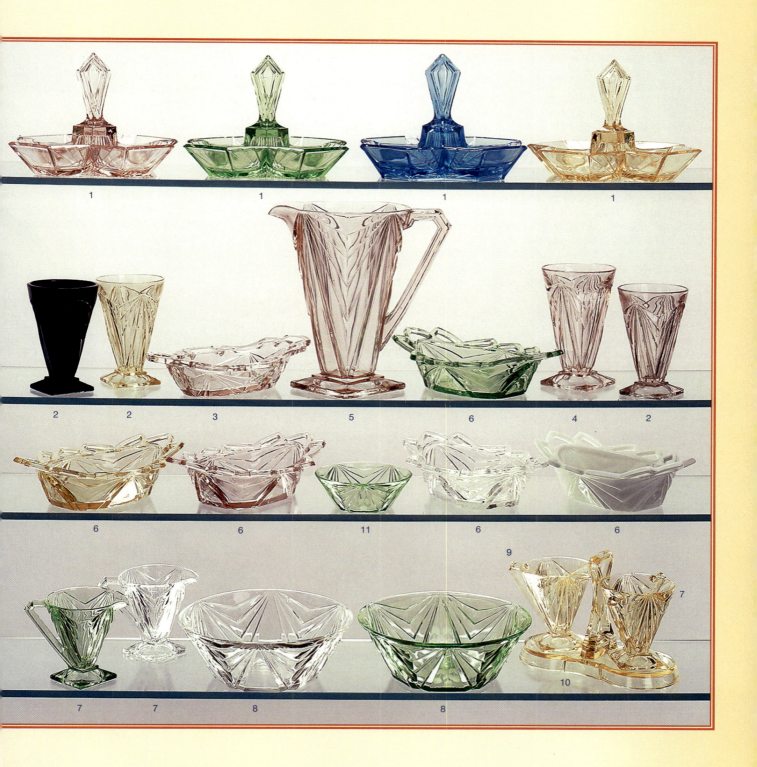

No. 612, "HORSESHOE," INDIANA GLASS COMPANY, 1930 – 1933

Colors: green, yellow, pink, and crystal

Indiana's pattern No. 612 has been called "Horseshoe" by collectors even though the design does not fit any form of horseshoe ever made. Prices have a propensity for scaring off new collectors for this beautiful pattern. If you honestly like something, even a piece or two can give you pleasure. You don't have to buy it all, just buy what you can afford — and enjoy!

The green "Horseshoe" butter dish rarely turns up, although tumblers, both flat and footed tea, grill plates (which not all collectors want), and pitchers are limited. We have been lucky enough to turn up two in the last year and both went galloping out of our booth at the first show displayed. The "Horseshoe" butter dish has always been highly priced. If you can find a first edition of this book, the butter dish was $90.00 in 1972. That was big money for a butter dish back then. There was a collector/dealer from southern Indiana who traveled every well known flea market and shop in a five state area looking for a butter top. He had a bottom and wanted a top. He bought another bottom from us explaining that way someone else wouldn't be searching for a top if they were to purchase our bottom.

No. 612 creates problems for collectors of yellow, also. There is no butter dish, and pitchers, grill plates, and footed iced tea are rarely seen. There are a few pieces found in crystal including creamer, sugar, and plates. Even that seemingly invisible grill plate has appeared in crystal. This grill in yellow or green is notorious for having inner rim roughness (irr) and most collectors will accept some roughness just to own it.

Platters come both plain in the center, or with the regular pattern. Be aware of scuffs on these. They were used.

Candy dishes only have the pattern on the top. The bottom is plain as you can see by the pink candy dish pictured. That candy is the only piece of "Horseshoe" that turns up in pink.

		Green	Yellow
	Bowl, 4½", berry	30.00	25.00
2 ▸	Bowl, 6½", cereal	32.00	35.00
	Bowl, 8½", vegetable	40.00	38.00
10 ▸	Bowl, 9½", large berry	50.00	50.00
	Bowl, 10½", oval vegetable	30.00	33.00
12 ▸	Butter dish and cover	895.00	
	Butter dish bottom	200.00	
	Butter dish top	650.00	
11 ▸	Candy in metal holder motif on lid	225.00	
	also, pink	235.00	
3 ▸	Creamer, footed	17.50	19.00
	Cup	11.00	12.00
	Pitcher, 8½", 64 ounce	350.00	395.00
	Plate, 6", sherbet	7.50	7.50

		Green	Yellow
	Plate, 8⅜", salad	13.00	11.00
	Plate, 9⅜", luncheon	14.00	17.00
4 ▸	Plate, 10⅜", grill	135.00	150.00
6 ▸	Plate, 11½", sandwich	30.00	28.00
	Platter, 10¾", oval	32.00	35.00
8 ▸	Relish, 3-part, footed	30.00	40.00
7 ▸	Saucer	4.00	4.00
1 ▸	Sherbet	16.00	20.00
9 ▸	Sugar, open	17.50	19.00
	Tumbler, 4¼", 9 ounce	185.00	
	Tumbler, 4¾", 12 ounce	195.00	
	Tumbler, 9 ounce, footed	32.00	32.00
5 ▸	Tumbler, 12 ounce, footed	175.00	195.00

No. 616, "VERNON," INDIANA GLASS COMPANY, 1930 – 1932

Colors: green, crystal, yellow

Over the years, No. 616 has given every photographer we have had a fit trying to capture this busy design so that it appears on the printed page. Light passes through it without picking up the design well. This one pattern is definitely better seen "in person" than viewed through a photographer's lens. Indiana's No. 616 pattern was labeled "Vernon" in homage to another glass author's spouse.

No. 616 was one of the first patterns we used as everyday dishes after purchasing most of a set in the late 60s. It was attractive; but we warn you from experience that there are rough mould lines protruding from the seams of the tumblers. This prickly problem comes from extra glass on the mould seam and not chips or flakes. After a cut lip or two from using the tumblers, this set was added to our sale box.

Crystal "Vernon" is still found today and some pieces are trimmed in platinum (silver). These decorated pieces seldom have worn platinum. Obviously, Indiana's process for attaching this border was superior to other companies whose platinum wore off easily.

The 11½" sandwich plate makes a great dinner or barbecue plate when grilling out. We used grill plates more than the luncheon plates for serving. Those 8" luncheon plates don't hold much food for big eaters. Do realize that sharp knives will damage glass rather easily.

Sets of yellow and green "Vernon" are not easy to finish, but there is even less green than yellow available. The green creamer and tumbler continue to elude us for photography.

		Green	Crystal	Yellow
7 ▸	Creamer, footed	28.00	12.00	28.00
2 ▸	Cup	16.00	10.00	16.00
1 ▸	Plate, 8", luncheon	10.00	6.00	10.00

		Green	Crystal	Yellow
6 ▸	Plate, 11½", sandwich	25.00	12.00	25.00
3 ▸	Saucer	4.00	2.00	4.00
4 ▸	Sugar, footed	28.00	11.00	20.00
5 ▸	Tumbler, 5", footed	45.00	20.00	45.00

No. 618, "PINEAPPLE & FLORAL," INDIANA GLASS COMPANY, 1932 – 1937

Colors: crystal, amber; some fired-on red, green, milk white; late 1960s, avocado; 1980s pink, cobalt blue, etc.

"Pineapple and Floral" is the only name anyone uses for this pattern that Indiana introduced as No. 618 in 1932. The diamond-shaped comports and 7" salad bowls were remade in the late 80s and early 90s in a multitude of colors and, unfortunately, in the original crystal. Most had sprayed-on colors, although the light pink was an excellent transparent color. ("Pineapple and Floral" was never originally made in pink.) Sadly, prices for older crystal comports and salads nose-dived as result and have never yet recovered. No other items have been reissued as of 2005. Amber and fired-on red are safe colors to collect since they were not remade.

"Pineapple and Floral" crystal sets (excluding comport and salad bowl) are not easily assembled; but it is not out of the question. Tumblers, cream soups, platters, and sherbets are the most worrisome pieces to find. As with most of Indiana's patterns, there is recurrent mould roughness on the seams. This roughness comes from excessive use and not missing glass. Always try to acquire the harder-to-find pieces first. This pattern is surprisingly attractive when several pieces are displayed together. Its luminous design often delights people who have not seen it displayed.

Two sizes of plates are found with an indented center ring. No tops have been discovered to fit either. The usual one seen is 11½" in diameter. The photographers have placed an amber cream soup on the one in the picture on page 153. It does not fit the ring which is much larger than the base of the soup. You may see these advertised as a servitor.

Amber No. 618 is not collected as often as the crystal since there is so little of it available. Only dinner plates have been found in light green. These are old and will glow under ultraviolet light.

The two-tier tidbit with a metal handle is not priced in my listings although they sell in the $25.00 to $30.00 range. Glass companies themselves seldom made tidbits. They can easily be assembled today if you can find the metal hardware. Many tidbits are a product of the early 70s when a dealer in St. Louis would make one from any pattern for $10.00 if you furnished the plates. He was prolific in making tidbits in patterns where tidbits never existed before 1970.

152

		Crystal	Amber, Red			Crystal	Amber, Red
9 ▸	Ashtray, 4½"	15.00			Plate, 11½", w/indentation	25.00	
	Bowl, 4¾", berry	22.00	18.00		Plate, 11½", sandwich	20.00	17.50
8 ▸	Bowl, 6", cereal	25.00	22.00	1 ▸	Platter, 11", closed handle	15.00	18.00
7 ▸	*Bowl, 7", salad	2.00	10.00	16 ▸	Platter, relish, 11½", divided	20.00	
9 ▸	Bowl, 10", oval vegetable	22.00	18.00	10 ▸	Saucer	4.00	4.00
3 ▸	*Comport, diamond-shaped	1.00	10.00	6 ▸	Sherbet, footed	15.00	18.00
7 ▸	Creamer, diamond-shaped	9.00	10.00	2 ▸	Sugar, diamond-shaped	9.00	10.00
5 ▸	Cream soup	22.00	22.00	13 ▸	Tidbit, 2-tier	35.00	
1 ▸	Cup	10.00	10.00	12 ▸	Tumbler, 4¼", 8 ounce	30.00	25.00
4 ▸	Plate, 6", sherbet	4.00	5.00		Tumbler, 5", 12 ounce	45.00	
4 ▸	Plate, 8⅜", salad	8.50	8.50	18 ▸	Vase, cone-shaped	55.00	
5 ▸	**Plate, 9⅜", dinner	15.00	15.00		Vase holder, metal $35.00		

* Reproduced in several colors   **Green $45.00

OLD CAFE, HOCKING GLASS COMPANY, 1936 – 1940

Colors: pink, crystal, and Royal Ruby

We were surprised to see satinized reproduction pieces of Old Café in an antique mall in Texas. You can see them pictured here. I do not know if these are from Anchor-Hocking moulds since they were not marked or labeled in any way. Just be aware that they exist and do not be duped into buying them as rare Old Café because they are unlisted in most books. The #10 in the bottom row is also new.

Collectors have always liked Old Cafe even if it is a rather small pattern. A few pieces were well disseminated over 60 years ago and surprisingly, you seldom go antiquing without finding a piece (usually the low candy or two-handled bowl). Old Café lamps, pitchers, and dinner plates are lacking in today's market. These pieces are costly when contrasted to prices for the rest of the pattern. Pitchers, shown in earlier editions, have alternating large panels with two small panels that constitute the make-up of all Old Cafe pieces. The pitcher that is often mislabeled Old Cafe can be seen under Hocking's Pillar Optic on page 179 – 180. Some collectors are mistakenly buying Pillar Optic (evenly spaced panels) for Old Cafe because some Internet sellers label them as such. A little time spent in a good book could save you money. The juice pitcher is moulded like the Mayfair juice pitcher, but with a large panel alternating with two smaller panels.

Reproductions

Pink and Royal Ruby lamps were sometimes made by drilling through a vase, but there are ones manufactured with ball feet to raise it enough to allow the cord to pass under the edge. The 5" bowl has an open handle while the 4½" bowl has tab handles, as does the 3¾" berry. There are two sherbets, footed and flat which measure 3¾".

Royal Ruby Old Cafe cups are found on crystal saucers. No Old Cafe Royal Ruby saucers have ever been seen. The 5½" crystal candy comes with a Royal Ruby lid and no Royal Ruby bottom is known.

The low candy (or footed tray) is 8⅜" including handles, and 6½" without.

Hocking made a cookie jar (a numbered line) which is an excellent "go-with" piece. It is ribbed up the sides similar to Old Cafe but is found with a crosshatched lid that does not match Old Cafe.

		Crystal, Pink	Royal Ruby			Crystal, Pink	Royal Ruby
5 ▸	Bowl, 3¾", berry, tab handles	11.00	9.00		Pitcher, 6", 36 oz.	150.00	
11 ▸	Bowl, 5½", cereal, no handles	35.00	28.00		Pitcher, 80 ounce	185.00	
6 ▸	Bowl, 5½", closed handles	15.00			Plate, 6", sherbet	10.00	
4 ▸	Bowl, 6½", open handles	20.00			Plate, 10", dinner	60.00	
7 ▸	Bowl, 9", closed handles	30.00			Saucer	5.00	
	Candy dish, 8", low, tab handles	16.00	20.00	9 ▸	Sherbet, 3¾", low ftd.	15.00	14.00
2 ▸	Candy jar, 5½", crystal with ruby cover		28.00	8 ▸	Sherbet, 3¾", no ft.	17.50	
	Cup	12.00	12.00	3 ▸	Tumbler, 3", juice	17.00	22.00
	Lamp	100.00	150.00	1 ▸	Tumbler, 4", water	26.00	35.00
	Olive dish, 6", oblong	10.00			Vase, 7¼"	50.00	55.00

OLD COLONY "LACE EDGE," "OPEN LACE," HOCKING GLASS COMPANY, 1935 – 1938

Colors: pink and some crystal and green

Old Colony's "lace" needs to be inspected carefully around the edge and underneath. Be sure to look for cracks running from each opening to the next as that is where most mistakes of inspection are made. It damaged easily and still does. Plates and bowls should be stacked carefully. A paper plate between each piece is crucial when stacking or packing delicate glassware.

Candlesticks, console bowls, and vases are limited in mint condition, but are available with chips, nicks, cracks. Many of these were satinized and sometimes painted with floral designs. We recently found the first frosted cereal bowls we have seen. Satinized or frosted pieces currently sell for a fraction of the cost of their unfrosted counterparts. Lack of demand is the reason. Possibly vases and candlesticks are rare because so many candles and vases were satinized. If satinized pieces still have the original painted floral decorations, they will fetch up to 25% more than the prices shown for plain satin. So far, only a few collectors think frosted Old Colony is beautiful; but I have noticed lately that more are noticing it because of its less expensive price.

A flower bowl with crystal frog converts to a candy jar when a cover is added in place of the frog. It was promoted and sold both ways. That cover also fits the butter dish or bonbon as Hocking actually cataloged it. The 7" comport becomes a footed candy with a cookie lid added. This piece was listed as a covered comport; but today, many dealers call it a footed candy jar. Since both these lids fit two separate items, it does not take a genius to realize why there is a severe lid shortage now. Moulds were expensive. It was a frequent practice for as many pieces as possible to be obtained from as few moulds as possible.

There are two styles of 7¾" and 9½" bowls, ribbed or not. The smaller, non-ribbed salad bowl serves as a butter bottom. Both sizes of ribbed bowls are harder to find than their non-ribbed counterparts. There is little price disparity on the large bowl, but price doubles for the smaller one.

Ribs on the footed tumbler reach roughly half way up the side as they do on the cup. This tumbler is often confused with the Coronation tumbler that has a comparable shape and design. Observe the Coronation photograph (page 47) and read there. Notice the fine ribbed effect from the middle up on the Coronation tumbler. Upper ribbing is absent on Old Colony tumblers.

The actual 9" comport in Old Colony has a rayed base. There is a similar comport that also measures 9". This "pretender" has a plain foot and was most likely made by Standard or Lancaster Glass. Both Lancaster and Standard had very similar designs. If the piece is not shown in my listing, or is in any color other than pink or crystal, the likelihood of your having an unknown Old Colony piece is doubtful.

We have detailed how we came upon the store window displays of Old Colony pictured here in previous books. So if you wish to learn about this 1990 discovery, check out an earlier copy.

	Pink
3 ▸ *Bowl, 6⅜", cereal	27.00
Bowl, 7¾", plain	30.00
10 ▸ Bowl, 7¾", ribbed, salad	67.50
Bowl, 8¼", crystal	12.00
9 ▸ Bowl, 9½", plain	28.00
4 ▸ Bowl, 9½", ribbed	32.00
**Bowl, 10½", 3 legs, frosted $65.00	275.00
Butter dish or bonbon with cover	70.00
Butter dish bottom, 7¾"	30.00
Butter dish top	40.00
**Candlesticks, pair, frosted $95.00	450.00
Candy jar and cover, ribbed	50.00
Comport, 7"	28.00
Comport, 7", and cover, footed	65.00
Comport, 9"	995.00
Cookie jar and cover, frosted $60.00	85.00
Creamer	30.00
11 ▸ Cup	30.00
Fish bowl, 1 gallon, 8 ounce (crystal only)	40.00

*Officially listed as cereal or cream soup, green $75.00

	Pink
2 ▸ Flower bowl, crystal frog	35.00
5 ▸ Plate, 7¼", salad	31.00
Plate, 8¼", luncheon	22.00
7 ▸ Plate, 10½", dinner	35.00
Plate, 10½", grill	24.00
Plate, 10½", 3-part relish	26.00
Plate, 13", solid lace	65.00
Plate, 13", 4-part, solid lace	65.00
Platter, 12¾"	42.00
Platter, 12¾", 5-part	35.00
Relish dish, 7½", 3-part, deep	88.00
12 ▸ Saucer	12.50
**Sherbet, footed	125.00
Sugar	30.00
6 ▸ Tumbler, 3½", 5 ounce, flat	215.00
13 ▸ Tumbler, 4½", 9 ounce, flat	25.00
8 ▸ Tumbler, 5", 10½ ounce, footed	100.00
1 ▸ Vase, 7", frosted $90.00	795.00

**Price is for absolute mint condition

Schreick's Studio
Columbus, Ohio

OLD ENGLISH, "THREADING," INDIANA GLASS COMPANY, Late 1920s

Colors: green, amber, pink, crystal, crystal with flashed colors, and forest green

Old English is not a copious pattern, but its prices remain rather steady. However, there are not enormous amounts of collectors pursuing it. Sets of green can be gathered, but not all pieces were made in pink. Regrettably, even luncheon sets cannot be assembled in any color, as there are no cups, saucers, or plates available.

All pieces listed are found in green. Some pieces have never been found in amber. Amber Old English is a deep color more suggestive of Cambridge or New Martinsville products which collectors find so appealing. Most of the amber pieces we have owned over the years have found passionate buyers, but green is simpler to purchase and sell. Note the unusual amber piece above with its ringed finger hold.

Crystal Old English is found with artistic deco decorations; unadorned crystal is rarely seen. While researching our Hazel-Atlas book, we discovered that the crystal egg cup is a Hazel-Atlas cataloged item, and not Old English as had been accepted for years.

There are two styles of sherbets. One is cone shaped and the other is straight sided. Both large and small berry bowls and the flat candy dish have inadequate supplies to meet demand. Sugar and candy jar lids have the same cloverleaf shaped knob as the pitcher. The flat candy lid is similar in size to the pitcher lid; but that pitcher lid is notched along the bottom rim to allow for pouring. You need to hold the lid when pouring. That flat candy is frequently found in a metal holder.

A fan vase is the only piece we have ever owned in dark green.

		Pink, Green, Amber				Pink, Green, Amber
8 ▶	Bowl, 4", flat	25.00		Tumbler, 4½", footed		25.00
14 ▶	Bowl, 9", footed fruit	35.00	9 ▶	Tumbler, 5½", footed		40.00
18 ▶	Bowl, 9½", flat	38.00	13 ▶	Vase, 5⅜", fan type, 7" wide		75.00
10 ▶	Candlesticks, 4", pair	50.00	17 ▶	Vase, 8¼", footed, 4¼" wide		65.00
15 ▶	Candy dish and cover, flat	75.00		Vase, 12", footed		85.00
3 ▶	Candy jar with lid	65.00		*Pink $165.00 **Pink $295.00		
2 ▶	Compote, 3½", ruffled top	30.00				
19 ▶	Compote, 3½" tall, 6⅜" across, 2-handle	22.50				
	Compote, 3½" tall, 7" across	25.00				
6 ▶	Compote, 3½", cheese for plate	20.00				
20 ▶	Creamer	20.00				
12 ▶	Egg cup (Hazel-Atlas)	8.00				
16 ▶	Fruit stand, 11", footed	45.00				
11 ▶	Goblet, 5¾", 8 ounce	35.00				
	*Pitcher	95.00				
5 ▶	**Pitcher and cover	155.00				
7 ▶	Plate, indent for compote	20.00				
23 ▶	Plate w/fingerhold	25.00				
4 ▶	Sandwich server, center handle	55.00				
1 ▶	Sherbet, 2 styles	22.00				
22 ▶	Sugar	17.50				
21 ▶	Sugar cover	40.00				

158

OLIVE, LINE #134, IMPERIAL GLASS COMPANY, Late 1930s

Colors: red, light blue, emerald, pink

Imperial's Olive Line #134 is a minor pattern whose major attraction is its mistaken identity with Imperial's Old English Line #166. Now, if you can keep Paden City's Popeye and Olive pattern out of the mix, you'll be fine.

Think round olives and that ought to help. Olive also has circles in its design near the bottom of the pieces along with ribbed feet. Old English Line #166 has elongated indentations reaching upward from its base with olive type balls. The plates in Old English, however, do have a kind of ribbed flower center design. You will notice that the plates in Olive Line #134 have plain centers. It is perplexing! Actually, they are so well-matched that should you care to collect both lines as one pattern, few will notice and you can get some tumblers from Old English that you will not have with Olive. Olive has handled mugs.

We see the blue and red pictured here in our travels; but those are the colors most sought; so, it all works out.

	Emerald, Pink	Blue, Red
Bowl, 6½", flared, footed	16.00	22.00
5 ▸ Bowl, 7", rose (cupped)	22.00	32.00
Bowl, 7", shallow	15.00	25.00
2 ▸ Bowl, 9", fruit, pedestal foot	20.00	35.00
Bowl, 9", bun or fruit tray	20.00	35.00
Bowl, 9", shallow	25.00	35.00
Bowl, 10¼", salad	30.00	45.00
3 ▸ Candle, 2½"	16.00	25.00
Candy jar w/lid	30.00	40.00
Compote, 6"	11.00	20.00

	Emerald, Pink	Blue, Red
Compote, 6½"	12.50	22.50
6 ▸ Creamer	11.00	16.00
7 ▸ Cup	9.00	12.00
Mayonnaise	15.00	18.00
Plate, 6"	4.00	5.50
Plate, 8"	8.00	10.00
4 ▸ Plate, 12"	18.00	25.00
8 ▸ Saucer	3.00	4.00
1 ▸ Sugar	11.00	16.00

"ORCHID," PADEN CITY GLASS COMPANY, Early 1930s

Colors: yellow, cobalt blue, crystal, green, amber, pink, red, and black

There are at least three "Orchid" arrangements found on Paden City blanks. Collectors used to not mind blending these varieties because so little of any one is found. However, with more attention paid to Paden City products of late, a single stemmed version has been singled out as a pattern unto itself.

All Paden City patterns were more restricted in production runs than those of some other glass companies, such as Heisey's Orchid which leaps to mind. Orchid growers once accounted for major interest in this and the Internet has helped unveil many pieces of Orchid. Instead of dozens buying at shows, there are now thousands eyeing pieces. It's very popular in today's market. Every piece of Paden's "Orchid" we have displayed at shows has sold not long after the show opened — if not before.

At first, many believed that "Orchid" etched pieces turned up only on #412 Line, the square, Crow's Foot blank made by Paden City. However, "Orchid" has turned up on the #890 rounded Crow's Foot blank, the #401 Mrs. B, and various vase blanks as well. "Orchid" may well be possible on any Paden City blank. The pattern displays better on the transparent pastel colors, but they do not seem to be as popular with the buying public. A few pieces of "Orchid" are being found on black. Red and cobalt blue are the preferred colors.

15

9

		All other colors	Red, Black, Cobalt Blue
	Bowl, 4⅞", square	33.00	55.00
2 ▸	Bowl, 8½", 2-handle	75.00	135.00
3 ▸	Bowl, 8¾", square	75.00	135.00
8 ▸	Bowl, 10", footed, square	95.00	195.00
11 ▸	Bowl, 11", square	85.00	195.00
	Cake stand, square, 2" high	75.00	155.00
10 ▸	Candlesticks, 5¾", pair	125.00	210.00
	Candy with lid, 6½", square, 3-part	110.00	195.00
	Candy with lid, cloverleaf, 3-part	95.00	195.00
	Comport, 3¼" tall, 6¼" wide	25.00	55.00
14 ▸	Comport, 4¾" tall, 7⅜" wide	65.00	100.00
	Comport, 6⅝" tall, 7" wide	65.00	135.00
12 ▸	Comport, 8" high		85.00
6 ▸	Creamer	55.00	100.00
	Ice bucket, 6"	110.00	225.00
1 ▸	Mayonnaise, 3-piece	85.00	165.00
13 ▸	Plate, 8½", square		125.00
7 ▸	Sandwich server, center handle	75.00	125.00
5 ▸	Sugar	55.00	100.00
9 ▸	Vase, 8"	110.00	275.00
15 ▸	Vase, 10"	135.00	295.00

OVIDE, "NEW CENTURY," HAZEL-ATLAS GLASS COMPANY, 1930 – 1935

Colors: green, black, white Platonite trimmed with fired-on colors in 1950s

Ovide is one pattern available today that can be started economically and collected in colors or certain designs that please you. You can buy a colorful, useable set as cheaply as buying new dishes to use. Wouldn't you rather own something with antique status (50 years for glass) than something that loses most of its value as you carry it out of the store?

Granted, finding a specific decoration may prove to be a chore, but possibly less so today with the Internet. Separating these decorations into time eras for my books has been a task. We are showing the "Art Deco" design here in a creamer and sugar set for the first time in years, so that all those who have never seen it can. New collectors have written over and over to ask what the "Art Deco" design looked like, so here it is.

Hazel-Atlas used a gaggle of different patterns on this popular Platonite, including one of flying geese. A popular one, considering the quantity found today, was the black floral design with red and yellow edge trim. That set included kitchenware items (stacking sets and mixing bowls) as well as a dinnerware line.

Very little black, transparent green, or plain yellow Ovide are ever seen at shows, but there are some collectors asking for it. A luncheon set should be possible; but it would be simpler to put together an Ovide set in black or yellow Cloverleaf which Depression glass dealers are apt to bring to shows while leaving plainer Ovide home.

Our new Hazel-Atlas book has eleven pages devoted to colors and decorations known on Ovide.

	Black	Green	Decorated White	Art Deco			Black	Green	Decorated White	Art Deco
Bowl, 4¾", berry	5.50		8.00		9 ▸ Plate, 6", sherbet	6.00	2.50	6.00	
▸ Bowl, 5½", cereal			13.00		10 ▸ Plate, 8", luncheon	4.00	3.00	14.00	75.00
Bowl, 8", large berry			22.50		7 ▸ Plate, 9", dinner			20.00	
Candy dish & cover	45.00	22.00	35.00		11 ▸ Platter, 11"			22.50	
Cocktail, footed, fruit	5.00	4.00			Salt and pepper, pair	28.00	27.50	24.00	
▸ Creamer	6.50	4.50	17.50	125.00	4 ▸ Saucer	3.50	2.50	6.00	25.00
▸ Cup	7.50	3.50	12.50	125.00	12 ▸ Sherbet	6.50	3.00	14.00	100.00
▸ Egg cup			18.00		1 ▸ Sugar, open	6.50	6.00	17.50	125.00
					5 ▸ Tumbler			18.00	125.00

OYSTER AND PEARL, ANCHOR HOCKING GLASS CORPORATION, 1938 – 1940

Colors: pink, crystal, Royal Ruby, Vitrock, and Vitrock with fired-on pink, blue, and green

The large Oyster and Pearl ruffled bowl pictured on the right did not create one letter or e-mail about its addition! We expected someone to say that they owned one or had found one in pink, but that did not happen. This was the first new piece to turn up in 34 years of writing and at least I was excited about it. Admittedly, I would have preferred pink, Royal Ruby, or even a fired-on Vitrock. Just know that colored varieties may exist. It was a rather lackluster day of antiquing in Ohio when Cathy noticed this bowl. She recognized that crystal was not frequently found, but had no concept that the ruffled top was the exhilarating part. It made my day! You don't have to know everything to spot something rare or different.

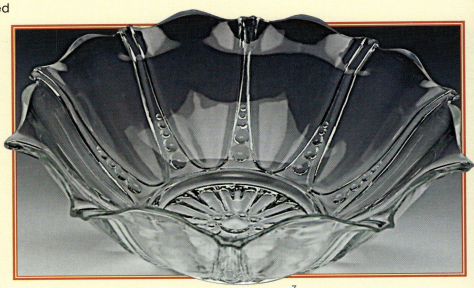

7

Royal Ruby Oyster and Pearl is pictured under the Royal Ruby pattern shown on page 203, but prices are also listed here. Pink Oyster and Pearl has regularly been used as harmonizing pieces for other Depression glass patterns. The pink relish dish and candlesticks sell well since they are reasonably priced in comparison to other patterns. Though not as true as it once was, Oyster and Pearl prices are generally cheaper than most patterns in this book.

Note: The Oyster and Pearl relish dish measures 11½" when the handles are included. We emphasize that because of letters we receive saying someone's dish is 11½" and all we list is a 10½" relish. All measurements in this book are specified without handles unless otherwise cited. Glass companies rarely measured the handles or included them in the measurements. There is no divided bowl in Oyster and Pearl; it was (and is) listed as a relish.

Pink fired over Vitrock was called Dusty Rose; the fired green was called Springtime Green by Hocking. Most collectors love these shades; but I've met a few who despise them. The non-colored Vitrock is intermittently seen, and is not as beguiling. Some pieces have been located with fired blue, but this is very scarce.

We have seen a few crystal pieces decorated, and most of them were trimmed in red as pictured on the large plate on page 165. They sell faster than undecorated crystal. The 10½" fruit bowl is a great salad bowl and the 13½" plate makes a great server or liner for the bowl.

The lipped, 5½" bowl is often referred to as "heart" shaped. It might serve as a gravy or sauce boat although most people use them for candy dishes. The same bowl is found without the spout in Royal Ruby. A spout-less bowl has not been seen in any other color. Dusty Rose and Springtime Green always have a spout when you can find them.

The report of a "lamp" made from candleholders turned out to be two candles glued together at their bases to form a ball. Obviously, someone had time on his hands. It was an entertaining idea.

	Crystal, Pink	Royal Ruby	White and Fired-On Green or Pink
3 ▸ Bowl, 5¼", heart-shaped, 1-handled	14.00		12.00
Bowl, 5½", 1-handled		22.00	
6 ▸ Bowl, 6½", deep-handled	18.00	22.00	
1 ▸ Bowl, 10½", deep fruit	25.00	60.00	28.00
7 ▸ Bowl, 10½", ruffled edge	55.00		
2 ▸ Candle holder, 3½", pair	42.00	65.00	30.00
5 ▸ Plate, 13½", sandwich	20.00	55.00	
4 ▸ Relish dish, 10½", oblong, divided		20.00	

"PARROT," SYLVAN, FEDERAL GLASS COMPANY, 1931 – 1932

Colors: green, amber; some crystal and blue

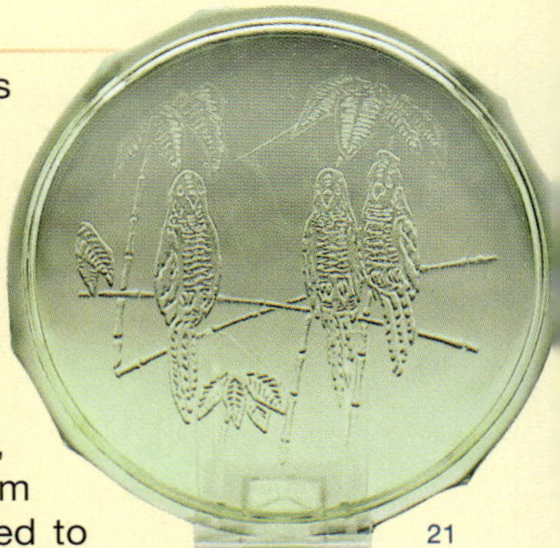

"Parrot" is a Depression glass pattern that has various rare pieces. The pattern has a history of brisk price accelerations, then periods of stability and then prices will take off again. When enthusiastic collectors covet "Parrot" at the same time, prices increase very rapidly. We have watched these recurring price cycles for years in several patterns.

Originally, a cache of 37 pitchers was found in the basement of an old hardware store in central Ohio. At least a couple of those original ones bit the dust. One cracked from a dealer dusting it out and bumping a diamond ring in a thin spot. The whole pitcher is thin; but where the pattern is designed, it gets even thinner. Today, there are still more than 30 in existence. Parrot pitchers have all but disappeared from the market at any price. At first, several of these sold for $35.00, but shortly jumped to $200.00. Prices for the few sold recently have reached a ballpark figure of $3,000.00. A few consumers were willing to pay that price and did. We heard of one being offered in the $4,000 range, but there were no buyers at that price the last we heard. One is listed for auction as we write.

There are two types of "Parrot" hot plates or possibly cold plates as described under Madrid or Georgian. One, pictured as a pattern shot, is moulded like the pointed edged Madrid; the other, round, is moulded like the one in Georgian. One of the round ones has emerged in amber.

Speaking of amber, the butter dish, creamer, and sugar lid are all more difficult to find than those in green; and even fewer mint butter dish tops or sugar lids have surfaced. Non-mint ones are available. (Damaged glassware should not bring mint prices.) Frequently found butter bottoms have an indented ridge or rest for the top. The jam dish is the same size as the butter bottom, but without that ridge. The jam dish has never been found in green, but is somewhat available in amber. There are fewer collectors of amber "Parrot"; so, prices are not as risky and exaggerated by demand, as are those for green.

"Parrot" tumblers are moulded on Madrid-like shapes except for the heavy-footed tumbler, whose pointy edges are easily chipped. The supply of those heavy, footed tumblers (in both colors), green water tumblers, and thin, flat iced tea in amber has met present demand. Mint ones are not easily found, but there are plenty of damaged ones available if you are willing to settle for damaged glass. Apparently, the thin, moulded, footed tumbler did not accept the "Parrot" design favorably and the heavier version was made. The thin, 10 ounce footed tumbler has only been found in amber and the parrot is often not vividly displayed on the glass. Prices for tumblers have stayed stable during the last few "Parrot" price increases. We have seen them priced for more, but not selling at the higher prices.

Yes, we know the shaker pictured is cracked as has been pointed out by several readers. It's our way to give glassware with little value a purpose. You still get to see size, shape, and color, and a collector gets to enjoy the good pieces we used to have. Actually, several dealers now offer us their damaged, hard-to-find pieces, at reasonable prices so we can photograph them for our books. Several craftsmen we've talked with use damaged and broken Depression glass for jewelry, ceramic decoration, glass window art, and the like. We furnished quite a number of boxes of broken glass to a lady creating artful items. There's great appreciation for this glassware and some find a way to enhance that which used to be thrown away. It's recycling we definitely approve.

Blue "Parrot" sherbets turn up occasionally, but no other pieces of blue have been found. The blue is the same shade as the Madonna blue of Madrid.

		Green	Amber			Green	Amber
7 ▸	Bowl, 5", berry	33.00	22.50	4 ▸ Plate, 9", dinner		58.00	48.00
	Bowl, 7", soup	55.00	38.00	10 ▸ Plate, 10½", round, grill		33.00	
	Bowl, 8", large berry	100.00	90.00	18 ▸ Plate, 10½", square, grill			32.00
12 ▸	Bowl, 10", oval vegetable	70.00	75.00	Plate, 10¼", square (crystal only)		26.00	
8 ▸	Butter dish and cover	450.00	1,500.00	6 ▸ Platter, 11¼", oblong		55.00	75.00
	Butter dish bottom	65.00	200.00	15 ▸ Salt and pepper, pair		295.00	
	Butter dish top	375.00	1,300.00	14 ▸ Saucer		15.00	18.00
16 ▸	Creamer, footed	55.00	85.00	19 ▸ *Sherbet, footed cone		22.50	22.50
13 ▸	Cup	40.00	42.50	Sherbet, 4¼" high		1,500.00	
21 ▸	Hot plate, 5", pointed	895.00	995.00	1 ▸ Sugar		40.00	50.00
	Hot plate, 5", round	995.00		2 ▸ Sugar cover		175.00	550.00
17 ▸	Jam dish, 7"		38.00	3 ▸ Tumbler, 4¼", 10 ounce		195.00	135.00
	Pitcher, 8½", 80 ounce	3,000.00		20 ▸ Tumbler, 5½", 12 ounce		225.00	165.00
5 ▸	Plate, 5¾", sherbet	35.00	24.00	9 ▸ Tumbler, 5¾", footed, heavy		195.00	165.00
11 ▸	Plate, 7½", salad	40.00		Tumbler, 5½", 10 oz., ftd (Madrid mould)			195.00

*Blue $225.00

166

"PARTY LINE," "SODA FOUNTAIN," LINE #191, 191½, #192, PADEN CITY GLASS
COMPANY, Late 1920s – 1951; CANTON GLASS COMPANY, 1950s

Colors: amber, blue, crystal, green, pink (Cheriglo), red, some turquoise green

"Party Line" was added to this book due to so many collectors asking for it to be listed. Paden City publicized it as being "the most complete tableware line in America." Actual dinnerware items are not very available even though it was produced into the 1950s. An early author, Jerry Barnett, stated in his Paden City book that factory workers called this pattern "Soda Fountain," definitely an apt name considering the plethora of those type items found.

Few pieces are found in light blue, so we were excited to find the crushed fruit jar pictured here. It is similar to the blue found in Hocking's Mayfair. We owned some mixing bowls in blue once. We're beginning to see this pattern pursued by collectors and perceptive dealers are carrying it to shows. The only drawback to "Party Line" is its thick and heavy pieces are not as admired as those of thinner more delicate patterns. However, if you should want a pattern that is sturdy, this might well be the pattern for you. Fountain ware would have needed to stand wear and tear.

Green is the color most often collected. One thing we have noticed is that "Party Line" is usually found in groups. Red Party Line shakers are pictured in the Penny Line photo.

*All colors			
Banana split, 8½", oval	25.00		
12 ▶ Bottle, 22 oz., wine w/stopper	50.00		
Bottle, 48 oz., water, no stopper	50.00		
Bowl, 4½", nappy	8.00		
Bowl, 6½", berry	10.00		
Bowl, 7", mixing	20.00		
Bowl, 8", mixing	25.00		
Bowl, 9", berry	25.00		
Bowl, 9", low foot comport, flare	27.50		
Bowl, 9", mixing	30.00		
Bowl, 10½", high foot, flare	35.00		
Bowl, 11", low foot comport	35.00		
Bowl, 11", vegetable, flare	35.00		
Butter box, w/cover, round flat lid	60.00		
2 ▶ Cake stand, low foot	30.00		
Candy, footed w/cover	35.00		
Cigarette holder w/cover, footed	45.00		
Cocktail shaker, 18 oz., w/lid	65.00		
Cologne, 1½ oz.	60.00		
9 ▶ Creamer, 7 oz.	10.00		
Cup, 6 oz.	8.00		

*All colors		
Custard, 6 oz.	8.00	
Ice tub & pail	60.00	
Ice tub, 6½", w/tab handle	50.00	
1 ▶‡ Jar w/lid, high, crushed fruit	75.00	
Marmalade, w/cover, 12 oz.	35.00	
6 ▶ Mayo, 6", footed	25.00	
Parfait, 5 oz. (2 styles)	14.00	
Pitcher, 30 oz., jug, w/cover	70.00	
Pitcher, 32 oz., grape juice w/lid	100.00	
Pitcher, 36 oz., measure w/5½" reamer	125.00	
Pitcher, 70 oz., jug w or w/optic, w/lid	135.00	
Plate 6"	6.00	
Plate, 8"	10.00	
Plate, 10½" cracker, w/covered cheese	65.00	
Saucer, 5¾"	3.00	
Server, 10", center handle	40.00	

*All colo	
Shaker, pair	35.00
Shaker, sugar	155.00
11 ▶ Sherbet, 3½ or 4½ oz., footed	10.00
Sherbet, 6 oz., high foot	12.50
Stem, 9 oz.	15.00
8 ▶ Sugar, 7 oz.	10.00
Sugar w/id, 10 oz., hotel	22.50
Sundae, 4 or 6 oz., tulip	15.00
5 ▶ Sundae, 9 oz., crimped	20.00
Syrup, 8 oz.	55.00
Syrup w/glass cover, 12 oz.	80.00
10 ▶ Tumbler, 1½ oz., footed, cordial	16.00
3 ▶ Tumbler, 2½ or 3½ oz., ftd, cocktail	12.50
7 ▶ Tumbler, 3 oz., wine	12.00
Tumbler, 4½ oz., juice	8.00
Tumbler, 5 oz., cola	12.00
Tumbler, 6 oz., 3 styles	12.00
Tumbler, 7 oz., 2 styles	12.00
Tumbler, 8 oz., 3 styles	14.00
Tumbler, 9 oz., barrel	12.00
4 ▶ Tumbler, 10 oz., 3 styles	12.00
Tumbler, 12 oz., blown	15.00
Tumbler, 12 oz., 4 styles	14.00
Tumbler, 14 oz., 3 styles	14.00
Vase, 6", fan	40.00
Vase, 7", fan	45.00
Vase, 7", crimped	50.00

*Double the price for red or blue and
 50% for crystal.
‡Blue 150.00

168

PATRICIAN, "SPOKE," FEDERAL GLASS COMPANY, 1933 – 1937

Colors: pink, green, crystal, and amber ("Golden Glo")

Patrician was one of the first Depression patterns we found in central Kentucky when we first started looking for glass. Amber was well distributed in our area. Amber Madrid was the other available pattern, so it looked like only amber hues were around to be gathered. That perception changed upon deeper digging; but buying those patterns and trying to make a profit selling them was not a great idea at first. Everyone else in our area had the same two amber patterns at flea markets, and the only way you could sell, was to beat their prices. It is a good idea to know what is plentiful in your market area.

Besides availability to recommend it, Patrician has never been reproduced. Sets of green or pink Patrician can probably be gathered with determination, but at a greater price. The abundant amber, 10½" "dinner" plates were premiums with 20-pound sacks of flour and promoted as cake plates. Exhibits of these plates sat on the counter near the cash register, and when you paid for your flour, you were handed one of these as an additional reward. Everyone baked and 20-pound bags of flour were bought regularly; so these plates stacked up at home. When we started buying Depression glass over 35 years ago, this was, and still is, known as a dinner plate, not a cake.

The jam dish is a butter bottom without the ridge for the top to rest against just like "Parrot" and Sharon patterns. It measures 6¾" wide and stands 1¼" deep. This is the same measurement as the butter bottom; however, Patrician cereal bowls are often offered as jam dishes. Cereals are 6" in diameter and 1¾" deep. Prices for these two items are close today; so that price is not as critical as it once was; but be cognitive of which is which. In the past, jam dishes were considered rare, and sold for almost double the price of the cereal. Today, collectors seek only one jam dish and varying amounts of cereals which have now attained the price range of the jam. That is another version of pricing concepts changing and developing over time.

Green Patrician is offered more than either pink or crystal. Even so, green dinner plates are scarce. Completing a set of crystal is a problem since not all crystal pieces have turned up.

Amber pitchers purportedly were made in two styles. One has a moulded handle. In crystal and green, the applied handled pitcher is the norm, but amber applied handled pitchers may not exist.

Mint condition Patrician sugar lids, footed tumblers, cookie and butter bottoms are harder to find than other pieces. The heavy cookie and butter tops have survived better than the thinner bottoms. Many a glass grinder has practiced on the curves of sugar lids, and some cut them shoddily. This is another pattern where saucers are harder to find than cups.

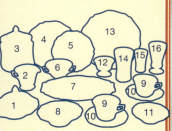

	Amber, Crystal	Pink	Green
6 ▸ Bowl, 4¾", cream soup	16.00	22.00	22.00
1 ▸ Bowl, 5", berry	14.00	12.00	13.00
8 ▸ Bowl, 6", cereal	23.00	25.00	32.00
Bowl, 8½", large berry	40.00	32.00	40.00
Bowl, 10", oval vegetable	35.00	30.00	35.00
1 ▸ Butter dish and cover	95.00	225.00	140.00
Butter dish bottom	60.00	175.00	80.00
Butter dish top	30.00	50.00	60.00
3 ▸ Cookie jar and cover	84.00		675.00
2 ▸ Creamer, footed	11.00	12.00	15.00
9 ▸ Cup	9.00	15.00	14.00
Jam dish	27.50	30.00	40.00
Pitcher, 8", 75 oz., moulded handle	135.00	125.00	165.00
Pitcher, 8¼", 75 oz., applied handle	*110.00	150.00	175.00

	Amber, Crystal	Pink	Green
Plate, 6", sherbet	9.00	8.00	10.00
5 ▸ Plate, 7½", salad	13.00	15.00	20.00
4 ▸ Plate, 9", luncheon	12.00	17.00	16.00
Plate, 10½", dinner	8.00	45.00	45.00
13 ▸ Plate, 10½", grill	14.00	15.00	20.00
7 ▸ Platter, 11½", oval	29.00	25.00	30.00
Salt and pepper, pair	60.00	120.00	80.00
10 ▸ Saucer	9.50	10.00	9.50
12 ▸ Sherbet	12.00	17.00	14.00
Sugar	9.00	9.00	15.00
Sugar cover	60.00	70.00	85.00
15 ▸ Tumbler, 4", 5 oz.	30.00	33.00	33.00
Tumbler, 4¼", 9 oz.	28.00	26.00	30.00
14 ▸ Tumbler, 5½", 14 oz.	45.00	45.00	55.00
16 ▸ Tumbler, 5¼", 8 oz., footed	58.00		75.00
*Crystal only			

"PATRICK," LANCASTER GLASS COMPANY, Early 1930s

Colors: yellow and pink

"Patrick" is rarely seen in anything except yellow luncheon sets today. A few pink "Patrick" luncheon sets are turning up in the St. Louis area; but the price has scared away all but fervent collectors even though prices have diminished somewhat for pink. Very few pieces of pink have come up for sale recently. "Patrick" seems to have been a restricted production before anyone ever considered the concept of limiting productions in order to sell commodities for more money.

A "Patrick" mayonnaise is presented with two plates. The raised circle one is the intended plate. The other is the salad plate. This difference holds true for Jubilee also. The other piece pictured came from a home in Lancaster, Ohio. The top of the candle has been ground flat so that the 11" console could be easily attached. (This was the tease of an interesting compor from last book.) How many of these exist, we have no idea. We priced it b adding the prices of the candle and bowl together and it sold the first da we put it on display at a show in Michigan.

"Patrick" serving pieces are rare. There are serving pieces to be found i other patterns on the same blanks used for "Patrick" and Jubilee. Howeve "Patrick" mould etchings and Jubilee cuttings are higher due to deman and collectability and not necessarily rarity. It is not "Patrick" unles "Patrick" etching is found on the piece.

	Pink	Yellow
Bowl, 9", handled fruit	165.00	125.00
12 ▸ Bowl, 11", console	145.00	125.00
13 ▸ Candlesticks, pair	195.00	150.00
Candy dish, 3-footed	225.00	225.00
Cheese & cracker set	135.00	110.00
6 ▸ Creamer	50.00	35.00
7 ▸ Cup	45.00	32.00
2 ▸ Goblet, 4", cocktail	80.00	80.00

	Pink	Yellow
Goblet, 4¾", 6 ounce, juice	70.00	65.00
3 ▸ Goblet, 6", 10 ounce, water	70.00	70.00
11 ▸ Mayonnaise, 3-piece	195.00	150.00
1 ▸ Plate, 7", sherbet	15.00	10.00
Plate, 7½", salad	20.00	14.00
9 ▸ Plate, 8", luncheon	30.00	18.00
8 ▸ Saucer	15.00	12.00
10 ▸ Sherbet, 4¾"	60.00	50.00
5 ▸ Sugar	50.00	35.00
4 ▸ Tray, 11", 2-handled	75.00	60.00
Tray, 11", center-handled	125.00	100.00

"PEACOCK REVERSE," DELILAH BIRD, "PHEASANT," LINE #411, #412 & #991, PADEN CITY GLASS COMPANY, 1930s

Colors: cobalt blue, red, amber, yellow, green, pink, black, and crystal

The "Peacock Reverse" bird etch is similar to that of "Peacock and Wild Rose" only the peacock's head is swiveled backwards to look over his shoulder. Paden City's Line #412 ("Crow's Foot"), Line #991 ("Penny Line"), and Line #411 (Mrs. "B" — square shapes with the corners cut off) are the prevailing lines on which "Peacock Reverse" has been found. Add to those an octagonal #701 Triumph plate, and no telling what other mould blank possibly will turn up with this etching. Paden City lines have various etched patterns ascribed to them. When you spot a piece by its shape from a distance, you are always wondering what etch will be found.

The #701 eight-sided plate is the only pink plate we have owned in "Peacock Reverse." Ruby seems to be the color most encountered. We turned up two colored sugars, but have yet to uncover a creamer in over 20 years of searching. Few collectors of cups and saucers have "Peacock Reverse" captured. Like "Cupid," cups and saucers may be the rarest pieces in the pattern. A lipped, footed comport on "Crow's Foot" blank has been called a gravy by collectors. You see this red comport without an etching, but finding it decorated is a coup.

There are several styles of candy dishes. Patterns are only on the lids, as was standard procedure for Paden City candies. Plain bases can be discovered with lids sporting other etches or even plain. That should make bases easier to find. It has been our experience that prices for "Peacock Reverse" are not set by color as much as other patterns. Pieces are so infrequently offered, collectors welcome any piece in any color, including crystal.

You could conceivably find this etch on almost any piece listed under "Crow's Foot" (squared) or "Orchid." We were informed by the granddaughter of a former Paden City worker that the workers at the plants called all these bird patterns "pheasants." When you look at them closely, we may well be hunting the wrong bird.

		All colors				All colors
10 ▸	Bowl, 4⅞", square	50.00			Creamer, 2¾", flat	125.00
4 ▸	Bowl, 8¾", square	125.00	6 ▸		Cup	155.00
9 ▸	Bowl, 8¾", square with handles	125.00			Plate, 5¾", sherbet	22.00
	Bowl, 11¾", console	150.00			Plate, 8½", luncheon	60.00
2 ▸	Candlesticks, 5¾", square base, pair	175.00			Plate, 10⅜", 2-handled	100.00
3 ▸	Candy dish, 6½", square	195.00	7 ▸		Saucer	45.00
	Comport, 3¼" high, 6¼" wide	75.00	5 ▸		Sherbet, 4⅝" tall, 3⅜" diameter	75.00
	Comport, 4¼" high, 7⅜" wide	85.00			Server, center-handled	80.00
11 ▸	Comport, footed, 2 spouts	125.00	1 ▸		Sugar, 2¾", flat	125.00
			8 ▸		Tumbler, 4", 10 ounce, flat	100.00
					Vase, 10"	250.00

"PEACOCK & WILD ROSE," "NORA BIRD," "PHEASANT LINE," LINE #300, PADEN CITY GLASS COMPANY, 1929 – 1930s

Colors: pink, green, amber, cobalt blue, black, light blue, crystal, and red

At a photography session where this pattern was being outlined with chalk to make it show in the photograph, Cathy noticed that "Nora Bird" etching was a condensed (or sectioned off) version of the larger "Peacock and Wild Rose" etching. Examine a tall vase; you will see the small bird at the bottom of the design that appears on the pieces of what was formerly known as a separate pattern, "Nora Bird." The bird on each piece can be found in flight or getting ready to take flight. Obviously, the entire larger pattern would not fit on smaller pieces; so, a condensed portion was used. That is why creamers, sugars, and luncheon pieces have never been found in "Peacock and Wild Rose." These pieces from Line #300 (formerly attributed to a separate pattern) are actually from the same etch. Copious amounts of accessory pieces in "Peacock and Wild Rose" can now be combined with cups, saucers, creamers, sugars, and luncheon plates of "Nora Bird" to give a complete pattern. Cups and saucers are rarely seen, but are, at least, possible now.

Bird patterns were popular during this era and a reader wrote to tell us that old time Paden City plant workers referred to all of the bird etches as "pheasant line."

The #300 line candy dish lid fits both the flat, three-part and the footed 5¼" candy dish. An octagonal flat candy pictured in an earlier book was from the #701 Triumph line. The green tray pictured was listed as a #210 Line refreshment tray and is sometimes found with a sugar and creamer. Light blue has been discovered in the form of a rolled edge bowl.

There are two styles of creamers and sugars (pointed handles and rounded handles). Both types are also found with "Cupid" etch. There is an individual (smaller) sugar and creamer with rounded handles.

		All colors
	Bowl, 8½", flat	135.00
12 ▸	Bowl, 8½", fruit, oval, footed	195.00
	Bowl, 8¾", footed	175.00
	Bowl, 9½", center-handled	165.00
	Bowl, 9½", footed	185.00
18 ▸	Bowl, 10½", center-handled	125.00
15 ▸	Bowl, 10½", footed	195.00
	Bowl, 10½", fruit	180.00
20 ▸	Bowl, 11", console	185.00
	Bowl, 14", console	195.00
1 ▸	Candlestick, 5" wide, pair	180.00
	Candlesticks, octagonal tops, pair	225.00
11 ▸	Candy dish w/cover, 6½", 3-part	195.00
	Candy dish w/cover, 7"	250.00
	Candy with lid, footed, 5¼" high	195.00
	Cheese and cracker set	185.00
	Comport, 3¼" tall, 6¼" wide	135.00
17 ▸	Comport, 6⅜" tall, 8" wide	150.00
3 ▸	Creamer, 4½", round handle	65.00
7 ▸	Creamer, 5", pointed handle	65.00
8 ▸	Cup	80.00
	Ice bucket, 6"	225.00
	Ice tub, 4¾"	210.00
	Ice tub, 6"	225.00
4 ▸	Mayonnaise	110.00

		All colors
19 ▸	Mayonnaise liner	25.00
	Pitcher, 5" high	395.00
	Pitcher, 8½", 64 ounce	495.00
5 ▸	Plate, 8"	25.00
	Plate, cake, low foot, 2"	150.00
	Relish, 3-part	125.00
9 ▸	Saucer	20.00
2 ▸	Sugar, 4½", round handle	65.00
6 ▸	Sugar, 5", pointed handle	65.00
16 ▸	Tray, 10¾", center handled	75.00
10 ▸	Tray, rectangular, handled	175.00
	Tumbler, 2¼", 3 ounce	65.00
	Tumbler, 3"	75.00
	Tumbler, 4"	95.00
	Tumbler, 4¾", footed	110.00
	Tumbler, 5¼", 10 ounce	110.00
13 ▸	Vase, 8¼", elliptical	395.00
14 ▸	Vase, 10", two styles	250.00
	Vase, 12"	295.00

173

"PEBBLED RIM," LINE #707, L. E. SMITH GLASS COMPANY, 1930s

Colors: amber, green, pink

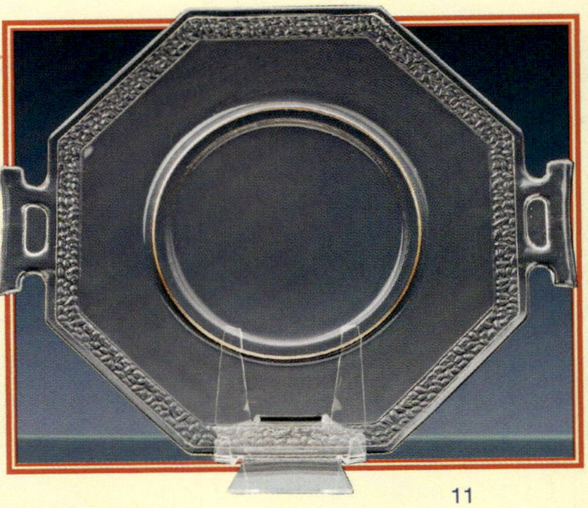

"Pebbled Rim" is a fairly plain L. E. Smith pattern that was advertised as a 40-piece dinner set. Some collectors appreciate the plainer patterns that are not as busy. Currently, there are two large sets being offered for sale we see in our travels in Pennsylvania and Texas. Both are being marketed as an entire set rather than individual pieces. Therefore, collectors who would buy parts or pieces are ignoring such a large initial outlay for an entire set. In addition, both sets have a premium price on them because they are large sets. Maybe they should be that expensive; but, right now, they are not and only a few collectors are presently searching for "Pebbled Rim." Demand drives prices and without demand, huge prices are not going to be accepted.

The large, ruffled edge vegetable and deep salad bowls, as well as the platter appear to be the hardest pieces to locate, although any green is more difficult than pink. This simple pattern blends well with other patterns. In fact, we believe that may account for the scarcity of some pieces. People are using them with other sets.

11

		All colors
	Bowl, 9½", oval	30.00
	Bowl, berry	8.00
10 ▸	Bowl, ruffled edge vegetable, deep	30.00
5 ▸	Bowl, ruffled edge vegetable, shallow	28.00
	Candleholder	20.00
3 ▸	Creamer	11.00

		All colors
1 ▸	Cup (two styles)	7.50
6 ▸	Plate, 6", bread/butter	3.00
7 ▸	Plate, 7", salad	4.00
	Plate, 9", dinner	10.00
9 ▸	Plate, 9", grill	10.00
11 ▸	Plate, 9", two-handle	18.00
8 ▸	Platter, oval	20.00
2 ▸	Saucer	2.00
4 ▸	Sugar	11.00

"PENNY LINE," LINE #991, PADEN CITY GLASS COMPANY, c. 1930

Colors: amber, crystal, green, Mulberry, pink (Cheriglo), primrose (light yellow), Royal blue, ruby

"Penny Line" is Paden City's Line #991 which is often confused with Paden City's "Party Line" #191. They are a different shape, but the name gets switched around in people's minds. The Deco age in which this pattern had its beginning was all about form, lines, and shapes. This circular, stacked rings appearance was a definite creation of that time and is prized as such by devotees of Deco and Depression wares. Notice the unusual handles on the cup and sugar pictured which echo the rippled bands

Low foot meant goblets with only one wafer and high foot pieces had two. The mayo was cataloged with a liner plate, which we assume was the 6" dessert plate also used as a sherbet liner. We have never found a mayo with liner; so, that is a guess. The candle pictured is often discovered used as a comport, due to its being set upside down.

Though we have seen it listed six times higher in a Paden City publication, the cobalt goblet price we list is a slow seller for us at our "undervalued" price.

Our picture here comes via a dealer friend who found it, called to ask if we needed a photo and then shipped a piece of everything to the photography studio. We can use all the extra help that we can get to bring you photos in these books. We should point out that the shakers pictured belong to Party Line #191. Obviously, the previous owner of this had blended his beautiful red ware.

	*All colors			***All colors**
▸ Bowl, 9", hdld.	30.00	10 ▸ Shaker, pair		40.00
Bowl, finger	15.00	Sherbet, low foot		9.00
▸ Candle	25.00	Stem, 1¼ ounce, cordial		22.00
Creamer	11.00	Stem, 3½ ounce, cocktail		12.50
▸ Cup	10.00	Stem, 3 ounce, wine		15.00
Decanter, 22 ounce w/stopper	45.00	Stem, 6 ounce, cocktail		12.50
Goblet, low foot, grapefruit	16.00	9 ▸ Stem, 9 ounce, water		20.00
Goblet, low foot, 9 ounce	15.00	2 ▸ Sugar		11.00
Goblet, high foot	17.50	3 ▸ Tray, rectangular, 2 handled, sugar/cream		25.00
Pitcher	55.00	1 ▸ Tumbler, 2½ ounce, wine		12.00
Plate, 6"	5.00	Tumbler, 5 ounce, juice		10.00
▸ Plate, 8", salad	11.00	7 ▸ Tumbler, 9 ounce, table		12.00
▸ Plate, 10", hdld.	30.00	Tumbler, 12 ounce, tea		14.00
▸ Saucer	3.00			
Server, 10½", center handle	35.00	*Add 50% for royal blue or red		

Colors: Monax, Ivrene, pink, crystal, cobalt, and fired-on red, blue, green, and yellow

Pink Petalware has fascinated many collectors. This delicate pink is still less costly than most other pink patterns in Depression glass and can be found reasonably priced at markets.

Petalware Mountain Flowers decoration continues to be hunted for its multicolored floral display on Monax, the (MacBeth-Evans name for their white glass). Original boxed sets of sherbets unveiled the Mountain Flowers name. Crystal Federal Star pitchers and decorated tumblers are shown on the opposite page. Pitchers are found satinized or plain as are the tumblers. Note the crystal sherbet; and look for a satinized one to turn up also. We had to buy six juice tumblers with the plain pitcher and even had to promise to sell it that way after photography; so we did. The owner didn't want the set separated.

An original boxed set on the right shows straight-sided tumblers with matching pastel bands were packed with Ivrene "Pastel Bands" sets. Even if these tumblers are not Petalware pattern, they wer decorated to go with it. These tumblers are found in several sizes, all presently selling in the $7.00 to $10.00 range. W can only guarantee the boxed ones on the right are accurate, but as long as the colored bands harmonize with the dir nerware, that is acceptable to most collectors. Regrettably, there is no name on the box for what we call "Pastel Bands. A dealer friend wants us to mention that the banded ring colors align differently on the Monax and Ivrene. The Ivren shows blue, green, and pink from center to rim: whereas that blue and green order is reversed on the Monax. The inf and color order placement was carefully provided us, but unfortunately, was stored in our computer which died.

Monax and Ivrene are names given these Petalware colors by MacBeth-Evans. Ivrene refers to the opaque, beig colored Petalware illustrated by the boxed set. That color is called Cremax in American Sweetheart. Pastel decorate Ivrene is the design now being pursued as avidly as Mountain Flowers. We are continually asked for serving pieces a shows. Taking into consideration the small amount of it available, prices are rising.

Collectors are enthralled with various Petalware decorations. This becomes noticeable when those items are put ou for sale and fly off the table shortly after the show opens.

Florette is the third most collected design. It is the pointed petal, red flower decoration without the red edge trin Since we now own a 1949 company magazine showing a woman painting this Florette design on stacks of plates, probably belongs in the 50s book.

Ivrene

	Crystal	Pink	Cremax, Monax, Plain	Cremax, Monax, Florette, Fired-On Decorations	Red Trim Floral
Bowl, 4½", cream soup	4.50	17.00	12.00	20.00	
2 ▸ Bowl, 5¾", cereal	4.00	15.00	9.00	20.00	42.00
Bowl, 7", soup			65.00	110.00	
12 ▸ *Bowl, 9", large berry	8.50	20.00	20.00	30.00	135.00
13 ▸ Cup	3.00	8.00	5.00	8.00	25.00
7 ▸ **Creamer, footed	3.00	10.00	8.00	10.00	35.00
Lamp shade (many sizes) $8.00 – $15.00					
18 ▸ Mustard with metal cover in cobalt blue only, $10.00					
5 ▸ Pitcher, (Mountain Flowers) juice (crystal or frosted)					300.00
Pitcher, 80 ounce (crystal decorated bands)	35.00				
1 ▸ Plate, 6", sherbet	2.00	5.00	3.00	4.00	22.00
9 ▸ Plate, 8", salad	2.00	7.00	6.00	8.00	25.00
11 ▸ Plate, 9", dinner	4.00	16.00	14.00	20.00	37.50
Plate, 11", salver	4.50	15.00	12.00	20.00	
10 ▸ Plate, 12", salver		16.00	17.00	20.00	40.00
15 ▸ Platter, 13", oval	8.50	25.00	15.00	30.00	
14 ▸ Saucer	1.50	2.00	2.00	3.50	10.00
Saucer, cream soup liner			15.00		
Sherbet, 4", low footed			30.00		
8 ▸ **Sherbet, 4½", low footed	3.50	10.00	8.00	18.00	38.00
6 ▸ **Sugar, footed	3.00	9.00	8.00	10.00	35.00
17 ▸ Tidbit servers or Lazy Susans, several styles					
12.00 to 17.50					
4 ▸ Tumbler, 3⅝", 6 ounce					50.00
3 ▸ Tumbler, 4⅝", 12 ounce					55.00
16 ▸ ‡Tumblers (crystal decorated pastel bands) $7.50 – $10.00					

*Also in cobalt at $65.00   **Also in cobalt at $35.00   ‡Several sizes

9   7   2   6   9

9   9   9   9   9

10   10

9   17   9

PILLAR OPTIC, "LOGS," "LOG CABIN," ANCHOR HOCKING GLASS COMPANY, 1937 – 1942

Colors: crystal, green, pink, Royal Ruby; amber and iridescent, possible Federal Glass Co.

Pillar Optic is familiar to collectors of kitchenware as it has been pictured in that book for years. The pretzel jar is often found with mugs and a pitcher which was originally promoted as pretzel set. We doubt the mugs were to be used for root beer, but you could. Most collectors call that 130-ounce jar a cookie, but it was not offered as such. The pretzel jar top is hard to find mint. These jars are sometimes found satinized and with hand-painted flowers.

On a recent trip my wife and son spotted one of these pretzel jars and were about to purchase it when my son's younger eyes noticed a chipped spot on the lid. After they declined it, the owner said, "Oh, I can fix that right up in just a minute with something I've

got behind the counter!" That didn't further enhance the piece in their eyes — but it provided quite a bit of merriment on the remainder of the trip in rehashing that rather startling pronouncement. That reminded me of a Miss America goblet that we turned down after spotting a chip on the rim. The owner followed us throughout the entire store with an Emory board grinding away. That sound drove us out of the shop rather quickly.

The 60-ounce pitcher came in three colors. The two 80-ounce ones are shown here. The panels of Pillar Optic are evenly spaced (note pretzel jars) and not like Old Café's alternating large panel with two smaller ones. Notice that there were two styles of Pillar Optic pitchers manufactured. It is only the ice lip style that is comparable to Old Café. We received a letter not long after adding this pattern to the book stating that we had sabotaged two sales of Old Café pitchers with our new listing. Pillar Optic pitchers are collectible, just not as the more expensive Old Café ones to collectors of that pattern.

Royal Ruby Pillar Optic items are hard to find though new pieces continue to be unearthed as you can see by the photo. It seems that cup, saucer, creamer, and sugar are all rare in red. We have added two additional pieces of Royal Ruby for this book including a saucer with indented ring, and a two-handled sandwich plate found at an estate sale in Florida.

Flat tumblers come in amber and iridescent. However, Federal Glass Company is known to have manufactured like patterned tumblers and it's most likely amber and iridescent wares have come from them rather than Anchor Hocking.

Two styles of cups are shown by the rounded cup pictured in green and the flatter red one, reminiscent of Colonial styled cups. We finally found a green saucer, but no pink one yet. We have not seen flat green cups or rounded pink ones. The pink sugar and creamer came out of the attic of a former Hocking employee.

Crystal Pillar Optic tumblers have been a fundamental part of Anchor Hocking's restaurant line for years. In fact, in one of their later catalogs, it is shown under the heading "Old Reliable." Many restaurants still use them.

	Crystal	Amber, Green, Pink	Royal Ruby			Crystal	Amber, Green, Pink	Royal Ruby
▸ Bowl, oval vegetable			150.00	4 ▸	Pretzel jar, 130 oz.	85.00	150.00	
▸ Bowl, 9", two-handle		65.00	150.00	1 ▸	Saucer w/indent	2.00	4.00	25.00
▸ Creamer, footed		65.00	100.00	13 ▸	Sherbet, 2 styles		12.00	50.00
▸ Cup, 2 styles	10.00	12.00	75.00	20 ▸	Sugar, footed		65.00	100.00
Mug, 12 oz.	12.00	35.00		14 ▸	Tumbler, 1½ oz., whiskey	8.00	15.00	
▸ Pitcher, w/o lip, 60 oz.	25.00	45.00		5 ▸	Tumbler, 3¼", 3 oz., footed	8.00	15.00	30.00
▸ Pitcher, w/lip, 80 oz.	30.00	55.00			Tumbler, 4", 5 oz., juice, ftd.	10.00	17.50	50.00
▸ Pitcher, w/o lip, 80 oz.	35.00	65.00		17 ▸	Tumbler, 5¼", 10 oz., ftd.	12.00	25.00	60.00
Plate, 6", sherbet	3.00	6.00	25.00	8 ▸	Tumbler, 7 oz., old fashioned	10.00	25.00	
▸ Plate, 8", luncheon	8.00	12.00	30.00	10 ▸	Tumbler, 9 oz., water	2.50	15.00	
▸ Plate, 12", 2 hdld.			150.00	6 ▸	Tumbler, 11 oz., ftd., cone	12.00	20.00	
▸ Platter, 11", oval			165.00	3 ▸	Tumbler, 13 oz., tea	4.00	25.00	

PRIMO, "PANELED ASTER," U.S. GLASS COMPANY, Early 1930s

Colors: green and yellow

Primo's grill pate with a raised rim cup seat made its appearance in green, but there are no reports of this piece in yellow. The normally found grill plate is difficult enough to find, but the cup ring one is almost invisible. Check it out in the picture. In 1932, Primo was promoted as a 14-piece bridge set (with plates, cups, saucers, and sugar and creamer), a 16-piece luncheonette (with grill plates, tumblers, cups, and saucers), an 18-piece occasional set (with plates, tumblers, sugar, creamer, cups, and saucers), a 19-piece hostess set (add a tray), or a 7-piece berry set.

That two-handled hostess tray finally materialized, so those 19-piece settings may not have been as popular as other assortments. The 11" three-footed console bowl (large berry in old ads) created a furor among Primo collectors when it was first pictured in a previous book. When found, that bowl (really abused over the years) was labeled rare because it wasn't listed in Gene Florence's book. No one seemed overly excited about the 6½" sherbet plate not previously listed. We were thrilled enough for everybody when they were first glimpsed in that antique mall. We bought the sherbet plates, but had to buy the sherbets to get them. Finding new pieces for patterns is now our "thrill." We can truly report there still is one 34 years later.

We have found that any bowls, dinner, grill, or cake plates would take some searching. Though we have discovered several new pieces in yellow and green, we have not yet found a green berry bowl to picture.

Aggravation in finding Primo is even worse when items are found with excessive mould roughness and inner rim damage. We have bought more Primo along the Gulf Coast than any place we have searched, so it seems likely it may have been a premium item for something in that area.

The tumbler exactly fits the coaster/ashtray. These coasters have been found in boxed sets with Primo tumblers that were advertised as "Bridge Service Sets." The coasters are also found in pink and black, but no Primo design is found on the coasters. Evidently, U.S. Glass used these as a universal item with other patterns.

	Yellow, Green			Yellow, Green
Bowl, 4½"	25.00		Plate, 10", dinner	30.00
1 ▸ Bowl, 7¾"	40.00	10 ▸	Plate, 10", grill	18.00
Bowl, 11", 3-footed	75.00	3 ▸	Plate, 10", grill w/indent	25.00
4 ▸ Cake plate, 10", 3-footed	50.00	7 ▸	Saucer	3.00
9 ▸ Coaster/ashtray	8.00	2 ▸	Sherbet	14.00
5 ▸ Creamer	14.00		Sugar	14.00
6 ▸ Cup	12.00		Tray, 2-handle hostess	50.00
Plate, 6¼"	15.00	8 ▸	Tumbler, 5¾", 9 ounce	22.00
Plate, 7½"	14.00			

PRINCESS, HOCKING GLASS COMPANY, 1931 – 1935

Colors: green, Topaz yellow, apricot yellow, pink, and light blue

11

Princess bowls in mint condition and footed iced tea tumblers are hard to locate in all colors. Collectors of green Princess have to search long and hard for the undivided relish and the obscure square-footed pitcher with tumblers to match. Some dealers sanction the undivided Princess relish as a soup bowl. It seems too shallow for a soup bowl; but if you can find one for sale, it will make a divot in your cash supply. Lovers of pink Princess have trouble acquiring coasters, ashtrays, and square-foot pitchers with matching tumblers. The hardest to find yellow pieces include the butter dish, juice pitcher, undivided relish, 10½" handled sandwich plate, coasters, and ashtrays. This handled sandwich is just like the handled grill plate without the dividers. We have only found two of these in all our years of searching for glass and they were bought reasonably because the dealer labeled them Patrician. He had called a friend and described them on the phone rather spend time to look them up — or buy a book. His friend thought he was describing Patrician. Sometimes, we are glad that dealers are too cheap to buy books. A good book in this business will save you money.

All Princess bowls present a problem due to inner rim roughness, "irr" in descriptions or ads. Stacking the bowls together over the years caused some of this "irr" damage; but the very sharply defined inner rims were problematic from the moulds. Mint condition bowls command a premium price.

A conspicuous color variation of yellow Princess exists. Topaz is the official color name listed by Hocking, and it is a bright, attractive shade of yellow. However, some yellow turned out looking more amber than yellow and has been labeled "apricot" by collectors. Most collect the Topaz, which makes the darker, amber shade troublesome to sell. The colors are so incompatible that it appears as if Hocking meant to produce two separate colors.

For some reason (possible distribution through premiums) yellow Princess cereal and berry bowls and sherbets proliferat in the Detroit area. We pointed that out to a dealer who had a table full of yellow at a show and he said he had never realized that yellow was as commonly found there until after he moved from New York to that area. On the other hand, all but one of the known yellow Princess juice pitchers have been found in northern and central Kentucky.

Blue Princess pieces are encountered on rare occasions. The cookie jar, cup, saucer, and dinner plate are finding a read market. There is some evidence that blue Princess was shipped to Mexico, which could explain its dearth here in the States. There was even an erroneous reproduction report published about blue dinner plates, but they turned out to be the real thing.

The grill plate without handles and dinner plate have been corrected to read 9½" in the listing instead of the 9" listed in Hocking catalogs. Measure perpendicularly and not diagonally

On a merely annoying level, reproductions in cobalt blue, green, pink, and amber (candy dishes) have been reported. The colors are not close to those original ones. Cobalt and amber were never made originally. The green will not glow under ultraviolet (black) light and the pink has an orange hue. We haven't wasted money to buy one to compare the actual design until colors are corrected which create a problem.

The different style Princess cup found near Lancaster is shown above left.

	Green	Pink	Topaz, Apricot
Ashtray, 4½"	80.00	95.00	125.00
13 ▸ Bowl, 4½", berry	35.00	35.00	58.00
1 ▸ Bowl, 5", cereal or oatmeal	40.00	42.00	42.00
Bowl, 9", octagonal, salad	45.00	58.00	175.00
5 ▸ Bowl, 9½", hat-shaped	52.00	50.00	150.00
19 ▸ Bowl, 10", oval vegetable	30.00	28.00	65.00
3 ▸ Butter dish and cover	105.00	135.00	850.00
Butter dish bottom	35.00	40.00	250.00
Butter dish top	70.00	95.00	600.00
Cake stand, 10"	32.50	35.00	
9 ▸*Candy dish and cover	60.00	95.00	
Coaster	55.00	85.00	125.00
22 ▸**Cookie jar and cover	58.00	70.00	
4 ▸ Creamer, oval	19.00	20.00	20.00
11 ▸‡Cup	11.00	11.00	8.00
Pitcher 6", 37 ounce	65.00	75.00	995.00
Pitcher, 7⅜", 24 ounce, ftd.	525.00	475.00	
Pitcher, 8", 60 ounce	60.00	65.00	110.00
12 ▸‡‡Plate, 5½", sherbet	9.00	9.00	3.00
6 ▸ Plate, 8", salad	16.00	18.00	15.00
§Plate, 9½", dinner	30.00	26.00	16.00

*Beware reproductions in cobalt blue and amber

	Green	Pink	Topaz, Apricot
**Plate, 9½", grill	20.00	20.00	8.00
Plate, 10¼", handled sandwich	25.00	30.00	195.00
15 ▸ Plate, 10½", grill, closed handles	10.00	12.00	5.50
10 ▸ Platter, 12", closed handles	32.00	32.00	67.50
20 ▸ Relish, 7½", divided, 4 pint	28.00	30.00	100.00
2 ▸ Relish, 7½", plain	200.00	200.00	265.00
8 ▸ Salt and pepper, 4½", pair	60.00	55.00	85.00
Spice shakers, 5½", pair	40.00		
12 ▸‡Saucer (same as sherbet plate)	9.00	9.00	3.00
14 ▸ Sherbet, footed	23.00	25.00	35.00
7 ▸ Sugar	10.00	15.00	8.50
21 ▸ Sugar cover	30.00	30.00	17.50
17 ▸ Tumbler, 3", 5 ounce, juice	35.00	38.00	32.50
Tumbler, 4", 9 ounce, water	30.00	32.00	25.00
Tumbler, 5¼", 13 oz., iced tea	50.00	45.00	30.00
Tumbler, 4¾", 9 oz., sq. ftd	65.00	60.00	
16 ▸ Tumbler, 5¼", 10 ounce, ftd.	33.00	30.00	22.00
18 ▸ Tumbler, 6½", 12½ oz., ftd.	120.00	100.00	175.00
23 ▸ Vase, 8"	45.00	60.00	

**Blue $995.00
‡Blue $125.00
‡‡Blue $60.00
§Blue $200.00

QUEEN MARY (PRISMATIC LINE), "VERTICAL RIBBED,"
ANCHOR HOCKING GLASS COMPANY, 1936 – 1949

Colors: pink, crystal, and some Royal Ruby

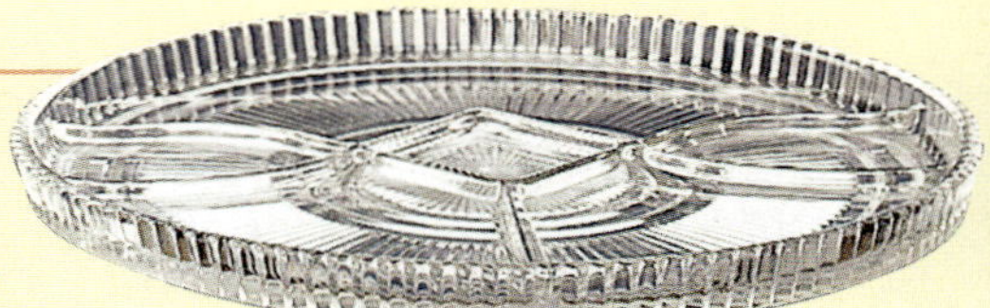

Crystal Queen Mary is attracting more new collectors than pink due to its being inexpensive and accessible; it has that same linear deco look of the pink. Nothing is as exasperating as trying to stumble onto pink Queen Mary dinner plates and footed tumblers. You should be warned that prices for those same items in crystal are exhibiting upward tendencies due to new demand. A crystal set can still be completed at manageable prices including dinner plates and footed tumblers.

A few pink Queen Mary prices have diminished because new collectors are not now latching onto it, as they are the crystal. Four dealers had pink Queen Mary dinner plates at a recent show. They were priced from $50.00 to $75.00. The $50.00 and $55.00 ones sold. Those higher priced were still sitting in the dealers' displays at the end of the show. Pink dinners will sell — at the right price!

The 6" cereal bowl has the same shape as the butter bottom but is smaller in diameter. What we call butter dishes were advertised as "preserve dishes" in Hocking's catalogs. There are two different cups. The smaller rests on the saucer with cup ring. The larger cup rests on the combination saucer/sherbet plate so typical of Hocking's patterns. The pink smaller cup and saucer have surpassed the larger in price. Some dealers are labeling the 5½" tab-handled bowl as a lug or cream soup. The price on that bowl has gone up due to that speculative description that is not in catalog listings.

The frosted crystal butter dish with metal band looks somewhat like a crown. These were made about the time of the English Coronation in the mid-1930s. We have seen these priced as high as $150.00 in an Art Deco shop and as low as $25.00 elsewhere. A couple of lampshades were found using frosted candy lids with metal-banded decorations.

We are now confident the little colored shakers pictured previously in amethyst and cobalt blue are Hazel Atlas; keep that in mind if they are offered to you as Queen Mary. They, alas, are not. However, they are quite collectible as Hazel-Atlas products.

A checkered appearing, cross-lined vase (shaped like Old Cafe with a 400 line number) is pictured along with Queen Mary items in early Hocking catalogs. As far as I am concerned, it is only pictured with the pattern; however, Cath thinks there's a chance it should be included in the listing as a Queen Mary item. You ultimately decide whether you use it with the pattern or not.

		Pink	Crystal
	Ashtray, 2" x 3¾", oval	5.00	4.00
6 ▸	*Ashtray, 3¼", round		3.00
	Ashtray, 4¼", square (#422)		4.00
	Bowl, 4", one-handle or none	5.00	3.50
	Bowl, 4½", berry	9.00	4.00
	Bowl, 5", berry, flared	11.00	5.50
	Bowl, 5½", two handle, lug soup	18.00	7.50
	Bowl, 6", cereal	22.00	6.50
14 ▸	Bowl, 6", 3-footed	12.00	
	Bowl, deep, 7½" (#477)	35.00	14.00
	Bowl, 8¾", large berry (#478)	25.00	15.00
17 ▸	Butter dish or preserve and cover (#498)	150.00	35.00
	Butter dish bottom (#498)	35.00	7.00
	Butter dish top (#498)	115.00	28.00
11 ▸	Candy dish and cover, 7¼" (#490)	65.00	20.00
	**Candlesticks, 4½", double branch, pair		22.00
9 ▸	Celery or pickle dish, 5" x 10" (#467)	50.00	15.00
	Cigarette jar, 2" x 3", oval	7.50	5.50
18 ▸	Coaster, 3½"	9.00	5.00
	Coaster/ashtray, 3¼", round (#419)	6.00	5.00
10 ▸	Comport, 5¾"	25.00	15.00
16 ▸	Creamer, footed	60.00	25.00

		Pink	Crystal
13 ▸	Creamer, 5½", oval (#471)	14.00	7.00
7 ▸	Cup, large	7.00	5.00
	Cup, small	6.00	8.00
	Mayonnaise, 5" x 2¾" h, 6" plate	35.00	20.00
	Plate, 6⅝"	5.00	4.00
4 ▸	Plate, 8¾", salad (#438)		5.50
	Plate, 9¾", dinner (#426)	58.00	30.00
	Plate, 12", sandwich (#450)	28.00	18.00
	Plate, 14", serving tray	22.00	12.00
1 ▸	Relish tray, cloverleaf		15.00
	Relish tray, 12", 3-part	18.00	9.00
18 ▸	Relish tray, 14", 5-part	20.00	12.00
5 ▸	Salt and pepper, 2½", pair (#486)		20.00
8 ▸	Saucer/cup ring	5.00	2.50
2 ▸	Sherbet, footed or flat	12.00	5.00
12 ▸	Sugar, footed	60.00	25.00
15 ▸	Sugar, 6", oval (#470)	14.00	7.00
	Tumbler, 3½", 5 ounce, juice	13.00	4.00
	Tumbler, 4", 9 ounce, water	15.00	6.00
3 ▸	Tumbler, 5", 10 ounce, footed	70.00	38.00
	Vase, 6½" (#441)		12.00

*Royal Ruby $5.00; Forest Green $3.00   **

Royal Ruby $150.00

RADIANCE, NEW MARTINSVILLE GLASS COMPANY, 1936 – 1939

Colors: red, cobalt and ice blue, amber, crystal, pink, and emerald green

Radiance punch, decanter, and condiment sets never appear in quantities to satisfy demand. Punch sets are laborious to find, but the punch ladle is practically impossible. The ladle was created by stretching and attaching a long handle to a punch cup. If not destroyed through use, collectors and dealers have added to their passing by bringing them to shows. We have been told several times that the handle detaches from the cup very easily. One dealer has had that tribulation twice. He is often teased that he, personally, has helped raise the price of red punch ladles. Be sure to notice the Canary Yellow (Vaseline) punch cup which is the only piece we have found in that color.

A 4" tall cake stand has been found in both red and crystal. Watch for other colors.

Viking made crystal punch bowls after they bought out New Martinsville in the mid 1940s. These are being found on large plates of emerald green and black. One such emerald green set was pictured previously. These are found rather frequently — unlike their older counterparts. The punch bowls flair outward rather than inward, like the older "bowling ball" design. Viking's ladle is plain, so it is not as desirable as the earlier ladle.

Several collectors are petitioning us to move Radiance to our Elegant book as it is too fine a glassware to be included in this book. They are probably right. However, Radiance was designated as Depression glass long before our "Elegant" term was born in 1980.

Radiance red and ice blue colors are easier found than any color except amber. They are the most sought colors, but they do not come inexpensively. The most troublesome pieces to locate in those colors include the butter dish and pitcher.

Vases have been made into lamps in several formats. It is doubtful this was a factory endeavor, but it could have been.

While shopping recently, we saw a pair of vases with decorations of gold and blue with flowers. We regretted leaving them, but they were so worn, it was difficult to justify the expense. Vases may be found in an array of colors.

Cobalt blue is striking, but few pieces surface in that color.

Pieces of pink Radiance including creamer, sugar, tray, cup, saucer, vase, and shakers are turning up occasionally. These are selling in the same range as the red since they are scarce at this time. Price crystal about 50% of amber; both colors are more difficult to sell. Only crystal pieces that item collectors seek sell well. These include pitchers, butter dishes, decanters, shakers, sugars, creamers, and cordials. Many crystal pieces were decorated with silver or gold.

6

		Ice & Cobalt Blue, Red	Amber				Ice & Cobalt Blue, Red	Amber
	Bowl, 5", nut, 2-handle	22.00	12.00			Condiment set, 4-piece w/tray	325.00	175.00
2▸	Bowl, 6", bonbon	33.00	17.50	14▸		Creamer	27.50	15.00
	Bowl, 6", bonbon, footed	35.00	20.00	22▸		Cruet, individual	90.00	50.00
	Bowl, 6", bonbon w/cover	115.00	55.00	18▸		Cup, footed	21.50	12.00
	Bowl, 7", relish, 2-part	35.00	20.00	6▸		Cup, punch	15.00	7.00
6▸	Bowl, 7", pickle	35.00	20.00	8▸		Decanter w/stopper, handle	225.00	125.00
2▸	Bowl, 8", relish, 3-part	40.00	35.00	9▸		Goblet, 1 ounce, cordial	33.00	23.00
	*Bowl, 9", punch	225.00	125.00			Honey jar, w/lid	125.00	75.00
	Bowl, 10", celery	45.00	22.00			Ladle for punch bowl	150.00	100.00
3▸	Bowl, 10", crimped	55.00	30.00			Lamp, 12"	125.00	65.00
	Bowl, 10", flared	50.00	25.00			Mayonnaise, 3-piece, set	115.00	65.00
	Bowl, 12", crimped	60.00	35.00	5▸		Pitcher, 64 ounce	325.00	175.00
	Bowl, 12", flared	65.00	32.00			Plate, 8", luncheon	20.00	10.00
1▸	Butter dish	465.00	210.00			**Plate, 14", punch bowl liner	85.00	45.00
0▸	Candlestick, 6", ruffled, pair	175.00	80.00	4▸		Salt & pepper, pair	95.00	50.00
	Candlestick, 8", pair	225.00	95.00	17▸		Saucer	8.50	5.50
	Candlestick, 2-lite, pair	175.00	95.00	7▸		Sugar	27.50	15.00
	Candy, flat, w/lid	100.00	50.00			Tray, oval	45.00	25.00
9▸	Cheese/cracker (11" plate) set	130.00	30.00	3▸		Tumbler, 9 ounce	34.00	22.00
	Comport, 5"	35.00	18.00			Vase, 10", flared or crimped	110.00	75.00
0▸	Comport, 6"	35.00	22.00			Vase, 12", flared or crimped	175.00	

* Emerald green $125.00   **Emerald green $25.00

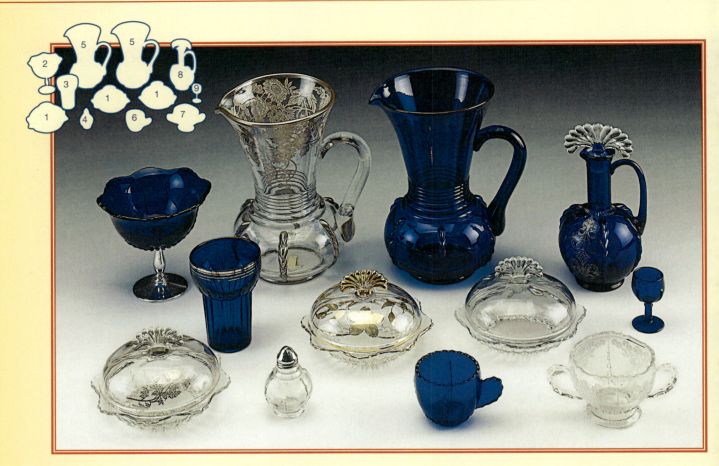

RAINDROPS, "OPTIC DESIGN," FEDERAL GLASS COMPANY, 1929 – 1933

Colors: green and crystal

Raindrops has rounded bumps and not elongated ones. Elongated bumps belong to another pattern commonly referred to as "Thumbprint." Almost all Raindrops pieces are embossed on the bottom with Federal's trademark F inside a shield. I want to emphasize that that mark is not a Fire-King mark as is being misrepresented over the Internet and in many antique malls we frequent. While we were working on our new Ovenware book, we bought large amounts of Federal glass to be included. I suspect that 20 – 25% of what we bought was labeled Fire-King and not Federal. Sellers knew Fire-King was valuable; so seeing an F on the bottom was good enough for them to label it wrong. The bad news is that we left quite a few we could have used in the book; but, being Federal, and not Fire-King, they were priced too expensively to buy.

Raindrops makes a great small luncheon or bridge set. It even has a few complementary pieces that other smaller sets do not. You can find three sizes of bowls in Raindrops. The 7½" bowl will be the one you will probably find last. That bowl has always been scarce and with new blood searching for it, the supply has shrunk rapidly. It is now the second most expensive piece of this pattern having by-passed the sugar lid. The shakers remain the items that rarely appear. I wonder how expensive they would be were there more people searching for this pattern. A couple of shaker collectors have told us that these are harder to find than yellow and green Mayfair. Both collectors had at least one of those elusive shakers, but neither one had the Raindrops. One Raindrops shaker is all we have owned. There is a slim possibility of your finding one; but never say never.

There are two styles of cups. One is flat bottomed and the other is slightly footed. The flat-bottomed is 2⁵⁄₁₆" high and the footed is 2¹¹⁄₁₆" (reported by an enthusiastic Raindrops collector). Prices have remained steady for the short supply being found. Prices for crystal tumblers run from 50% to 60% less than for green.

Raindrops will blend well with many other green sets; so, give that a try if you want extra pieces.

		Green
4 ▸	Bowl, 4½", fruit	7.00
5 ▸	Bowl, 6", cereal	14.00
6 ▸	Bowl, 7½", berry	60.00
1 ▸	Cup	9.00
4 ▸	Creamer	7.50
5 ▸	Plate, 6", sherbet	2.50
8 ▸	Plate, 8", luncheon	6.00
	Salt and pepper, pair	420.00
2 ▸	Saucer	2.00

		Green
3 ▸	Sherbet	8.00
13 ▸	Sugar	7.50
12 ▸	Sugar cover	42.50
	Tumbler, 3", 4 ounce	5.00
9 ▸	Tumbler, 2⅛", 2 ounce	5.00
11 ▸	Tumbler, 3⅞", 5 ounce	6.50
7 ▸	Tumbler, 4⅛", 9½ ounce	9.00
	Tumbler, 5", 10 ounce	9.00
	Tumbler, 5⅜", 14 ounce	14.00
10 ▸	Whiskey, 1⅞", 1 ounce	7.00

REEDED, WHIRLSPOOL, "SPUN," LINE #701, IMPERIAL GLASS COMPANY, c. 1936 – 1960s

Colors: black, crystal, cobalt, dark green, amber, tangerine, Midas gold, turquoise, pink, milk, mustard

Reeded is the name given this pattern by Imperial, but it has been called "Spun" by collectors for years. It was heavily promoted as beverage sets which must have sold well due to the quantity found today. A rather unusual vanity set (powder and perfume) was included amongst its mostly dinnerware items. The perfume has a spade shaped stopper. Additional items (vases and decanters) were added to the line in the 1960s. We were encouraged to put Reeded in the book due to Imperial's closure making their wares more collectible.

Do notice the black Reeded cocktail shaker pictured which surfaced a couple of years ago at a show in New York. Candles were made from a small ivy ball vase fitted with a crystal glass candle insert (see the cobalt one pictured here). It is the insert that is difficult to find and valued as much as the vase. You might find these in crystal vases reasonably priced; so buy them for the inserts. Along with a larger ball, these were promoted as a console set in the 1950s.

The two jars on the top row below are called Whirlspool and are found with glass lids as pictured or with triangular metal knobs. Glass lids are preferred, but the metal knobbed variety is accepted by collectors.

		*All colors
	Ashtray, 2¼", cupped	10.00
	Bottle, 3 oz., bitters	38.00
	Bowl, 4½", fruit	20.00
	Bowl, 7", nappy, straight side	33.00
8 ▶	Bowl, 8", nappy	33.00
	Bowl, 10", deep salad	45.00
	Candle, 2½", ball w/crystal glass insert	45.00
2 ▶	Candy box, footed w/cone lid	50.00
	Cigarette holder, wider mouth, 2½" ball	20.00
1 ▶	Cocktail shaker, 36 oz., w or w/o handles	75.00
	Creamer, footed	25.00
	Cup	20.00
	Ice tub	60.00
5 ▶	Jar, Whirlspool, 4", tall, w/lid or w/metal knob	55.00
6 ▶	Jar, Whirlspool, 5", tall, w/lid or w/metal knob	65.00
	Jar, Whirlspool, 6", tall, w/lid or w/metal knob	75.00
	Jar, Whirlspool, 7", tall, w/lid or w/metal knob	85.00
	Muddler, 4½"	10.00
	Perfume w/triangle stop	50.00
4 ▶	Pitcher, 80 oz., ice lip	70.00
	Plate, 8", salad, belled rim	20.00
	Plate, 13½", cupped edge	30.00
	Plate, 14", server, flat	32.50
	Powder jar w/lid	50.00
	Saucer	8.00
	Sherbet	17.50
	Sugar, footed	25.00
	Syrup, ball w/chrome spout & handle	50.00
	Tumbler, 2 oz., shot	20.00
	Tumbler, 3½ oz., cocktail	10.00
	Tumbler, 5 oz., juice, straight	10.00
	Tumbler, 7 oz., old fashioned	12.00
3 ▶	Tumbler, 9 oz.	12.00
	Tumbler, 12 oz., tea, straight side	13.00

		*All colors
	Tumbler, 12 oz., tea, bulb top	14.00
7 ▶	Vase, 2½", ball	20.00
	Vase, 3½", ivy ball, footed	35.00
	Vase, ivy ball, 6½", footed	55.00
	Vase, 4", ball	17.50
	Vase, 5", bud	35.00
	Vase, 5", bulbous, tall neck rose	45.00
	Vase, 5", rose	40.00
9 ▶	Vase, 6", ball, rose	45.00
	Vase, 6", bud	40.00

	*All colors
Vase, 6", slender	40.00
Vase, 8½"	40.00
Vase, 9"	50.00

*Add 50% for red or blue; deduct 25% for crystal

188

"RIBBON," HAZEL-ATLAS GLASS COMPANY, Early 1930s

Colors: green; some black, crystal, and pink

"Ribbon" is a Hazel-Atlas pattern that is representative of the era in which it was launched. "Ribbon" has clean lines and shapes, which manage to convey elegance and movement at the same time.

We hardly ever see "Ribbon" for sale at glass shows except for candy dishes. These have sold very well to new collectors as a "Ribbon" example piece. However, some dealers have begun to "jump" the price for these and we see more sitting than leaving with buyers. A candy dish makes a great first piece of a collection due to its practicality for the owner. New collectors love to buy a usable piece as a display item and candies fit that niche quite well.

"Ribbon" is another of the patterns not uncovered in the west according to dealers who travel those areas. We find more in Ohio and Pennsylvania than any place. Tumblers, sugars, and creamers are not yet as hard to find as bowls, but even they are beginning to disappear.

"Ribbon" bowls are among the most elusive in all of Depression glass. They are in shorter supply than those of its sister pattern, Cloverleaf. Prices are beginning to reflect that. We had a letter from a long-time collector explaining that we were wrong in listing the cereal because it did not exist in Ribbon. (He had an older book. We told him it was pictured now.) He wanted to buy the bowl. We had to turn him down since this is the only one we have been able to buy since we started writing. Others surely are there to be found.

The panel design on pieces that flare at the top expands, as shown by the sugar and creamer in the picture. The normally found "Ribbon" design has evenly spaced small panels. This natural flared expansion is especially noticeable on a belled rim vegetable bowl found in both black and green coloring. We received a letter wondering if that flared bowl was the "Ribbon" pattern because it looked so different. This flared version has been accepted as "Ribbon" for as long as we have been in the business. The 8" bowl with straight sides is pictured here shaped like the berry and cereal.

We have never been convinced that shakers exist in green although some found are similar. We would suspect real ones would be Ovide shaped as in Cloverleaf.

		Green	Black			Green	Black
1	Bowl, 4", berry	38.00		7	Plate, 6¼", sherbet	5.00	
2	Bowl, 5", cereal	48.00			Plate, 8", luncheon	9.00	14.00
	Bowl, 8", large berry, flared	35.00	40.00		*Salt and pepper, pair	30.00	45.00
4	Bowl, 8", straight side	85.00			Saucer	2.50	
3	Candy dish and cover	65.00		9	Sherbet, footed	12.00	
6	Creamer, footed	15.00		5	Sugar, footed	14.00	
10	Cup	5.00		8	Tumbler, 6", 10 ounce	37.50	

* Pink $35.00

189

RING, "BANDED RINGS," LINE #300, HOCKING GLASS COMPANY, 1927 – 1933

Colors: crystal, crystal w/bands of pink, red, blue, orange, yellow, black, silver, etc.; green, pink, "Mayfair" blue, and Royal Ruby

Green "Ring-like" pieces began showing up a few years ago in the form of goblets and tumblers. These are not old Hocking Ring and will not glow under ultra-violet light as the older green does. (Green glows due to uranium oxide used in the formula for making it. It is not Vaseline which is yellow in color.) Each new piece is marked MSE for Martha Stewart Everyday. They are not Depression glass.

Crystal with colored bands intrigues more collectors than the ever-abundant, unadorned crystal. Crystal with platinum (silver) bands is the next favored form of Ring. Worn platinum trims frustrate collectors, as there is presently no inexpensive way to restore them. Colored rings do not seem to suffer from that malady, possibly because the colors did not adorn rims, as did platinum. To be Ring, *molded* rings have to be in the design — not just applied colored bands.

There is a colored Ring arrangement of black, yellow, red, and orange in that order. Assorted other arrangements were made. The foot of Ring stems and tumblers are found plain or with a block/grid design. Both these styles are also found in Mayfair and Princess, which makes finding one style a problem only when buying by mail or ordering online. Be sure to specify whether you want a plain foot or a block/grid design on the foot.

A subscription to *Country Gentleman* in the 1930s gave you a premium of a green Ring berry bowl set consisting of an 8" berry and six 5" berry bowls. Green Ring berry bowls have not been plentiful over the years; so that enticement may have not worked well in a gentleman's magazine. A set of green Ring can be put together over time as a couple of our dealer friends have recently proved.

Pink pitcher and tumbler sets are the only pieces we see regularly in that color in Florida. Maybe a few Wisconsin retirees brought them south since a Wisconsin collector testified that the pink was a dairy premium in her area. The tumblers were packed with cottage cheese and she could not remember what you had to do to receive the pitcher. Pink sets remain plentiful in that dairy country.

Royal Ruby and "Mayfair" blue pieces of Ring are found occasionally. The luncheon plate and 10-ounce tumbler are fairly common in Royal Ruby, and flat juice tumblers and cups have appeared in small groups, but no saucers.

Remember, for a piece to be Hocking's Ring, it must have the moulded ring lines, not just painted stripes.

	Crystal	Green, Dec.
8 ▸ Bowl, 5", berry, tab handles	4.00	8.00
Bowl, 7", soup	10.00	15.00
9 ▸ Bowl, 5¼", divided	12.00	40.00
7 ▸ Bowl, 8", large berry, tab handles	7.00	14.00
Butter tub or ice tub	25.00	40.00
Cocktail shaker	20.00	27.50
10 ▸**Cup	6.00	9.00
Creamer, footed	6.00	10.00
Decanter and stopper	28.00	45.00
Goblet, 7¼", 9 ounce	14.00	20.00
Goblet, 3¾", 3½ ounce, cocktail	12.00	18.00
Goblet, 4½", 3½ ounce, wine	13.00	20.00
Ice bucket	20.00	40.00
Pitcher, 8", 60 ounce	17.50	35.00
5 ▸*Pitcher, 8½", 80 ounce	22.00	45.00
13 ▸ Pitcher, 9¼", 84 ounce		60.00
Plate, 6¼", sherbet	2.00	2.50
2 ▸ Plate, 6½", off-center ring	6.00	9.00
‡Plate, 8", luncheon	5.00	7.00

	Crystal	Green, Dec
Plate, 11¼", sandwich	7.00	14.00
‡‡Salt and pepper, pair, 3"	25.00	55.00
Sandwich server, center handle	20.00	27.50
11 ▸ Saucer	1.50	2.00
1 ▸ Sherbet, low (for 6½" plate)	8.00	15.00
6 ▸ Sherbet, 4¾", footed	6.50	11.00
Sugar, footed	6.00	10.00
Tumbler, 3", 4 ounce	4.00	12.00
3 ▸ Tumbler, 3½", 5 ounce	5.00	12.00
Tumbler, 4", 8 ounce, old fashioned	12.00	18.00
Tumbler, 4¼", 9 ounce	4.50	15.00
4 ▸ Tumbler, 4¾", 10 ounce	7.50	13.00
*Tumbler, 5⅛", 12 ounce	8.00	10.00
Tumbler, 3½" footed, juice	6.00	10.00
Tumbler, 5½" footed, water	6.00	12.00
Tumbler, 6½" footed, iced tea	10.00	15.00
12 ▸ Vase, 8"	17.50	38.00
Whiskey, 2", 1½ ounce	7.00	15.00

*Also found in pink. Priced as green.   **Red $65.00 Blue $45.00   ‡Red $17.50   ‡‡Green $55.00

ROCK CRYSTAL, "EARLY AMERICAN ROCK CRYSTAL," McKEE GLASS COMPANY,
1920s and 1930s in colors

Colors: four shades of green, aquamarine, Canary yellow, amber, pink and frosted pink, red slag, dark red, red, amberina red, crystal, frosted crystal, crystal with goofus decoration, crystal with gold decoration, amethyst, milk glass, blue frosted or "Jap" blue, and cobalt blue

Crystal Rock Crystal pieces are sometimes purchased by collectors of other patterns to use as complementary items. Vases, cruets, candlesticks, and an abundance of serving pieces are some of the favored items. Serving pieces display well; enjoy using them.

Rock Crystal had the longest production run of patterns in this book. It was introduced around 1915 in crystal and marketed as one of their Prescut lines. Prescut was McKee's trademarked name for moulded patterns near the end of the cut glass production era. Early Rock Crystal pieces will be embossed Prescut, usually inside the piece. All major glass companies designed moulded wares to simulate cut glass when mechanization became possible and experienced cut glass workers left the glass shops for the war.

Supposedly, hand-cut wares made for a king's table centuries ago inspired the design. Crystal was made until the early 1940s, so that quarter of a century run makes crystal readily available. Some items were only made for a short time and are not so easily found.

Color production ran from the 1920s until the late 1930s. Long years of production made for a vast volume of this glassware with a large assortment of pieces produced. Some pieces designed had only been made in earlier pattern glass production or elegant glassware of the time such as salt dips, syrups, cruets, and egg cups.

Catalogs depicting all the pieces have not been found. Colored glassware production years are well authenticated, but unexpected pieces still show up. A red syrup pitcher was discovered a few years ago. Syrup pitchers were supposedly not made during the time red was produced. Evidently an older syrup pitcher mould was revived and used during the red production. Often older moulds were pulled out to experiment with a color being run at that time; according to older glass-makers, up to 50 pieces would be run to see if the mould were usable. Those short or experimental runs give us some of the rarest and most desirable glassware today. That gives hope for shakers, cruets, and other pieces not yet seen in red.

We bought a large collection of red Rock Crystal from a former McKee employee in the late 1970s. He had eight or nine flat candy bottoms in this lot, which, he explained, were soup bowls. We assume that may have been a method to get rid of excess stock. One problem with McKee's red is its variety of color hues. Note the yellow center in the plate below. That yellow and red mixture is called amberina by collectors. Some red is so dark it almost looks black.

Red, crystal, and amber sets can be finished with determination. An assortment of pieces is available; you need to decide what items you want. Instead of buying every tumbler and stem made, you can select a couple of each, choosing a style you favor. Even collectors with limited budgets can start a small crystal or amber set. Red will take a deeper pocket.

There are two different sizes of punch bowls. The base for the larger bowl has an opening 5" across, and stands 7¹⁄₁₆" tall. This base fits a punch bowl that is 4³⁄₁₆" across the bottom. The other style base has only a 4³⁄₁₆" opening, but is also 6¹⁄₁₆" tall. This base only fits the bowl that is 3½" across the bottom.

Egg plates are often found with gold trim; they were probably a promotional item. In central Florida, we see a dozen or more Lazy Susans each year. They consist of a revolving metal stand with a Rock Crystal relish for a top.

For your information, in the 20s and 30s, Tiffin also made a Rock Crystal similar to McKee's. Their wares had one 8- to 11-petaled daisy flower with ruffled rim lines above it, round pedestal feet and ribbed handles.

191

ROCK CRYSTAL

		Crystal	All other colors	Red
	* Bonbon, 7½", s.e.	22.00	35.00	60.00
19 ▸	Bowl, 4", s.e.	12.00	22.00	32.00
	Bowl, 4½", s.e.	20.00	22.00	32.00
27 ▸	**Bowl, 5", finger bowl with 7" plate, p.e.	35.00	45.00	70.00
31 ▸	Bowl, 5½", s.e.	22.00	24.00	45.00
	Bowl, 7", pickle or spoon tray	40.00	40.00	75.00
	Bowl, 7", salad, s.e.	24.00	37.50	75.00
	Bowl, 8", salad, s.e.	27.50	37.50	85.00
	Bowl, 8½", center handle			220.00
8 ▸	Bowl, 9", salad, s.e.	45.00	50.00	125.00
	Bowl, 10½", salad, s.e.	25.00	50.00	100.00
	Bowl, 11½", 2-part relish	38.00	50.00	80.00
	Bowl, 12", oblong celery	27.50	45.00	95.00
‡	Bowl, 12½", footed center bowl	85.00	125.00	295.00
29 ▸	Bowl, 12½", 5-part relish	38.00	60.00	
	Bowl, 13", roll tray	45.00	60.00	125.00
	Bowl, 14", 6-part relish	50.00	65.00	
	Butter dish and cover	335.00		
	Butter dish bottom	200.00		
	Butter dish top	135.00		
⧥	Candelabra, 2-lite, pair	40.00	105.00	295.00
16 ▸	Candelabra, 3-lite, pair	65.00	195.00	395.00
	Candlestick, flat, stemmed, pair	40.00	65.00	150.00
24 ▸	Candlestick, 5½", low, pair	40.00	65.00	195.00
	Candlestick, 8", tall, pair	100.00	165.00	475.00
	Candy and cover, footed, 9¼"	75.00	90.00	295.00
21 ▸	Candy and cover, round	75.00	85.00	225.00
28 ▸	Cake stand, 11", 2¾" high, footed	35.00	52.50	120.00
	Cheese stand, 2¾"	22.00	30.00	50.00
22 ▸	Comport, 7", s.e.	50.00	45.00	95.00
25 ▸	Comport, 7", p.e.	22.00	28.00	
	Creamer, flat, s.e.	37.50		
	Creamer, 9 oz., footed	20.00	32.00	67.50
	Cruet and stopper, 6 oz., oil	115.00		
11 ▸	Cup, 7 oz.	15.00	27.50	72.00
	Egg plate	38.00		
17 ▸	Goblet, 7½ oz., 8 oz., low footed	20.00	27.50	57.50
7 ▸	Goblet, 11 oz., low footed, iced tea	20.00	30.00	67.50
	Ice dish (3 styles)	40.00		
	Jelly, 5", footed, s.e.	30.00	27.50	52.50
	Lamp, electric	295.00	395.00	695.00
14 ▸	Parfait, 3½ oz., low footed	20.00	35.00	75.00
	Pitcher, quart, s.e.	165.00	225.00	
	Pitcher, ½ gallon, 7½" high	130.00	195.00	
	Pitcher, 9", large covered	175.00	295.00	895.00
	Pitcher, fancy tankard	195.00	695.00	995.00
18 ▸	Plate, 6", bread and butter, s.e.	8.00	9.50	22.00
4 ▸	Plate, 7½", p.e. & s.e.	10.00	10.00	25.00
5 ▸	Plate, 8½", p.e. & s.e.	15.00	12.50	35.00
3 ▸	Plate, 9", s.e.	18.00	22.00	55.00
	Plate, 10½", s.e.	25.00	30.00	65.00
6 ▸	Plate, 10½", dinner, s.e. (large center design)	47.50	70.00	195.00
2 ▸	Plate, 11½", s.e.	18.00	25.00	57.50
	Punch bowl and stand, 14" (2 styles)	695.00		
	Punch bowl stand only (2 styles)	250.00		
	Salt and pepper (2 styles), pair	90.00	125.00	
	Salt dip	60.00		
	Sandwich server, center-handle	30.00	40.00	145.00

* s.e. McKee designation for scalloped edge   **p.e. McKee designation for plain edge
‡ Red Slag $350.00; Cobalt $325.00   ⧥ Cobalt $325.00

		Crystal	All other colors	Red
12 ▸	Saucer	7.50	8.50	18.00
13 ▸	Sherbet or egg, 3½ oz., footed	14.00	28.00	55.00
30 ▸	Sherbet, 6 oz.	12.00	20.00	35.00
	Spooner	45.00		
	Stemware, 1 oz., footed, cordial	18.00	35.00	48.00
	Stemware, 2 oz., wine	22.00	28.00	43.00
9 ▸	Stemware, 3 oz., wine	16.00	33.00	55.00
20 ▸	Stemware, 3½ oz., footed, cocktail	16.00	21.00	45.00
	Stemware, 6 oz., footed, champagne	16.00	20.00	35.00
	Stemware, 7 oz.	16.00	25.00	50.00
1 ▸	Stemware, 8 oz., large footed goblet	22.00	26.00	57.50
	Sundae, 6 oz., low footed	12.00	18.00	35.00
	Sugar, 10 oz., open	15.00	22.00	45.00
	Sugar lid	35.00	50.00	135.00
	Syrup with lid	225.00		895.00
	Tray, 5⅜" x 7⅜", ⅞" high	65.00		
	Tumbler, 2½ oz., whiskey	20.00	30.00	50.00
10 ▸	Tumbler, 5 oz., juice	16.00	25.00	57.50
	Tumbler, 8 oz., old fashioned	20.00	30.00	60.00
	Tumbler, 9 oz., concave or straight	22.00	26.00	52.50
15 ▸	Tumbler, 12 oz., concave or straight	30.00	35.00	75.00
	Vase, 6", cupped	90.00		
	Vase, cornucopia	125.00	165.00	275.00
26 ▸	Vase, 11", footed	85.00	145.00	225.00

"ROMANESQUE," L. E. SMITH GLASS COMPANY, Early 1930s

Colors: black, amber, crystal, pink, yellow, and green

"Romanesque" is a small pattern that few collectors noticed before the Internet. There were a few avid collectors, but they were sparsely scattered across the country. We'd sell a piece here and there as we set up at shows. In the last four or five years, we rarely leave a show with a piece of "Romanesque" remaining. On a trip to New York, we found about a dozen pieces of "Romanesque" including a pair of fan vases. We pulled several pieces for photography and priced the rest. All of it sold at the New York show save one amber plate. That fan vase often goes unrecognized as "Romanesque." We should point out that we've recently encountered two different collectors of only fan vases.

9

Green and amber colors seem to be widespread; we have, so far, found plates, candles, ruffled sherbets, and the bowl part of the console in amber. Notice the newly listed amber, two-handled plate in th photo. The yellow being found is a bright, canary yellow that is often called "vaseline" by collectors.

Pink "Romanesque" seems to be the seldom seen color. There have been some wild prices bandied about on th footed console in that particular color.

Console bowls also come with a separate base, usually black, but sometimes amber. The black pattern is on the bottor so it has to be displayed upside down to identify it as "Romanesque." We have only seen bowls and cake stands in black.

The console bowl sits atop a plain, octagonal detached base. These have to be aligned properly with the bottom the bowl, but are still shaky if a little weight is added to one side of the bowl and not the other. A number of companie made bowls during this era, which resided on matched or different colored stands. Usually these type bowls held a glas frog in the center for mounting floral arrangements which would have worked just fine. You may find the bowl separat from the base these days, making it appear something like a turned edge plate. These were originally designed as consol sets, having a pair of candles at each side, to be used as centerpieces. The stands elevated the bowls for visual appeal.

Snack trays were sold with a sherbet to hold fruit or dessert. An original ad called these a luncheon set which is no what most companies considered as their luncheon set.

If you have other information or unlisted pieces in this pattern, please let us know. This pattern seems to still ho surprises which keep turning up.

	* All colors			* All colors
8 ▸ Bowl, 10", footed, 4¼" high	80.00	4 ▸ Plate, 10", octagonal		25.00
Bowl, 10½"	50.00	6 ▸ Plate, 10", octagonal, 2-handled		30.00
Cake plate, 11½" x 2¾"	45.00	Powder jar		45.00
3 ▸ Candlestick, 2½", pair	30.00	9 ▸ Tray, snack		15.00
7 ▸ Plate, 5½", octagonal	7.00	Sherbet, plain top		10.00
5 ▸ Plate, 7", octagonal	10.00	Sherbet, scalloped top		12.00
1 ▸ Plate, 8", octagonal	13.00	Vase, 7½", fan		65.00
Plate, 8", round	10.00	*Black or canary add 30%		

ROSE CAMEO, BELMONT TUMBLER COMPANY, 1931

Color: green

Belmont Tumbler Company patented Rose Cameo which previously had been attributed to Hazel-Atlas. Rose Cameo only has seven known pieces and it is possible that the actual production was fulfilled by Hazel-Atlas. In any case Belmont was fundamentally a tumbler-making company. Glass shards have been found in digs at a Hazel-Atlas factory site in West Virginia. Conversely, a yellow Cloverleaf shaker was unearthed at the site of Akro Agate's factory in Clarksburg, West Virginia; and we seriously question that Akro had anything to do with making Hazel-Atlas Cloverleaf. (Did you know some glass collectors engage in archaeological digs for glass?)

Actually, as we learn more about how the companies lent out their moulds and/or, contracted glass runs, anything is possible. Rather than lose a contract, a company could make some agreement with another who was running the requested color rather than change over vats to run it themselves. A bonded person transferred the valuable moulds between the plants. We talked with a man whose job was just that. He made an average of three runs per week between glass factories.

All three Rose Cameo bowls are difficult to find; but the smaller berry turns up more often than the others. Most collectors are not finding the straight-sided 6" bowl at any price. Rose Cameo is not confusing new collectors as it once did. Cameo, with its dancing girl, and this cameo-encircled rose were often misidentified in the past when we were all learning. A well educated collecting public rarely makes those mistakes today.

There are two styles of tumblers; one flares and one does not.

3▸	Bowl, 4½", berry	17.00	4▸	Plate, 7", salad	14.00
1▸	Bowl, 5", cereal	22.00	6▸	Sherbet	15.00
5▸	Bowl, 6", straight sides	32.00	2▸	Tumbler, 5", footed (2 styles)	23.00

ROSE POINT BAND, "WATER LILY," "CLEMATIS,"
INDIANA GLASS COMPANY, c. 1915

Color: crystal

Although production began in 1915, Rose Point Band became a contemporary of Depression glass due to its long run and as such, we have included it simply because it's charming and can be found residing alongside Depression wares on flea market shelves. Some collectors assume this is much older Pattern glass rather than Depression era.

When it was first distributed, a wholesaler could buy 240 pounds of it for $13.20 and command a net profit of $5.78. Most items were priced from 10¢ to 15¢, though the pitcher was 25¢. These prices were not as inexpensive as some patterns, but it evidently sold well.

It was advertised to dealers as a "sure repeater and money maker" and was their "peerless common sense assortment" of eight dozen pieces. You got a half dozen of sixteen different items. That did not include the plate, sauce bowl, and small-footed sugar and creamer. The plate an footed sugar shown in the picture were not even included in the catalog listing we have; so, there may be other items t be found as well.

5 ▸	Bowl, sauce, 3 ftd.	8.00			Creamer, ftd.	12.50
	Bowl, 7½", deep berry	15.00	4 ▸		Creamer, flat	12.50
	Bowl, 7½", footed salad	15.00			Cruet (vinegar)	50.00
6 ▸	Bowl, 8½", footed fruit	22.50			Pitcher, ½ gal.	58.00
	Bowl, 9½", footed, "fancy"	27.50	2 ▸		Plate, 11¾" ped. foot	28.00
	Bowl, 10", crimped berry	30.00			Spoon (cupped tumbler for spoons)	25.00
	Bowl, 10", orange (flared, straight rim)	30.00	3 ▸		Sugar, ftd.	12.50
1 ▸	Butter w/cover	45.00	7 ▸		Sugar w/cover	20.00
	Compote (footed jelly)	18.00			Tray, 8½", footed (flat compote)	22.00
	Compote w/cover, 5½"	28.00			Vase (celery)	35.00

ROSEMARY, "DUTCH ROSE," FEDERAL GLASS COMPANY, 1935 – 1937

Colors: amber, green, pink; some iridized

The Rosemary pattern was a redesign of Federal's delightful Mayfair pattern because of Hocking's earlier patent of the Mayfair name. The story of Rosemary's having been redesigned from Federal's Mayfair pattern can be read on page 128. Rosemary is a charming pattern particularly in green or pink. We've never heard anybody say they were regretful they chose to collect Rosemary. An exception was one exasperated collector searching for pink tumblers which remain fairly invisible today.

An amber set can be put together without much difficulty; there are only a few limited pieces, namely the cereal and tumblers. Other than that, the supply is more than adequate for the market. If you like amber, this would be one set we can recommend as a possibility to gather.

Pink or green cream soups, cereals, or tumblers are the pieces driving collectors' searches. Pink Rosemary grill plates, oval bowls, and platters can be added to the short supply list. We understand it is exasperating to try to collect a color or pattern that does not seem to appear at any price. If you saw the sad letters we get relating how Depression glass was given away, sold for next to nothing, or plain trashed in their relative's estate, there should be quite a bit more out there becoming available to the market. Speaking of trashed, one of the biggest collections in the country comes via a trash collecting business. He recycled old glass before recycling became in vogue. You'd be surprised how many mon-eyed people used to throw away (and maybe still do) a pair of Elegant candles if one were damaged. In their defense, this colored glass used to have little value to people — and perhaps the "throw away generation" started before the cur-rent one, too.

New collectors should know that grill plates are the three-part divided plates usually associated with diners or grills (restaurants) of that time. Food was kept from running together by those raised partitions (normally three).

The sugar has no handles and is often misidentified as a sherbet. There is no sherbet.

	Amber	Green	Pink			Amber	Green	Pink
9 ▸ Bowl, 5", berry	6.00	9.00	14.00	5 ▸ Plate, dinner	10.00	15.00	25.00
Bowl, 5", cream soup	18.00	33.00	48.00	2 ▸ Plate, grill	10.00	20.00	30.00
1 ▸ Bowl, 6", cereal	30.00	40.00	52.00	4 ▸ Platter, 12", oval	17.00	27.00	40.00
▸ Bowl, 10", oval vegetable	18.00	30.00	45.00	8 ▸ Saucer	2.00	5.00	6.00
Creamer, footed	10.00	12.50	25.00	1 ▸ Sugar, footed	10.00	12.50	25.00
7 ▸ Cup	7.50	9.50	12.00	3 ▸ Tumbler, 4¼", 9 ounce	30.00	40.00	75.00
▸ Plate, 6¾", salad	6.00	8.50	12.00				

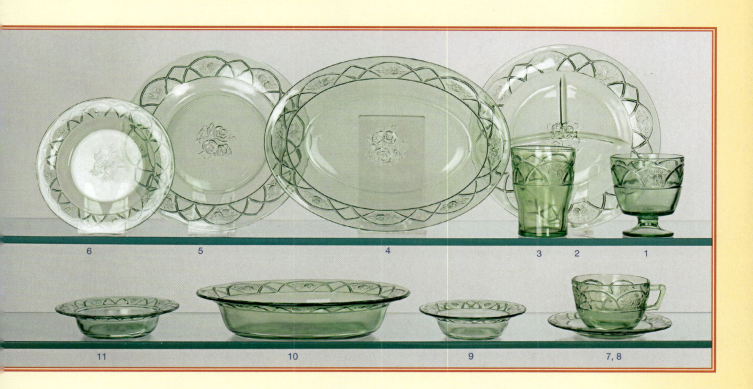

ROULETTE, "MANY WINDOWS," HOCKING GLASS COMPANY, 1935 – 1938

Colors: green, pink, and crystal

Roulette is the bona fide name of the pattern which collectors formerly called "Many Windows. The indentations are sup posed to remind one of the slots on a roulette wheel.

Hocking once promoted Roulette as a "winning" pattern. Hopefully, that gamble paid off better than the roulette wheel nor mally does. Roulette has six assorted tumblers which were used for promotion with pitchers as beverage sets. Pitchers wer packaged with various tumblers and presented to retailers as advertising baits to lure customers to their stores. Once there fo the "bargain" (usually a pitcher and six tumblers for around $1.00), it was up to the shop owner to convince the customer h needed more of his products. These promotions evidently worked and seemed to be the norm of the time. Pink pitchers an tumblers are easier to find than green ones, but pink Roulette was not made in additional pieces. There are five sizes of pin flat tumblers; but we have never heard of a pink-footed tumbler.

Sometimes an entire luncheon set of 14 or 19 pieces was the bait. Green Roulette was peddled for these promotions. may never have been advertised as a pattern by itself.

Cups, saucers, sherbets, and luncheon plates can be acquired in green. The 12" sandwich plate and fruit bowls are not s easily unearthed. Juice tumblers and the old fashioned are most elusive. We have not found a green juice in several year Whiskeys sell very well to the shot-glass collecting group that is making its presence known in collecting spheres. Crystal an pink whiskeys are available with some searching, but green ones are a different story. We rarely see green ones for sale; so, you spot some, know they are in demand.

Crystal tumbler and pitcher sets are more limited in supply; however, there is less demand for the few that have surface Some crystal beverage sets are decorated with colored stripes. In fact, this striped effect gives them an Art Deco appearanc that pleases the Deco crowd.

		Crystal	Pink, Green			Crystal	Pink, Green
10 ▸	Bowl, 9", fruit	9.50	28.00	3 ▸ Tumbler, 3¼", 5 ounce, juice		7.00	28.00
1 ▸	Cup	4.00	8.00	12 ▸ Tumbler, 3¼", 7½ oz., old fashioned		23.00	50.00
11 ▸	Pitcher, 8", 65 ounce	32.00	45.00	5 ▸ Tumbler, 4⅛", 9 ounce, water		13.00	22.00
	Plate, 6", sherbet	3.50	5.00	4 ▸ Tumbler, 5⅛", 12 ounce, iced tea		16.00	35.00
6 ▸	Plate, 8½", luncheon	5.00	9.00	7 ▸ Tumbler, 5½", 10 ounce, footed		14.00	38.00
8 ▸	Plate, 12", sandwich	11.00	18.00	9 ▸ Whiskey, 2½", 1½ ounce		14.00	17.00
2 ▸	Saucer	1.50	3.50				
	Sherbet	3.50	7.00				

"ROUND ROBIN," ECONOMY GLASS CO., Probably early 1930s

Colors: green, iridescent, and crystal

Round Robin's Domino tray is the expensive, unexpected piece in this diminutive pattern. Hocking's Cameo is the only other pattern in Depression glass which offers a sugar cube tray. The Domino tray name came from the sugar brand that furnished cubes of sugar. The indentation in the center is for a cream pitcher as pictured. "Loaf sugar" was fashionable, elegant even, with tiny silver sugar tongs made especially to serve it. So, having this piece in this small pattern is slightly incongruous. If they were more abundant, we'd speculate they were from a premium contract with the sugar company. This tray has, so far, only been found in green "Round Robin." Few of these have ever been displayed at shows and they have been grabbed up for collections of sugar related items or by the few collectors of "Round Robin" who are lucky enough to find one.

Green sherbets and berry bowls are few and far between. We have never found a green berry bowl to photograph. Green saucers seem to be harder to find than the cups. Only a few patterns can claim that. The "Round Robin" cup is footed, a style not plentiful in Depression glass. Sherbets and berry bowls abound in iridescent, but where are the cup and saucers?

Some crystal "Round Robin" is found today. Crystal was sprayed and baked to accomplish the iridized look. Obviously, not all the crystal was sprayed, since we find it occasionally. In addition, Cathy found a "Round Robin" creamer that the top half is iridized and bottom half crystal. Their spraying hand, or technique, wasn't too meticulous, either.

	Green	Iridescent
1 ▸ Bowl, 4", berry	10.00	9.00
8 ▸ Cup, footed	6.00	7.00
3 ▸ Creamer, footed	12.50	9.00
7 ▸ Domino tray	125.00	
6 ▸ Plate, 6", sherbet	3.50	2.50
5 ▸ Plate, 8", luncheon	8.00	4.00
Plate, 12", sandwich	12.00	10.00
9 ▸ Saucer	2.00	2.00
4 ▸ Sherbet	10.00	10.00
2 ▸ Sugar	12.50	9.00

ROXANA, HAZEL-ATLAS GLASS COMPANY, 1932

Colors: "Golden Topaz," crystal, and some white

Roxana has seven known pieces that are pictured below. We said that in a previous book and a reader wrote to say we couldn't count as there were eight. There are eight pieces, but only seven different since the gold decorated plate also appears as plain. This small pattern was obviously created strictly as promotional ware for some product, thus, its shortage of pieces. We know it was offered in Star brand oats as you received one piece of "Golden Topaz" table glassware in every package. This "Golden Topaz" is what we now call yellow Roxana. We have pictured an ad promoting this offer in previous books. It can now be found in our new Hazel-Atlas book. That ad may show why the deep 4½" bowl and the 5½" plates are so hard to find. They were not packed as a premium in these oats. Roxana was recorded for only one year by Hazel-Atlas.

Only the 4½" deep bowl has been found in Platonite; if you find any other item in Platonite, please let us know.

		Yellow	White
6 ▸	Bowl, 4½" x 2⅜"	15.00	17.00
4 ▸	Bowl, 5", berry	18.00	
1 ▸	Bowl, 6", cereal	20.00	
2 ▸	Plate, 5½"	9.00	
5 ▸	Plate, 6", sherbet	10.00	
3 ▸	Sherbet, footed	10.00	
7 ▸	Tumbler, 4¼", 9 ounce	23.00	

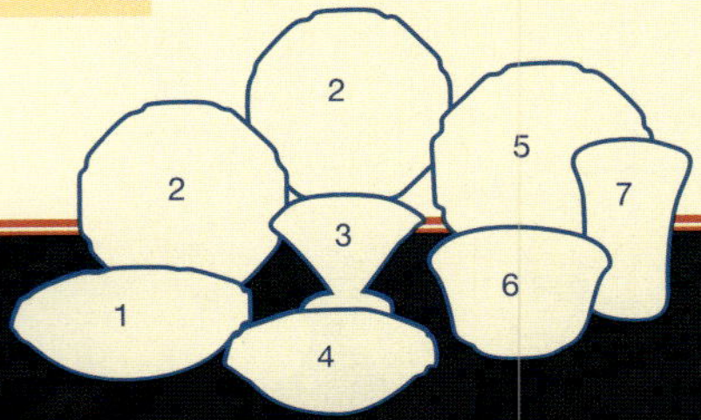

ROYAL LACE, HAZEL-ATLAS GLASS COMPANY, 1934 – 1941

Colors: cobalt blue, crystal, green, pink; some amethyst (See Reproduction Section.)

Royal Lace collectors have always favored the blue, but in recent years more green is funneling into the market and new collectors have noticed its availability as well as the lesser price and have adopted that as the color of choice. Green is found in quantities unknown before in England. Many of these pieces are coming home via Internet selling. English container shipments of furniture used to have glassware added to fill the empty spaces. Today, there are shippers specializing in gathering American glassware and other "smalls" to send back rather than large pieces of furniture. I know the owner of a mall who gets English shipments regularly and can usually sell the Depression glass cheaper than I can find it here.

An abundance of green basic "tea" sets are there, i.e. cups, saucers, creamers, and sugars. For some reason sugar lids did not seem to appear with the sugar bowls; so, they are still rarely seen. The straight-sided pitcher must have been the predominant style in England as we bought a half dozen or more from a dealer there. He never found any other style pitcher and only water tumblers to go with them. Shakers with original Hazel-Atlas labels declaring, "Made in America" were on several sets we purchased. You have to wonder if Hazel-Atlas named this pattern specifically for this "royal" market. It seems possible since this would have been made during the English royalty hoopla that so captivated the world. Little blue is found in England, but cobalt was not made until 1938 and may have been too late a production time wise due to the beginnings of the war.

Royal Lace in cobalt blue remains dear to our hearts because of box loads of it that I took to the first Depression glass show I ever attended in Springfield, Missouri, in 1971. Selling it to dealers and authors alike vastly improved my paltry teaching salary. I met the established authors, Weatherman and Stout, and met dealers I would ship glass to in the future. Weatherman told me that the cobalt color for Royal Lace pattern was something of a stroke of luck according to a factory employee. The cereal contractor cancelled his order more for Shirley Temple cobalt glassware causing Hazel-Atlas to make the Royal Lace they were already running in that color, too, in order to use up tanks of cobalt blue that were on hand. I asked her had she had any reports of green cookie jars or yellow indented butter bottoms in Mayfair. She also told me in a very straight forward manner the wisdom of that time, that Hocking did not make green cookie jars or yellow Mayfair indented butter dish bottoms and that I did not have any such items. Imagine her surprise when I pulled those from my little box. Showing her these was my reason for the trip because I knew she hadn't listed these items. So yes, I do know how exciting it is to show an unknown to an author. I had found two of the butter bottoms in Dayton, Ohio, and selling one for $30.00 paid all my expenses for the trip. Gas was $0.199 per gallon and the motel was $6.00. Those were the fun days when we were all learning new things about the glass every other day or so it seemed.

There were five different pitchers made in Royal Lace: a) 48 ounce, straight side; b) 64 ounce, 8", no ice lip; c) 68 ounce, 8", w/ice lip; d) 86 ounce, 8", no ice lip; e) 96 ounce, 8½", w/ice lip. The 10-ounce difference in the last two listed is caused by the spout on the pitcher without lip dipping below the top edge of the pitcher. This causes the liquid to run out before you get to the top. All spouted pitchers will vary in ounce capacity (up to eight ounces) depending upon how the spout tilts or dips. Always measure ounce capacities until no more liquid can be added without running out. The 68-ounce pitcher with ice lip and the 86 ounce without lip may not exist in cobalt blue. A crystal 68 ounce pitcher just sold for a record price to someone who had searched for years for it. Speaking of records, a crystal nut cup just brought more than cobalt ones are fetching. Two collectors really sparred for it.

ROYAL LACE

	Crystal	Pink	Green	Blue
10 ▶ Bowl, 4¾", cream soup	17.50	32.00	38.00	48.00
2 ▶ Bowl, 5", berry	18.00	40.00	50.00	75.00
12 ▶ Bowl, 10", round berry	20.00	35.00	30.00	87.50
Bowl, 10", 3-legged, straight edge	35.00	65.00	75.00	95.00
*Bowl, 10", 3-legged, rolled edge	295.00	135.00	145.00	750.00
17 ▶ Bowl, 10", 3-legged, ruffled edge	45.00	105.00	135.00	850.00
3 ▶ Bowl, 11", oval vegetable	28.00	40.00	45.00	75.00
Butter dish and cover	80.00	225.00	275.00	695.00
Butter dish bottom	55.00	140.00	180.00	495.00
Butter dish top	25.00	55.00	95.00	200.00
22 ▶ Candlestick, straight edge, pair	40.00	75.00	95.00	165.00
**Candlestick, rolled edge, pair	60.00	160.00	175.00	550.00
11 ▶ Candlestick, ruffled edge, pair	50.00	150.00	195.00	575.00
6 ▶ Cookie jar and cover	35.00	65.00	100.00	395.00
21 ▶ Creamer, footed	15.00	22.00	28.00	60.00
19 ▶ Cup	9.00	21.00	20.00	42.50
Nut bowl	550.00	550.00	550.00	1,695.00

	Crystal	Pink	Green	Blue
7 ▶ Pitcher, 48 ounce, straight sides	40.00	100.00	135.00	190.00
Pitcher, 64 oz., 8", w/o lip	45.00	110.00	120.00	325.00
Pitcher, 8", 68 oz., w/lip	350.00	115.00	225.00	
23 ▶ Pitcher, 8", 86 oz., w/o lip		135.00	175.00	
Pitcher, 8½", 96 oz., w/lip	65.00	150.00	160.00	495.00
Plate, 6", sherbet	8.00	10.00	12.00	17.00
16 ▶ Plate, 8½", luncheon	8.00	25.00	16.00	48.00
14 ▶ Plate, 9⅞", dinner	18.00	30.00	38.00	50.00
13 ▶ Plate, 9⅞", grill	11.00	25.00	28.00	40.00
18 ▶ Platter, 13", oval	24.00	42.00	42.00	70.00
9 ▶ Salt and pepper, pair	42.00	65.00	140.00	325.00
20 ▶ Saucer	5.00	7.00	10.00	12.50
24 ▶ Sherbet, footed	17.00	20.00	25.00	65.00
1 ▶ ‡Sherbet in metal holder	6.00			40.00
5 ▶ Sugar	11.00	20.00	22.00	40.00
4 ▶ Sugar lid	20.00	60.00	75.00	195.00
Tumbler, 3½", 5 ounce	20.00	33.00	40.00	55.00
8 ▶ Tumbler, 4⅛", 9 ounce	15.00	25.00	32.00	50.00
15 ▶ Tumbler, 4⅞", 10 ounce	60.00	85.00	100.00	165.00
Tumbler, 5⅜", 12 ounce	55.00	95.00	75.00	130.00
‡‡Toddy or cider set includes cookie jar, metal lid, metal tray, 8 roly-poly cups, and ladle				295.00

*Amethyst $900.00   ** Amethyst $900.00
‡Amethyst $40.00   ‡‡ Amethyst $195.00

202

ROYAL RUBY, ANCHOR HOCKING GLASS COMPANY, 1938 – 1940

Color: Ruby red

Anchor Hocking's patented Royal Ruby (red) color was inaugurated in 1938 using their existing moulds. A smidgen of Royal Ruby has been found in Anchor Hocking lines including Colonial, Ring, Manhattan, Queen Mary, Pillar Optic, and Miss America. These Royal Ruby pieces are generally thought rare in these highly collected patterns and most are of extraordinary quality for Anchor Hocking, having ground bottoms, which are usually not found on their normal mass-produced glassware.

This book identifies and prices only pieces of Royal Ruby produced before 1940. Royal Ruby pieces made after 1940 are now in the *Collectible Glassware from the 40s, 50s, 60s....* Remember, only Anchor Hocking's red can technically be called Royal Ruby even though many collectors use that term for any red glassware. Oyster and Pearl, Old Cafe, and Coronation were among the familiar patterns used in the original Royal Ruby production. There were other designs produced that were numbered lines and never given pattern names. None of those items is priced in the listing below.

We feel that the name of the color was probably inspired by our country's fascination with the English coronation of Edward VIII in 1936 and his subsequent renouncing of that royal crown.

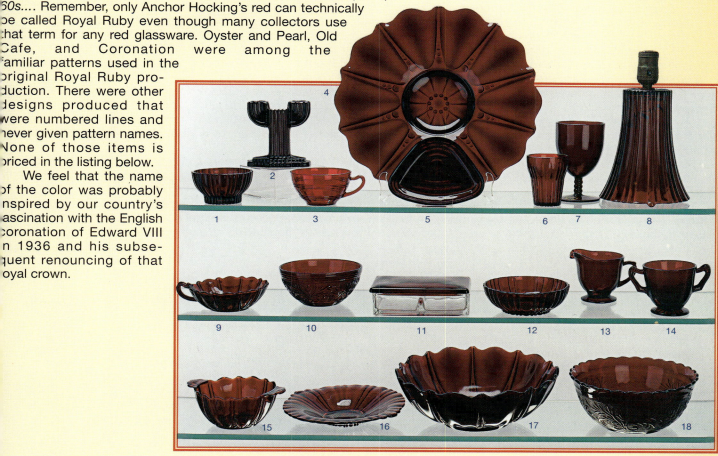

Bonbon, 6½"		8.50
Bowl, 3¾", berry (Old Cafe)		9.00
Bowl, 4½", handled (Coronation)		8.00
10 ▸ Bowl, 4⅞", smooth (Sandwich)		12.50
Bowl, 5¼", scalloped (Sandwich)		20.00
9 ▸ Bowl, 5½", 1-handled (Oyster & Pearl)		22.00
12 ▸ Bowl, 5½", cereal (Old Cafe)		35.00
15 ▸ Bowl, 6½", deep-handled (Oyster & Pearl)		22.00
Bowl, 6½", handled (Coronation)		18.00
Bowl, 6½", scalloped (Sandwich)		27.50
Bowl, 8", handled (Coronation)		18.00
18 ▸ Bowl, 8¼", scalloped (Sandwich)		50.00
17 ▸ Bowl, 10½", deep fruit (Oyster & Pearl)		60.00
Candle holder, 3½", pair (Oyster & Pearl)		65.00
2 ▸ Candle holder, 4½", pair (Queen Mary)		150.00
16 ▸ Candy dish, 8" mint, low (Old Cafe)		20.00
Candy jar, 5½", crystal w/Ruby cov. (Old Cafe)		28.00
11 ▸ Cigarette box/card holder, 6⅛" x 4", crystal w/Ruby top		65.00
13 ▸ Creamer, footed		9.00
Cup (Coronation)		6.50
Cup (Old Cafe)		12.00
3 ▸ Cup (Ring)		20.00
Cup, round		6.00
7 ▸ Goblet, ball stem		12.00
Jewel box, 4¼", crystal w/Ruby cov.		12.50
8 ▸ Lamp (Old Cafe)		150.00
Marmalade, 5⅛", crystal w/Ruby cov.		7.50
Plate, 8½", luncheon (Coronation)		10.00
Plate, 9⅛", dinner, round		11.00
4 ▸ Plate, 13½", sandwich (Oyster & Pearl)		55.00
Puff box, 4⅝", crystal w/Ruby cov.		9.00
5 ▸ Relish tray insert (Manhattan)		4.00
Saucer, round		2.50
1 ▸ Sherbet, low footed (Old Cafe)		14.00
14 ▸ Sugar, footed		7.50
Sugar, lid		11.00
Tray, 6" x 4½"		12.50
6 ▸ Tumbler, 3", juice (Old Cafe)		22.00
Tumbler, 4", water (Old Cafe)		35.00
Vase, 7¼" (Old Cafe)		55.00
Vase, 9", two styles		17.50

"S" PATTERN, "STIPPLED ROSE BAND," MacBETH-EVANS GLASS COMPANY, 1930 – 1933

Colors: crystal; crystal w/trims of silver, blue, green, amber; pink; some amber, green, fired-on red; ruby, Monax, and light yellow

"S" Pattern was avidly collected when Depression glass first became a phenomenon the early '70s. There was real excitement toward it because it came in various colors and trims, with a couple of styles of pitchers and a huge cake plate like the much-adored Dogwood one. A spring vacation trip to Ohio in 1972 brought a discovery of six or seven red "S" pattern luncheon plates like those of American Sweetheart, but they had never been documented. We sold those for $70.00 each. Since then, we had only seen one other priced for $100.00 several years ago. Last fall we ran into a group of five and have been unable to sell them for $30.00 each, some 30 years later. The interest in rarely seen red "S" Pattern has waned.

Times change as do collectors' interests. Early on, color and unusual pieces were highly fashionable; but today, collectors shy from big prices for odd colors and unusual pieces unless they are in a major, highly desired pattern. Now, we see this delicate little pattern, which wasn't long in production, being ignored at markets. It would be a great pattern for a beginning collector to latch onto. We found a setting for eight with a platinum band in a mall last summer. After photographing one of each piece for this book, we priced it and put it out for show. Everything sold except a luncheon plate. It sold because it was inexpensive and displays beautifully as a striking glass setting.

Amber, blue, or green-banded crystal was made. Crystal luncheon plates display to advantage against a colored charger plate that helps to emphasize the eye-catching fleur-de-lis pattern occurring in its scrolled rim design.

Amber "S" Pattern sometimes appears more yellow than amber. The color is almost the hue of Hocking's Princess. A dinner plate does occur in amber "S" Pattern and the amber pitcher in this pattern is rare. No crystal (nor crystal with trim) dinner plates have been spotted.

Pink or green pitcher and tumbler sets appear occasionally. Years ago, there were a number of pitcher collectors per se; rare pitchers sold fast in the $200.00 – 500.00 range. Now, those same pitchers are establishing four-figure prices but, alas, not those of "S" pattern.

Finding a pink tumbler that has a moulded blossom design will indicate a Dogwood moulded tumbler and not "S" Pattern. The only pink or green tumblers found in "S" Pattern have an applied, silk-screened "S" Pattern design on the glass like those of Dogwood. However, crystal tumblers are found with moulded "S" Pattern designs.

	Crystal	Yellow, Amber, Crystal w/Trims			Crystal	Yellow, Amber, Crystal w/Trims
7 ▶ *Bowl, 5½", cereal	5.00	9.00	5 ▶ Plate, grill	6.50	9.00
Bowl, 8½", large berry	15.00	20.00	Plate, 11¾", heavy cake	50.00	65.00
9 ▶ *Creamer, thick or thin	6.00	7.00	‡Plate, 13", heavy cake	70.00	90.00
10 ▶ *Cup, thick or thin	3.50	4.50	11 ▶ Saucer	2.00	2.50
Pitcher, 80 ounce (like "Dogwood"), green or pink $550.00	65.00	160.00	2 ▶ Sherbet, low footed	4.50	7.00
			8 ▶ *Sugar, thick and thin	6.00	6.50
Pitcher, 80 ounce (like "American Sweetheart")	90.00		3 ▶ Tumbler, 3½", 5 ounce	5.00	8.00
			Tumbler, 4", 9 ounce, green or pink $50.00	10.00	12.00
6 ▶ Plate, 6", sherbet, Monax 8.00	2.50	3.00	1 ▶ Tumbler, 4¾", 10 ounce	12.00	12.00
4 ▶ **Plate, 8¼", luncheon	8.00	7.00	Tumbler, 5", 12 ounce	14.00	16.00
Plate, 9¼", dinner		10.00			

* Fired-on red items will run approximately twice price of amber   **Red $40.00; Monax $10.00   ‡Amber $77.50

SANDWICH, INDIANA GLASS COMPANY, 1920s – 1980s

Colors: crystal late 1920s – today; teal blue 1950s – 1980s; milk white mid-1950s; amber late 1920s – 1980s; red 1933, 1970s; Smokey Blue 1976 – 1977; pink, green 1920s – early 1930s

Since green Indiana Sandwich was chosen for the cover of our *Pocket Guide to Depression Glass, 12th Edition*, we have received numerous calls and letters from people who think they have old Indiana Sandwich, but who actually have Tiara's 1980s version called Chantilly. You can test out green with an ultraviolet (black) light. Tiara's Chantilly will not glow under that light. This is not a general test for age of glass. There is glass made yesterday which will glow under black light. It is a test for this particular green Sandwich vs. Chantilly pattern. Any green piece encountered that has no price listed below is presumably new. Indiana also made a lighter pink in recent years.

Amber Sandwich is priced here with crystal. Realize that the majority of amber found today is from the Tiara issues and is not Depression-era glass. Early amber Sandwich was very light in color. There is no easy way to distinguish old crystal from new as most of the new was made from Indiana's original moulds.

Only six items in red Sandwich can be dated from 1933, i.e., cups, saucers, luncheon plates, water goblets, creamers, and sugars. In the 1970s, Tiara Home Products marketed red Sandwich. This was not a large production and most of it is more ambena in color than red. Today, there is little pricing difference for red unless you have some marked 1933 Chicago World's Fair, which will command considerably more as guaranteed old and a World's Fair collectible.

	Amber, Crystal	Teal Blue	Red	Pink, Green
▸ Ashtrays (club, spade, heart, diamond shapes, each)	3.00			
Basket, 10" high	32.00			
Bowl, 4¼", berry	3.50			
Bowl, 6"	4.00			
▸ Bowl, 6", hexagonal	5.00	14.00		
▸ Bowl, 8½"	11.00			
▸ Bowl, 9", console	16.00			40.00
Bowl, 11½", console	18.50			50.00
Butter dish and cover, domed	22.00	*155.00		
Butter dish bottom	6.00	42.50		
Butter dish top	16.00	112.50		
▸ Candlesticks, 3½", pair	16.00			45.00
Candlesticks 7", pair	30.00			
▸ Creamer	9.00		45.00	
▸ Celery, 10½"	16.00			
▸ Creamer and sugar on diamond shaped tray	16.00	32.00		
Cruet, 6½ oz. and stopper	26.00	135.00		175.00
▸ Cup	3.50	8.50	27.50	
Decanter and stopper	25.00		80.00	150.00

	Amber, Crystal	Teal Blue	Red	Pink, Green
2 ▸ Goblet, 9 oz.	13.00		45.00	
8 ▸ Mayonnaise, footed, 3 pc.	18.00			40.00
Pitcher, 68 oz.	20.00		130.00	
Plate, 6", sherbet	3.00	7.00		
Plate, 7", bread and butter	4.00			
Plate, 8", oval, indent for cup	5.50			15.00
3 ▸ Plate, 8⅜", luncheon	4.75		20.00	
Plate, 10½", dinner	8.00			20.00
Plate, 13", sandwich	13.00	24.00	35.00	25.00
Puff box	16.00			
Salt and pepper, pair	17.50			
Sandwich server, center	18.00		45.00	35.00
Saucer	2.50	4.50	7.50	
Sherbet, 3¼"	5.50	14.00		
Sugar, large	9.00		45.00	
Sugar lid for large size	12.00			
Tumbler, 3 oz., footed, cocktail	6.00			
Tumbler, 8 oz., footed, water	9.00			
Tumbler, 12 oz., footed, iced tea	10.00			
Wine, 3", 4 oz.	6.00		12.50	25.00

205   *Beware recent vintage sell $22.00

SHARON, "CABBAGE ROSE," FEDERAL GLASS COMPANY, 1935 – 1939

Colors: pink, green, amber; some crystal (See Reproduction Section.)

In the last few books, we have pictured an old advertising page where coupons from some product could be redeemed for an assortment of items of Federal's "Golden Glow" (amber) glassware. We emphasized that the plain pitcher in that ad (without design), would sell in the $35.00 range. It did not occur to us that someone would presuppose that plain pitcher without design to be Sharon. However, we received an e-mail from someone trying to sell one of these plain green pitchers as rare green Sharon on an Internet auction. As with all patterns in this book, if the pattern is not on the piece, it is only moulded like the item and not the pattern itself.

Green Sharon pitchers and tumblers in all sizes are difficult to find. You will find thick or thin flat iced teas and waters. The thick tumblers are easier to find in green; and the price reflects that. Unfortunately, the price of the pitcher and tumblers precludes many collectors from owning them. At that first Depression show in 1971, a collector paid $20.00 for a green Sharon pitcher and everyone thought he had lost a few marbles on his way there. Little we knew then. In amber and pink, the heavy iced teas are more rarely seen than the waters. Those differences do not mean as much today as they once did, as most collectors are happy to find any tumbler.

Prices have softened a bit for common dinnerware pieces of amber and pink Sharon. Footed amber tumblers in Sharon are rare and amber pitchers with ice lips are twice as difficult to locate as pink. However fewer collectors for amber right now, translate into fewer dollars offered due to lack of demand.

The decreasing requests for pink Sharon have caused some reduction in those prices. New collectors were timid about starting this extremely popular pink pattern a few years ago due to some reproductions flooding markets. However, once everyone learned how to recognize them (see the reproduction section), demand for this durable, 70-year-old pattern flourished once again. Then the latest economic problems hit and collecting has slowed and prices simply followed.

Cathy's grandmother told her she remembered the drummer who came around selling Sharon put the plate on the floor upside down and stood on it to show how sturdy this ware was. Someone tried that feat and it didn't work for him as it broke into hundreds of pieces. However, we do not know the size of the drummer.

The price for a pink Sharon cheese dish has leaped into four figures. The top for the cheese and butter dish is the same piece. The bottoms are different. The butter bottom is a 1½" deep bowl with a sloping, indented ledge while the cheese bottom is a flat salad plate with a raised band of glass on its surface within which the lid rests. The bottom piece is the rare part of this cheese.

Amber cheese dishes were made; but none has ever surfaced in green. A collector told me he'd found an old ad showing these were a special promotion item run for some cheese products. It would appear no one much wanted the product, else more of these dishes would have been produced and we wouldn't have such a scarcity of them, today. Other infrequently found pink Sharon items include flat, thick iced teas and jam dishes. The jam dish is like the butter bottom except it has no indentation for the top. It differs from the 1⅞" deep soup bowl by standing only 1½" tall. Occasionally, you can find a jam dish priced as a soup bowl; but that happens infrequently in today's world of informed collectors and dealers. There are no green soup bowls, only jam dishes.

		Amber	Pink	Green
20 ▸	Bowl, 5", berry	8.00	13.00	18.00
8 ▸	Bowl, 5", cream soup	22.00	50.00	55.00
4 ▸	Bowl, 6", cereal	19.00	26.00	30.00
26 ▸	Bowl, 7¾", flat soup, 1⅞" deep	55.00	55.00	
8 ▸	Bowl, 8½", large berry	6.00	32.00	35.00
0 ▸	Bowl, 9½", oval vegetable	18.00	32.00	33.00
9 ▸	Bowl, 10½", fruit	21.00	39.00	42.50
6 ▸	Butter dish and cover	45.00	60.00	85.00
	Butter dish bottom	20.00	30.00	40.00
	Butter dish top	25.00	30.00	50.00
7 ▸	*Cake plate, 11½", footed	27.50	42.00	65.00
	Candy jar and cover	45.00	50.00	175.00
	Cheese dish and cover	225.00	1,750.00	
2 ▸	Creamer, footed	14.00	17.00	20.00
1 ▸	Cup	8.00	12.00	20.00
7 ▸	Jam dish, 7½"	35.00	250.00	65.00
6 ▸	Pitcher, 80 oz., w/ice lip	135.00	195.00	450.00
3 ▸	Pitcher, 80 oz., w/o ice lip	140.00	185.00	475.00
9 ▸	Plate, 6", bread and butter	4.00	8.00	8.00
2 ▸	**Plate, 7½", salad	15.00	23.00	25.00
3 ▸	Plate, 9½", dinner	11.00	18.00	25.00

		Amber	Pink	Green
3 ▸	Platter, 12½", oval	17.50	30.00	29.00
11 ▸	Salt and pepper, pair	38.00	55.00	70.00
27 ▸	Saucer	7.00	7.00	11.00
5 ▸	Sherbet, footed	11.00	15.00	37.50
15 ▸	Sugar	9.00	12.00	16.00
14 ▸	Sugar lid	22.00	32.00	40.00
25 ▸	Tumbler, 4⅛", 9 oz., thick	26.00	42.00	80.00
21 ▸	Tumbler, 4⅛", 9 oz., thin	26.00	45.00	85.00
24 ▸	Tumbler, 5¼", 12 oz., thin	53.00	57.50	110.00
	Tumbler, 5¼", 12 oz., thick	65.00	100.00	110.00
22 ▸	‡Tumbler, 6½", 15 oz., footed	80.00	50.00	

*Crystal $10.00   **Crystal $50.00   ‡Crystal $20.00

Child's bowl on Sharon mould blank

"SHIPS" or "SAILBOAT" also known as "SPORTSMAN SERIES,"
HAZEL-ATLAS GLASS COMPANY, Late 1930s

Colors: cobalt blue w/white, yellow, and red decoration, crystal w/blue

Moderntone cobalt blue decorated with white "Ships" is now seldom seen particularly in mint condition. Ship decorated sherbet plates are harder to find than dinner plates, but both have vanished into long-standing collections. There is no Moderntone cup with a "Ships" decoration that fits the saucer, which does have a "Ships" decoration. The cup is just a normal Moderntone cup. Prices below are for mint pieces. Discolored (beige) or worn items should sell for less, but some collectors will shy away from less than perfect decorations. Admittedly, they don't get to buy as much that way and they may pay higher prices, but they are happier to find mint pieces. When the "Ships" pattern is partially missing, would be easier to sell if the whole ship had sunk and you only had a cobalt blue Moderntone piece left.

The baffling "Ships" shot glass is the smallest (2½", two-ounce) tumbler, not the heavy bottomed tumbler that hold four-ounces and is 3¼" tall. We receive letters from people who purchased this 4-ounce tumbler under the impression (having been told) it was a shot glass. We have tried to explain this is not the shot glass for at least 20 years. The 4-ounce heavy bottomed tumbler was sold as a liquor tumbler with the cocktail shaker, but never as the shot. No shot glass ever holds more than 2-ounces according to some of my drinking friends. There is a large price difference between the authentic, 2-ounce shot and the 4-ounce tumbler. The price for that 4-ounce tumbler has increased, maybe due to its sale as the supposed shot glass. Do you suppose they made that tumbler heavy bottomed for unsteady hands and fuzzy eyesight?

At least one yellow "Ships" old-fashioned tumbler has surfaced in "raincoat" yellow.

We enjoy the decorations that have the red boats with white sails on blue. So far, only pitchers and tumblers are found with this patriotic red, white, and blue combination. Have you spotted other items?

We should mention that no red glass pitcher has ever been found to go with the red glass (different design) ship tumblers ($10.00) often found in the markets. To our knowledge the red tumblers are not a Hazel-Atlas product.

	Blue, White			Blue, White
8 ▸ Bowl, 6", white rings	22.00	15 ▸ Plate, 8", salad		35.00
18 ▸ Cup (Plain), "Moderntone"	11.00	16 ▸ Plate, 9", dinner		50.00
Cocktail mixer w/stirrer	35.00	19 ▸ Saucer		22.00
2 ▸ Cocktail shaker	40.00	17 ▸ Tumbler, 2 oz., 2¼", shot glass		235.00
5 ▸ Ice bowl	40.00	Tumbler, 3½", whiskey		25.00
10 ▸ Ice tub	35.00	7 ▸ Tumbler, 4 oz., 3¼", heavy bottom		25.00
12 ▸ Pitcher w/o lip, 82 ounce	70.00	1 ▸ Tumbler, 5 oz., 3¾", juice		16.00
11 ▸ Pitcher w/lip, 86 ounce	75.00	9 ▸ Tumbler, 6 ounce, roly poly		14.00
13 ▸ Plate, 5⅞", sherbet	35.00	6 ▸ Tumbler, 8 oz., 3⅜", old fashioned		20.00
		14 ▸ Tumbler, 9 oz., 3¾", straight, hi-ball		16.00
		20 ▸ Tumbler, 9 oz., 4⅝", water		13.00
		4 ▸ Tumbler, 10½ oz., 4⅞", iced tea		16.00
		3 ▸ Tumbler, 12 oz., iced tea		28.00
		Tumbler, 15 oz.		45.00

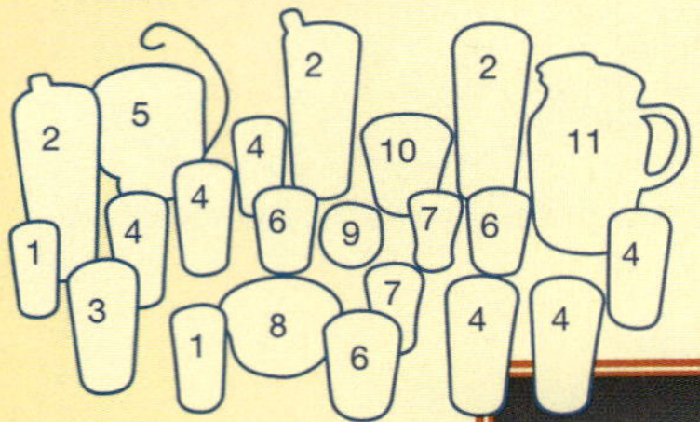

208

"Go-with" accessories

SIERRA, "PINWHEEL," JEANNETTE GLASS COMPANY, 1931 – 1933

Colors: green, pink, and some Ultra Marine and Delphite

Sierra is a word of Spanish origin meaning saw or sawtooth, which makes this an excellent name choice for this pleasing 1930s Jeannette glassware. Those pointed edges are readily noticed, but also easily damaged. Collectors are charmed by it though it is now all but disappearing from the market in both colors. Pink and green pitchers, tumblers, and oval vegetable bowls are safely tucked into collections and few are being offered for sale. I rushed over to check out a vegetable bowl in a mall, recently, only to notice one of the points was missing. It was priced as if it were all there, but it will be difficult to get a collector to pay for mint when it is definitely not. A consummate problem with Sierra is finding mint condition items. If pieces were used much, one or more of those points is usually chipped or nicked. Many time these chips are underneath the point, so look there too.

Always closely examine any pink Sierra butter dishes to check for the Adam/Sierra combination lid. That is how found my first one. Be sure to read about this elusive and pricey butter under Adam.

Wrong cups are often offered for sale on Sierra saucers. Any pink cup of nondescript origin can be found atop the saucers. Be sure to note that original cups have the design on the cup without the serrated rim. You would have a first rate dribble cup if the rim were serrated.

The cups, pitchers, and tumblers all have smooth, not serrated, edges. Therefore, they do not chip as easily.

Mint sugar bowls are harder to find than lids because of the points on the bowl. Years ago, lids were priced higher than the bowls, but times have changed.

There have been four Sierra Ultra Marine cups found, but no saucer has been reported. Were these a sample run made at the time Jeannette was making Ultra Marine Doric and Pansy or Swirl?

Did you note the Delphite bowl on the cover discovered in the Pittsburgh area last year? There could be more.

		Pink	Green			Pink	Green
11 ▸	Bowl, 5½", cereal	15.00	16.00	3 ▸ Platter, 11", oval		58.00	80.00
13 ▸	Bowl, 8½", large berry	35.00	40.00	Salt and pepper, pair		45.00	45.00
12 ▸	Bowl, 9¼", oval vegetable	100.00	160.00	2 ▸ Saucer		8.00	9.00
10 ▸	Butter dish and cover	75.00	80.00	7 ▸ Serving tray, 10¼", 2 handles		25.00	20.00
6 ▸	Creamer	20.00	25.00	8 ▸ Sugar		25.00	30.00
1 ▸	Cup	15.00	15.00	9 ▸ Sugar cover		20.00	20.00
5 ▸	Pitcher, 6½", 32 ounce	140.00	175.00	4 ▸ Tumbler, 4½", 9 ounce, footed		72.00	100.00
14 ▸	Plate, 9", dinner	22.00	29.00				

SPIRAL, HOCKING GLASS COMPANY, 1928 – 1930

Colors: green, crystal, and pink and fired-on red

Hocking's Spiral is one of numerous spiraling patterns from the Depression era which had its origin in older, pattern glass lines. A few pieces of Hocking Spiral have turned up in crystal. At this stage of collecting, I am beginning to wonder if pink Spiral exists, even though it's listed in an old catalog. Do you own a piece? Do not mistake the pink swirling pattern marked "made in France" as Spiral. It is newly made and not Depression glass as it is so often labeled by sellers.

The true complication lies in recognition of Hocking's Spiral among the others produced during this period. First, observe shape. Most pieces of Hocking's Spiral, the ice tub, platter, cake plate, creamer, and sugar, are shaped like their popular Cameo and Block Optic patterns. The seldom seen platter has closed or tab handles, as do many made by Hocking. There is a 5¾" vase shaped like Cameo's footed one. It can be found iridized with a green foot or as part of Hocking's Rainbow line. We have found a Spiral one in Tangerine; so watch for other possible colors.

A Spiral luncheon set can be put together quite inexpensively when compared to other Depression patterns. Spiral is not a pattern often offered for sale at glass shows. You may have to ask for it, and you will probably buy it more economically from someone who actually knows what the pattern really is.

The Hocking Spiral center-handled server has a solid handle while its confusing Imperial Glass Company counterpart, Twisted Optic (Line #313), has an open handle. The Spiral pitcher shown has the rope top treatment like those found in Cameo and Block Optic. There is also a 7⅝", 54-ounce bulbous based one (like shown in Block Optic) available with Spiral pattern.

There are two styles of sugars and creamers found in Spiral, one a flat utilitarian style, like the Block Optic flat style, and one is footed with a fancier handle, like Cameo. Generally speaking, Hocking's Spiral swirls go to the left or clockwise while Imperial's Twisted Optic spirals go to the right or counterclockwise. (Westmoreland's #1710 Spiral line and Duncan's Spiral Flutes have hand-polished bottoms on flat pieces, something not found on Hocking's machine-made Spiral. Those items confused with Hocking Spiral all have different shapes from the Hocking line.)

You might find a footed cake plate with an embossed ad for White Lily flour around the edge which tickles those looking for advertising items. There are several Depression items that have embossed product names, but not many.

	Green			Green
Bowl, 4¾", berry	8.00	8 ▸ Plate, 8", luncheon		3.50
Bowl, 7", mixing	15.00	4 ▸ Platter, 12"		35.00
Bowl, 8", large berry	12.50	5 ▸ Preserve and cover		40.00
Cake plate	20.00	Salt and pepper, pair		35.00
▸ Creamer, flat or footed	10.00	12 ▸ Sandwich server, center handle		25.00
3 ▸ Cup	7.00	14 ▸ Saucer		2.00
▸ Ice or butter tub	32.00	3 ▸ Sherbet		5.00
▸ Pitcher, 7⅝", 54 ounce, bulbous	48.00	2 ▸ Sugar, flat or footed		10.00
Pitcher, 7⅝", 58 ounce	42.00	Tumbler, 3", 5 ounce, juice		4.50
▸ Plate, 6", sherbet	3.00	Tumbler, 5", 9 ounce, water		10.00
		10 ▸ Tumbler, 5⅞", footed		18.00
		6 ▸ Vase, 5¾", footed		75.00

SPRINGTIME, MONONGAH GLASS COMPANY, c. 1927

Color: crystal w/24-karat gold band decoration

Monongah, who promoted themselves as "pioneers in the manufacture of the automatic machine pressed tumbler," was taken over by Hocking; and Springtime was the inspiration for Hocking's enormously popular Cameo pattern. Springtime etching was by hand. Cameo pattern was translated to an automatic mould process by Hocking.

Springtime was only made in crystal, and most often with a 24-karat gold band trim. Three quarters of a century later, that gold trim is mostly absent from pieces you find. Gold is particularly vulnerable to dishwater treatment. The mould blanks have an optic rib effect, often found in older wares, but it is very faint. You find Springtime only occasionally; so I would suggest that you buy whatever crosses your path if you wish to collect this lovely older design. Usually, the price is inexpensive since it often is unrecognized. However, since including Springtime in our book, recognition has increased and there may not be as many bargains as in the past.

Item	Price
Bowl, finger	45.00
Creamer	37.50
Decanter, 26 oz., w/cut facet stop	125.00
Pitcher, 30 oz., juice w/lid	100.00
Pitcher, 50 oz., water, straight rim	135.00
Pitcher, 50 oz., tea w/lid	195.00
Pitcher, 60 oz., water, slope rim	165.00
Plate, 6½"	10.00
4 ▸ Plate, 8½", luncheon	17.50
1 ▸ Stem, ¾ oz., brandy cordial	145.00
Stem, 1½ oz., ftd., almond	35.00
2 ▸ Stem, 2½ oz., wine	45.00
Stem, 2½ oz., cocktail	35.00
Stem, 4 oz., claret	50.00
Stem, 5½ oz., parfait	45.00

Item	Price
Stem, 5½ oz., high sherbet	25.00
Stem, 5½ oz., low sherbet	25.00
3 ▸ Stem, 9 oz., goblet	30.00
Stem, 6" confection stand (compote)	30.00
Sugar, open	37.50
7 ▸ Tumbler, 2½ oz., whiskey	60.00
6 ▸ Tumbler, 5 oz., juice	35.00
Tumbler, 7 oz., ginger ale	35.00
Tumbler, 8 oz., water	30.00
5 ▸ Tumbler, 9 oz., water	30.00
Tumbler, 10 oz., tea	35.00
Tumbler, 13 oz., hdld. ice tea	70.00
Tumbler, 13 oz., tea	50.00

* Deduct 10 – 20% for missing gold trim

1   2   3   4   5   6   7

SQUARE, "HAZEN," LINE #760 et al., IMPERIAL GLASS COMPANY, c. 1930s

Colors: crystal, green, pink, ruby

Square is an attractive small line of Imperial's which was advertised in luncheon sets having 15, 21, or 27 pieces. Imperial used it as a blank for etchings. We were lucky enough to find a large red set in an antique mall. The owner had no idea what it was, but priced it as if it were gold. When I first saw the price, I left it. The unusual style handles and rich, ruby coloring are truly captivating in square design.

As a separate observation, it is often not easy to buy red, cobalt blue, black, or older canary glass from sellers who do not know what they have. Color is habitually highly priced, and frequently inflated. As an example, I picked up a piece of Emerald green Cambridge to look for a price at a recent antique fair. The owner informed me that it was an old piece of "vaseline" and he only wanted $125.00 (for that $40.00 item on a good day). I casually mentioned that the company that made it called it Emerald green and he looked at me as if I had sprouted horns. No form of green is "vaseline" no matter what you are told. "Vaseline" was a term used by collectors for vibrant yellow colored glassware. Today this is emphasized by showing it glowing under an ultraviolet light. Some green colors will also glow due to uranium oxide content of the glass formula, but that does not make it "vaseline" yellow. My experience has been that you cannot deal with uninformed sellers who already know more than you do, however. So, just watch for their mistakes in pricing; they will make some.

	Crystal, Pink, Green	Ruby
Bowl, 4½", nappy	15.00	22.00
Bowl, 7", square, soup/salad	20.00	30.00
5 ▸ Creamer, footed	35.00	35.00
2 ▸ Cup	20.00	32.00
Plate, 6", dessert	7.50	10.00

	Crystal, Pink, Green	Ruby
4 ▸ Plate, 8", salad	15.00	20.00
3 ▸ Saucer	5.00	10.00
1 ▸ Server, 10½", center handled	40.00	55.00
Shaker, square, foot, pair	50.00	75.00
6 ▸ Sugar, footed	25.00	35.00

STARLIGHT, HAZEL-ATLAS GLASS COMPANY, 1938 – 1940

Colors: crystal, pink; some white, cobalt

Starlight is another inexpensively priced pattern; the impediment lies in tracking it down. Starlight has never been accumulated by large numbers of collectors, but the ones who have tried for a set report shortages of sherbets, cereals, and the large salad bowl and liner/serving plate. A bowl with a metal base and rim make up a small punch or cider set. This set is similar to the Royal Lace toddy set, having a bowl in a metal holder with an extending flat rim to accommodate cups. A metal ladle with a red knob rests in the bowl. This was not made at Hazel-Atlas, but by some other company who bought the glass and added their own accoutrements to it. Buying wares for decorating was a standard practice at this time, and Hazel-Atlas furnished several patterns that are found with metal attachments today.

Pink and cobalt blue bowls make nice accessory pieces with crystal, but only bowls are available in those colors.

The 5½" cereal is tab handled and measures 6" including the handles. Measurements in this book do not normally include handles, unless specified in the price listing.

Shakers are the item most often spotted in Starlight. We see them regularly in Florida and finally found out why there are so many here. The tops were expressly designed to keep the salt "moisture proof." Labeled Airko shakers with these tops are often found in southern areas where the humid air caused shaker holes to clog. One of these moisture-proof shakers is pictured here with an original label. Some unused pairs have been found in boxes packed for gift giving or souvenirs. They evidently sold well!

		Crystal, White	Pink			Crystal, White	Pink
10 ▸	Bowl, 5½", cereal, closed handles	9.00	12.00	1 ▸ Plate, 9", dinner	8.00	
12 ▸	* Bowl, 8½", closed handles	12.00	20.00	4 ▸ Plate, 13", sandwich	15.00	18.00
13 ▸	Bowl, 11½", salad	30.00		6 ▸ Relish dish	15.00	
	Bowl, 12", 2¾" deep	40.00		3 ▸ Salt and pepper, pair	25.00	
11 ▸	Creamer, oval	7.00		9 ▸ Saucer	2.00	
8 ▸	Cup	6.00		2 ▸ Sherbet	15.00	
5 ▸	Plate, 6", bread and butter	3.00		7 ▸ Sugar, oval	7.00	
	Plate, 8½", luncheon	5.00		* Cobalt $32.50		

STRAWBERRY, U.S. GLASS COMPANY, Early 1930s

Colors: pink, green, crystal; some iridized

Collectible Depression glass patterns that U.S. Glass made are often reminiscent of earlier pattern glassware designs of the late 1890s and early 1900s. To some extent, Strawberry pattern itself, is a throwback to pattern glass. New styles and newly designed glassmaking equipment were emerging that left the heavier, bulkier, roughly moulded glass behind. However, Strawberry and its sister pattern, Cherryberry, are popular with today's collectors. This shows a certain age-less, continuity of appreciation, which is nice to see. Strawberry, particularly, is asked for at every show we do.

Crystal and iridescent pitchers are in few collections, but it is not necessarily only Strawberry collectors who are picking them. Carnival collectors treasure iridescent Strawberry pitchers and tumblers more highly than Depression glass collectors do. By that, we mean they will pay more for them. One problem exists which makes carnival collectors run in the opposite direction. If the color fades at the bottom or goes toward crystal, they will not consider buying it at any price. The pitcher or tumbler has to have full, vivid color to be considered by them at all. This prejudice carries over somewhat with Depression glass collectors who want strong color also. Crystal is priced with iridescent because it is, categorically, rare. Only two or three crystal pitchers have ever been seen and those probably escaped being sprayed as iridescent.

Green Strawberry requires more attention than pink and matching green color hues seems to be a trivial issue here unlike other patterns where color is a primary concern. Green or pink Strawberry can be collected as a set; however, there are no cups, saucers, or dinner-sized plates. There is the usual mould roughness on the seams. Even pieces that are acknowledged as mint may have extra glass burrs on seams where it came out of the mould.

Strawberry sugar covers and the 6¼", 2" deep bowl are hard to find. Some older sellers erroneously label the sugar with no lid and no handles as a spooner which was a common piece sold that way in earlier times; however, by the Depression era, spooners were rarely used. Of course selling a sugar with no lid is difficult, so marketing it a spooner might sell it faster.

Strawberry has a plain butter dish bottom that is analogous to other U.S. Glass patterns. Some of those other U.S. Glass pattern butters have been robbed of their bottoms over the years to use with Strawberry tops. Strawberry butter dishes have been desirable to collectors since day one. In fact, in the "pioneering" days of Depression glass collecting, there was a strong nucleus of butter dish collectors. That hobby would be unaffordable, today, without a large stash of cash. Many of the rarer butters are already in collections and rarely appear on the market at any price.

	Crystal, Iridescent	Pink, Green		Crystal, Iridescent	Pink, Green
4 ▸ Bowl, 4", berry	6.50	12.00	14 ▸ Olive dish, 5", one-handle	9.00	22.00
Bowl, 6¼", 2" deep	65.00	165.00	5 ▸ Pickle dish, 8¼", oval	9.00	20.00
2 ▸ Bowl, 6½", deep salad	15.00	25.00	11 ▸ Pitcher, 7¾"	175.00	225.00
3 ▸ Bowl, 9", oval	30.00	30.00	9 ▸ Plate, 6", sherbet	5.00	12.00
Butter dish and cover	135.00	155.00	15 ▸ Plate, 7½", salad	12.00	18.00
3 ▸ Butter dish bottom	77.50	90.00	Sherbet	8.00	10.00
2 ▸ Butter dish top	57.50	65.00	6 ▸ Sugar, small, open	12.00	22.00
7 ▸ Comport, 5¾"	18.00	35.00	8 ▸ Sugar, large	22.00	45.00
8 ▸ Creamer, small	12.00	22.00	1 ▸ Sugar cover	45.00	75.00
0 ▸ Creamer, 4⅝", large	22.50	40.00	17 ▸ Tumbler, 3⅝", 8 ounce	22.00	40.00

"SUNBURST," "HERRINGBONE," JEANNETTE GLASS COMPANY, Late 1930s

Color: crystal

You may not know the name "Sunburst" but we'll bet you have spied the candlesticks while treasure hunting for other patterns. Outside of those easily spotted pieces, you will have some difficulty rounding up a sizeable set. Sherbets, dinner plates, and tumblers are the hardest to corral. The tumbler is similar in style to the flat Iris one with a flared top. "Sunburst" was made from the same shaped moulds as Iris. We wish we could show you one, but the tumbler has successfully eluded us. Every known piece of "Sunburst" is pictured save for that tumbler.

Wouldn't one of these stylish berry bowls or the divided relish have been great additions to the Iris pattern? As with Iris, those straight sided inner rims are easily nicked and need to be checked just as carefully as those of the Iris pattern; and to protect rims, items should be stacked with paper plates between each one. The clear areas on plates will showcase any excessive wear and scratches, so check that out when buying plates.

Collectors would probably not have noticed "Sunburst" had it not been for the popular sister pattern, Iris. Several collectors told us they started buying "Sunburst" after Iris attained those lofty prices that it fetches today. They liked the Iris shapes; so this gave them a less expensive pattern to collect. Any number of patterns are collected due to shaping or the blanks being thought equally as pleasing as the pattern.

Additional items may be found. Let us know of anything not found in the listing.

10 ▸	Bowl, 4¾", berry	10.00
9 ▸	Bowl, 8½", berry	20.00
14 ▸	Bowl, 10¾"	25.00
3 ▸	Candlesticks, double, pair	25.00
1 ▸	Creamer, footed	10.00
11 ▸	Cup	8.00
13 ▸	Plate, 5½"	10.00
6 ▸	Plate, 9¼", dinner	20.00
8 ▸	Plate, 11¾", sandwich	26.00
5 ▸	Relish, 2-part	15.00
12 ▸	Saucer	3.00
7 ▸	Sherbet	17.50
2 ▸	Sugar	10.00
4 ▸	Tray, small, oval	12.00
	Tumbler, 4", 9 ounce, flat	38.00

SUNFLOWER, JEANNETTE GLASS COMPANY, 1930s

Colors: pink, green, some Delphite; some opaque colors and Ultra Marine

8   10

Sunflower is an easily recognized pattern of Depression glass even by non-collectors. The ubiquitous cake plate may help recognition due to the quantities found today. Cake plates were packed in or given away with 20-pound bags of flour, which sold in huge quantities in the 1930s because home baking was the norm then. With a 50-pound bag, you received two. Sometimes, displays of the give-away items were near the cash register and you were handed one when you made your purchase. However, I've been told these were packaged in the sacks themselves.

You not only got the flour sack from which you made everything from dresses to curtains, but you also got a cake plate on which to display your baking skills. How many cake plates can one use? Many were stored away or passed down through the family.

A pink cake plate is pictured. If you look closely, you can see a couple of the legs showing through. A predicament taking place with the green cake plate is that many are uncovered in a deep, dark green that does not even come close to other pieces of green Sunflower. That heavy, round green piece is a paperweight found in a former Jeannette employee's home. Some cake plates are found darker than that paperweight shown.

There is still some puzzlement over the cake plate and the rarely found Sunflower trivet. Think 7 inches! The 7" trivet has an edge that is slightly upturned and it is 3" smaller than the omnipresent 10" cake plate. The 7" trivet remains the most elusive piece of Sunflower. Collector demand for the rare trivet keeps prices ascending.

Green Sunflower pieces are found less often than pink as evidenced by our photo; accordingly, prices for green are greater than for those of pink.

Sunflower saucers are in short supply. The last few sets of Sunflower we have seen have had more cups than saucers. Perhaps cups were a premium, or cups were offered longer than the saucers.

The Ultra Marine ashtray pictured is the only piece we have found in that color. Opaque colors show up sporadically, usually creamers and sugars. Only a creamer, plate, 6" tab-handled bowl, cup, and saucer have been documented in Delphite blue. They have all been pictured in previous books.

	Pink	Green			Pink	Green
2 ▸ *Ashtray, 5", center design only	9.00	11.00	8 ▸ Plate, 9", dinner		25.00	25.00
5 ▸ Cake plate, 10", 3 legs	15.00	15.00	7 ▸ Saucer		8.00	10.00
4 ▸ **Creamer, opaque $85.00	28.00	28.00	3 ▸ Sugar, opaque $85.00		28.00	28.00
6 ▸ Cup, opaque $75.00	18.00	20.00	9 ▸ Tumbler, 4¾", 8 ounce, footed		38.00	38.00
1 ▸ Paperweight		150.00	Trivet, 7", 3 legs, turned up edge		395.00	395.00
10 ▸ Plate, 8", luncheon	35.00		*Found in Ultra Marine $30.00 **Delphite $95.00			

217

SUNSHINE, LINES #731 – #737, LANCASTER GLASS COMPANY, c. 1932

Colors: pink, green w/crystal

Sunshine comes both satinized and non-satinized as you can see from our photo. We received numerous inquiries asking about non-satinized Sunshine after our photo only showed satinized pieces. We kept running into satinized when first buying items for the book. In the last two years, we have found several items which illustrate both styles.

This was another of those small lines sold as an assortment of pieces. There appears to have been a series of hexagonal blanks used for the pattern. You could buy up to a 36-piece assortment of Sunshine; so there should be more of it available than seems to be showing up. We have never heard of any dinner plates, though they may have been made judging from the other luncheon type pieces we do know were available. Notice the use of plates being turned into bowls, a practice employed to get as many items as possible from a single mould. As in Beaded Block, plates may simply be harder to find than bowls since plates were turned up for bowls.

You will seldom find a piece of this line inexpensively priced, not because the dealer has any notion what it is, just because it "looks like better glass." Most of the pieces pictured here were at least $40.00 when we found them for sale.

Thanks to several readers, there are some new listings added. Thank you for that information and keep it coming.

		Pink, Green			Pink, Green
1 ▸	Bowl, 6", 2-handled, hex edge	30.00	9 ▸	Mayonnaise, 5½", 2-handled, hex edge	38.00
2 ▸	Bowl, 8", 2-handled, hex edge	55.00	5 ▸	Mayonnaise, liner, 7¼", 2-handled, hex edge	20.00
	Bowl, 9", 2-handled, hex edge	65.00	3 ▸	Plate, 10½", 2-handled, hex edge	40.00
8 ▸	Bowl, 10½ x 8", oval, 2 raised sides,		4 ▸	Plate, 14", serving, hex edge	50.00
	2-handled, hex edge	75.00		Server, 10", center handled sandwich,	
6 ▸	Bowl, 12", flat rim, hex edge	65.00		hex edge	50.00
	Candle, single, hex foot	35.00	7 ▸	Sugar, round, footed	27.50
	Creamer, round, footed	27.50		Tray, 10", roll edge, "bun" tray,	
				hex edge	60.00

SWANKY SWIGS, 1930s – Early 1940s

We have tried a new format to portray these. One problem was that we could not come up with every type of the earlier styles we pictured previously.

"Why, I remember those. We used them when I was growing up!" or "Look, Mommy, those are like I used at Granny's house!" These are the type comments we often hear when Swanky Swigs are spotted. Serious collectors seek all types and sizes; casual collectors like flowers, particularly daffodils, red tulips, violets, and bachelor buttons. See *Collectible Glassware from the 40s, 50s, 60s...* for later made Swanky Swigs and a sample of their various metal lids, which have become collectible themselves.

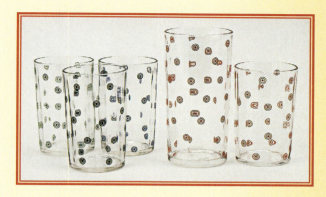

Band No.1, 3⅜": Blue, 3.50 – 5.00; red & black (not shown), 2.00 – 3.00; red & blue (not shown), 3.00 – 4.00. Band No. 2: Red & black, 3⅜", 3.00 – 4.00; red & black, 4¾" (not shown), 4.00 – 5.00. Band No. 3, 3⅜": Red & blue, 3.00 – 4.00.

Circle & Dot: Green, 3½", 4.00 – 5.00; black, 3½", 5.00 – 6.00; blue, 3½", 5.00 – 6.00; red, 4¾", 8.00 – 10.00; red, 3½", 4.00 – 5.00; blue, 4¾" (not shown), 8.00 – 10.00; green, 3½" (not shown), 4.00 – 5.00. Dot (not shown): Black, 4¾", 7.00 – 9.00; blue, 3½", 5.00 – 6.00.

Star: Black, 3½", 3.00 – 4.00; blue, 3½", 3.00 – 4.00; blue, 4¾", 7.00 – 8.00; green, 3½", 3.00 – 4.00; red, 3½", 3.00 – 4.00; cobalt w/white stars, 4¾" (not shown), 18.00 – 20.00.

Centennials: Texas, cobalt, 4¾", 35.00 – 40.00; Texas, blue (not shown), black, or green, 3½", 35.00 – 40.00; West Virginia, cobalt (not shown), 4¾", 22.00 – 25.00.

Checkerboard: Red, blue, or green, 3½", 30.00 – 35.00.

Sailboat: Red or blue, 3½", 10.00 – 12.00; green or light green, 3½", 12.00 – 15.00; blue, 4½" (not shown), 12.00 – 15.00; red or green, 4½" (not shown), 12.00 – 15.00.

Tulip No. 1: Blue, 3½", 3.00 – 4.00; blue, 3½", w/label, 15.00 –
20.00; blue, 4½", 15.00 – 20.00: black, 3½", w/label, 15.00 –
20.00; 3½", 3.00 – 4.00.

Tulip No. 1: Light green, 3½", 3.00 – 4.00; 3½", w/label, 15.00
– 20.00; 4½", 15.00 – 20.00 3½", 3.00 – 4.00.

Tulip No. 1: Red, 3½", 3.00 – 4.00; red, 4½", 15.00 – 20.00;
Yellow, 3½", 3.00 – 4.00.

Tulip No. 2: Red, blue, green, or black, 3½", 30.00 – 35.00.

Tulip No. 3: Yellow, red, 3¾", 3.00 – 4.00; 3¼", 15.00 – 20.00;
4½", 15.00 – 20.00.

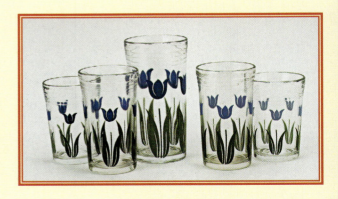

Tulip No. 3: Dark blue, light blue, 3¼", 15.00 – 20.00; 3¾", 2.50
3.50; 4½", 15.00 – 20.00.

SWIRL, "PETAL SWIRL," JEANNETTE GLASS COMPANY, 1937 – 1938

Colors: Ultra Marine, pink, Delphite; some amber and "ice" blue

Swirl can be found with two different edgings on most bowls and plates, ruffled and plain. Ultra Marine can be found with both, but pink is customarily found with plain borders. You need to stipulate what style you want if ordering by mail or off the Internet, though there should be no difference in price.

A Swirl Ultra Marine pitcher (pictured in previous editions) is found with great difficulty. So far, we know of only three that have turned up since the first one was found in 1974. None have been available in pink. Some collectors of Jeannette Swirl integrate this pattern with Jeannette's "Jennyware" kitchenware line that does have a flat, 36-ounce pink pitcher in it. If you find mixing bowls, measuring cups, or reamers, then you have crossed into the kitchenware line and out of Swirl dinnerware. See *Kitchen Glassware of the Depression Years* for complete "Jennyware" listings and pricing.

Swirl candy and butter dish bottoms are more numerous than tops. Bear that in mind before you buy only a bottom unless it is very reasonably priced. That dearth of tops holds true for 90% of the butter and candy dishes in Depression glass. Unless you have the ability to remember color hues, it might be beneficial to take your half piece with you when trying to match this Ultra Marine color. Swirl has some green-tinged pieces as well as the normally found color. This green tint is hard to match, and some collectors steer clear of this shade. For that reason, you can usually buy this green tint at a discounted price if you are willing to assemble that shade. This coloration problem occurs with all Jeannette patterns made in Ultra Marine.

Pink candleholders are not regarded as rare even though they were absent from the listings in some of our earlier editions.

Pink coasters are regularly found inside a small rubber tire and used for ashtrays. These tire advertisements have become collectible. Those with a tire manufacturer's name on the glass insert are more in demand; but those with a non-advertising glass insert are collected if the miniature tire is embossed with the name of a tire company. Many of these tires dried up or came apart over the years leaving only the glass inserts as reminders, particularly here in Florida. Rubber and Florida's heat do not co-exist well. You should see what it does for elastic in clothing.

Swirl was produced in several experimental colors, but most of these are found as bowls. However, a smaller set can be compiled in Delphite blue; it would only have basic pieces and a serving dish or two.

SWIRL

	Pink	Ultra Marine	Delphite
1 ▸ Bowl, 4⅞" & 5¼", berry	13.00	16.00	14.00
2 ▸ Bowl, 9", salad	26.00	28.00	30.00
Bowl, 9", salad, rimmed	30.00	35.00	
15 ▸ Bowl, 10", footed, closed handles	40.00	35.00	
Bowl, 10½", footed, console	20.00	32.00	
Butter dish	185.00	350.00	
Butter dish bottom	35.00	60.00	
Butter dish top	150.00	290.00	
11 ▸ Candle holders, double branch, pair	90.00	60.00	
Candle holders, single branch, pair			125.00
13 ▸ Candy dish, open, 3 legs	14.00	18.00	
Candy dish with cover	130.00	185.00	
Coaster, 1" x 3¼"	15.00	25.00	
7 ▸ Creamer, footed	11.50	15.00	15.00
Cup	11.00	15.00	12.00
Pitcher, 48 ounce, footed		2,000.00	

	Pink	Ultra Marine	Delphite
17 ▸ Plate, 6½", sherbet	7.00	7.00	6.00
10 ▸ Plate, 7¼"	12.00	16.00	
Plate, 8", salad	10.00	15.00	9.00
9 ▸ Plate, 9¼", dinner	18.00	22.00	12.00
4 ▸ Plate, 10½"			25.00
16 ▸ Plate, 12½", sandwich	22.00	29.00	
3 ▸ Platter, 12", oval			38.00
14 ▸ Salt and pepper, pair		50.00	
Saucer	3.00	4.00	5.00
Sherbet, low footed	16.00	23.00	
Soup, tab handle (lug)	45.00	55.00	
6 ▸ Sugar, footed	11.50	17.00	15.00
5 ▸ Tray, 10½", 2-handle			27.50
Tumbler, 4", 9 ounce	23.00	40.00	
Tumbler, 4⅝", 9 ounce	20.00		
Tumbler, 5⅛", 13 ounce	60.00	135.00	
Tumbler, 9 ounce, footed	25.00	46.00	
Vase, 6½" footed, ruffled	26.00		
12 ▸ Vase, 8½" footed, two styles		27.50	

222

TEA ROOM, INDIANA GLASS COMPANY, 1926 – 1931

Colors: pink, green, amber, and some crystal

24   11   24

We mentioned before that the Internet was expanding finds of Tea Room in New Zealand and Australia. Measurements from there have been a problem as the reported a 9½" amber ruffled vase shrunk an inch in shipping. Once it reached the States, it only was 8½" tall. Maybe it was a metric conversion problem. Several smaller 6½" amber Tea Room ruffled vases have been uncovered "down under." A green tumbler from there exhibited a slightly different green hue from those we normally find here. We have known for years that rare pieces in some patterns were only rare in the States. This may have to do with their being used as ballast materials in the ships. With the Internet, more discoveries are being found to the extent it is difficult to keep up. Let us know what you discover.

We would like to thank a reader for compiling a listing of Tea Room prices realized from Internet auctions. Having bought a large collection, we have been aware of pricing changes in this pattern, but pricing comparisons help. Many prices have been adjusted — both up and down.

As the name suggests, the very Deco styled Tea Room pattern was marketed for use in the tea rooms and ice cream parlors of that day. That is the reason you find so many soda fountain items not seen in other patterns. Two styles of banana splits are found with the flat green one twice as costly as the footed one. In pink, the two styles are priced about the same. In the past you, could often find flat banana splits reasonably priced because they were unrecognized; now that rarely happens in this world of educated collectors.

The biggest problem in Tea Room is finding mint condition pieces. Check the underneath sides of flat pieces, which are inclined to chip and flake on all the unprotected ridges. The pink set we bought had four or five pieces listed as damaged and the rest listed as mint. Upon examining it, there were other pieces that were not exactly mint. Mint means no damage at all. Imperfections in the glass may exist, but no chips or small cracks anywhere. It is perfectly fine to buy and use flawed pieces; just don't pay mint prices for them. Prices below are for mint items. These prices are high because mint condition items are difficult to obtain. Damaged pieces are often bought to supplement sets until mint items can be found. Not everyone can afford to buy only mint items were they readily available. They are willing to accept Tea Room pieces with some minor flaws at lesser prices. New collectors may have to accept some damage on items or do without. If you've sought an item forever and find it damaged slightly, you might want to own the item anyway since this may be your only chance to do so. You have to weigh all factors as they fit you in regards to your glass and your pocketbook. We're sure that pieces pulled from moulds were marred at that moment. It was an inherent flaw in the design and manufacturing process. We've told you before about examining original boxed Tea Room that was not in really mint condition when closely examined.

Green Tea Room is sought more than pink; and some people are starting to search for crystal. Some crystal pieces are fetching the prices listed in pink except for the commonly found 9½" ruffled vase and the rarely found pitcher.

	Green	Pink			Green	Pink
Bowl, finger	90.00	85.00	31 ▸	*Saucer	30.00	30.00
Bowl, 7½", banana split, flat	165.00	200.00	19 ▸	Sherbet, low, footed	35.00	30.00
Bowl, 7½", banana split, footed	100.00	125.00	27 ▸	Sherbet, low, flared edge	35.00	30.00
Bowl, 8¼", celery	32.00	37.50	13 ▸	Sherbet, tall, footed, 4½"	70.00	65.00
Bowl, 8¾", deep salad	100.00	125.00		Sugar w/lid, 3"	150.00	150.00
Bowl, 9½", oval vegetable	70.00	65.00	2 ▸	Sugar, 4"	22.00	22.00
Candlestick, low, pair	85.00	65.00	7 ▸	Sugar, 4½", footed, amber $125.00	25.00	20.00
Creamer, 3¼"	25.00	25.00	22 ▸	Sugar, rectangular	25.00	20.00
Creamer, 4½", footed, amber $125.00	25.00	20.00		Sugar, flat with cover	225.00	200.00
Creamer, rectangular	35.00	35.00	4 ▸	Sundae, footed, ruffled top	135.00	175.00
Creamer, 4"	22.00	22.00	28 ▸	Tray, center-handle	200.00	145.00
*Cup	75.00	65.00	3 ▸	Tray, handled, sugar/creamer	40.00	40.00
Goblet, 9 ounce	85.00	75.00	23 ▸	Tray, rectangular sugar & creamer	95.00	60.00
Ice bucket	95.00	90.00	16 ▸	Tumbler, 8 ounce, 4³⁄₁₆", flat	160.00	150.00
Lamp, 9", electric	155.00	140.00		Tumbler, 6 ounce, footed	40.00	35.00
Marmalade, notched lid	255.00	225.00	9 ▸	Tumbler, 8 ounce, 5¼", high, footed,		
Mustard, w/plain or notched lid	210.00	175.00		amber $125.00	35.00	35.00
Parfait	165.00	165.00	26 ▸	Tumbler, 11 ounce, footed	55.00	55.00
**Pitcher, 64 ounce, amber $695.00	185.00	150.00	17 ▸	Tumbler, 12 ounce, footed	75.00	80.00
Plate, 6½", sherbet	32.00	30.00	12 ▸	‡Vase, 6½", ruffled edge	100.00	85.00
Plate, 8¼", luncheon	55.00	50.00	39 ▸	‡‡Vase, 9½", ruffled edge	130.00	
Plate, 10½", 2-handle	65.00	60.00	6 ▸	Vase, 11", ruffled edge	295.00	295.00
Relish, divided	27.00	30.00		Vase, 11", straight	160.00	165.00
Salt and pepper, pair	110.00	100.00				

Prices for absolutely mint pieces   ** Crystal $695.00   ‡ Amber $350.00   ‡‡ Crystal $16.00

THISTLE, MacBETH-EVANS, 1929 – 1930

Colors: pink, green; some yellow and crystal

MacBeth Evans Thistle pattern has been one of the most difficult patterns to capture on film and in print. We have had seven or eight photographers try to keep the thistles showing and sometimes they do, but more often they do not. Photography lights cause Thistle to do a vanishing act, something all too familiar for Thistle collectors. Our photographer seems to have captured it, but you will never know how many Polaroid test shots were made before both the delicate color and the pattern were captured.

If you encounter a thick butter dish, pitcher, tumbler, creamer, sugar, or other heavy moulded pieces with impressed Thistle designs, they are probably newly made. Mosser Glass Company in Cambridge, Ohio, is making these pieces in various colors. They are not a part of this pattern, but are designs based on a much older Cambridge pattern glass. Should you encounter the older Cambridge ware, it will probably be embossed with the words "near cut" in its center. If you have a piece of Thistle not in the photograph, then you probably do not have a piece of Depression glass Thistle made by MacBeth-Evans. All seven pieces known in the pattern are shown here. Many companies made thistle designs sometime during their productions.

Green Thistle is even less available than pink except for the large fruit bowl that is practically a fantasy in pink. We have owned the one pictured here for over 30 years. Our arms have been twisted many times over the years to sell it and that day may come.

Thistle pieces have the same mould shapes as thin Dogwood; however, no Thistle creamer or sugar has ever been found. The Thistle grill plate has the pattern only on the edge. None have been found with an allover pattern as in Dogwood. Those plain centers scratched easily; beware of that should you locate a grill plate. Frankly, they are so scarce now, if you find one with a distinguishable pattern, be thankful and buy it.

		Pink	Green
7 ▸	Bowl, 5½", cereal	35.00	38.00
4 ▸	Bowl, 10¼", large fruit	595.00	395.00
1 ▸	Cup, thin	28.00	30.00
5 ▸	Plate, 8", luncheon	17.00	18.00
3 ▸	Plate, 10¼", grill	30.00	35.00
6 ▸	Plate, 13", heavy cake	210.00	235.00
2 ▸	Saucer	10.00	12.00

"TOP NOTCH," "SUNBURST," NEW MARTINSVILLE, c. 1930s

Colors: amethyst, red, green, cobalt, amber

In the northeast, the name "Top Notch" or "Top Prize" is used; but in the south, "Sunburst" is the label. We will use the "Top Notch" moniker for now until the real name is discovered. Most of the pieces we have found have been in the northeast. Cathy asked one southern dealer where her name label came from and she said she "found it in some old magazine a couple of years ago" though she couldn't pinpoint which one. No matter what it's being called, it is a wonderful design and comes in rich jewel colors. We had a letter from a lady who thought she had some pieces in amethyst, but they were packed away and she would contact us when they were unpacked. So far, that has not happened.

We know the items pictured are from a luncheon set, but whether there are additional items available is a mystery. We have, however, run into a second set in Florida having the green items depicted here. Finding glassware patterns here does not help much in pinpointing sources, since no one knows where it was before being transplanted to this state. A lot of excellent collectible glass was brought here by retirees and much of that is now reaching the market.

We purchased the red cup and saucer in Kentucky and have seen one set in blue. A friend with whom we were discussing the pattern believes she's seen amber. That would fit with New Martinsville colors from this period; so, I feel confident in listing that color.

		All colors
5 ▸	Cup	20.00
2 ▸	Creamer	30.00
6 ▸	Plate, luncheon	20.00
3 ▸	Plate, serving tray	38.00
4 ▸	Saucer	8.00
1 ▸	Sugar	30.00

TULIP, DELL GLASS COMPANY, Late 1930s – Late 1940s

Color: amethyst, turquoise (blue), crystal, green

The amethyst Tulip decanter picture exposed a couple of others. The decanter bottom is not tulip design, though it does have an optic in the glass. Only the stopper shows Tulip design. Even showing it in the previous book, we were still able to find a blue decanter sans stopper for $6.00 in an antique mall. Know what to look for when shopping.

We started buying Tulip about 15 years ago when we ran across nine green sugar bowls for $10.00. We did not know whether there were collectors for this pattern or not, but we soon found out. Those sugars are regularly found in groups of four or more, making us surmise they may have been sold as cream soups, also. Another clue toward that theory is finding around a dozen sugars for every creamer.

We find that the scalloped rims have a proclivity to damage and most of it occurs under the rim edge. Be sure to turn the piece over and check each of the pointed scallops from the opposite side. Many times a scallop or two will be almost absent and not show from the top side.

Candleholders are found in two varieties. One style is made from an ivy bowl (not a sherbet as the piece was formerly believed to be). That ivy bowl (sherbet) is pictured in the 1946 Montgomery Ward catalog with ivy growing in it. We have pictured that ad in past books. For clarification, the violin vase pictured here (#18 below) and in the ad is not considered to be part of the pattern although the neck of the violin is rather like the neck on the decanter. Also, that violin vase can be found in all Tulip colors.

The juice tumbler (shown as a cigarette holder in an ad in previous books) is 2¾" tall and holds three ounces; the whiskey is only 1¾" and holds one ounce. Prices are similar, but shot glass collectors add to the numbers buying the latter. That ad for Tulip showed no stippling on some pieces. Early in buying Tulip, we ignored some pieces without stippling. That changed after conversations with a collector who told us both styles are acceptable to collectors.

Crystal is priced with the green since you will not see much of it. Crystal may be the rarest "color."

	Amethyst, Blue	Crystal, Green			Amethyst, Blue	Crystal, Green
15 ▸ Bowl, oval, oblong, 13¼"	110.00	95.00	8 ▸ Decanter stopper	25.00	25.00
13 ▸ Candleholder, 3¾" (ivy bowl)	38.00	30.00	17 ▸ Decanter w/stopper	495.00	
16 ▸ Candleholder, 5¼" base, 3" tall	65.00	45.00	12 ▸ Ice tub, 4⅞" wide, 3" deep	75.00	65.00
9 ▸ Candy w/lid, footed (6" w/o lid)	225.00	185.00	10 ▸ Plate, 6"	10.00	9.00
2 ▸ Creamer	20.00	22.00	14 ▸ Plate, 7¼"	16.00	13.00
4 ▸ Cup	18.00	14.00	6 ▸ Plate, 10"	35.00	32.00
			5 ▸ Saucer	7.00	6.00
			1 ▸ Sherbet, 3¾", flat (ivy bowl)	22.00	20.00
			3 ▸ Sugar	20.00	20.00
			11 ▸ Tumbler, 2¾", juice	33.00	22.00
			7 ▸ Tumbler, whiskey	35.00	25.00

228

TWISTED OPTIC, LINE #313, IMPERIAL GLASS COMPANY, 1927 – 1930 and onward

Colors: pink, green, amber; some blue and Canary yellow, ruby and iridized crystal

First, you should realize that many other glass companies made twisting patterns besides this Twisted Optic from Imperial or Hocking's Spiral previously presented in this book.

The Canary yellow color photographed here is often mislabeled "vaseline." "Vaseline" was a term used by collectors for vibrant yellow colored glassware. We were able to buy enough pieces from a dealer selling a set to illustrate the Canary color wonderfully. Seeing all the items he had accumulated besides these was breathtaking and we were very tempted to buy it all. However, we only need one of each for illustration purposes.

If we pay $100.00 for a piece to get it photographed, then sell it for $100.00 afterwards, that doesn't make sense to some dealers; but it was worth it to us… and we hope, you, too.

Of course, there are more pieces of Twisted Optic than we show. Space limitations are forcing us to cut back a page or two on some of the less collected patterns, but you can refer to previous editions to see larger quantities of Twisted Optic.

	Blue, Canary Yellow	All other colors		Blue, Canary Yellow	All other colors
Basket, 10", tall	95.00	60.00	Plate, 7", salad	8.00	4.00
Bowl, console, scroll tab hdld., oval, ftd.	65.00	50.00	Plate, 7½" x 9", oval with indent	12.00	5.00
Bowl, 4¾", fruit	25.00	15.00	Plate, 8", luncheon	8.00	7.00
Bowl, 5", cereal	16.00	9.00	Plate, 9½", cracker	30.00	18.00
Bowl, 7", crimped	30.00	20.00	Plate, 10", sandwich	25.00	9.00
Bowl, 7", salad	25.00	15.00	Plate, 12"	30.00	15.00
Bowl, 9"	35.00	15.00	Plate, 14", buffet	40.00	25.00
Bowl, 9¼", salad	40.00	25.00	Platter, oval	35.00	25.00
Bowl 10", salad	45.00	30.00	Powder jar w/lid	80.00	45.00
Bowl, 10½", console	45.00	25.00	Preserve (same as candy w/slotted lid)		30.00
Bowl, 11½", 4¼" tall	55.00	30.00	7 ▸ Sandwich server, open center handle, 2 styles	40.00	20.00
Candlesticks, 3", pair (3 styles)	45.00	50.00	Sandwich server, two-handle	18.00	12.00
Candlesticks, 8½", pair	75.00	55.00	9 ▸ Saucer	5.00	2.00
2 ▸ Candy jar w/cover, flat	90.00	50.00	Server, center handle, bowl shape	42.00	20.00
Candy jar w/cover, flat, flange edge	100.00	55.00	4 ▸ Sherbet	12.00	6.00
Candy jar w/cover, ftd., flange edge	100.00	55.00	Sugar	18.00	10.00
3 ▸ Candy jar w/cover, ftd., short, fat	110.00	60.00	Tumbler, 4½", 9 ounce		6.00
Candy jar w/cover, footed, tall	135.00	60.00	Tumbler, 5¼", 12 ounce		8.00
Compote, cheese	20.00	12.00	6 ▸ Vase, 7¼", 2-handle, rolled edge	75.00	45.00
Creamer	18.00	10.00	Vase, 7¼", flat rim	65.00	40.00
8 ▸ Cup	13.00	7.00	Vase, 8", 2-handle, fan	95.00	50.00
Mayonnaise	50.00	30.00	1 ▸ Vase, 8", 2-handle, straight edge	95.00	45.00
Pitcher, 64 ounce		45.00	Vase, 8½", 2-handle, bulbous neck	11.00	65.00
5 ▸ Plate, 6", sherbet	6.00	3.00			

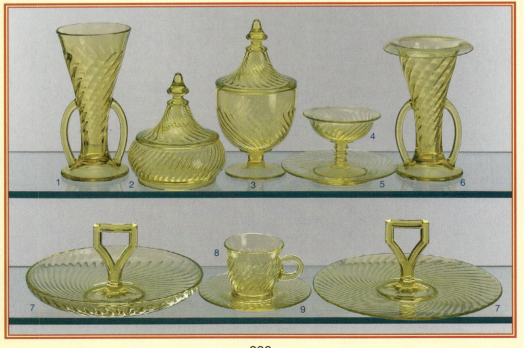

"U.S. SCROLL," "STAR FLOWER," "PINWHEEL," UNITED STATES GLASS COMPANY, c. 1925

Colors: black, green, pink

The intertwined U.S.G. (United States Glass) symbol is usually found on this smaller pattern with the octagonal shape. We uncovered a few more black items to display, but notice they have to be shown from the bottom or back to see the "Scroll" pattern.

Although cataloged in pink, we have been unable to come up with a piece in that color. It is generally found in small groups rather than a piece at a time. Unfortunately, damaged pieces are the norm. This may have been from excessive use or the angular shapes which invite bumps. You will see green most often. This should answer those 50 or more letters we receive each year asking what we know about this pattern.

A recent e-mail from Canada told us that a green 10", three-footed cake plate was found there. One is shown at right.

	Black	Green, Pink
6▸ Cake plate, 10", 3-footed		25.00
5▸ Creamer	12.00	8.00
2▸ Cup	8.00	7.00
Plate, 7½"	8.00	5.00
4▸ Plate, 8½"	12.00	9.00
3▸ Saucer	3.00	2.00
1▸ Sugar	12.00	8.00

"U.S. SWIRL," U.S. GLASS COMPANY, Late 1920s

Colors: green, some pink, iridescent, and crystal

"U.S. Swirl" is an easily recognized swirling pattern because it has shapes and pieces very similar to the popula[r] Aunt Polly and Strawberry patterns made by U.S. Glass. The 24-pointed star on the bottom of most pieces is a dead give-away. Most other swirled and spiral patterns have plain bottoms. Pink, iridescent, and crystal items are happened upon once in a while in "U.S. Swirl." We have only found one pink shaker, a butter dish, and a tumbler in all the years we have been hunting. Obviously, very little pink was distributed, or possibly only some special items for promotional use. I[n] the listings, we have separated the colors based on demand for green outweighing that of pink, but not all pink items may exist. If more pink were available, it would surely bypass green prices due to rarity. Since it is so rarely seen, there are few searching for it; so the demand factor does not influence price yet.

Occasionally, we spot crystal sherbets. The 5⅜" tall, rarely found comport was labeled a large sherbet when we found it. Comports were mostly used as an open candy, but some, today, favor them for martini glasses. (That's why Hocking's Manhattan comport supplies have dried up. Collectors are buying six or more for drink use instead of one for candy.)

"U.S. Swirl" iridescent butter dishes appear once in a while, as do sherbets. In early days of collecting, those butters would have been snapped up by collectors of those. Today, with few butter dish collectors, they are harder to sell. The 8 ounce tumbler listing 3⅝" conforms with the only known size of Aunt Polly and Cherryberry/Strawberry tumblers; but the 12-ounce tumbler, pictured, has only been found in "U.S. Swirl."

"U.S. Swirl" has the plain butter bottom that is compatible with other patterns made by U.S. Glass. The butter dish in this pattern is the one that many Strawberry or Cherryberry collectors have purchased over the years to borrow the base for their butter lids. This plundering has reduced the number of butters in "U.S. Swirl" pattern, particularly in scarce pink. Had there ever been iridescent butter dishes found in Cherryberry/Strawberry patterns, the iridescent "U.S. Swirl" but[-]ters might have disappeared entirely with the crossover butter bottom usage.

		Green	Pink			Green	Pink
	Bowl, 4⅜", berry	5.50	6.50		Creamer	25.00	25.00
1▸	Bowl, 5½", 1-handle	9.50	10.50	10▸ Pickle dish, 8¼", oval	30.00	30.00
6▸	Bowl, 7⅞", large berry	15.00	16.00	11▸ Pitcher, 8", 48 ounce	90.00	90.00
	Bowl, 8¼", oval (2¾" deep)	50.00	45.00		Plate, 6⅛", sherbet	2.50	2.50
	Bowl, 8⅜", oval (1¾" deep)	60.00	55.00	8▸ Plate, 7⅞", salad	5.50	6.50
	Butter and cover	120.00	120.00		Salt and pepper, pair	75.00	75.00
3▸	Butter bottom	90.00	90.00		Sherbet, 3¼"	4.50	5.00
2▸	Butter top	30.00	30.00	9▸ Sugar w/lid	50.00	50.00
	Candy, footed, 2-handled	35.00	30.00	7▸ Tumbler, 3⅝", 8 ounce	10.00	10.00
	Candy w/cover, 2-handled	27.50	35.00	4▸ Tumbler, 4¾", 12 ounce	15.00	16.00
5▸	Comport	35.00	30.00		Vase, 6½"	32.00	28.00

"VICTORY," DIAMOND GLASS-WARE COMPANY, 1928 – 1931

Colors: amber, pink, green; some cobalt blue and black

"Victory" was one of the last of Diamond's patterns produced before the factory burned in 1931. Luckily, it was around for the 1929 cobalt blue introduction phase.

"Victory" is a pattern where colors are often blended by collectors. Notice how well the amber and black complement each other. One new collector told us that photo combination in a previous book prompted her search for "Victory." Since she lived in New England, she had a better chance of selection than is found elsewhere. We have purchased almost all the "Victory" pictured here from the northeast part of the country.

Intermixing colors is really catching on amongst collectors. It gives you more than just one color to pursue. Many times, you will observe your pattern for sale only to have it be a wrong color. This is disappointing and does not happen as often if you are searching for several colors. The black with gold trim stands out better in the photo than the gold-trimmed amber. As with most black glass of this era, the pattern is on the reverse; you have to flip it over to see the piece is "Victory" unless you can recognize it from the indented edges shape. Collectors of black glass are more apt to own black "Victory" than Depression glass people. Those collectors often bring "Victory" to shows for identification since they have no clue it's an actual named pattern.

Several enrichment techniques besides the 22K gold trim are found on "Victory." There are floral decorations and even a Deco looking black design on pink and green. I have spied more floral decorated console sets (bowl and candlesticks) than anything in this pattern. I suppose that complete sets of gold decorated pink and green can be located while black pieces decorated with gold appear to be available only in luncheon or console sets. The decorations other than gold trimmed may have been added by a decorating company rather than Diamond.

Sets of "Victory" can be accumulated in pink, green, or amber with a great deal of searching. Cobalt blue or black will take more hunting and some good fortune. It can be done even in today's market, but it will be expensive. After we previously mentioned that "Victory" was being found in the northeast, especially in Maine, we have been notified of other sets there, the latest of which was bought in an antique mall rather reasonably.

Gravy boats with platters are the most sought pieces to own in all colors. We have owned one amber and one green set, but three cobalt blue ones. A green gravy and platter can be seen at the bottom of page 234. The "Victory" goblet, candlestick, cereal, soup, and oval vegetable bowls will keep you looking long and hard no matter what color you desire.

"VICTORY"

	Black, Amber, Pink, Green	Blue
Bonbon, 7"	11.00	20.00
8 ▸ Bowl, 5", 2 handled	15.00	
9 ▸ Bowl, 6½", cereal	14.00	45.00
Bowl, 8½", flat soup	22.00	70.00
Bowl, 9", oval vegetable	35.00	115.00
Bowl, 11", rolled edge	30.00	50.00
Bowl, 12", console	35.00	65.00
11 ▸ Bowl, 12½", flat edge	30.00	70.00
Candlesticks, 3", pair	35.00	135.00
Cheese & cracker set, 12" indented plate & compote	40.00	
6 ▸ Comport, 6" tall, 6¾" diameter	15.00	
3 ▸ Creamer	15.00	50.00
1 ▸ Cup	12.00	30.00
Goblet, 5", 7 ounce	25.00	95.00
10 ▸ Gravy boat and platter	250.00	300.00
Mayonnaise set: 3½" tall, 5½" across, 8½" indented plate, w/ladle	42.00	100.00
Plate, 6", bread and butter	6.00	16.00
5 ▸ Plate, 7", salad	7.00	20.00
Plate, 8", luncheon	7.00	32.00
Plate, 9", dinner	20.00	55.00
12 ▸ Platter, 12"	30.00	95.00
7 ▸ Sandwich server, center handle	35.00	78.00
2 ▸ Saucer	4.00	8.00
Sherbet, footed	14.00	26.00
4 ▸ Sugar	15.00	50.00

Colors: white and white w/fired-on colors, usually red or green

Vitrock was Hocking's impetuous leap into the milk glass market. It was not an authentic named pattern per se; rather a mid-1930s milk white color of Hocking's similar to Hazel-Atlas's Platonite. There are different patterns found on this very robust line, but collectors have embraced the decorated Lake Como (page 108) and the "Flower Rim" dinnerware sets as Vitrock patterns to collect.

Vitrock's main claim to fame with collectors is its kitchenware line of reamers, measuring cups, and mixing bowls. Of late, shakers and grease sets have been the most desired items made in Vitrock. It was promoted as ware that "will not craze or check," a major flaw in many pottery lines of the time and thus, a good selling point. Those large Vitrock mixing bowls are probably so hard to find today because they cost a quarter, which may have accounted for a half-day's wage for a worker then and been too dear a price to pay. At the time, Vitrock competed with Hazel-Atlas's Platonite; and from all conclusions now, Platonite won.

Today, the "Flower Rim" decorated platters, soup plates, and cream soups are pieces that are nearly impossible to find. We finally found a regular Vitrock flat soup with label pictured in the bottom row. These are rarer than I previously thought as we have found a dozen or more decorated with Lake Como before spotting this one. Also turning out harder to find than they should be are the 9½" vegetable bowls. Several collectors have suggested that the fired-on Vitrock is even less available. Since we only have two fired color pieces, we have no hesitation in believing that.

You can see more Vitrock items in our book *Kitchen Glassware of the Depression Years*. Some collectors are fusing patterns that cross fields. Vitrock is a prime example of a color/pattern that fits into both kitchen and dinnerware arenas. Hazel-Atlas did the same with their Platonite wares. It made business sense to sell supporting items that matched your everyday dishes.

	White			White
9 ▸ Bowl, 4", berry	4.00	4 ▸ Plate, 7¼", salad		4.00
1 ▸ Bowl, 5½", cream soup	16.00	2 ▸ Plate, 8¾", luncheon		5.00
2 ▸ Bowl, 6", fruit	5.50	11 ▸ Plate, 9", soup		35.00
Bowl, 7½", cereal	9.00	3 ▸ Plate, 10", dinner		10.00
10 ▸ Bowl, 9½", vegetable	15.00	Platter, 11½"		30.00
5 ▸ Creamer, oval	7.00	8 ▸ Saucer		2.00
7 ▸ Cup	6.00	6 ▸ Sugar		7.00

235

WATERFORD, "WAFFLE," HOCKING GLASS COMPANY, 1938 – 1944

Colors: crystal, pink; some yellow, Vitrock; forest green 1950s

Waterford was Hocking's answer for the common man's opportunity to own a pattern that reflects light and pattern well. It was not an expensive, cut lead crystal, like Irish Waterford; but it evokes images of that. This Waterford sells very well because it is available and priced reasonably. It also looks impressive when displayed as a setting. We bought a set of over 300 pieces of crystal last year, and over half of it sold immediately.

Regrettably, pink is rarely spotted any more outside of major glass shows. Those searching for pink would be ecstatic about pink cereal bowls, a pitcher, or a butter dish inhabiting their table setting. Of these three pieces, the cereal is the most elusive. It has always been perplexing to find, and worse, challenging to find mint. The inside rim is unavoidably damaged from stacking or use. A little roughness is expected; do not let that keep you from owning a hard-to-find piece. Because of the scalloped rim design, Waterford chips or flakes more easily on the inside than most other patterns.

Some scarce crystal pieces include cereal bowls, pitchers, and water goblets. There is a 7¾" bowl standing 2" high that turns up occasionally, but is missing from most collections. Those crystal shakers pictured were used by many restaurants through the 1960s and into the 1970s, which is why they are commonly seen today. There are two styles of crystal sherbets. One has a scalloped top and base. It is not as commonly found and is not as accepted as the regular, plain edged one.

Advertising ashtrays, such as the "Post Cereals" shown below, are selling for $20.00 to $25.00 depending upon the significance of the advertising on the piece. A promotional one for Anchor Hocking itself will fetch $35.00 to $40.00.

A few pieces of Vitrock Waterford and some Dusty Rose and Springtime Green decorated ashtrays turn up once in a while, and sell near crystal prices. Examples of those rose and green colors can be seen in the Oyster and Pearl pattern (page 165). Large Forest Green Waterford 13¾" plates were made in the 1950s promotion of Forest Green; these are usually found in the $30.00 range, but are presently not fast sellers. Many of these are found with five Ivory sections sitting around them similar to those relish tray inserts found in Manhattan. The large green plate was used as the E 2900/100 7 piece relish base. Some crystal has also been found trimmed in red. There is not enough of the red trim to collect a set unless you get lucky and find it all at once.

Items listed below with Miss America shape noted in parentheses are Waterford patterned pieces with the same mould shapes as Miss America, having three rings above the pattern. Examples of these can be found in the seventh edition of this book and our *Treasures of Very Rare Depression Glass* book.

Those yellow and amber goblets shown below are compliments of Anchor Hocking's photographer from items stored in their morgue. I have never seen yellow ones for sale, but amber ones sell for around $25.00 when they can be found.

	Crystal	Pink			Crystal	Pink
21 ▶ *Ashtray, 4"	7.50			Plate, 6", sherbet	4.00	7.00
1 ▶ Bowl, 4¾", berry	7.00	19.00	11 ▶	Plate, 7⅛", salad	7.00	15.00
13 ▶ Bowl, 5½", cereal	18.00	37.50	12 ▶	Plate, 9⅝", dinner	12.00	26.00
4 ▶ Bowl, 8¼", large berry	14.00	28.00	6 ▶	Plate, 10¼", handled cake	12.00	18.00
16 ▶ Butter dish and cover	30.00	225.00	5 ▶	Plate, 13¾", sandwich	14.00	40.00
Butter dish bottom	8.00	30.00		Relish, 13¾", 5-part	20.00	
Butter dish top	22.00	205.00	17 ▶	Salt and pepper, 2 types	10.00	
18 ▶ Coaster, 4"	3.00		8 ▶	Saucer	3.00	6.00
3 ▶ Creamer, oval	6.00	12.00	9 ▶	Sherbet, footed	5.00	20.00
Creamer (Miss America shape)		45.00	23 ▶	Sherbet, footed, scalloped top	6.00	
7 ▶ Cup	6.50	15.00	2 ▶	Sugar	6.00	12.50
Cup (Miss America shape)		50.00	22 ▶	Sugar cover, oval	12.00	32.50
19 ▶ Goblets, 5¼", 5⅝"	17.00			Sugar (Miss America shape)		45.00
Goblet, 5½" (Miss America shape)	40.00	135.00		Tumbler, 3½", 5 oz. juice		
Lamp, 4", spherical base	26.00			(Miss America shape)		125.00
20 ▶ Pitcher, 24 ounce, tilted, juice	24.00		10 ▶	Tumbler, 4⅞", 10 ounce, footed	14.00	28.00
14 ▶ Pitcher, 80 ounce, tilted, ice lip	42.00	175.00				

* With ads $15.00 – 40.00 depending on item popularity

236

WHITE BAND, DECORATION #97, HOCKING GLASS COMPANY, 1932 – 1936

Color: crystal w/white band and red stripes

The wide White Band with contrasting red stripes "produces a pleasing effect" according to Hocking's 1935 catalog. Our listing below is taken from that catalog and we need to address some terminology there. First are the "shell" tumblers in 6, 10, and 12 ounces. These are straight sided, flat tumblers sometimes referred to by other companies as cylinder tumblers. This is the only time we can find that shell designation in any Hocking pattern. It is usually reserved for restaurant plain tumbler listings. The term saucer champagne we found unusual for Hocking since most other patterns such as Cameo and Mayfair call these high sherbets, a practice begun during Prohibition.

White Band is available, particularly in central Ohio, but you need to find pieces that were not heavily used. It's easy to spot them when still showing both the wide White Band and the red stripes. While gathering this pattern for photography, we saw dozens of pieces unsuitable for exhibiting. White Band is an apropos name as the red stripes go AWOL with usage and sometimes the white is all that is left. You will not want to use this in the dishwasher. As late as the 60s, glass makers were still trying to get their painted trims to adhere to items placed in the dishwasher.

We might point out that the martini mixer is usually called a cocktail shaker by collectors. There is a quart cocktail shaker in this pattern, but the martini mixer is only a pint, or half the cocktail size. We couldn't put our hands on a #78 pitcher; it is large, holds 80 ounces, is without an ice lip, and has optic panels should you spot one. Luncheon items including plates, cups, and saucers are not easy to find in mint condition. Evidently, these were well used and the decoration did not hold up well to 70 years of use. Goblets in excellent condition seem more available than tumblers. Most of the tumblers we find have little red left.

	Cocktail shaker, 32 oz.	30.00	12 ▸	Plate, 6", sherbet	4.00
9 ▸	Cup	8.00	7 ▸	Plate, 8", salad	10.00
13 ▸	Decanter, w/ground stopper, 32 oz.	35.00	10 ▸	Saucer, 6"	3.00
1 ▸	Goblet, 3 oz., cocktail	9.00		Sherbet, 5 oz.	8.00
2 ▸	Goblet, 3 oz., wine	10.00	8 ▸	Tumbler, 1½ oz., whiskey	15.00
	Goblet, 7 oz., saucer champagne	8.00		Tumbler, 3½ oz., ftd., cocktail	6.00
6 ▸	Goblet, 9½ oz., water	12.00		Tumbler, 6 oz., shell	7.00
11 ▸	Ice bowl, 5⅞"	27.50		Tumbler, 7½ oz., old fashioned	9.00
	Martina mixer, flat lid, 16 oz.	22.50		Tumbler, 9 oz., table	8.00
	Pitcher, 80 oz.	45.00	5 ▸	Tumbler, 10 oz., ftd., tumbler	12.00
			3 ▸	Tumbler, 10 oz., shell	9.00
			4 ▸	Tumbler, 12 oz., shell	10.00
				Tumbler, 13 oz., ftd., iced tea	15.00

WINDSOR, "WINDSOR DIAMOND," JEANNETTE GLASS COMPANY, 1936 – 1946

Colors: pink, green, crystal; some Delphite, amberina red, and ice blue

Windsor crystal has items never found in pink or green. The one-handled candlestick, 10½" pointed edge tray, three-part platter, and three sizes of footed tumblers come to mind, but there are others if you look at our price list. There are numerous collectors for colored Windsor, but fewer hunt crystal. Due to war time shortages, color was discontinued about 1940 in many glass factories, but crystal pieces were cataloged at Jeannette as late as 1946. Redesigned moulds for the Windsor butter, creamer, and sugar were later passed on to the Holiday pattern when that was introduced in 1947. This redesign caused there to be two styles of sugars and lids. One is shaped like Holiday and has no ledge for the lid to rest upon; the other sugar has a ledge for the lid. The pink sugar and lid shaped like Holiday are rare and expensive when found.

Green Windsor tumblers are elusive. The water tumbler, commonly found in pink, is scarce. Mould roughness is found on seams of tumblers; and Windsor tumblers have a proclivity to chip on the protruding sides. The diamond pattern pokes outward, making the sides an easy target for chips and flakes. Check these vigilantly before you buy. There are color variations in green; be mindful of that.

Square relish trays can be found with or without tabbed (closed) handles. Trays without handles commonly appear in crystal, but pink trays without handles are seldom found. Two styles of sandwich plates were produced. The normally found one is 10¼" and has open handles. The recently discovered one is 10", and has closed handles.

The large pink 13⅝" is often seen in ads as an underliner tray for a beverage set with a pitcher and six water tumblers. This set may have been a premium item since so many pitchers and water tumblers are discovered today. Prices for pink tumblers and the 11¾" x 7" boat shaped bowl have dipped due to the quantities available outpacing demand. Green tumblers do not experience this profusion and prices are holding steady at present.

The 8" pointed edge rim bowl is rarely seen in pink, but is being found in crystal and even crystal with red trim. Pointed edge bowls are rarely found undamaged. Those points are targets for any mishandling. The large crystal bowl, along with a comport, make up a punch bowl and stand. The upended comport fits snugly inside the base of the bowl to keep it from sliding off. In recent years, there have been newly made comports in crystal with sprayed colors that have a beaded edge. This recently made version will not work as a punch stand because the beaded edge will not fit inside the base of the bowl.

Unusual Windsor colors and items can be found pictured in our *Treasures of Very Rare Depression Glass* book.

WINDSOR

	Crystal	Pink	Green
*Ashtray, 5¾"	13.50	40.00	55.00
18 ▸ Bowl, 4¾", berry	4.00	12.00	12.00
36 ▸ Bowl, 5", pointed edge	9.00	33.00	
36 ▸ Bowl, 5", cream soup	7.00	30.00	33.00
3 ▸ Bowls, 5⅛", 5⅜", cereal	8.50	25.00	35.00
25 ▸ Bowl, 7⅛", three legs	9.00	30.00	
15 ▸ Bowl, 8", pointed edge	18.00	60.00	
35 ▸ Bowl, 8½", large berry	10.00	25.00	25.00
26 ▸ Bowl, 9", 2-handle	10.00	22.00	25.00
21 ▸ Bowl, 9½", oval vegetable	8.00	22.00	32.00
Bowl, 10½", salad	15.00		
13 ▸ Bowl, 10½", pointed edge	32.00	165.00	
31 ▸ Bowl, 12½", fruit console	30.00	135.00	
9 ▸ Bowl, 7" x 11¾", boat shape	20.00	20.00	37.50
1 ▸ Butter dish (two styles)	26.00	65.00	95.00
33 ▸ Cake plate, 10¾", footed	8.50	25.00	28.00
Candleholder, one handle	15.00		
19 ▸ Candlesticks, 3", pair	25.00	110.00	
Candy jar and cover	20.00		
24 ▸ Coaster, 3¼"	6.00	15.00	20.00
35 ▸ Comport	10.00		
16 ▸**Creamer	5.00	14.00	18.00
4 ▸ Creamer (shaped as "Holiday")	7.50		
8 ▸**Cup	5.00	10.00	12.50
Pitcher, 4½", 16 ounce	24.00	195.00	
34 ▸ ‡Pitcher, 6¾", 52 ounce	26.00	35.00	65.00
Plate, 6", sherbet	2.50	5.00	8.00
6 ▸ Plate, 7", salad	4.50	20.00	25.00

	Crystal	Pink	Green
**Plate, 9", dinner	8.00	22.00	25.00
Plate, 10", sandwich, closed handle		25.00	
Plate, 10½", pointed edge	10.00		
30 ▸ Plate, 10¼", sandwich, open handles	6.00	20.00	25.00
32 ▸ Plate, 13⅝", chop	18.00	40.00	45.00
22 ▸ Platter, 11½", oval	15.00	26.00	28.00
2 ▸‡‡Powder jar	15.00	60.00	
Relish platter, 11½", divided	15.00	250.00	
10 ▸ Salt and pepper, pair	20.00	40.00	50.00
23 ▸ Saucer, ice blue $15.00	2.50	5.00	6.00
Sherbet, footed	3.50	13.00	17.50
5 ▸ Sugar & cover	12.00	30.00	33.00
Sugar & cover (like "Holiday")	15.00	135.00	
7 ▸ Tray, 4", square, w/handle	5.00	10.00	12.00
Tray, 4", square, w/o handle	10.00	50.00	
Tray, 4⅛" x 9", w/handle	4.00	10.00	16.00
17 ▸ Tray, 4⅛" x 9", w/o handle	12.00	60.00	
14 ▸ Tray, 8½" x 9¾", 3-part	20.00	90.00	
Tray, 8½" x 9¾", w/handle	6.50	24.00	35.00
Tray, 8½" x 9¾", w/o handle	15.00	110.00	
27 ▸**Tumbler, 3¼", 5 ounce	12.00	22.00	35.00
28 ▸**Tumbler, 4", 9 ounce, red 55.00	7.00	16.00	30.00
29 ▸ Tumbler, 5", 12 ounce	10.00	28.00	52.00
Tumbler, 4⅝", 11 ounce	9.00		
11 ▸ Tumbler, 4", footed	8.00		
Tumbler, 5", footed, 11 ounce	11.00		
Tumbler, 7¼", footed	18.00		

*Delphite $45.00   **Blue $65.00   ‡Red $450.00   ‡‡Yellow $175.00; Blue $185.00

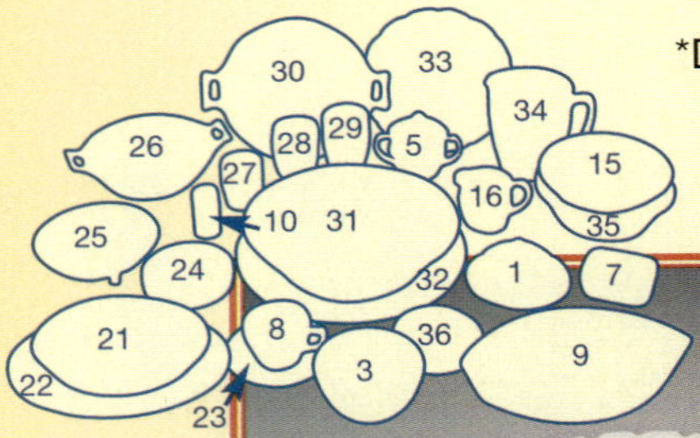

240

"WOOLWORTH," "STIPPLED GRAPE," "OREGON GRAPE," WESTMORELAND GLASS COMPANY, c. 1930s

Colors: crystal, green, pink

This grape pattern has been dubbed "Woolworth" because it was mainly marketed in that chain of stores during the 1930s. A grape name would seem more in line with the design, but no authentic name has surfaced. This smaller Westmoreland pattern has fascinated collectors over the years. Somehow Internet buyers became ecstatic about this embossed fruit design and prices increased dramatically. Due to the demand and requests for "Woolworth," we included it in the last book and now supplies have really dried up.

The creamer and sugar are seen most often, but plates and bowls are another story. "Woolworth" is another pattern where plates were formed into bowls by turning up the sides, so measurements vary greatly. Our measurements are taken from the pieces pictured. We discovered up to ½" discrepancy on similar pieces due to the amount of flaring and ruffling on each item. These ruffles and flares were done by hand with a wooden tool. A heavy-handed worker might push down harder making a bowl shallower than one made by a light-handed worker. We have never spotted a smooth edged bowl, so evidently it was the scalloped edge plates that were used for this reworking. Green plates and bowls appear less often than the pink.

Crystal prices approach those of pink or green except for creamer and sugars which sell in the $10.00 ballpark. Scarcity of other items increases the price more than demand. Most collectors we have talked to buy all colors and not just one. That is a different concept than collecting most other patterns. One collector said he bought every piece he could find in the Atlanta area. He also picked every grape we had at last year's Peach State Depression Glass show.

		Crystal	Green, Pink			Crystal	Green, Pink
2 ▸	Basket, 5½", hdld.	20.00	28.00	Bowl, 7⅝", round, 1⅞" shallow nappy	20.00	25.00
	Bowl, 5½", hdld.	18.00	22.00	4 ▸ Creamer	15.00	20.00
1 ▸	Bowl, 5⅞", square nappy	22.00	30.00	6 ▸ Plate, 8½", scalloped rim	20.00	25.00
	Bowl, 6⅜", round, 2¼" deep nappy	15.00	20.00	5 ▸ Plate, 8⅝", plain rim	22.00	28.00
3 ▸	Bowl, 6¾", round, 2¼" deep nappy	17.50	22.50	7 ▸ Sugar	15.00	20.00
3 ▸	Bowl, 7⅜", round, 2" shallow nappy	20.00	28.00			

241

REPRODUCTIONS

NEW "ADAM," PRIVATELY PRODUCED OUT OF KOREA THROUGH ST. LOUIS IMPORTING COMPANY ONLY THE ADAM BUTTER DISH HAS BEEN REPRODUCED.

The reproduction Adam butter dish is finally off the wholesale market as far as I can determine. Identification of the reproduction is easy. *Do not use any of the following information for any piece of Adam save the butter dish.*

Top: Notice the veins in the leaves.

New: Large leaf veins do not join or touch in center of leaf.

Old: Large leaf veins all touch or join the center vein.

A further note about the original Adam butter dish: the veins of all the leaves at the center of the design are very clear cut and precisely moulded; in the new, these center leaf veins are very indistinct and almost invisible in one leaf of the center design.

Bottom: Place butter dish bottom upside down for observation. Square it, flat side, to your body.

New: Four arrowhead-like points line up in northwest, northeast, southeast, and southwest directions of compass. These points head in the wrong directions from old. There are very bad mould lines and a very glossy light pink color on the butter dishes I examined.

Old: Four arrowhead-like points line up in north, east, south, and west directions of compass.

NEW "AVOCADO," INDIANA GLASS COMPANY Tiara Exclusives Line, 1974 – 1980s

Colors: pink, green, and fifteen additional colors never made originally

In 1979, a green Avocado pitcher was reproduced. It was darker than the original green and was a limited hostess gift item. Yellow pieces are all recently made. Yellow was never made originally.

The old pink color Indiana made was a delicate, attractive pink. The first reproduced pink pitcher appeared in 1973. The newer, tends to be more orange than the original color. The other colors shown pose little threat since none of those colors were made originally.

We understand that Tiara sales counselors told potential customers that their newly made glass was collectible because it was made from old moulds. We do not share this view. We feel it's like saying that since you were married in your grandmother's wedding dress, you will have the same happy marriage for the 57 years she did. All you can truly say is that you were married in her dress. We think all you can say about the new Avocado is that it was made from the old moulds. Time, scarcity, and people's whims determine collectibility as far as we're able to determine it. It has taken nearly 50 years or more for people to turn to collecting Depression glass — and that's done, in part, because of what we call the "nostalgia factor" — everyone remembers it; they had some in their home at one time or another; it has universal appeal. Who is to say what will be collectible in the next 50 years? If we knew, we could all get rich! Now, that Tiara is out of business, perhaps some of their wares will become collectible. Unhappily, there are many collectors who were taken in by some of this glass being represented as old, and most of them have long enough memories to avoid it during their generation.

If you like Tiara products then of course buy them; but don't do so depending upon their being collectible. You have an equal chance, we feel, of going to Las Vegas and depending upon getting rich at the blackjack table.

NEW "CAMEO"

Colors: green, pink, cobalt blue (shakers); yellow, green, and pink (children's dishes)

We hope you can still see how very weak the pattern is on this reproduction shaker. It was originally made by Mosser Glass Company in Ohio, but is now being made overseas. In addition, you can see how much glass remains in the bottom of the shaker; and, of course, the new tops all make this easy to spot at the market. These were to be bought wholesale at around $6.00 but did not sell well. An importer made shakers in pink, cobalt blue, and a terrible green color. These, too, are weakly patterned. They were never originally made in the blue, but beware of pink.

Children's dishes in Cameo (called "Jennifer" by the manufacturer) pose no problem to collectors since they were never made originally. These, also made by Mosser, are *scale* models of the larger size. This type of production we have no quarrel with since they are not made to dupe anyone.

There are over 50 of these smaller pieces; thus, if you have a piece of glass that looks like a miniature (child's) version of a larger piece of Cameo, then you probably have a newly manufactured item.

NEW "AVOCADO"

REPRODUCTIONS

NEW "CHERRY BLOSSOM"

Colors: pink, green, blue, Delphite, cobalt, red, and iridized colors

Use information provided only for the piece described. Do not apply the information on the tumbler for the pitcher etc. Realize that with various importers now reproducing glass, there are more modifications than we can possibly scrutinize for you. Know your dealer and *hope* he knows what he is doing.

Due to all the altered reproductions of the same pieces over and over, please understand this is only a guide as to what you should look for when buying. We've now seen some reproductions of those reproductions. All the items pictured on the next page are easy to spot as reproductions once you know what to look for with the possible exception of the 13" divided platter pictured in the center. It's too heavy, weighing 2¾ pounds, and has a thick ⅜" of glass in the bottom; but the design isn't too bad. The edges of the leaves aren't smooth; but neither are they serrated like old leaves.

There are many differences between old and new scalloped bottom, AOP Cherry pitchers. The easiest way to tell the difference is to turn the pitcher over. The branch crossing the bottom of my old Cherry pitchers looks like a branch. It's knobby and gnarled and has several leaves and cherry stems directly attached to it. One variation of the new pitcher just has a bald strip of glass cutting the bottom of the pitcher in half. Further, the old Cherry pitchers have a plain glass background for the cherries and leaves in the bottom of the pitcher. In the new pitchers, there's a rough, filled in, straw-like background. You see no plain glass.

As for the new tumblers, look at the ring dividing the patterned portion of the glass from the plain glass lip. The old tumblers have three indented rings dividing the pattern from the plain glass rim. The new has only one. Again, the pattern at the bottom of the new tumblers is brief and practically nonexistent in the center curve of the glass bottom. The pattern, when there is one, mostly hugs the center of the foot.

two-handled tray — old: 1⅞ lb.; 3/16" glass in bottom; leaves and cherries east/west from north/south handles (some older trays were rotated so this is not always true); leaves have real spine and serrated edges; cherry stems end in triangle of glass. **new:** 2⅛ lb.; ¼" glass in bottom; leaves and cherries north/south with the handles; canal type leaves (but uneven edges; cherry stem ends before canal shaped line).

cake plate — new: color too light pink; leaves have too many parallel veins that give them a feathery look; arches at plate edge don't line up with lines on inside of the rim to which the feet are attached.

8½" bowl — new: crude leaves with smooth edges; veins in parallel lines.

cereal bowl — new: wrong shape, looks like 8½" bowl, small 2" center. **old:** large center; 2½" inside ring; nearly 3½ if you count the outer rim before the sides turn up.

dinner plate — new: smooth-edged leaves, fish spine type center leaf portion; weighs one pound plus; feels thicker at edge with mould offset lines clearly visible. **old:** center leaves look like real leaves with spines, veins, and serrated edges; weighs ¾ pound; clean edges; no mould offset (a slight step effect at the edge).

cup — new: area in bottom left free of design; canal centered leaves; smooth, thick top to cup handle (old has triangle grasp point).

saucer — new: offset mould line edge; canal leaf center.

The Cherry child's cup (with a slightly lopsided handle) having the cherries hanging upside-down when the cup was held in the right hand appeared in 1973. After we reported this error, it was quickly corrected by re-inverting the inverted mould. These later cups were thus improved in design but slightly off color. The saucers tended to have slightly off center designs, too. Next came the child's butter dish that was never made by Jeannette. It was essentially the child's cup without a handle turned upside-down over the saucer and having a little glob of glass added as a knob for lifting purposes.

Pictured are some of the colors of butter dishes made so far. Shaker reproductions were introduced in 1977 and some were dated '77 on the bottom. Shortly afterward, the non-dated variety appeared. How can you tell new shaker from old — should you get the one in a million chance to do so?

First, look at the tops. New tops could indicate new shakers. Next, notice the protruding edges beneath the tops. In the new they are squared off juts rather than the nicely rounded scallops on the old. The design on the newer shakers is often weak in spots. Finally, notice how far up inside the shakers the solid glass (next to the foot) remains. The newer shakers have almost twice as much glass in that area. They appear to be ¼ full of glass before you ever add the salt.

In 1989, a new distributor began making reproduction glass in the Far East. He made shakers in cobalt blue, pink and a hideous green, that is no problem to spot. These shakers are similar in quality to those made before. However, the present pink color is good; yet the quality and design of each batch could vary greatly. Realize that only two original pair of pink Cherry shakers have ever been found and those were discovered before any reproductions were made in 1977.

Butter dishes are naturally more deceptive in pink and green since those were the only original colors. The major flaw in the new butter is that there is one band encircling the bottom edge of the butter top; there are two bands very close together along the skirt of the old top.

REPRODUCTIONS

NEW "FLORAL," IMPORTING COMPANY OUT OF GEORGIA

Reproduction Floral shakers can now be found in pink, red, cobalt blue, and a dark green color. Cobalt blue, red, and the dark green Floral shakers are of little concern since they were never made in those colors originally. The green is darker than the original green, but not as deep as forest green. The pink shakers are not only a very good pink, but they are also a very good copy. There are many minor variations in design and leaf detail to someone who knows glassware well; but the easy way to tell the Floral reproductions is to take off the top and look at the threads where the lid screws onto the shaker. On the old, there is a pair of parallel threads on each side or a least a pair on one side, which end right before the mold seams down each side. The new Floral has one continuous line thread that starts at one side and continues around the shaker until it ends above the beginning line on the other side. There is approximately one inch of overlapped thread making two lines for that inch; but the whole thread is one continuous line and not two separate ones as on the old. No other Floral reproductions have been made as of May 2005.

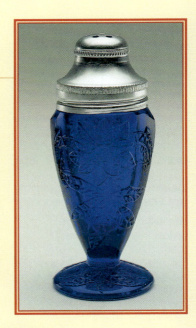

NEW "FLORENTINE" NO. 1, IMPORTING COMPANY OUT OF GEORGIA

Although a picture of a reproduction shaker is not shown, we would like you to know it exists.

Florentine No. 1 shakers have been reproduced in pink, red, and cobalt blue. There may be other colors to follow. No red or cobalt blue Florentine No. 1 shakers have ever been found, so those colors are no problem. We have only examined one reproduction shaker, and it is difficult to know if all shakers will be as badly molded as this is. There is little or no design on the bottom. We compared the pink shaker to several old pairs. The old shakers have a major open flower on each side. There is a top circle on this blossom with three smaller circles down each side. The seven circles form the outside of the blossom. The new blossom looks more like a strawberry with no circles forming the outside of the blossom. This repro blossom looks like a poor drawing. Do not use the Floral thread test for the Florentine No. 1 shakers, however. It won't work for Florentine although the same importing company out of Georgia makes these.

NEW "FLORENTINE" NO. 2, IMPORTING COMPANY OUT OF GEORGIA

A reproduced footed Florentine No. 2 pitcher and footed juice tumbler appeared in 1996. First to surface was a cobalt blue set that alerted knowledgeable collectors that something was strange. Next, sets of red, dark green, and two shades of pink began to be seen at the local flea markets. All these colors were dead giveaways since the footed Florentine No. 2 pitcher was never made in any of those shades.

The new pitchers are approximately ¼" shorter than the original and have a flatter foot as opposed to the domed foot of the old. The mold line on the lip of the newer pitcher extends ½" below the lip while only ⅜" below on the original. All of the measurements could vary over time with the reproductions and may even vary on the older ones. The easiest way to tell the old from the new, besides color, is by the handles. The new handles are ⅞" wide, but the older ones were only ¾" wide. That ⅛" seems even bigger than that when you set them side by side as shown at right.

The juice tumbler differences are not as apparent; but there are two. The old juice stands 4" tall and the diameter of the base is 2⅛". The reproduction is only 3¹⁵⁄₁₆" tall and 2" in base diameter.

NEW "IRIS," IMPORTING COMPANY

New Iris cocktails appeared in August 2004. The easiest way to tell the new ones is to look inside from the top. The new ones have what looks like a dot, looking down into it (see top right photo). The old ones do not have a dot.

New Iris iced tea tumblers have two distinct differences. First, turn these upside down and feel the rays on the foot. New rays are very sharp and will almost cut your finger if you press on them hard. Old tumbler rays are rounded and feel smooth in comparison. The paneled design on the new tumbler gets very weak in several places as you rotate it in your hand. Old tumbler paneled designs stay bold around the entire tumbler.

New dinner plates have two characteristics. The extreme edge of the pattern on the new dinners is pointed outward (upside down V). Old dinner plate designs usually end looking like a stack of the letter V, though optical illusions sometimes distort that a bit. In addition, the inside rim of the new dinner slopes inward toward the center of the plate, whereas original inside rims are almost perpendicular and steeper sided against the center portion of the plate.

New flat tumblers do not have herringbone in the bottom pattern design. There are other differences, especially the crystal, clear color of the new ones; however, missing herringbone is the easiest to observe.

In the fall of 2000, several large lots of Iris coasters appeared on an internet auction site. All of these coasters had origins in Ohio and were like the tumblers and dinner plates in one major respect. The crystal color was too good. If you take any old piece of Iris and place it on a white background, it will have a gray or yellow tint to it. If you place the new dinner plates or iced tea tumblers on white, they have no tinted hue of any sort. The coasters and cocktails are the same — no tint. The other sure-fire way to tell these newer coasters is to look from the side across the coaster edge. New ones look half-full of glass or slightly over. The older ones are only a quarter-full of glass. You can keep up with current reproductions through a website where I have posted pictures. Go to www.glassshow.com and then the Reading Room. Click on Reproductions for the latest information available.

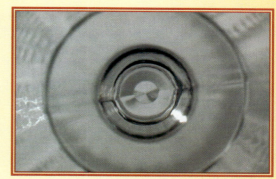

Iris 6½" footed ice tea tumblers (new on left).

New flat tumblers (left) do not have herringbone in the pattern. There are many other minor differences, but that is the easiest to observe.

Iris dinner plate (new on left).

Iris coasters (new on right).

REPRODUCTIONS

NEW "MADRID" CALLED "RECOLLECTION," RECENTLY BEING MADE

I hope you have already read about Recollection Madrid on page 123. Indiana Glass made Madrid in teal after making it in blue, pink, and crystal. This light teal color was never made originally, so there is no problem of it being confused with old. The teal was sold through all kinds of outlets ranging from better department stores to discount catalogs. In the past couple of years, we have received several ads stating that this is genuine Depression glass made from old moulds. None of this is made from old glass moulds unless you consider 1976 old. Most of the pieces are from moulds never made originally.

The light blue was a big seller for Indiana according to reports we are receiving around the country. It is a brighter, more fluorescent looking blue than the soft, original color. More and more of it is turning up in antique malls. Buy it if you like it; just don't pay antique prices for it.

Look at the picture below. Only the cup, saucer, and oval vegetable were ever made in old Madrid. The new grill plate has one division splitting the plate in half, but the old had three sections. A goblet or vase was never made. The vase is sold with a candle making it a hurricane lamp. The heavy tumbler was placed on top of a candlestick to make this a vase/hurricane lamp. That candlestick gets a workout. It was attached to a plate to make a pedestal cake stand and to a butter dish to make a preserve stand. That's a clever idea, actually. You would not believe the mail spawned by those last two, newly manufactured pieces.

The new shakers are short and heavy. The latest item we have seen is a heavy 11-ounce flat tumbler being sold in a set of four or six called "On the Rocks." The biggest giveaway to this newer pink glass is the pale, washed out color.

The only concerns in new pink Madrid pieces are the cups, saucers, and oval vegetable bowl. These three pieces were made in pink in the 1930s. None of the others shown were ever made in the 1930s in pink; so realize that when you see the butter dish, dinner plate, soup bowl, or sugar and creamer. These are new items. Once you have learned what this washed-out pink looks like by seeing these items for sale, the color will be a clue when you see other pieces.

The least difficult piece for new collectors to tell new from old is the candlestick. The new ones all have three raised ridges inside to hold the candle more firmly. Old ones do not have any inside ridges. You may even find new candlesticks in black.

NEW "MAYFAIR," IMPORTING COMPANY

Colors: pink, green, blue, cobalt (shot glasses), 1977; pink, green, amethyst, cobalt blue, red (cookie jars), 1982; cobalt blue, pink, amethyst, red, and green (odd shade), shakers 1988; green, cobalt, pink, juice pitchers, 1993

Only the pink shot glass need cause any concern for collectors because that glass was not made in any other color originally. At first glance, the color of the newer shots is often too light pink or too orange. Dead giveaway is the stem of the flower design, however. In the old that stem branched to form an "A" shape at the bottom; in the new, you have a single stem. Further, in the new design, the leaf is hollow with the veins moulded in. In the old, the leaf is moulded in and the veining is left hollow. In the center of the flower on the old, dots (anther) cluster entirely to one side and are rather distinct. Nothing like that occurs in the new design. *Do not use this information for any piece except shot glass.*

As for the cookie jars, at cursory glance the base of the cookie has a very indistinct design. It will feel smooth to the touch, because it's so faint. In the old cookie jars, there's a distinct pattern that feels like raised embossing to the touch. Next, turn the bottom upside-down. The new bottom is perfectly smooth. The old bottom contains a 1¾" mould circle rim that is raised enough to catch your fingernail in it. There are other distinctions as well; but that is the quickest and easiest way to tell old from new.

In the Mayfair cookie lid, the new design (parallel to the straight side of the lid) at the edge curves gracefully toward the center "V" shape (rather like bird wings in flight); in the old, that edge is a flat straight line going into the "V" (like airplane wings sticking straight out from the side of the plane as you face it head on).

The green color of the cookie, as you can see from the picture, is not the pretty, yellow/green color of true green Mayfair. It also doesn't glow under black light as the old green does; so, that is a simple test for green.

NEW "MAYFAIR"

The corner ridges on the old Mayfair shaker rise half way to the top and then smooth out. The new shaker corner ridges rise to the top and are quite pronounced. The measurement differences are listed below, but the diameter of the opening is the critical and easiest way to tell old from new. New lids will not fit old shakers as they are too small.

	OLD	NEW
Diameter of opening	¾"	⅝"
Diameter of lid	⅞"	¾"
Height	4¹⁄₁₆"	4"

OLD　　　　　**NEW**

Mayfair juice pitchers were reproduced in 1993. The old pitchers have a distinct mould circle on the bottom that is missing on the newly made ones. This and the oddly applied handles on the repros make these easily spotted. The blue pitcher is the old one in the photos.

OLD　　　　　**NEW**

NEW "MISS AMERICA"

Colors: crystal, green, pink, ice blue, red amberina, cobalt blue

Miss America reproduction creamers and sugars are smaller than the originals; Miss America was not made in cobalt, but other colors have followed. These creamer and sugars are poorly made. There are many bubbles in the glass of the ones we have seen.

The reproduction butter dish in the Miss America design is probably the best of the newer products; yet there are three differences to be found between the original butter top and the newly made ones. The obvious thing is how the top knob sticks up away from the butter caused by a longer than usual stem at the knob.

Pick up the top of the new dish and feel up inside it. If the butter top knob is filled with glass so that it is convex (curved outward), the dish is new; the old inside knob area is concave (curved inward).

Finally, from the underside, look through the top toward the knob. In the original butter dish, you would see a perfectly formed multi-sided star; in the newer version, you see distorted rays with no visible points.

Miss America shakers have been made in green, pink, cobalt blue, and crystal. The latest copies of shakers are becoming more difficult to distinguish from the old. The measurements given below for shakers do not hold true for all the latest reproductions. It is impossible to know which generation of shaker reproductions that you will encounter, so you have to be careful on these.

New shakers most likely will have new tops; but since some old shakers have been given new tops, that isn't conclusive at all. Unscrew the lid. Old shakers have a very neatly formed ridge of glass on which to screw the lid. It overlaps a little and has rounded off ends. Old shakers stand 3⅜" tall without the lid. Most new ones stand 3¼" tall. Old shakers have almost a forefinger's depth inside (female finger) or a fraction short of 2½". Most new shakers have an inside depth of 2", about the second digit bend of a female's finger. (I'm doing finger depths since most of you will carry those with you to the flea market, rather than a tape measure.) In men, the old shaker's depth covers my knuckle; the new shaker leaves my knuckle exposed. Most new shakers simply have more glass on the inside of the shaker — something you can spot from 12 feet away. The hobs are more rounded on the newer shaker, particularly near the stem and seams; in the old shaker, these areas remained pointedly sharp.

New Miss America tumblers have ½" of glass in the bottom, have a smooth edge on the bottom of the glass with no mould rim, and show only two distinct mould marks on the sides of the glass. Old tumblers have only ¼" of glass in the bottom, have a distinct mould line rimming the bottom of the tumbler, and have four distinct mould marks up the sides of the tumbler.

New Miss America pitchers (without ice lip only) are all perfectly smooth rimmed at the top edge above the handle. All old pitchers that I have seen have a hump in the top rim of the glass above the handle area, rather like a camel's hump. The very bottom diamonds next to the foot in the new pitchers squash into elongated diamonds. In the old pitchers, these get noticeably smaller, but they retain their diamond shape. As of May 2005, these are the only pieces of Miss America that has been reproduced.

NEW "ROYAL LACE," IMPORTING COMPANY

Color: Cobalt blue

The first thing you notice about the reproduced pieces of Royal Lace is the harsh, extra dark, vivid cobalt blue color or the orange cast to the pink. It is not the soft cobalt blue originally made by Hazel-Atlas. So far, only the cookie jar, juice, and water tumblers have been made as of May 2005.

The original cookie jar lid has a mould seam that bisects (cuts in half) the center of the pattern on one side, and runs across the knob and bisects the pattern on the opposite side. There is no mould line at all on the reproduction.

There are a multitude of bubbles and imperfections on the bottom of the new cookie jar that I am examining. The bottom is poorly moulded and the pattern is extremely weak. Original bottoms are plentiful anyway; learn to distinguish the top and it will save you money.

As for tumblers, the first reproduction tumblers had plain bottoms without the four-pointed design. The new juice tumbler has a bottom design, but it is as large as the one on the water tumbler and covers the entire bottom of the glass. Originally, this design was very small and did not encompass the whole bottom, as does this reproduction. Additionally, there are design flaws on both size tumblers that stand out. The four ribs between each of the four designs on the side of the repro tumblers protrude far enough to catch your fingernail. The original tumblers have a very smooth, flowing design that you can only feel. The other distinct flaw is a semi-circular design on the rim of the glass above those four ribs. Originally, these were very tiny on both tumblers with five oval leaves in each. There are three complete diamond-shaped designs in the new tumblers with two being doubled diamonds (diamond shapes within diamonds); and the semi-circular design almost touches the top rim. There's at least an ⅛" of glass above the older fan.

Also, on the bottom of the tumblers, the four flower petal center designs in the old is open-ended leaving ⅛" of open glass at the tip of each petal. In the new version, these ends are closed, causing the petals to be pointed on the end.

NEW "SHARON," PRIVATELY PRODUCED 1976...(continued page 253)

Colors: blue, dark green, light green, pink, cobalt blue, opalescent blue, red, burnt umber

A blue Sharon butter turned up in 1976 and turned our phone line to liquid fire. The color was Mayfair blue — a fluke and dead giveaway as far as real Sharon is concerned. The original mastermind of reproductions did not know his patterns very well and mixed up Mayfair and Sharon. (He admitted that when we talked to him.)

When Sharon butters are found in colors similar to the old pink and green, you can immediately tell that the new version has more glass in the top where it changes from pattern to clear glass. It is a thick, defined ring of glass as opposed to a thin, barely defined ring of glass in the old. The knob of the new dish tends to stick up more. In the old butter dish, there is barely room to fit your finger to grasp the knob. The new butter dish has a sharply defined ridge of glass in the bottom around which the top sits. The old butter has such a slight rim that the top easily scoots off the bottom.

In 1977 a cheese dish appeared having the same top as the butter and having all the flaws inherent in that top which were discussed in detail above. However, the bottom of this dish was wrong. It was about half way between a flat plate and a butter dish bottom — bowl shaped; and it was very thick, giving it an awkward appearance. The real cheese bottom was a salad plate (not bowl) with a rim of glass for holding the top inside that rim. These round bottomed cheese dishes are but a parody of the old and are easily spotted.

NEW "SHARON" (continued)

Some of the latest reproductions in Sharon are a too-light-pink creamer and sugar with lid. They are pictured with the "Made in Taiwan" label. These retail for around $15.00 for the pair and are easy to spot as reproductions. I'll just mention the most obvious differences. Turn the creamer so you are looking directly at the spout. In the old creamer, the mould line runs dead center of that spout; in the new, the mould line runs decidedly to the left of center spout.

On the sugar, the leaves and roses are "off" but not enough to describe it to new collectors. Therefore, look at the center design, both sides, at the stars located at the very bottom of the motif. A thin leaf stem should run directly from that center star upward on both sides. In this new sugar, the stem only runs from one; it stops way short of the star on one side; or look inside the sugar bowl at where the handle attaches to the bottom of the bowl; in the new bowl, this attachment looks like a perfect circle; in the old, its an upside down "v"-shaped teardrop.

As for the sugar lid, the knob of the new lid is perfectly smooth as you grasp its edges. The old knob has a mould seam running mid circumference (equator). You could tell these two lids apart blindfolded.

While there is a slight difference between the height, mouth-opening diameter, and inside depth of the old Sharon shakers and those newly produced, we will not attempt to upset you with those sixteenths and thirty-seconds of an inch of difference. It is safe to say that in physical appearance, they are very close. However, when documenting design on the shaker, they are miles apart.

The old shakers have true appearing roses. The flowers really look like roses. On the new shakers, the roses appear as poorly drawn circles with wobbly concentric rings. The leaves are not as clearly defined on the new shakers as the old are. However, forgetting all that, in the old shakers, the first design you see below the lid is a rose bud. It is angled like a rocket shooting off into outer space with three leaves at the base of the bud (where the rocket fuel would burn out). In the new shakers, this bud has become four paddles of a windmill. It is the difference between this ❀ and this ❁.

New "Sharon" candy dishes have been made in pink, green, cobalt blue, red, and opaque blue that goes to opalescent. These candy jars are among the easiest items to discern old from new. Pick up the lid and look from the bottom side. On the old there is a 2" circle ring platform below the knob; on the new, that ring of glass below the knob is only ½". This shows from the top also but it is difficult to measure with the knob in the center. There are other major differences, but this one will not be easily corrected. The bottoms are also simple to distinguish. The base diameter of the old bottom is 3¼" and the new is only 3". On the example we have, quality of the new is rough, poorly shaped and moulded; but I do not know if that will hold true for all reproductions of the candy. We hope so.

OTHER TITLES FROM THE FLORENCES

NEWEST RELEASE

FLORENCES' OVENWARE
FROM THE 1920S TO THE PRESENT
Item #6641 • ISBN: 1-57432-449-7 • 8½ x 11 • 208 Pgs. • HB • $24.95

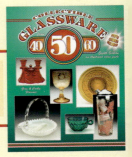

NEWEST EDITION

COLLECTIBLE GLASSWARE FROM THE 40S, 50S & 60S, EIGHTH EDITION
Item #6821 • ISBN: 1-57432-460-8 • 8½ x 11 • 256 Pgs. • HB • $19.95

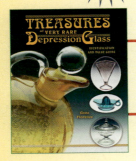

TREASURES OF VERY RARE DEPRESSION GLASS
Item #6241 • ISBN: 1-57432-336-9 • 8½ x 11 • 368 Pgs. • HB • $39.95

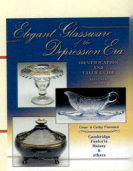

ELEGANT GLASSWARE, OF THE DEPRESSION ERA, ELEVENTH EDITION
Item #6559 • ISBN: 1-57432-417-9 • 8½ x 11 • 256 Pgs. • HB • $24.95

KITCHEN GLASSWARE OF THE DEPRESSION YEARS, SIXTH EDITION
Item #5827 • ISBN: 1-57432-220-6 • 8½ x 11 • 272 Pgs. • HB • $24.95

POCKET GUIDE TO DEPRESSION GLASS & MORE, FOURTEENTH EDITION
Item #6556 • ISBN: 1-57432-414-4 • 5½ x 8½ • 224 Pgs • PB • $12.95

THE HAZEL-ATLAS GLASS
IDENTIFICATION AND VALUE GUIDE
Item #6562 • ISBN: 1-57432-420-9 • 8½ x 11 • 224 Pgs. • HB • $24.95

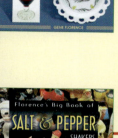
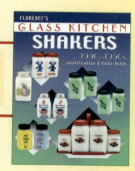
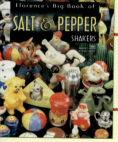

Schroeder's
ANTIQUES
Price Guide

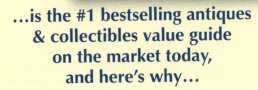

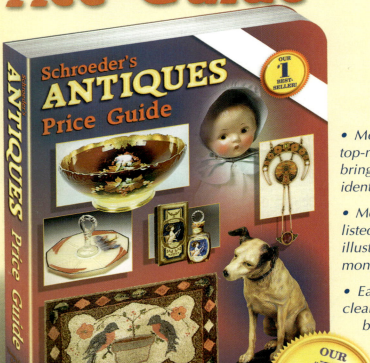

8½" x 11"
608 pgs.
$14.95

...is the #1 bestselling antiques & collectibles value guide on the market today, and here's why...

• More than 400 advisors, well-known dealers, and top-notch collectors work together with our editors to bring you accurate information regarding pricing and identification.

• More than 50,000 items in over 500 categories are listed along with hundreds of sharp original photos that illustrate not only the rare and unusual, but the common, popular collectibles as well.

• Each large close-up shot shows important detail clearly. Every subject is represented with histories and background information, a feature not found in any of our competitors' publications.

• Our editors keep abreast of newly developing trends, often adding several new categories a year as the need arises.

Without doubt, you'll find

Schroeder's Antiques Price Guide

the only one to buy for reliable information and values.

If it merits the interest of today's collector, you'll find it in *Schroeder's*. And you can feel confident that the information we publish is up-to-date and accurate. Our advisors thoroughly check each category to spot inconsistencies, listings that may not be entirely reflective of market dealings, and lines too vague to be of merit. Only the best of the lot remains for publication.

COLLECTOR BOOKS
P.O. Box 3009, Paducah, KY 42002–3009
www.collectorbooks.com